DIAL H FOR HERO

NEW HEROES OF METROPOLIS

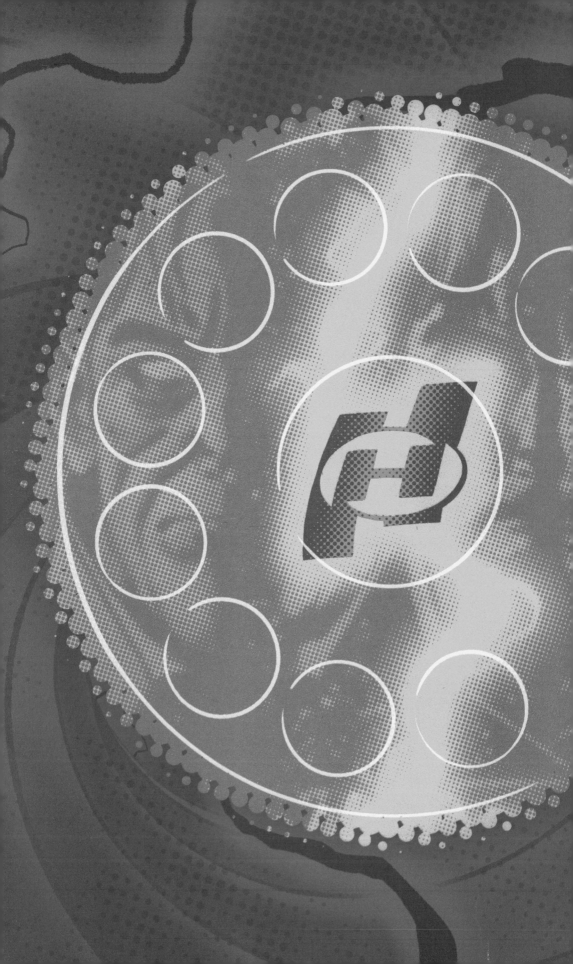

DIAL H FOR HERO

NEW HEROES OF METROPOLIS

SAM HUMPHRIES
writer

JOE QUINONES
with
COLLEEN DORAN
MICHAEL AVON OEMING
ERICA HENDERSON
STACEY LEE
PAULINA GANUCHEAU
artists

JORDAN GIBSON
with
JOE QUINONES
colorists

DAVE SHARPE
letterer

JOE QUINONES
collection cover artist

JOE QUINONES
EVAN "DOC" SHANER
original series cover artists

SUPERMAN created by JERRY SIEGEL and JOE SHUSTER
By special arrangement with the Jerry Siegel family

ALEX ANTONE
BRITTANY HOLZHERR
Editors – Original Series
ANDREA SHEA Assistant Editor – Original Series
JEB WOODARD Group Editor – Collected Editions
SCOTT NYBAKKEN Editor – Collected Edition
STEVE COOK Design Director – Books
CURTIS KING JR. Publication Design
CHRISTY SAWYER Publication Production

BOB HARRAS Senior VP – Editor-in-Chief, DC Comics

DAN DiDIO Publisher
JIM LEE Publisher & Chief Creative Officer
BOBBIE CHASE VP – New Publishing Initiatives
DON FALLETTI VP – Manufacturing Operations & Workflow Management
LAWRENCE GANEM VP – Talent Services
ALISON GILL Senior VP – Manufacturing & Operations
HANK KANALZ Senior VP – Publishing Strategy & Support Services
DAN MIRON VP – Publishing Operations
NICK J. NAPOLITANO VP – Manufacturing Administration & Design
NANCY SPEARS VP – Sales
JONAH WEILAND VP – Marketing & Creative Services
MICHELE R. WELLS VP & Executive Editor, Young Reader

DC Comics, 2900 West Alameda Ave., Burbank, CA 91505
Printed by LSC Communications, Owensville, MO, USA. 5/1/20.
First Printing. ISBN: 978-1-77950-176-9.

Library of Congress
Cataloging-in-Publication Data
is available.

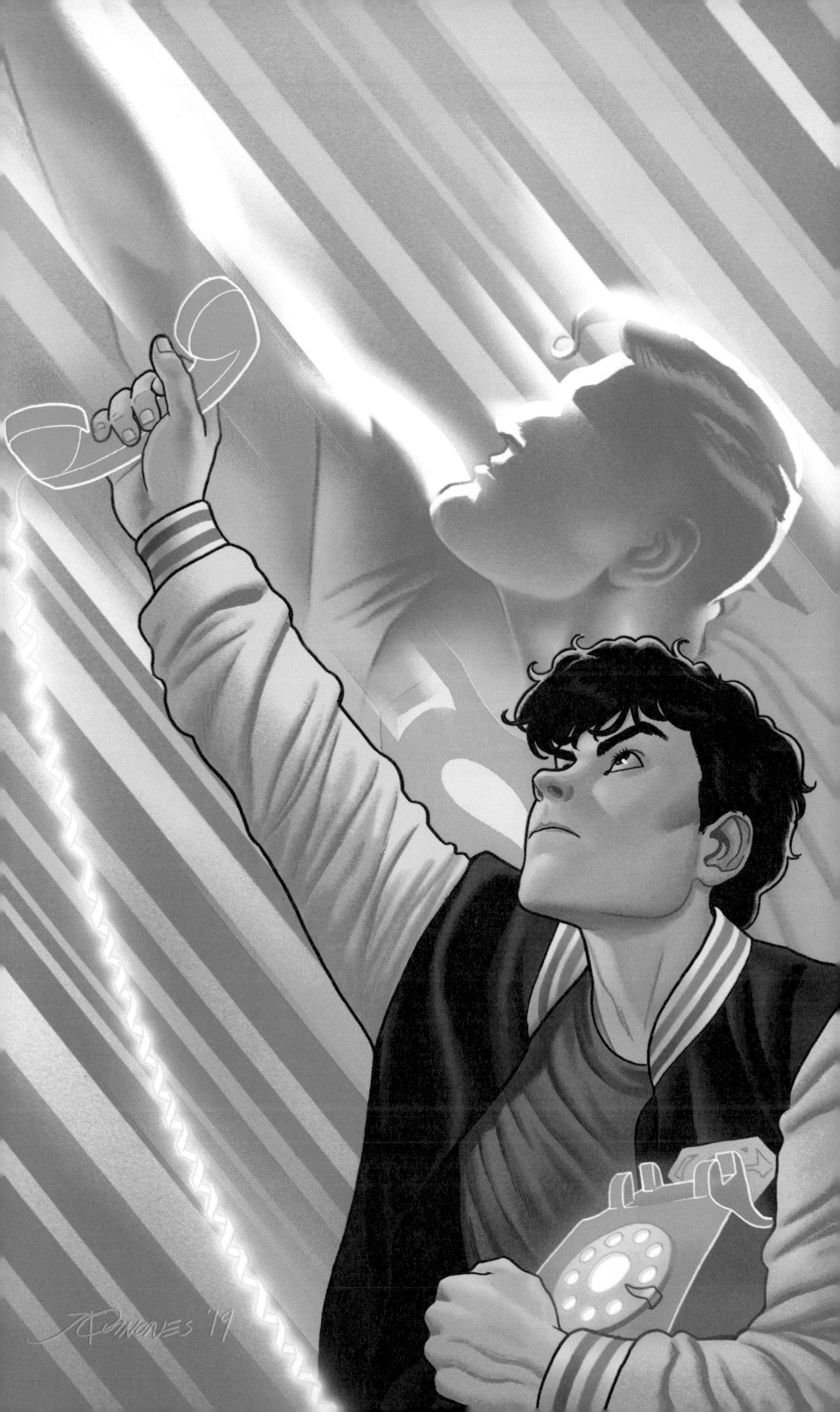
JQUINONES '19

THE NEW HEROES OF METROPOLIS

art by
(in order of appearance)
JOE QUINONES, COLLEEN DORAN, MICHAEL AVON OEMING,
ERICA HENDERSON, and STACEY LEE

colors by
JORDAN GIBSON

cover art by
JOE QUINONES

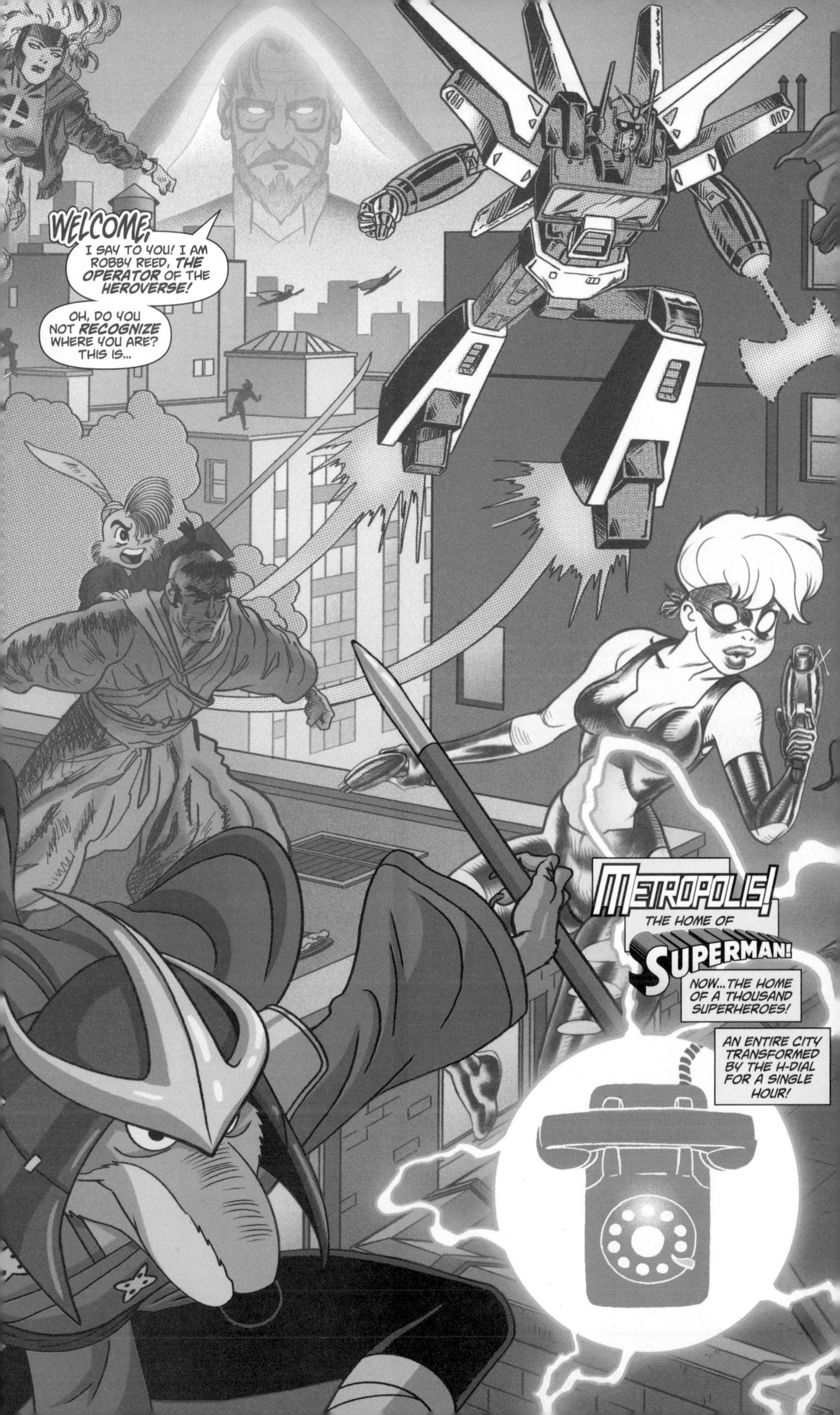
WELCOME, I SAY TO YOU! I AM ROBBY REED, THE OPERATOR OF THE HEROVERSE!
OH, DO YOU NOT RECOGNIZE WHERE YOU ARE? THIS IS...
METROPOLIS!
THE HOME OF SUPERMAN!
NOW...THE HOME OF A THOUSAND SUPERHEROES!
AN ENTIRE CITY TRANSFORMED BY THE H-DIAL FOR A SINGLE HOUR!

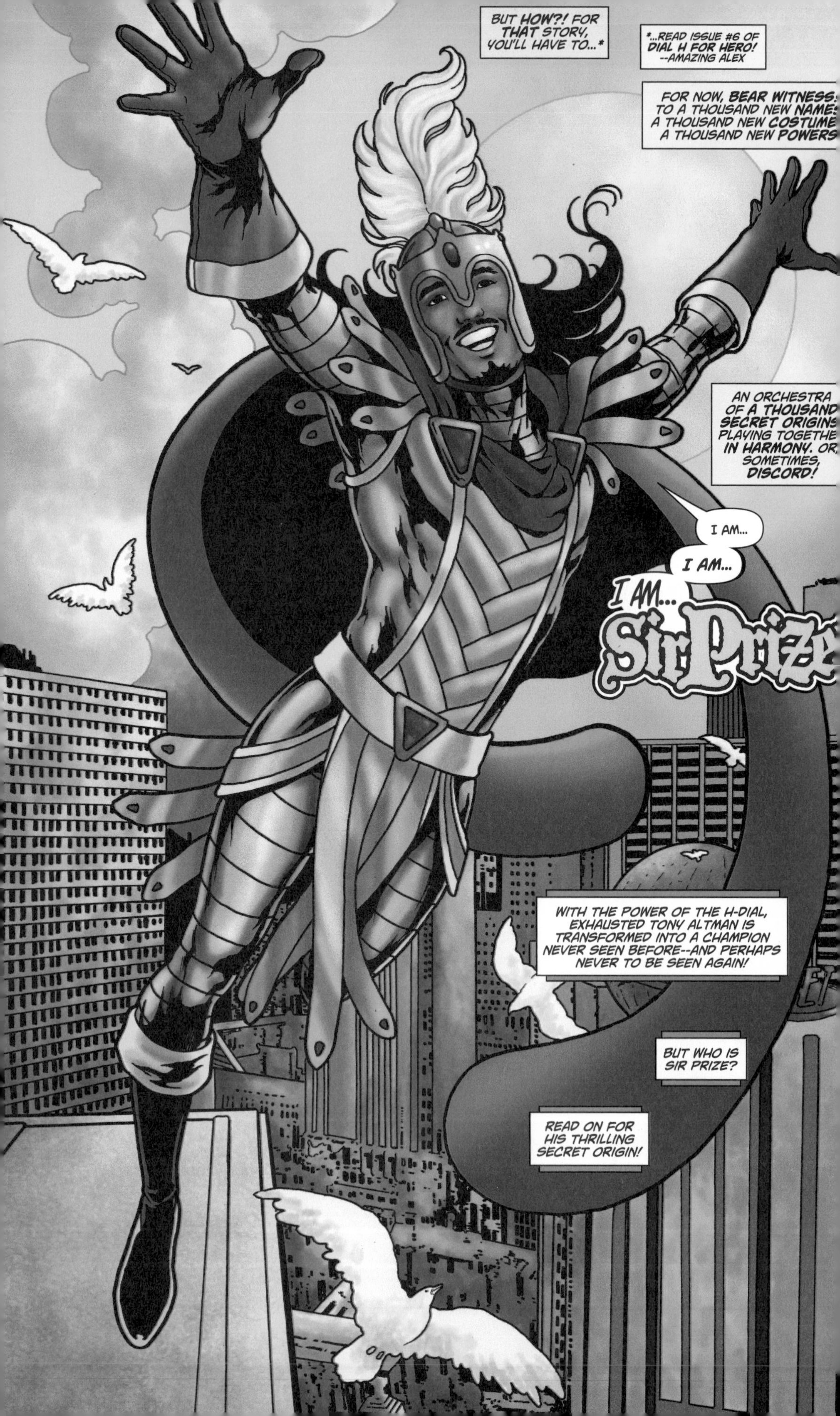

BUT HOW?! FOR THAT STORY, YOU'LL HAVE TO...*
*...READ ISSUE #6 OF DIAL H FOR HERO! --AMAZING ALEX
FOR NOW, BEAR WITNESS: TO A THOUSAND NEW NAMES A THOUSAND NEW COSTUMES A THOUSAND NEW POWERS
AN ORCHESTRA OF A THOUSAND SECRET ORIGINS PLAYING TOGETHER IN HARMONY. OR, SOMETIMES, DISCORD!
I AM...
I AM...
I AM... Sir Prize
WITH THE POWER OF THE H-DIAL, EXHAUSTED TONY ALTMAN IS TRANSFORMED INTO A CHAMPION NEVER SEEN BEFORE--AND PERHAPS NEVER TO BE SEEN AGAIN!
BUT WHO IS SIR PRIZE?
READ ON FOR HIS THRILLING SECRET ORIGIN!

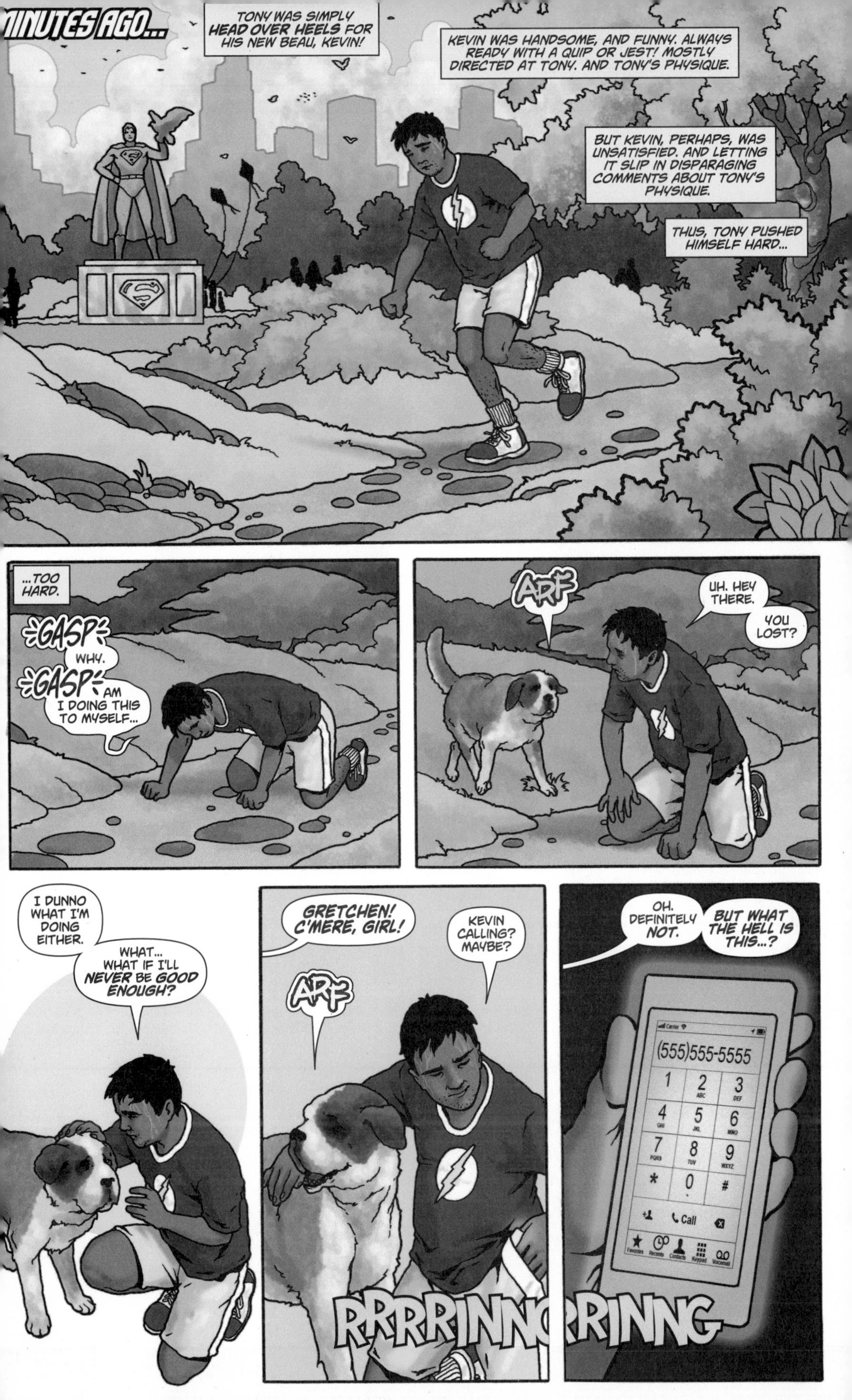
MINUTES AGO...
TONY WAS SIMPLY HEAD OVER HEELS FOR HIS NEW BEAU, KEVIN!
KEVIN WAS HANDSOME, AND FUNNY. ALWAYS READY WITH A QUIP OR JEST! MOSTLY DIRECTED AT TONY. AND TONY'S PHYSIQUE.
BUT KEVIN, PERHAPS, WAS UNSATISFIED. AND LETTING IT SLIP IN DISPARAGING COMMENTS ABOUT TONY'S PHYSIQUE.
THUS, TONY PUSHED HIMSELF HARD...
...TOO HARD.
GASP
WHY.
GASP
AM I DOING THIS TO MYSELF...
ARF
UH. HEY THERE.
YOU LOST?
I DUNNO WHAT I'M DOING EITHER.
WHAT... WHAT IF I'LL NEVER BE GOOD ENOUGH?
GRETCHEN! C'MERE, GIRL!
ARF
KEVIN CALLING? MAYBE?
OH. DEFINITELY NOT.
BUT WHAT THE HELL IS THIS...?
(555)555-5555
RRRRINNGRRINNG

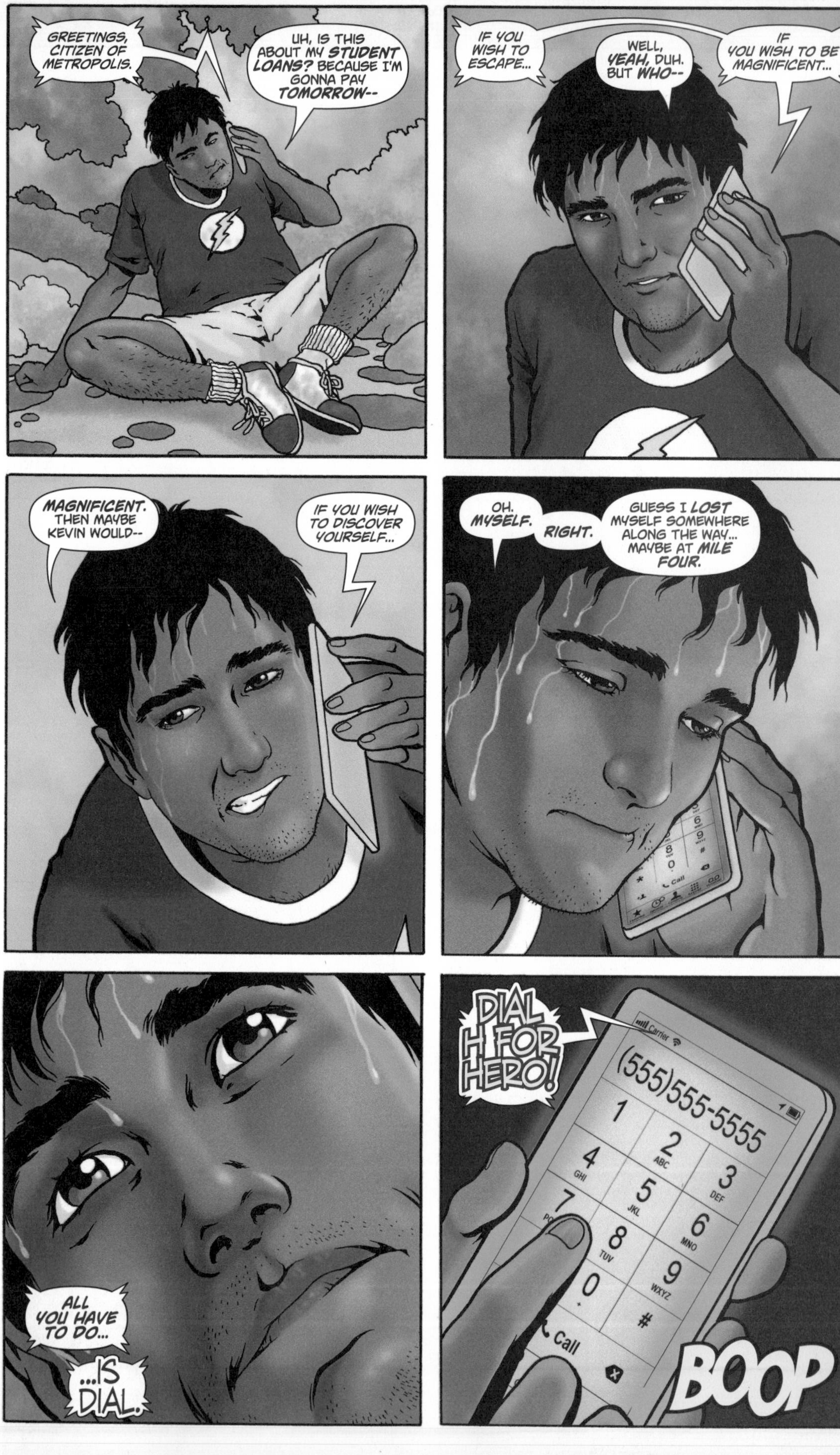
GREETINGS, CITIZEN OF METROPOLIS.
UH, IS THIS ABOUT MY STUDENT LOANS? BECAUSE I'M GONNA PAY TOMORROW--
IF YOU WISH TO ESCAPE...
WELL, YEAH, DUH. BUT WHO--
IF YOU WISH TO BE MAGNIFICENT...
MAGNIFICENT. THEN MAYBE KEVIN WOULD--
IF YOU WISH TO DISCOVER YOURSELF...
OH. MYSELF.
RIGHT.
GUESS I LOST MYSELF SOMEWHERE ALONG THE WAY... MAYBE AT MILE FOUR.
ALL YOU HAVE TO DO...
...IS DIAL.
DIAL H FOR HERO!
Carrier
(555)555-5555
1
2 ABC
3 DEF
4 GHI
5 JKL
6 MNO
8 TUV
9 WXYZ
0
#
Call
BOOP

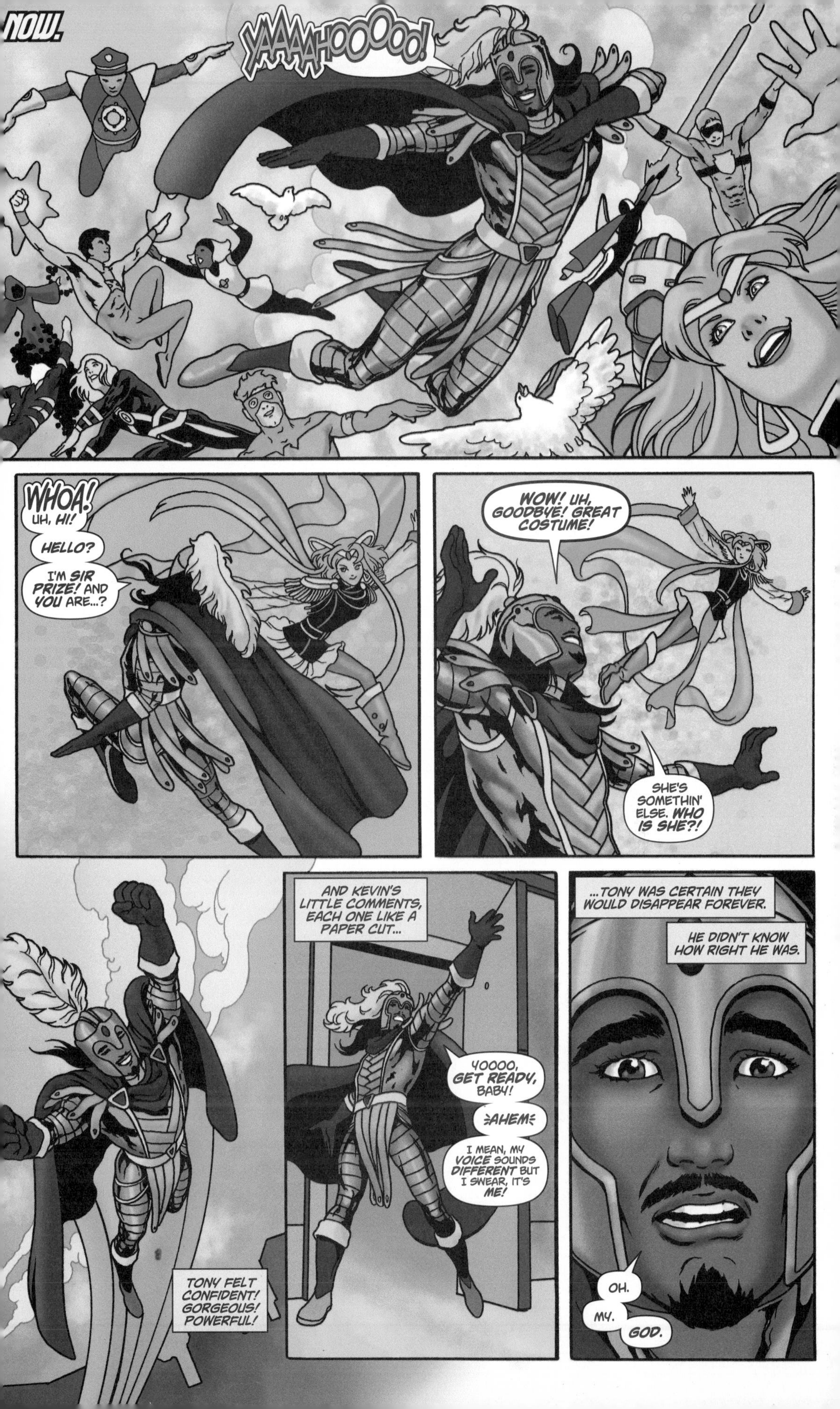
NOW.
YAAAAHOOOOoo!
WHOA! UH, HI!
HELLO?
I'M SIR PRIZE! AND YOU ARE...?
WOW! UH, GOODBYE! GREAT COSTUME!
SHE'S SOMETHIN' ELSE. WHO IS SHE?!
TONY FELT CONFIDENT! GORGEOUS! POWERFUL!
AND KEVIN'S LITTLE COMMENTS, EACH ONE LIKE A PAPER CUT...
YOOOO, GET READY, BABY!
AHEM
I MEAN, MY VOICE SOUNDS DIFFERENT BUT I SWEAR, IT'S ME!
...TONY WAS CERTAIN THEY WOULD DISAPPEAR FOREVER.
HE DIDN'T KNOW HOW RIGHT HE WAS.
OH.
MY.
GOD.

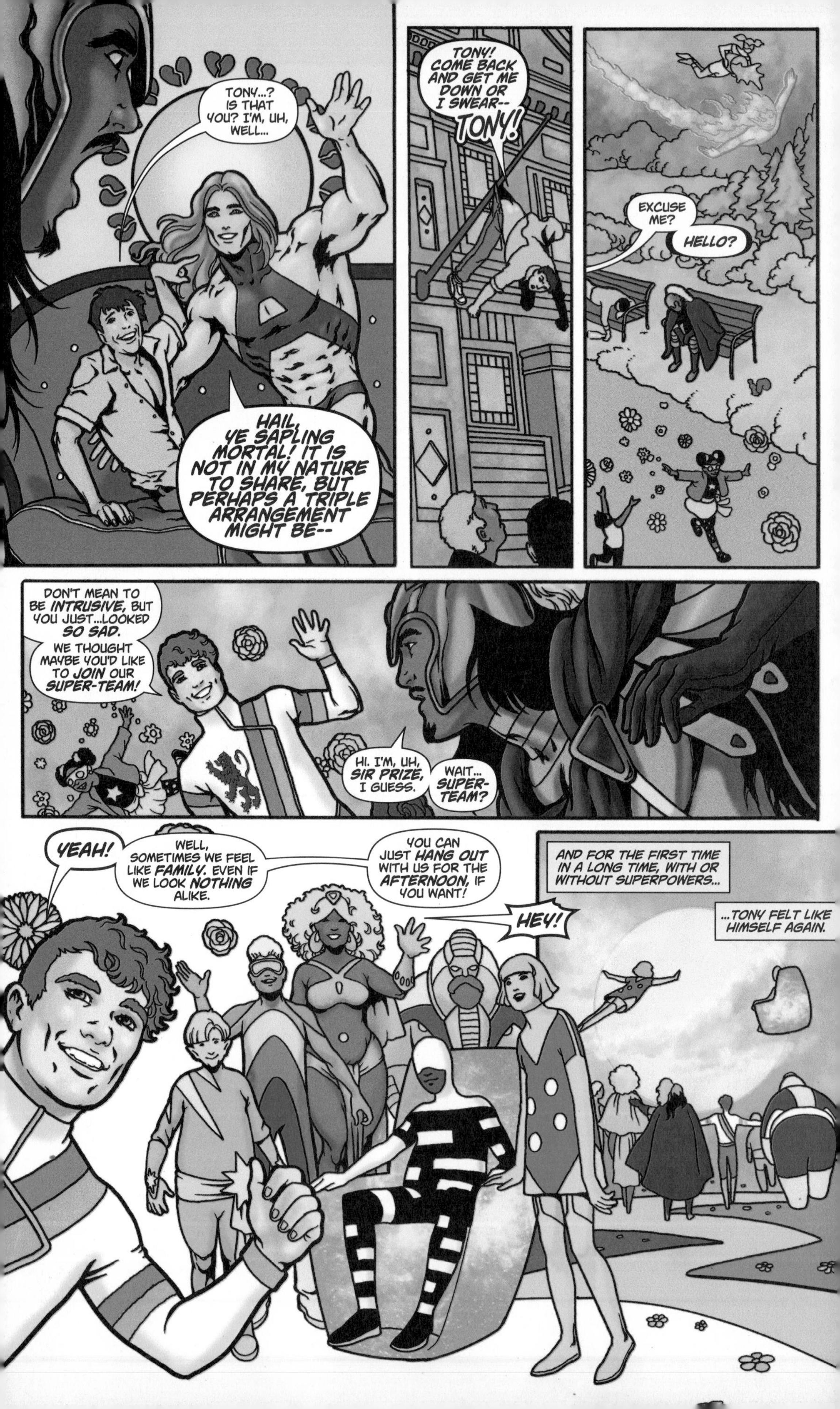

TONY...? IS THAT YOU? I'M, UH, WELL...
HAIL, YE SAPLING MORTAL! IT IS NOT IN MY NATURE TO SHARE, BUT PERHAPS A TRIPLE ARRANGEMENT MIGHT BE--
TONY! COME BACK AND GET ME DOWN OR I SWEAR--
TONY!
EXCUSE ME?
HELLO?
DON'T MEAN TO BE INTRUSIVE, BUT YOU JUST...LOOKED SO SAD.
WE THOUGHT MAYBE YOU'D LIKE TO JOIN OUR SUPER-TEAM!
HI. I'M, UH, SIR PRIZE, I GUESS.
WAIT... SUPER-TEAM?
YEAH!
WELL, SOMETIMES WE FEEL LIKE FAMILY. EVEN IF WE LOOK NOTHING ALIKE.
YOU CAN JUST HANG OUT WITH US FOR THE AFTERNOON, IF YOU WANT!
HEY!
AND FOR THE FIRST TIME IN A LONG TIME, WITH OR WITHOUT SUPERPOWERS...
...TONY FELT LIKE HIMSELF AGAIN.

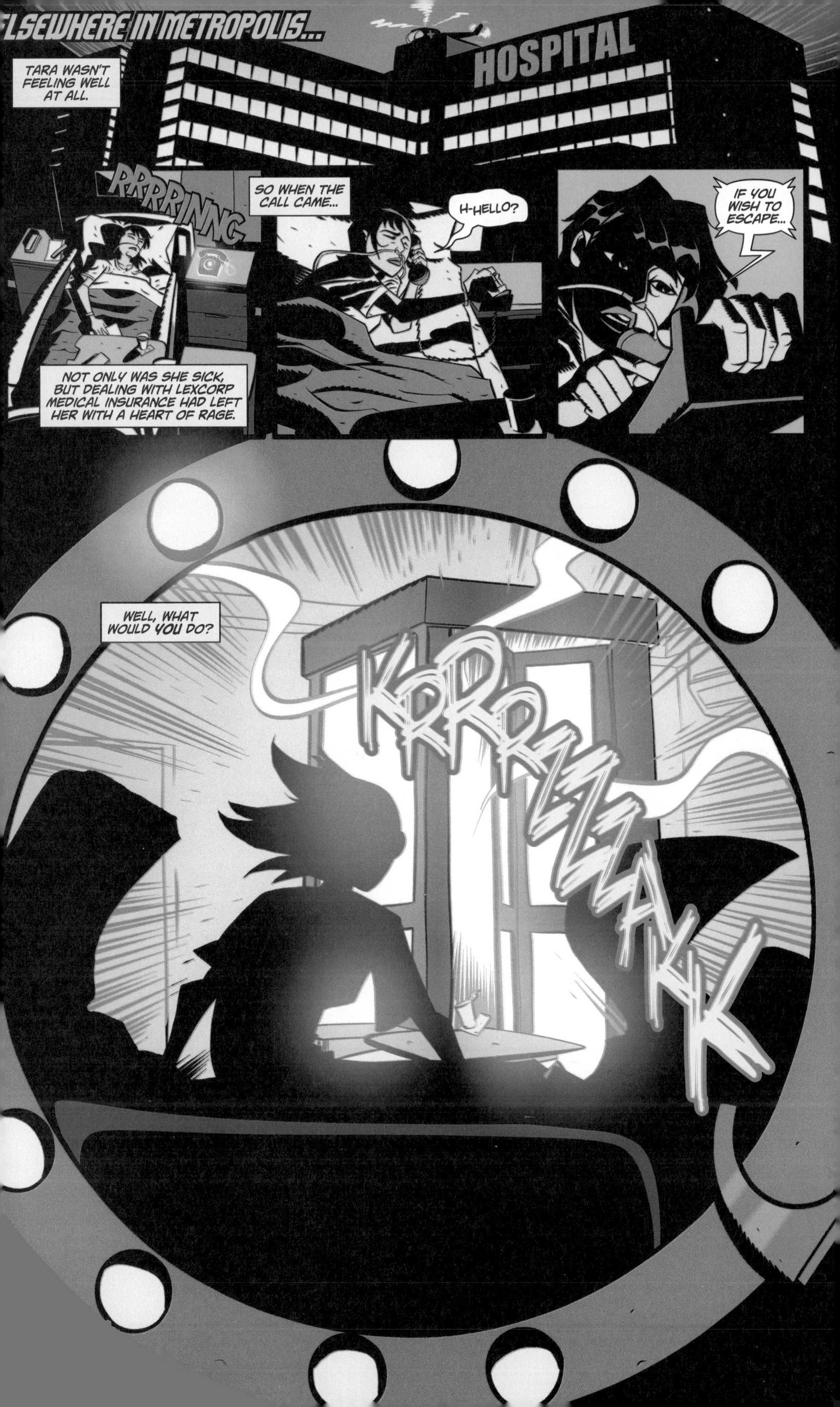

ELSEWHERE IN METROPOLIS...
HOSPITAL
TARA WASN'T FEELING WELL AT ALL.
RRRRINNG
NOT ONLY WAS SHE SICK, BUT DEALING WITH LEXCORP MEDICAL INSURANCE HAD LEFT HER WITH A HEART OF RAGE.
SO WHEN THE CALL CAME...
H-HELLO?
IF YOU WISH TO ESCAPE...
WELL, WHAT WOULD YOU DO?
KRRZZZAKK

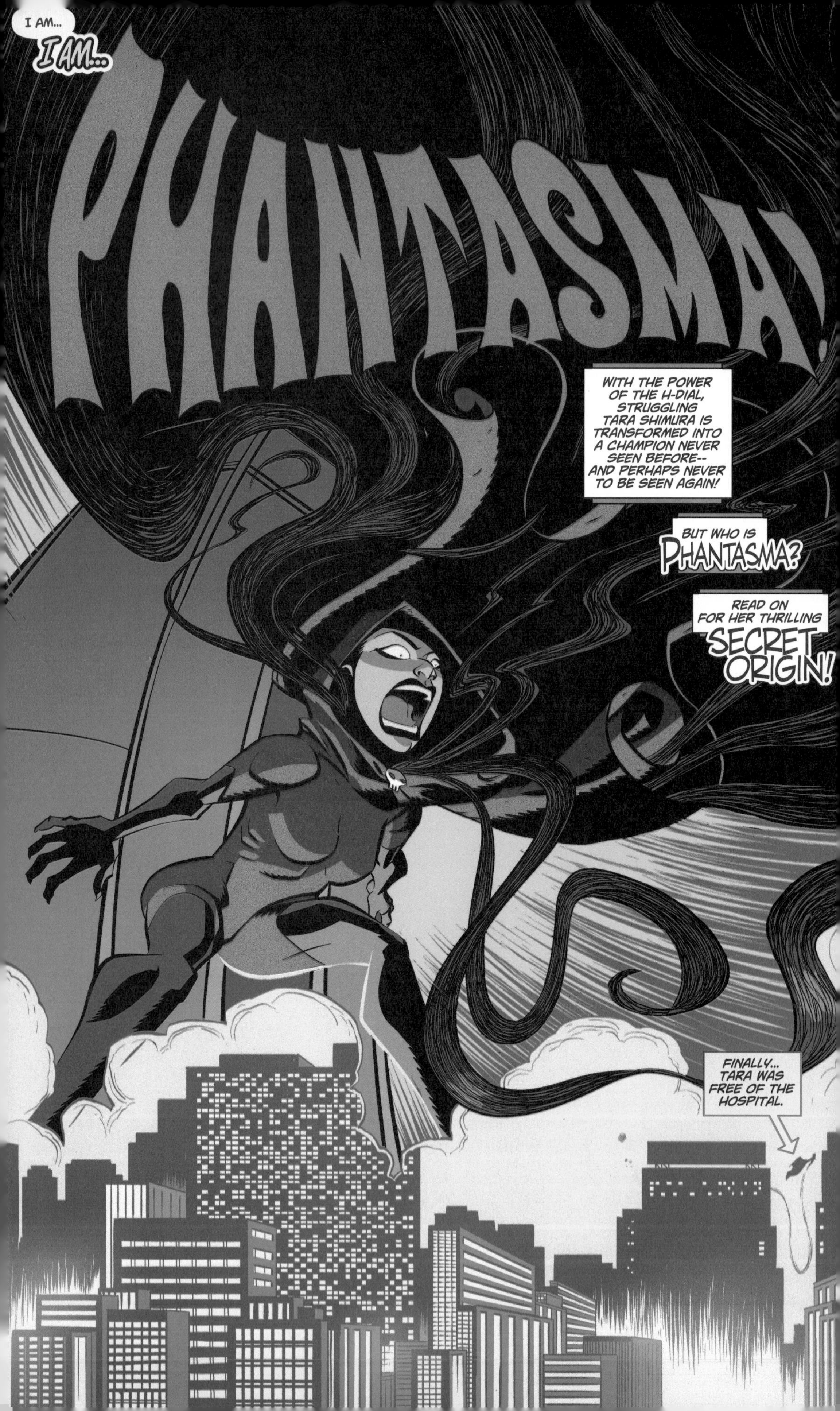

I AM...
I AM...
PHANTASMA!
WITH THE POWER OF THE H-DIAL, STRUGGLING TARA SHIMURA IS TRANSFORMED INTO A CHAMPION NEVER SEEN BEFORE-- AND PERHAPS NEVER TO BE SEEN AGAIN!
BUT WHO IS PHANTASMA?
READ ON FOR HER THRILLING SECRET ORIGIN!
FINALLY... TARA WAS FREE OF THE HOSPITAL.

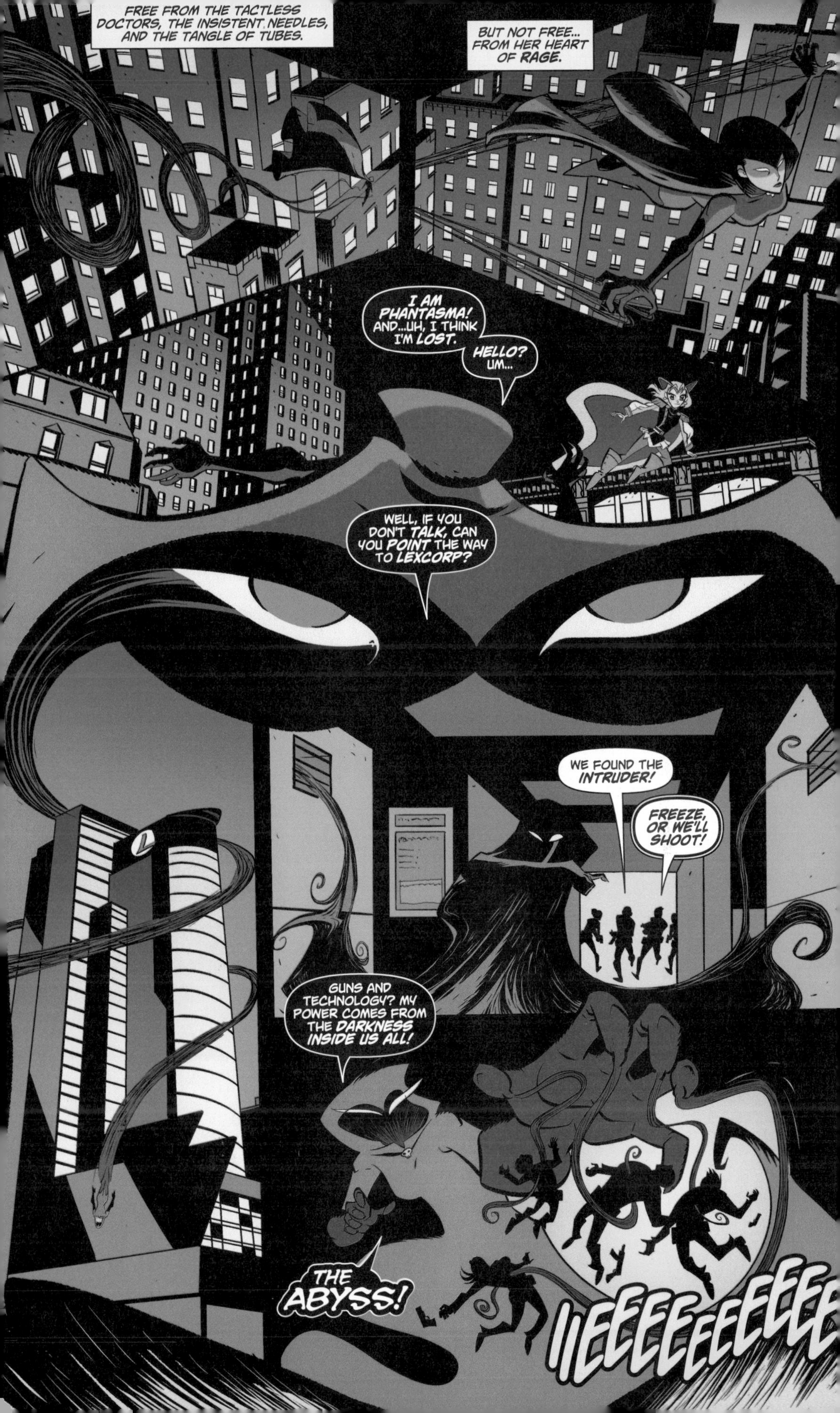

FREE FROM THE TACTLESS DOCTORS, THE INSISTENT NEEDLES, AND THE TANGLE OF TUBES.
BUT NOT FREE... FROM HER HEART OF RAGE.
I AM PHANTASMA! AND...UH, I THINK I'M LOST.
HELLO? UM...
WELL, IF YOU DON'T TALK, CAN YOU POINT THE WAY TO LEXCORP?
WE FOUND THE INTRUDER!
FREEZE, OR WE'LL SHOOT!
GUNS AND TECHNOLOGY? MY POWER COMES FROM THE DARKNESS INSIDE US ALL!
THE ABYSS!
IIEEEEEEEEEEE

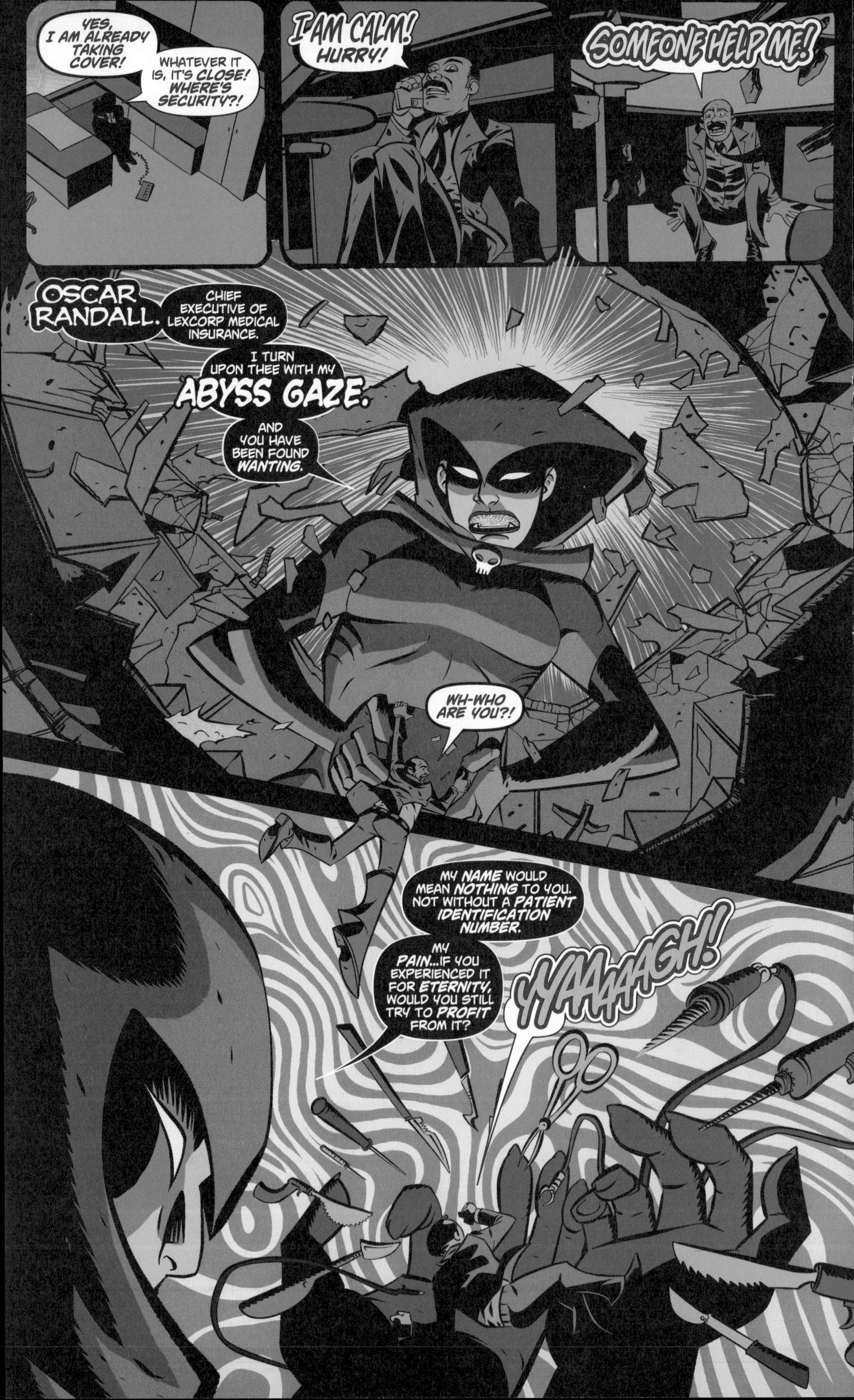

YES, I AM ALREADY TAKING COVER!
WHATEVER IT IS, IT'S CLOSE! WHERE'S SECURITY?!
I AM CALM! HURRY!
SOMEONE HELP ME!
OSCAR RANDALL.
CHIEF EXECUTIVE OF LEXCORP MEDICAL INSURANCE.
I TURN UPON THEE WITH MY ABYSS GAZE.
AND YOU HAVE BEEN FOUND WANTING.
WH-WHO ARE YOU?!
MY NAME WOULD MEAN NOTHING TO YOU. NOT WITHOUT A PATIENT IDENTIFICATION NUMBER.
MY PAIN...IF YOU EXPERIENCED IT FOR ETERNITY, WOULD YOU STILL TRY TO PROFIT FROM IT?
YAAAAAGH!

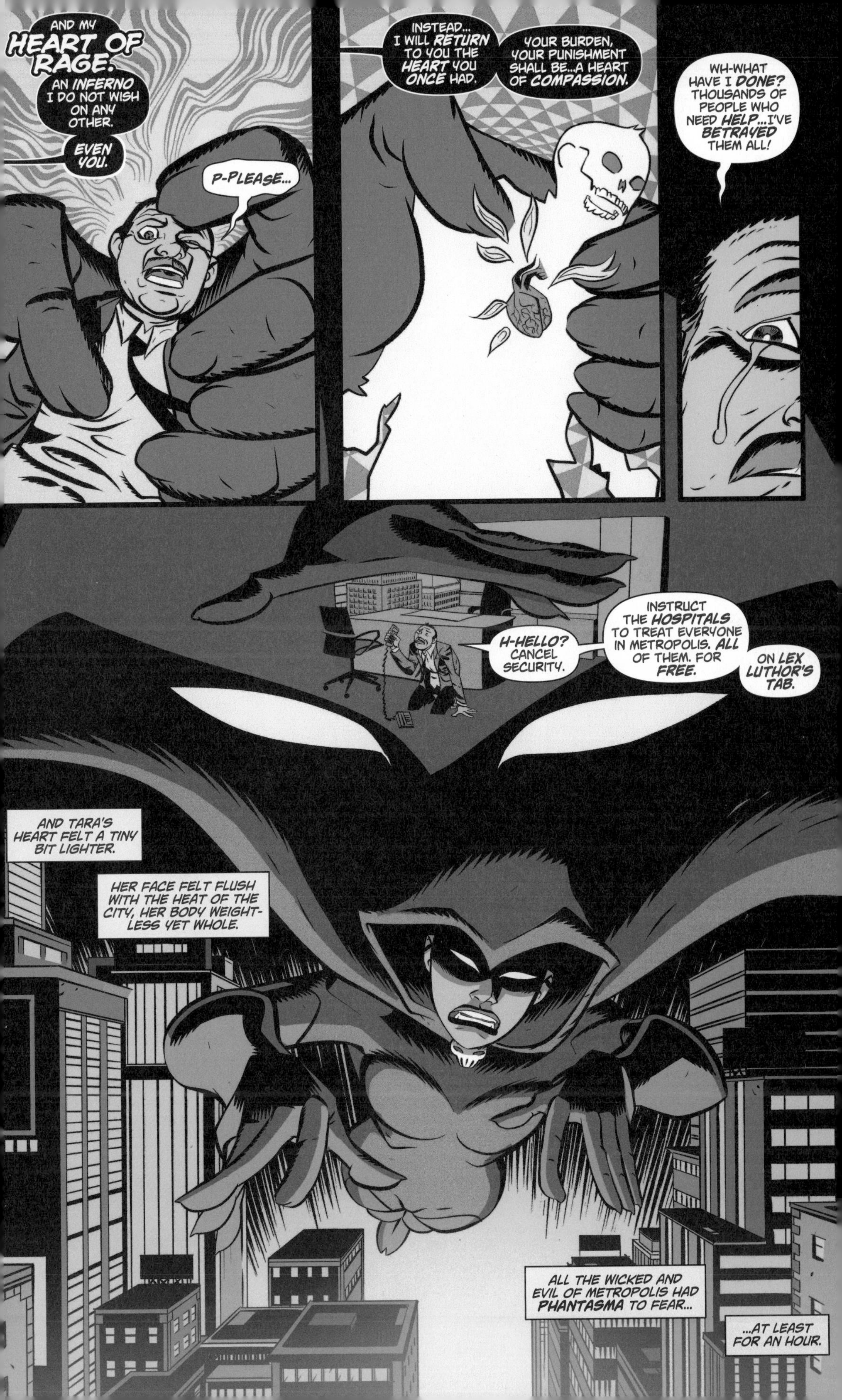
AND MY HEART OF RAGE.
AN INFERNO I DO NOT WISH ON ANY OTHER.
EVEN YOU.
P-PLEASE...
INSTEAD... I WILL RETURN TO YOU THE HEART YOU ONCE HAD.
YOUR BURDEN, YOUR PUNISHMENT SHALL BE...A HEART OF COMPASSION.
WH-WHAT HAVE I DONE? THOUSANDS OF PEOPLE WHO NEED HELP...I'VE BETRAYED THEM ALL!
H-HELLO? CANCEL SECURITY.
INSTRUCT THE HOSPITALS TO TREAT EVERYONE IN METROPOLIS. ALL OF THEM. FOR FREE.
ON LEX LUTHOR'S TAB.
AND TARA'S HEART FELT A TINY BIT LIGHTER.
HER FACE FELT FLUSH WITH THE HEAT OF THE CITY, HER BODY WEIGHT-LESS YET WHOLE.
ALL THE WICKED AND EVIL OF METROPOLIS HAD PHANTASMA TO FEAR...
...AT LEAST FOR AN HOUR.

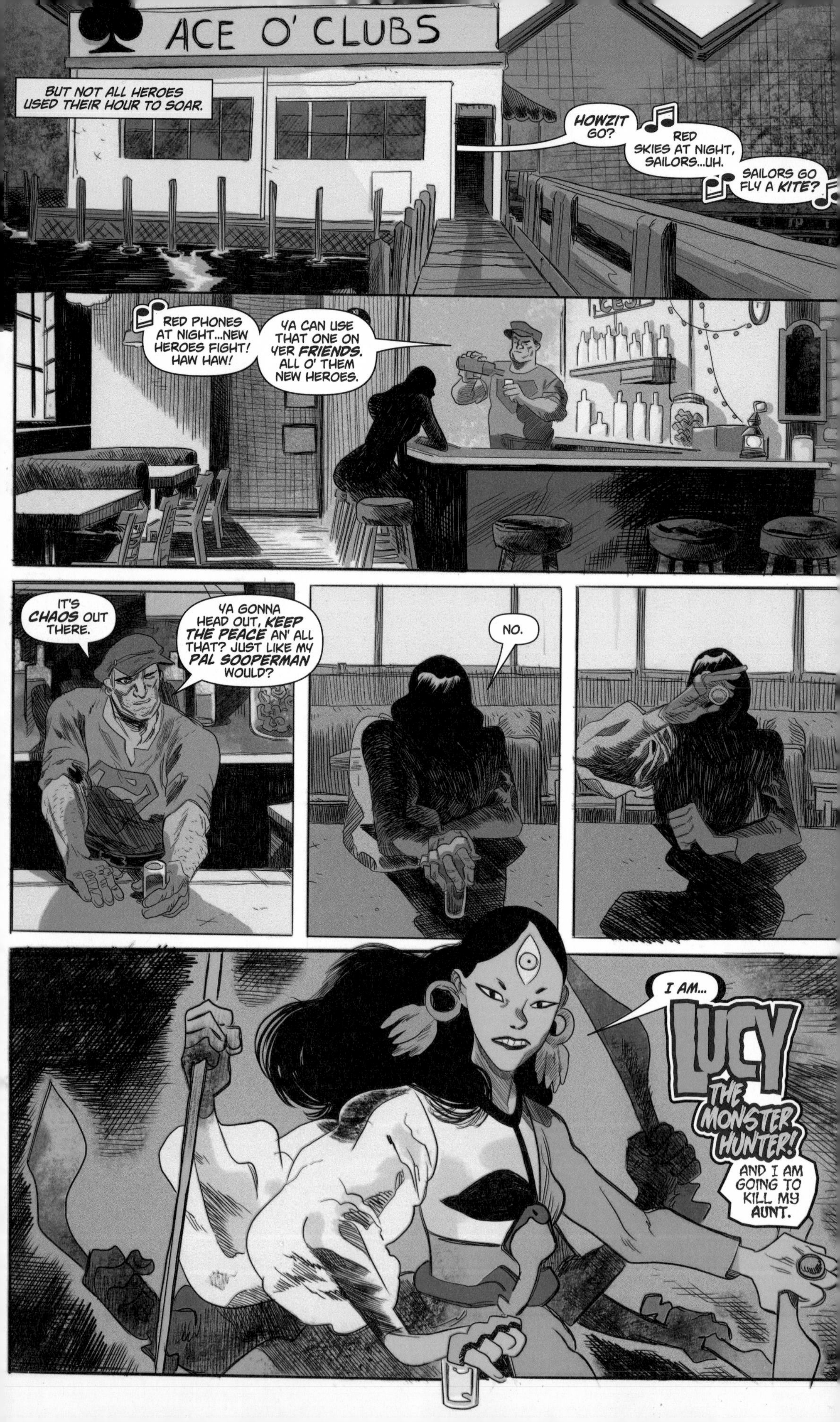
ACE O' CLUBS
BUT NOT ALL HEROES USED THEIR HOUR TO SOAR.
HOWZIT GO?
RED SKIES AT NIGHT, SAILORS...UH.
SAILORS GO FLY A KITE?
RED PHONES AT NIGHT...NEW HEROES FIGHT! HAW HAW!
YA CAN USE THAT ONE ON YER FRIENDS. ALL O' THEM NEW HEROES.
IT'S CHAOS OUT THERE.
YA GONNA HEAD OUT, KEEP THE PEACE AN' ALL THAT? JUST LIKE MY PAL SOOPERMAN WOULD?
NO.
I AM...
LUCY THE MONSTER HUNTER!
AND I AM GOING TO KILL MY AUNT.

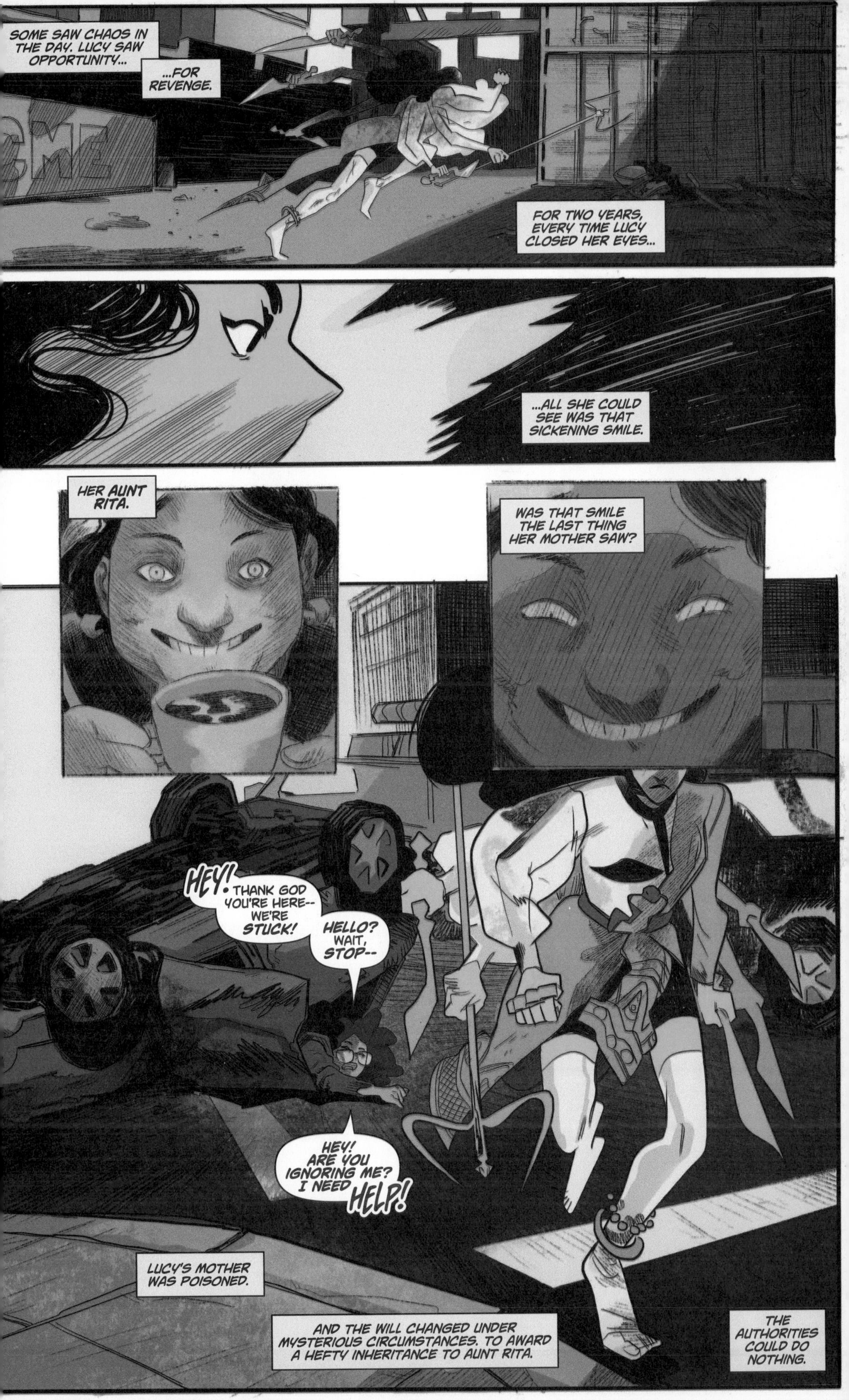
SOME SAW CHAOS IN THE DAY. LUCY SAW OPPORTUNITY...
...FOR REVENGE.
FOR TWO YEARS, EVERY TIME LUCY CLOSED HER EYES...
...ALL SHE COULD SEE WAS THAT SICKENING SMILE.
HER AUNT RITA.
WAS THAT SMILE THE LAST THING HER MOTHER SAW?
HEY! THANK GOD YOU'RE HERE-- WE'RE STUCK!
HELLO? WAIT, STOP--
HEY! ARE YOU IGNORING ME? I NEED HELP!
LUCY'S MOTHER WAS POISONED.
AND THE WILL CHANGED UNDER MYSTERIOUS CIRCUMSTANCES. TO AWARD A HEFTY INHERITANCE TO AUNT RITA.
THE AUTHORITIES COULD DO NOTHING.

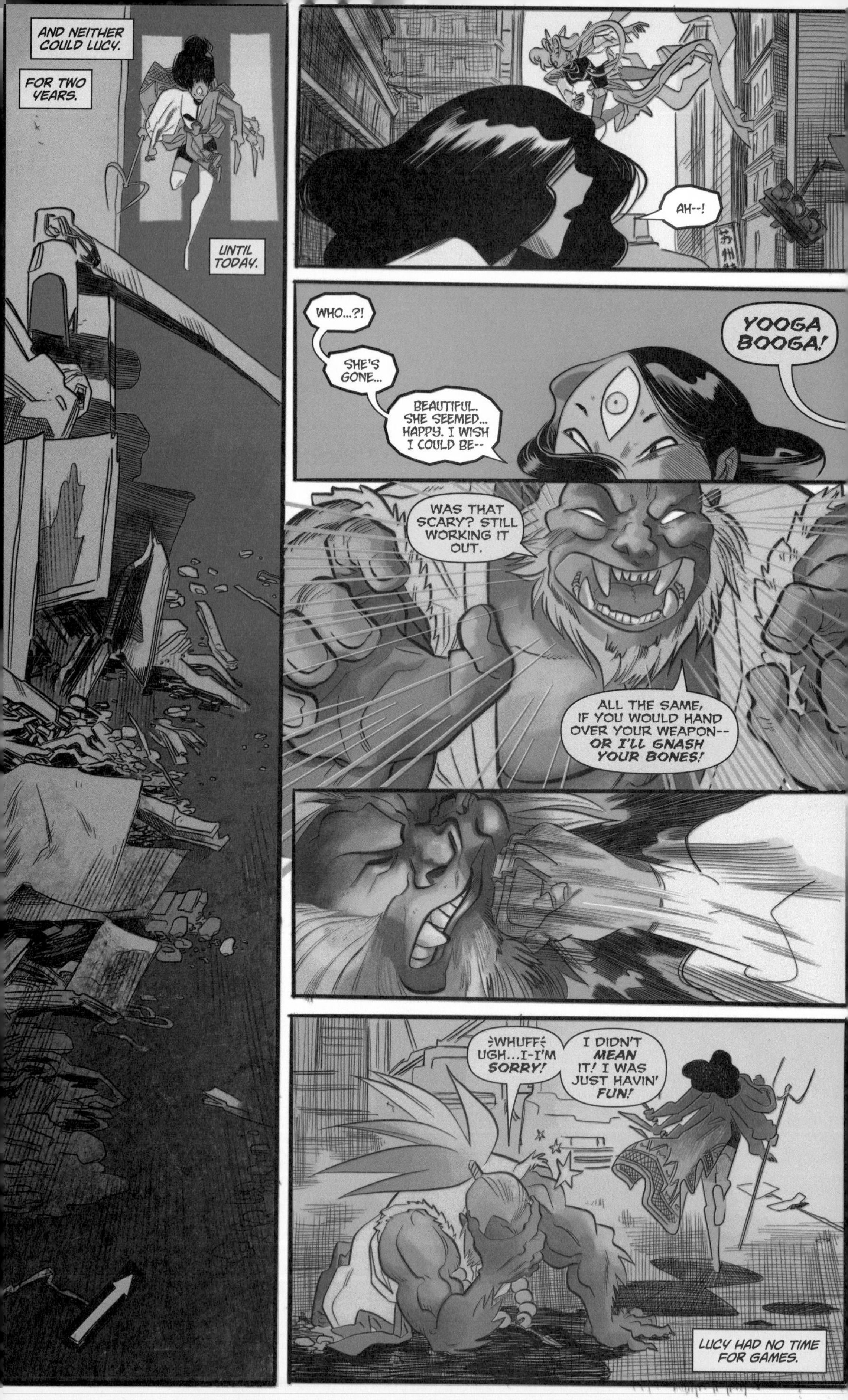

AND NEITHER COULD LUCY.
FOR TWO YEARS.
UNTIL TODAY.
AH--!
WHO...?!
SHE'S GONE...
BEAUTIFUL. SHE SEEMED... HAPPY. I WISH I COULD BE--
YOOGA BOOGA!
WAS THAT SCARY? STILL WORKING IT OUT.
ALL THE SAME, IF YOU WOULD HAND OVER YOUR WEAPON-- OR I'LL GNASH YOUR BONES!
WHUFF UGH...I-I'M SORRY!
I DIDN'T MEAN IT! I WAS JUST HAVIN' FUN!
LUCY HAD NO TIME FOR GAMES.

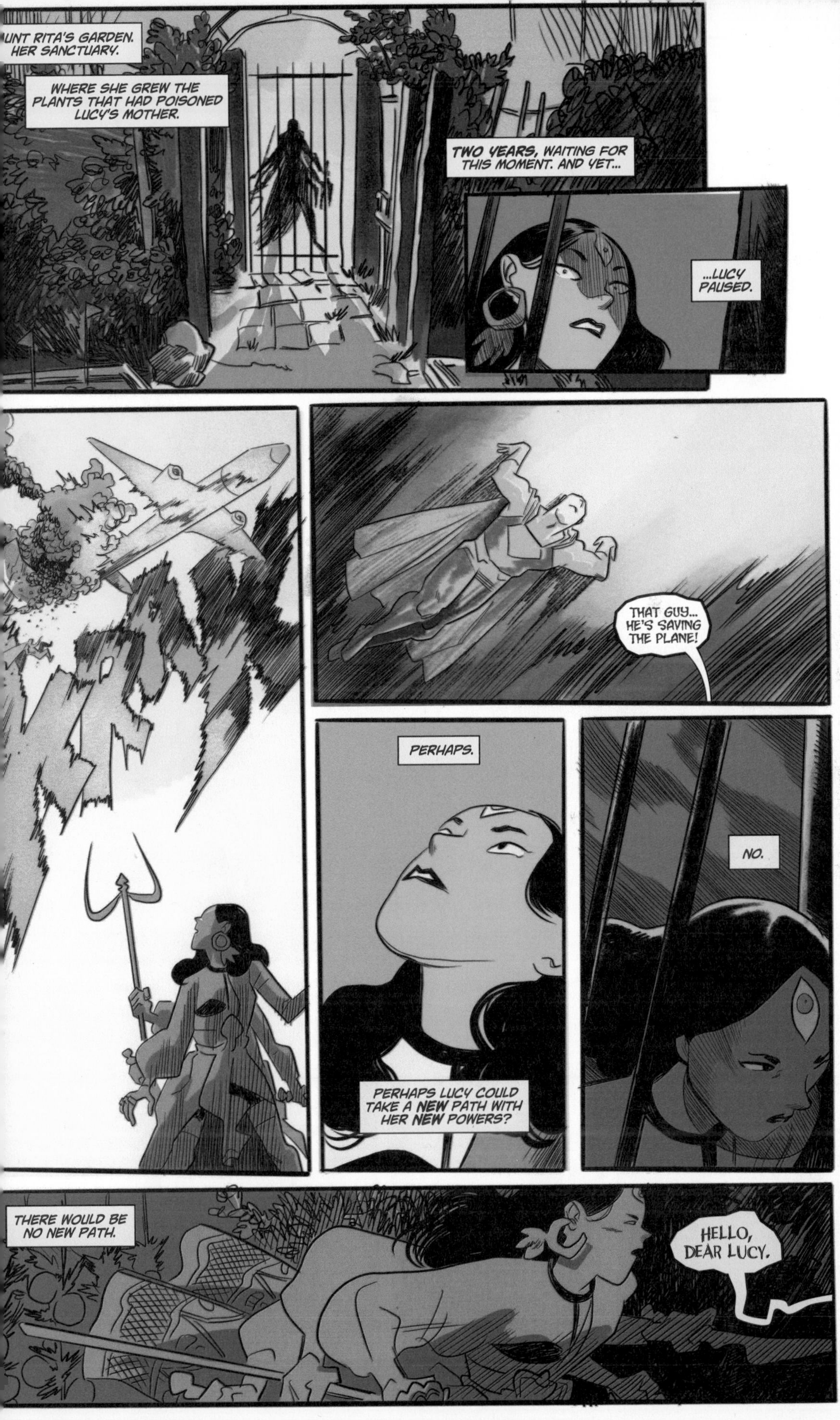
UNT RITA'S GARDEN. HER SANCTUARY.
WHERE SHE GREW THE PLANTS THAT HAD POISONED LUCY'S MOTHER.
TWO YEARS, WAITING FOR THIS MOMENT. AND YET...
...LUCY PAUSED.
THAT GUY... HE'S SAVING THE PLANE!
PERHAPS.
PERHAPS LUCY COULD TAKE A NEW PATH WITH HER NEW POWERS?
NO.
THERE WOULD BE NO NEW PATH.
HELLO, DEAR LUCY.

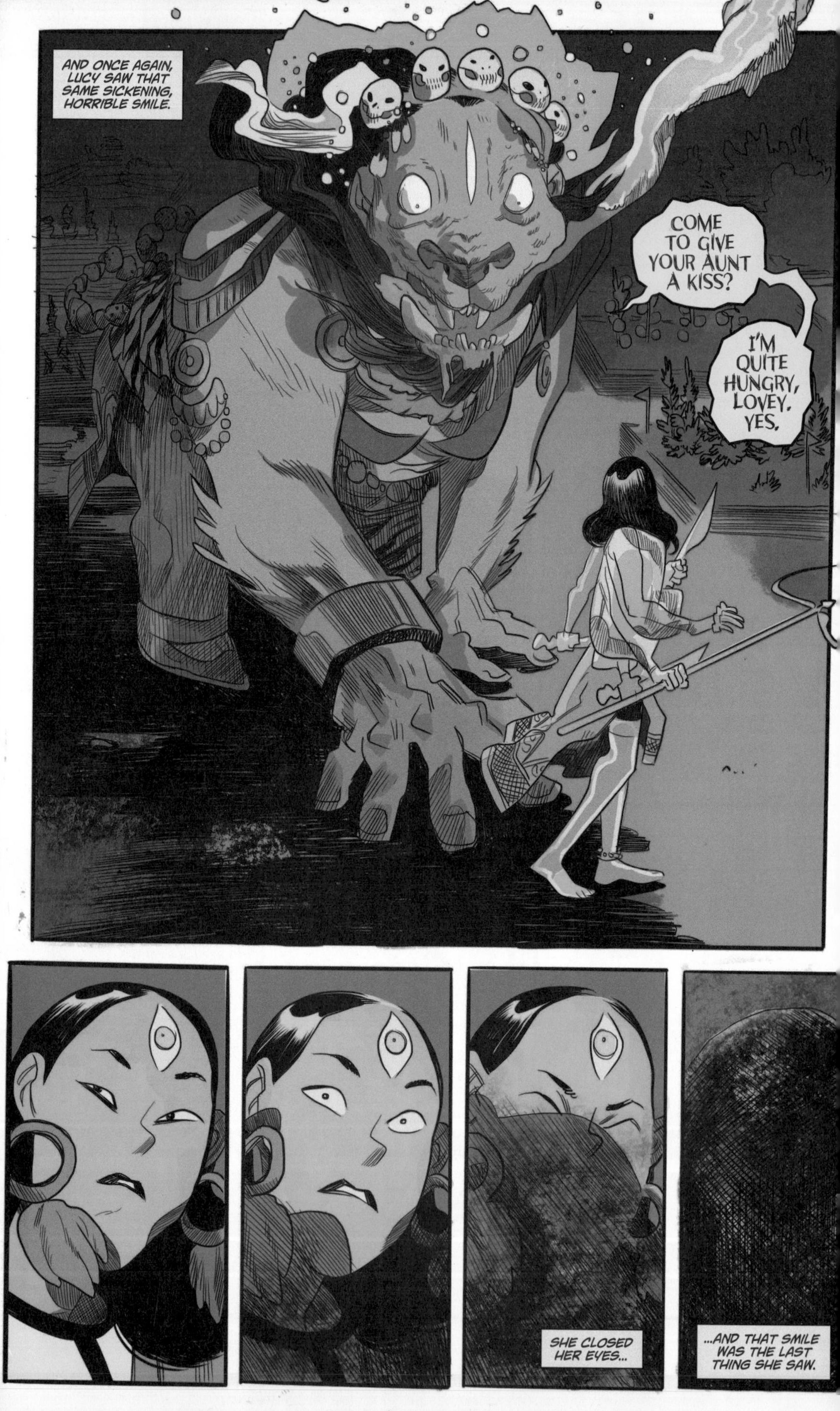
AND ONCE AGAIN, LUCY SAW THAT SAME SICKENING, HORRIBLE SMILE.
COME TO GIVE YOUR AUNT A KISS?
I'M QUITE HUNGRY, LOVEY. YES.
SHE CLOSED HER EYES...
...AND THAT SMILE WAS THE LAST THING SHE SAW.

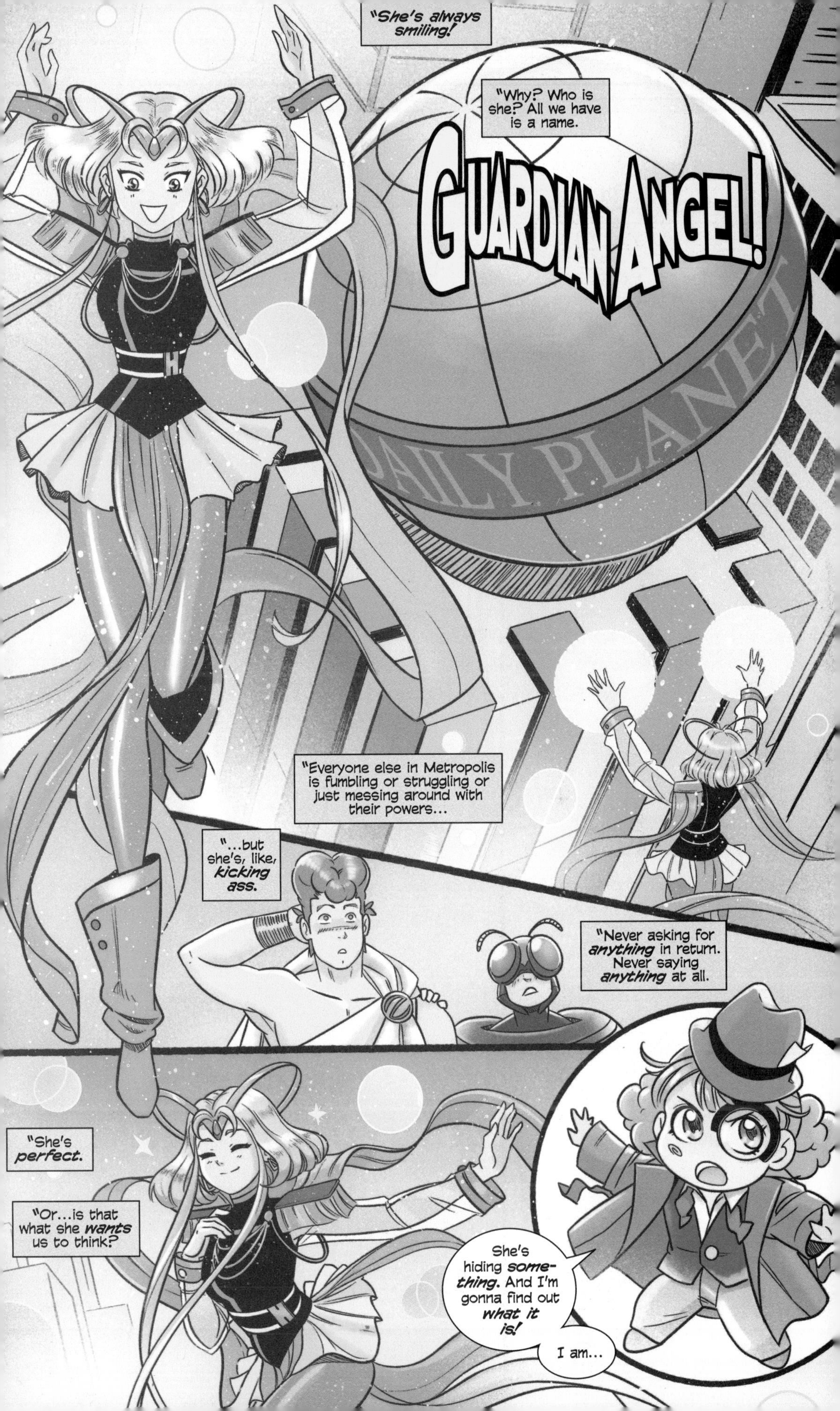
"She's always smiling!
"Why? Who is she? All we have is a name.
GUARDIAN ANGEL!
DAILY PLANET
"Everyone else in Metropolis is fumbling or struggling or just messing around with their powers...
"...but she's, like, *kicking ass.*
"Never asking for *anything* in return. Never saying *anything* at all.
"She's *perfect.*
"Or...is that what she *wants* us to think?
She's hiding *something.* And I'm gonna find out *what it is!*
I am...

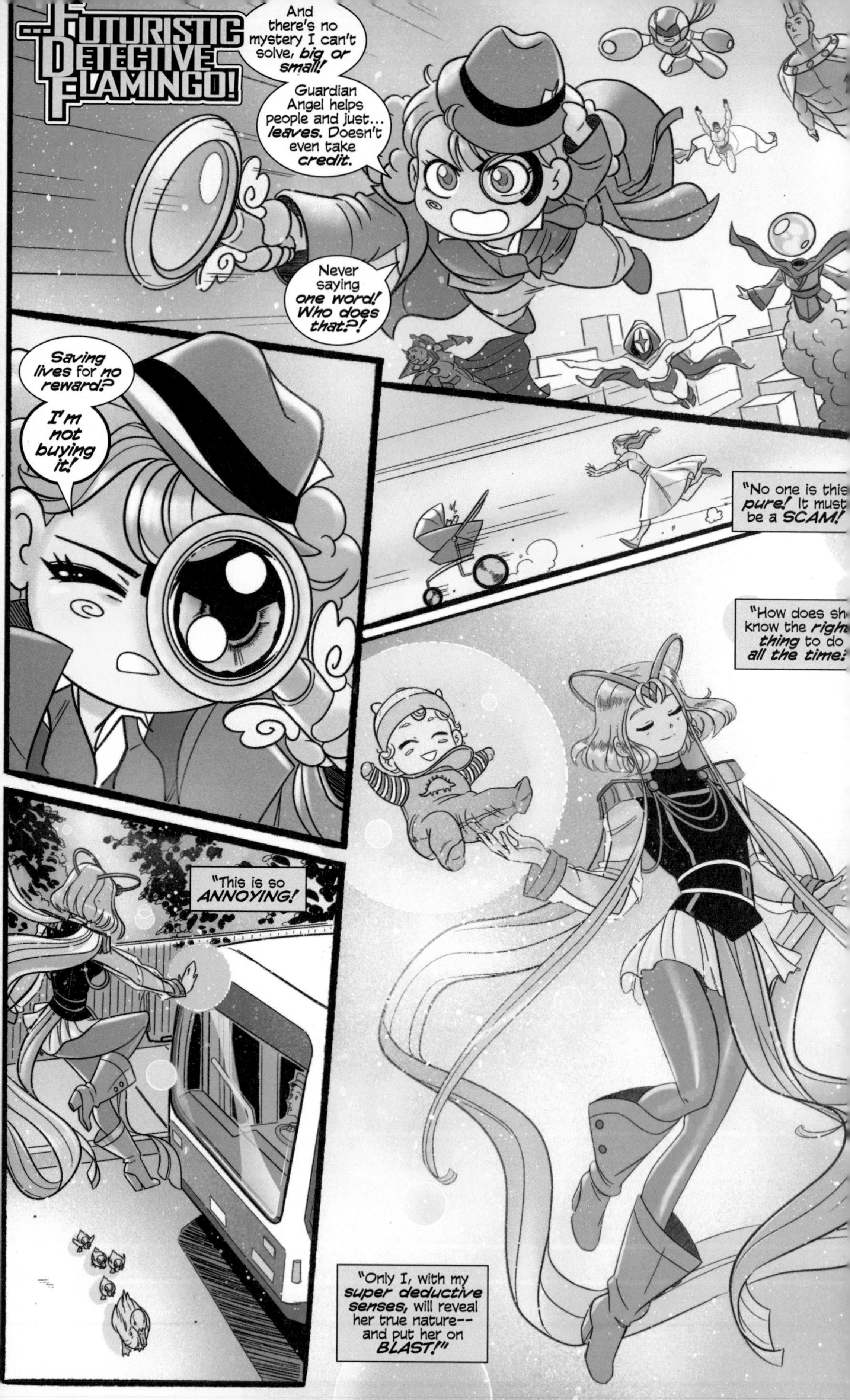
...FUTURISTIC DETECTIVE FLAMINGO!
And there's no mystery I can't solve, big or small!
Guardian Angel helps people and just... leaves. Doesn't even take credit.
Never saying one word! Who does that?!
Saving lives for no reward?
I'm not buying it!
"No one is this pure! It must be a SCAM!
"How does she know the right thing to do all the time?
"This is so ANNOYING!
"Only I, with my super deductive senses, will reveal her true nature--and put her on BLAST!"

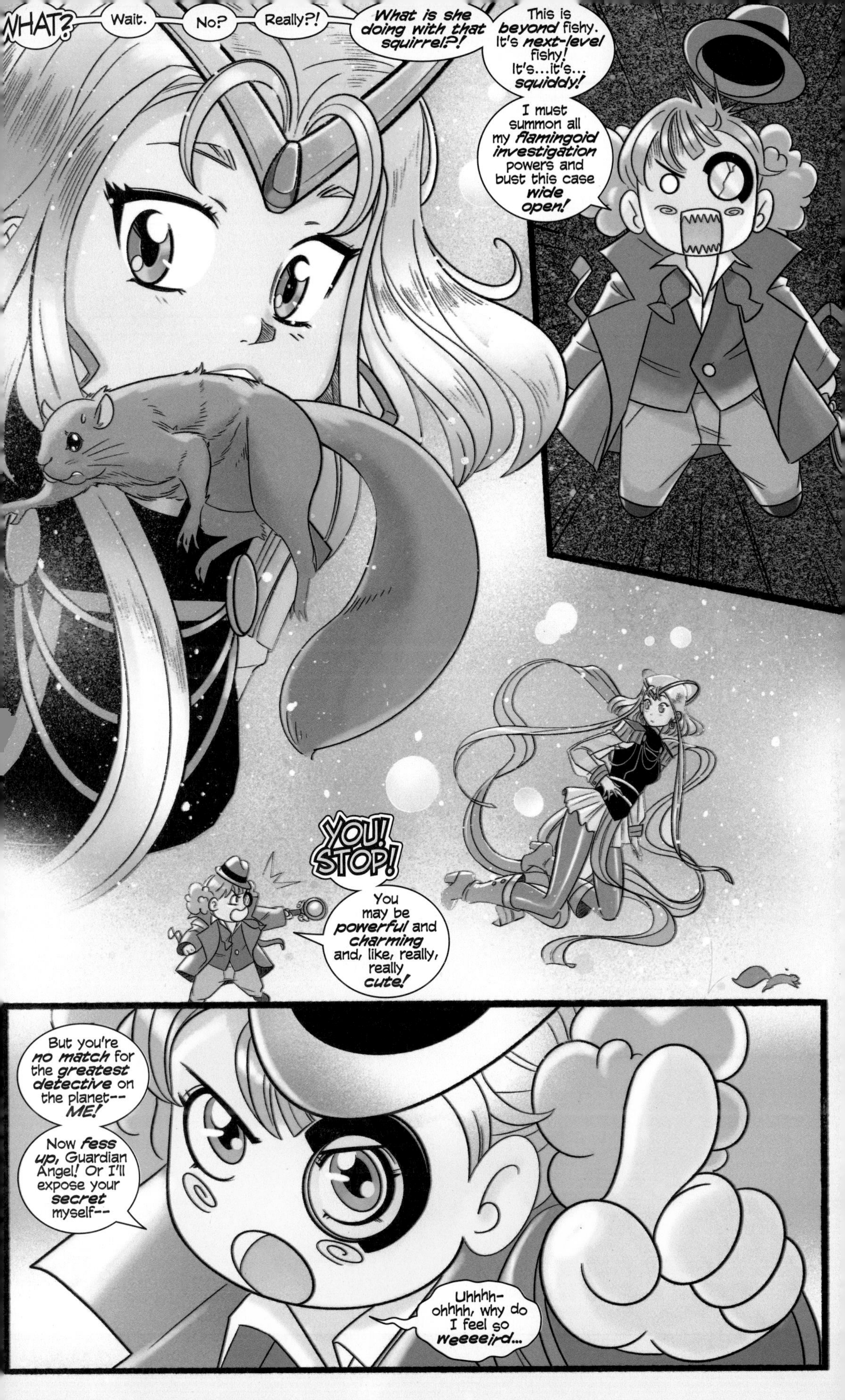
WHAT?
Wait.
No?
Really?!
What is she doing with that squirrel?!
This is beyond fishy. It's next-level fishy! It's...it's... squiddy!
I must summon all my flamingoid investigation powers and bust this case wide open!
YOU! STOP!
You may be powerful and charming and, like, really, really cute!
But you're no match for the greatest detective on the planet-- ME!
Now fess up, Guardian Angel! Or I'll expose your secret myself--
Uhhhh-ohhhh, why do I feel so weeeeird...

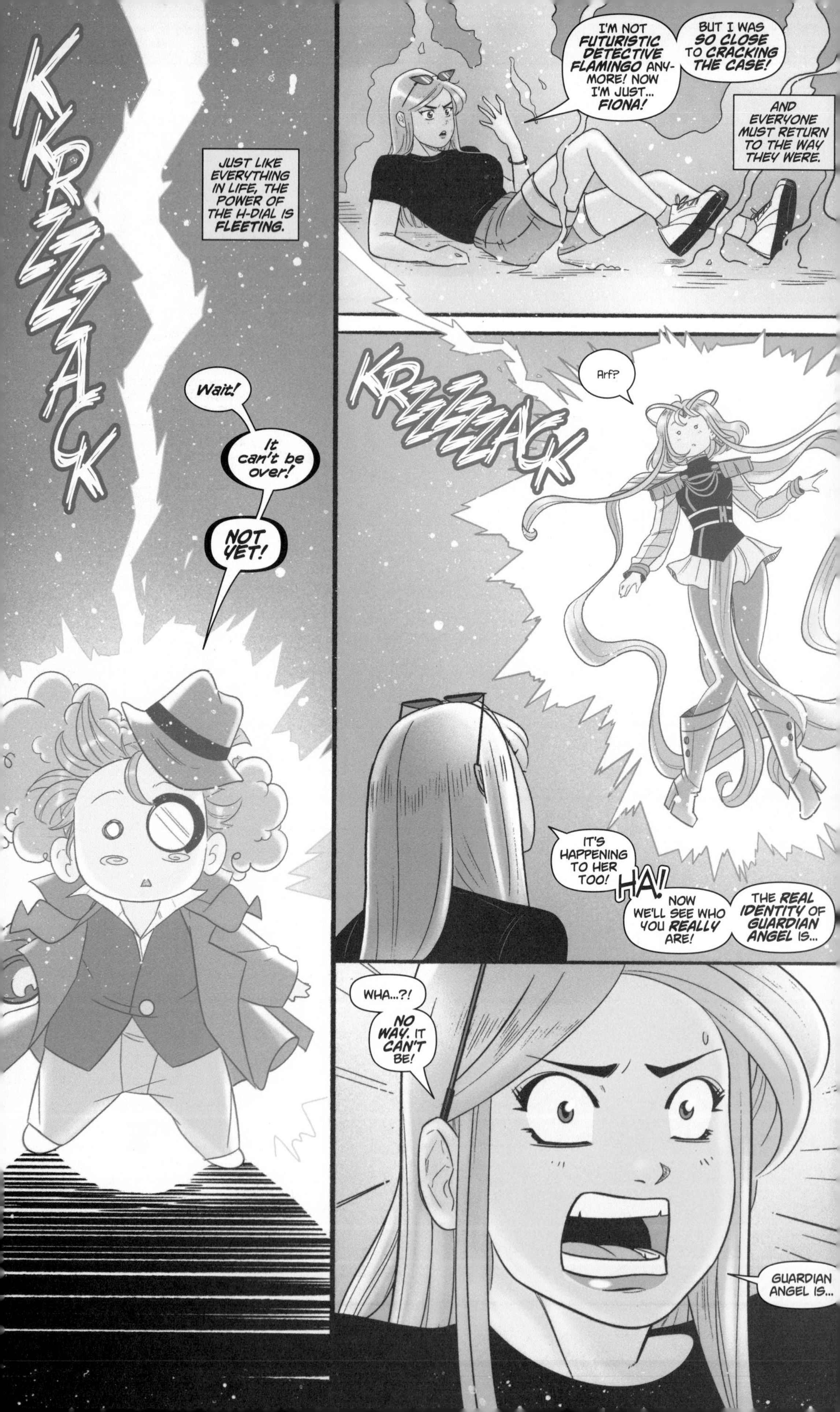
KKRZZZZACK
JUST LIKE EVERYTHING IN LIFE, THE POWER OF THE H-DIAL IS FLEETING.
Wait!
It can't be over!
NOT YET!
I'M NOT FUTURISTIC DETECTIVE FLAMINGO ANY-MORE! NOW I'M JUST... FIONA!
BUT I WAS SO CLOSE TO CRACKING THE CASE!
AND EVERYONE MUST RETURN TO THE WAY THEY WERE.
KRZZZZACK
Arf?
IT'S HAPPENING TO HER TOO!
HA!
NOW WE'LL SEE WHO YOU REALLY ARE!
THE REAL IDENTITY OF GUARDIAN ANGEL IS...
WHA...?!
NO WAY. IT CAN'T BE!
GUARDIAN ANGEL IS...

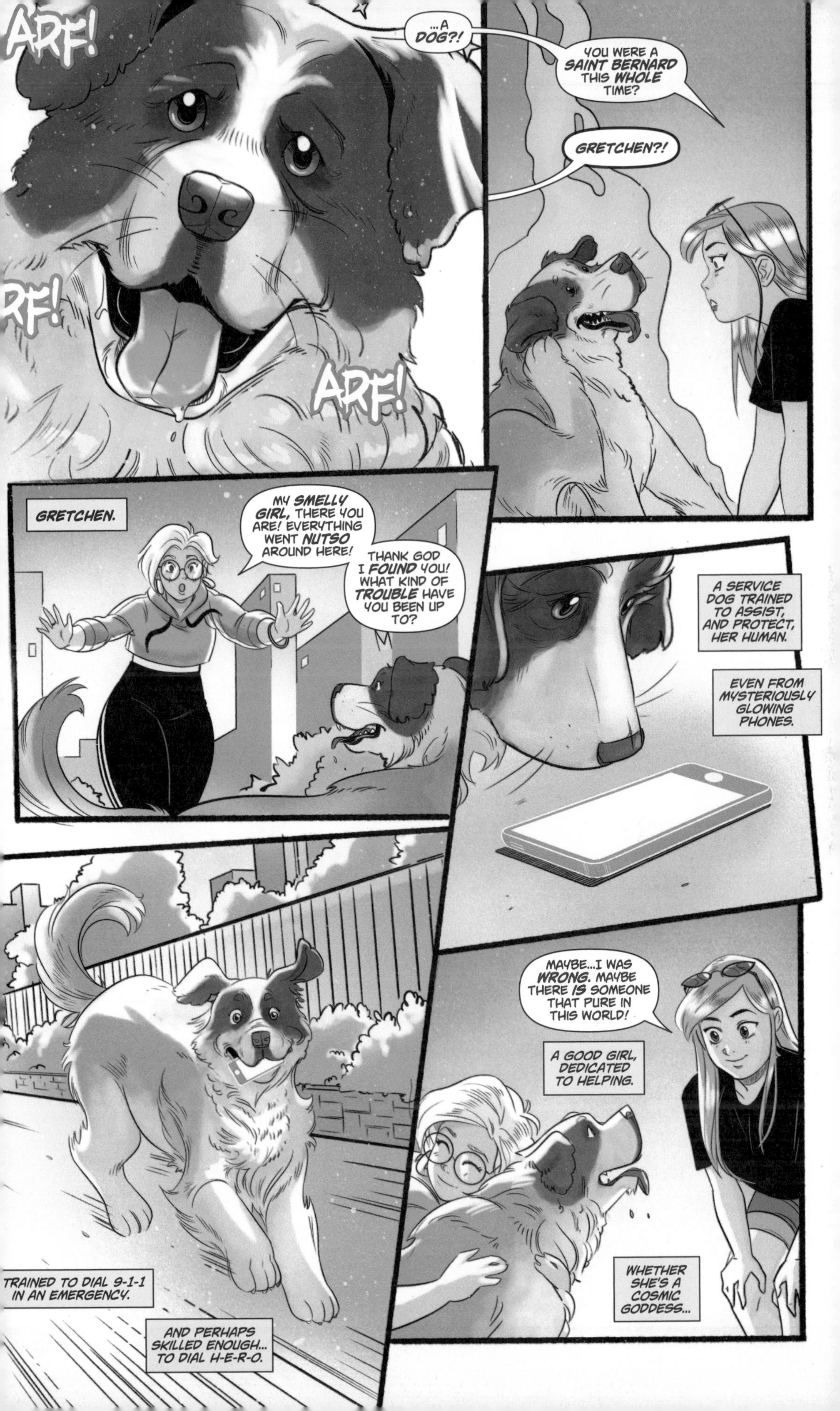
ARF!
ARF!
ARF!
...A DOG?!
YOU WERE A SAINT BERNARD THIS WHOLE TIME?
GRETCHEN?!
GRETCHEN.
MY SMELLY GIRL, THERE YOU ARE! EVERYTHING WENT NUTSO AROUND HERE!
THANK GOD I FOUND YOU! WHAT KIND OF TROUBLE HAVE YOU BEEN UP TO?
A SERVICE DOG TRAINED TO ASSIST, AND PROTECT, HER HUMAN.
EVEN FROM MYSTERIOUSLY GLOWING PHONES.
TRAINED TO DIAL 9-1-1 IN AN EMERGENCY.
AND PERHAPS SKILLED ENOUGH... TO DIAL H-E-R-O.
MAYBE...I WAS WRONG. MAYBE THERE IS SOMEONE THAT PURE IN THIS WORLD!
A GOOD GIRL, DEDICATED TO HELPING.
WHETHER SHE'S A COSMIC GODDESS...

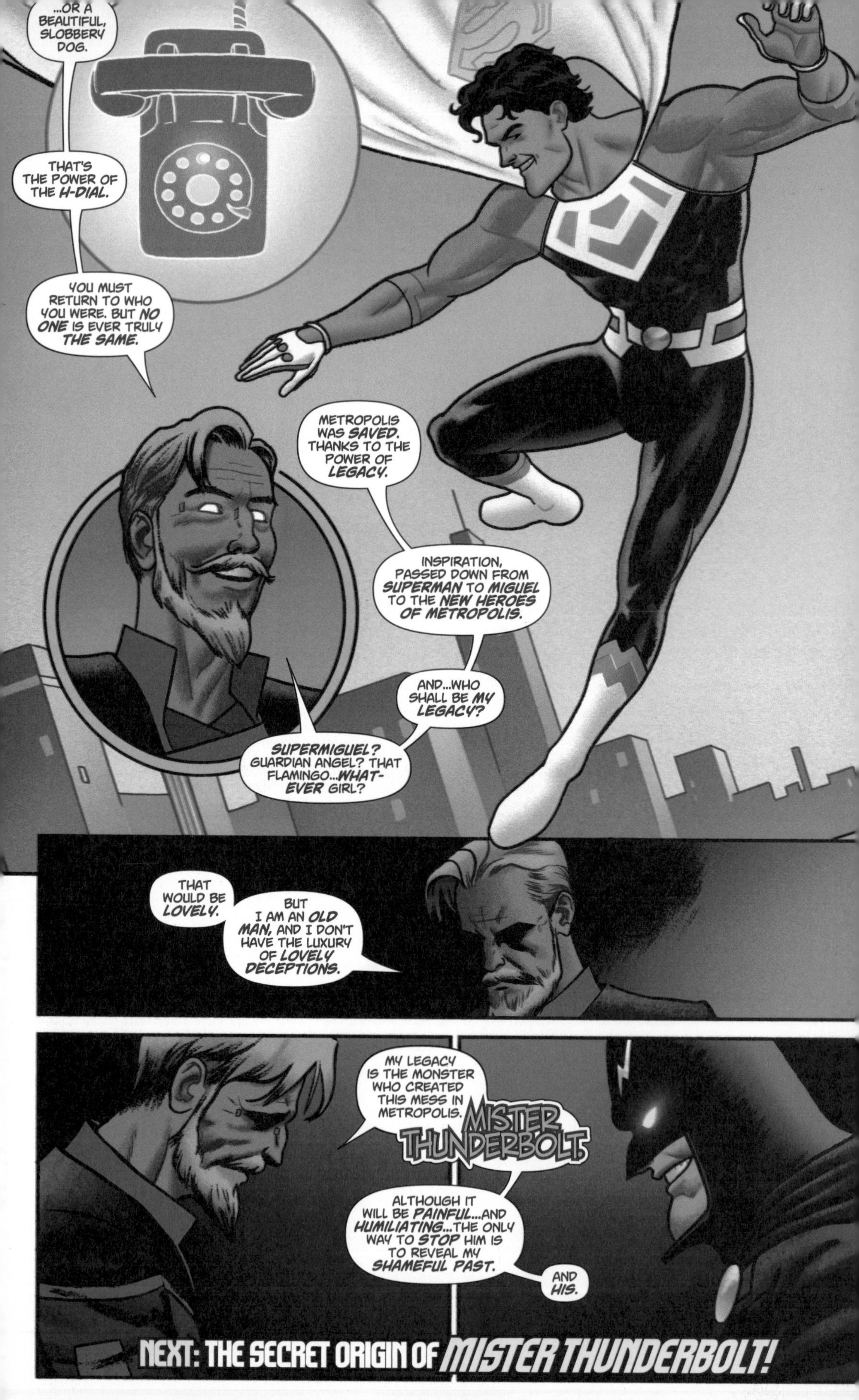
...OR A BEAUTIFUL, SLOBBERY DOG.
THAT'S THE POWER OF THE H-DIAL.
YOU MUST RETURN TO WHO YOU WERE. BUT NO ONE IS EVER TRULY THE SAME.
METROPOLIS WAS SAVED. THANKS TO THE POWER OF LEGACY.
INSPIRATION, PASSED DOWN FROM SUPERMAN TO MIGUEL TO THE NEW HEROES OF METROPOLIS.
AND...WHO SHALL BE MY LEGACY?
SUPERMIGUEL? GUARDIAN ANGEL? THAT FLAMINGO...WHAT-EVER GIRL?
THAT WOULD BE LOVELY.
BUT I AM AN OLD MAN, AND I DON'T HAVE THE LUXURY OF LOVELY DECEPTIONS.
MY LEGACY IS THE MONSTER WHO CREATED THIS MESS IN METROPOLIS.
MISTER THUNDERBOLT.
ALTHOUGH IT WILL BE PAINFUL...AND HUMILIATING...THE ONLY WAY TO STOP HIM IS TO REVEAL MY SHAMEFUL PAST.
AND HIS.
NEXT: THE SECRET ORIGIN OF MISTER THUNDERBOLT!

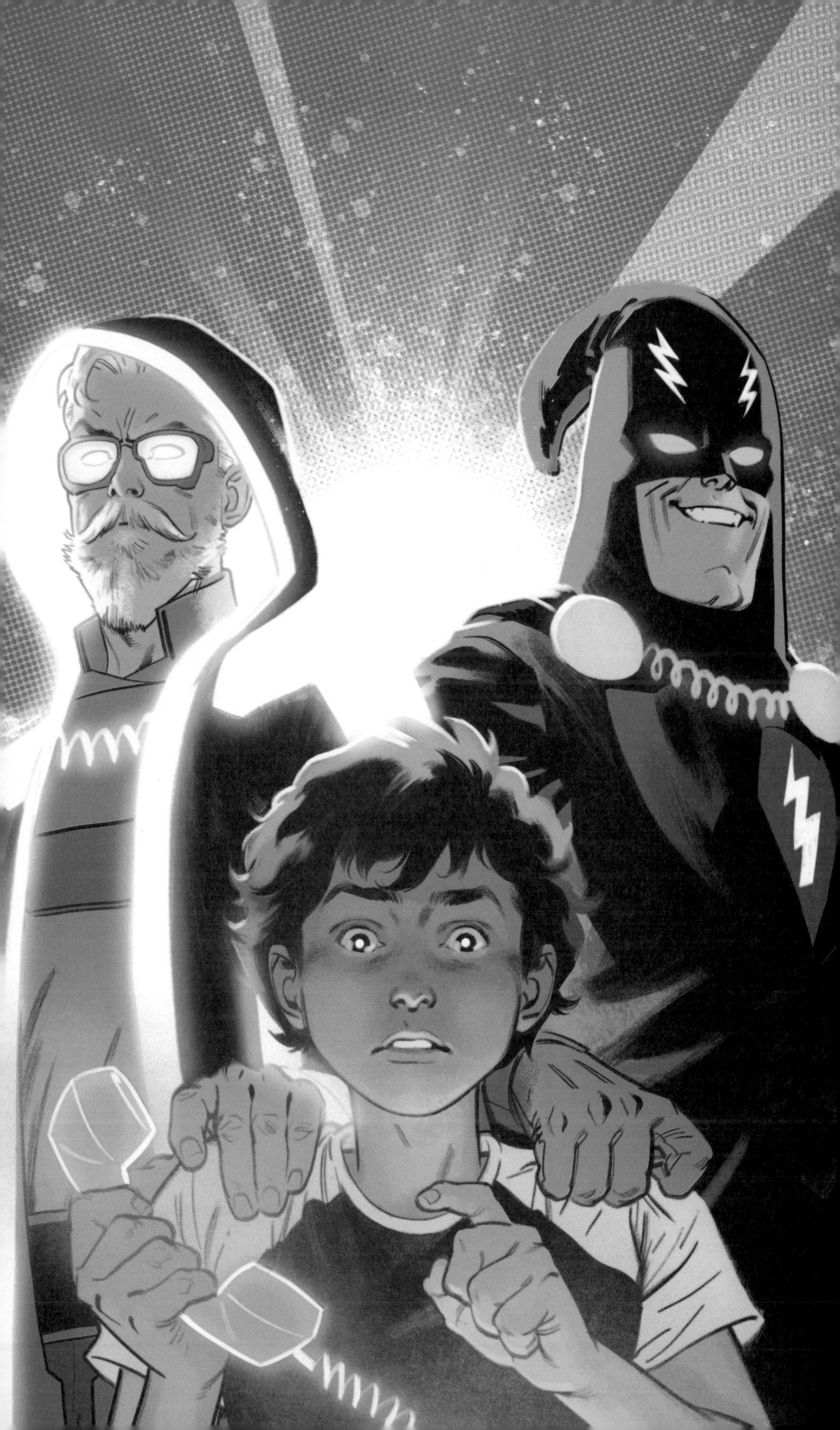

THE MANY TRANSFORMATIONS OF ROBBY REED

art by
PAULINA GANUCHEAU and **JOE QUINONES**

colors by
JORDAN GIBSON and **JOE QUINONES**

cover art by
JOE QUINONES

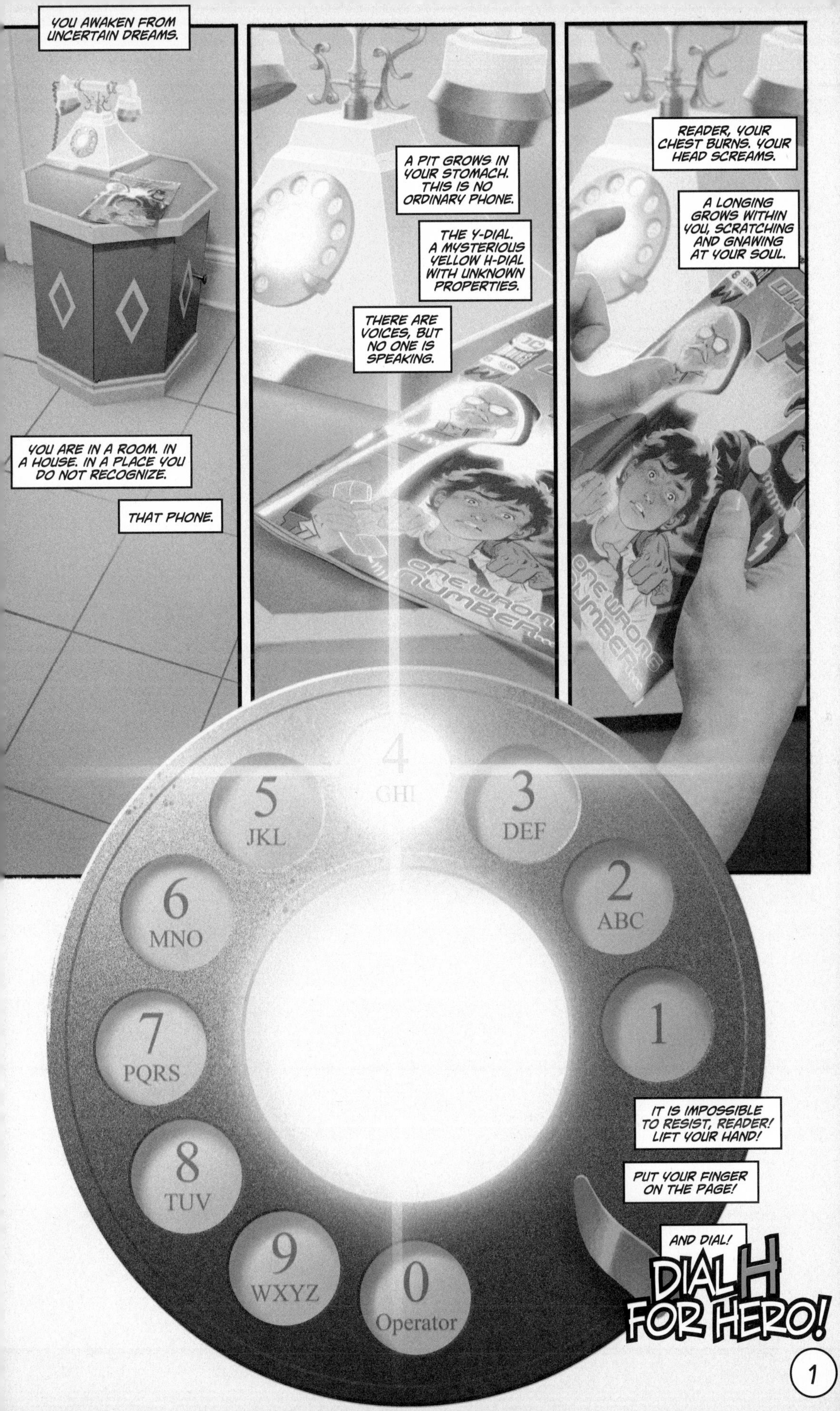
YOU AWAKEN FROM UNCERTAIN DREAMS.
YOU ARE IN A ROOM. IN A HOUSE. IN A PLACE YOU DO NOT RECOGNIZE.
THAT PHONE.
A PIT GROWS IN YOUR STOMACH. THIS IS NO ORDINARY PHONE.
THE Y-DIAL. A MYSTERIOUS YELLOW H-DIAL WITH UNKNOWN PROPERTIES.
THERE ARE VOICES, BUT NO ONE IS SPEAKING.
ONE WRONG NUMBER...
READER, YOUR CHEST BURNS. YOUR HEAD SCREAMS.
A LONGING GROWS WITHIN YOU, SCRATCHING AND GNAWING AT YOUR SOUL.
5 JKL
4 GHI
3 DEF
2 ABC
6 MNO
1
7 PQRS
8 TUV
9 WXYZ
0 Operator
IT IS IMPOSSIBLE TO RESIST, READER! LIFT YOUR HAND!
PUT YOUR FINGER ON THE PAGE!
AND DIAL!
DIAL H FOR HERO!

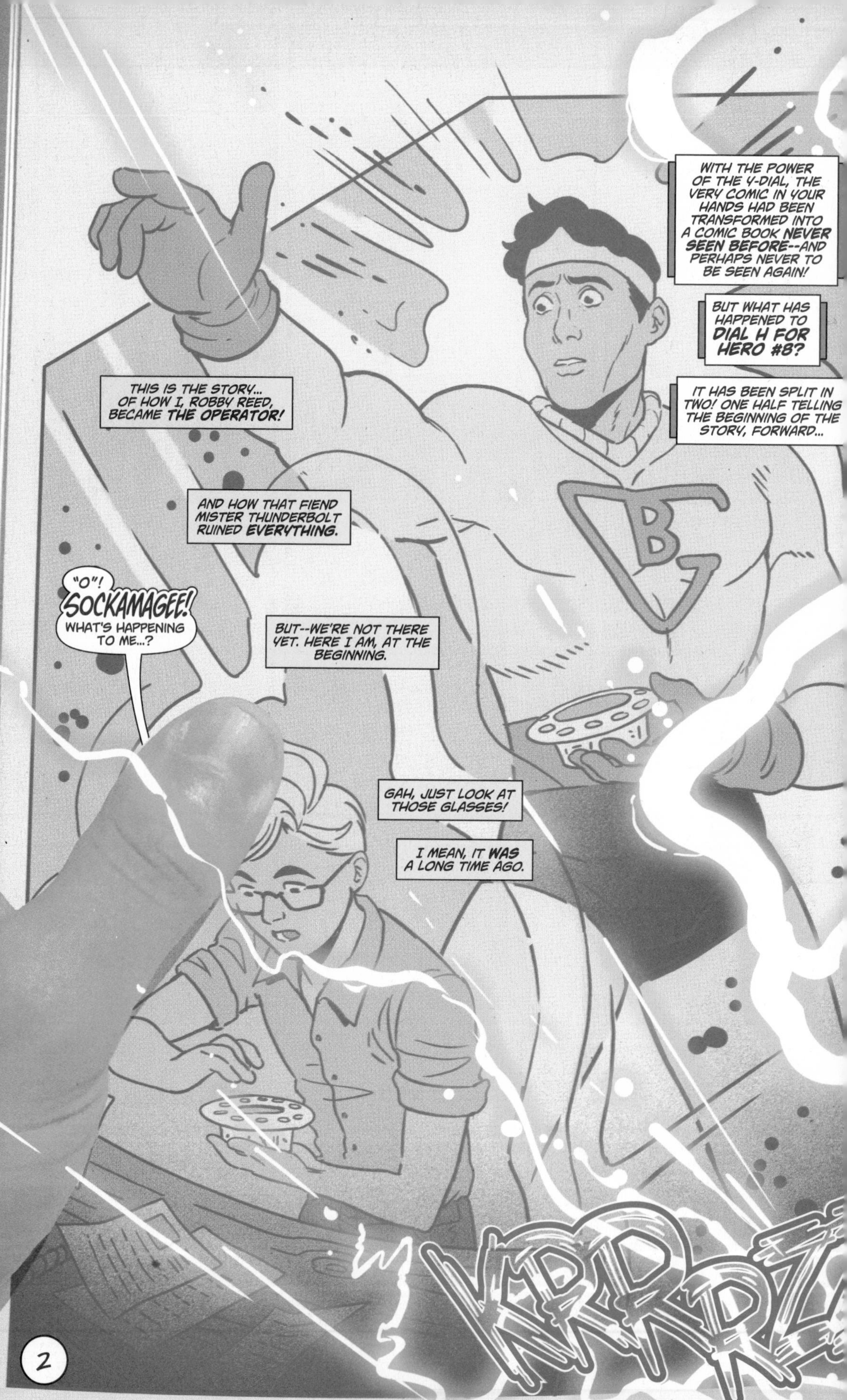

WITH THE POWER OF THE Y-DIAL, THE VERY COMIC IN YOUR HANDS HAD BEEN TRANSFORMED INTO A COMIC BOOK NEVER SEEN BEFORE--AND PERHAPS NEVER TO BE SEEN AGAIN!
BUT WHAT HAS HAPPENED TO DIAL H FOR HERO #8?
IT HAS BEEN SPLIT IN TWO! ONE HALF TELLING THE BEGINNING OF THE STORY, FORWARD...
THIS IS THE STORY... OF HOW I, ROBBY REED, BECAME THE OPERATOR!
AND HOW THAT FIEND MISTER THUNDERBOLT RUINED EVERYTHING.
"O"! SOCKAMAGEE! WHAT'S HAPPENING TO ME...?
BUT--WE'RE NOT THERE YET. HERE I AM, AT THE BEGINNING.
GAH, JUST LOOK AT THOSE GLASSES!
I MEAN, IT WAS A LONG TIME AGO.
KRRRZZT

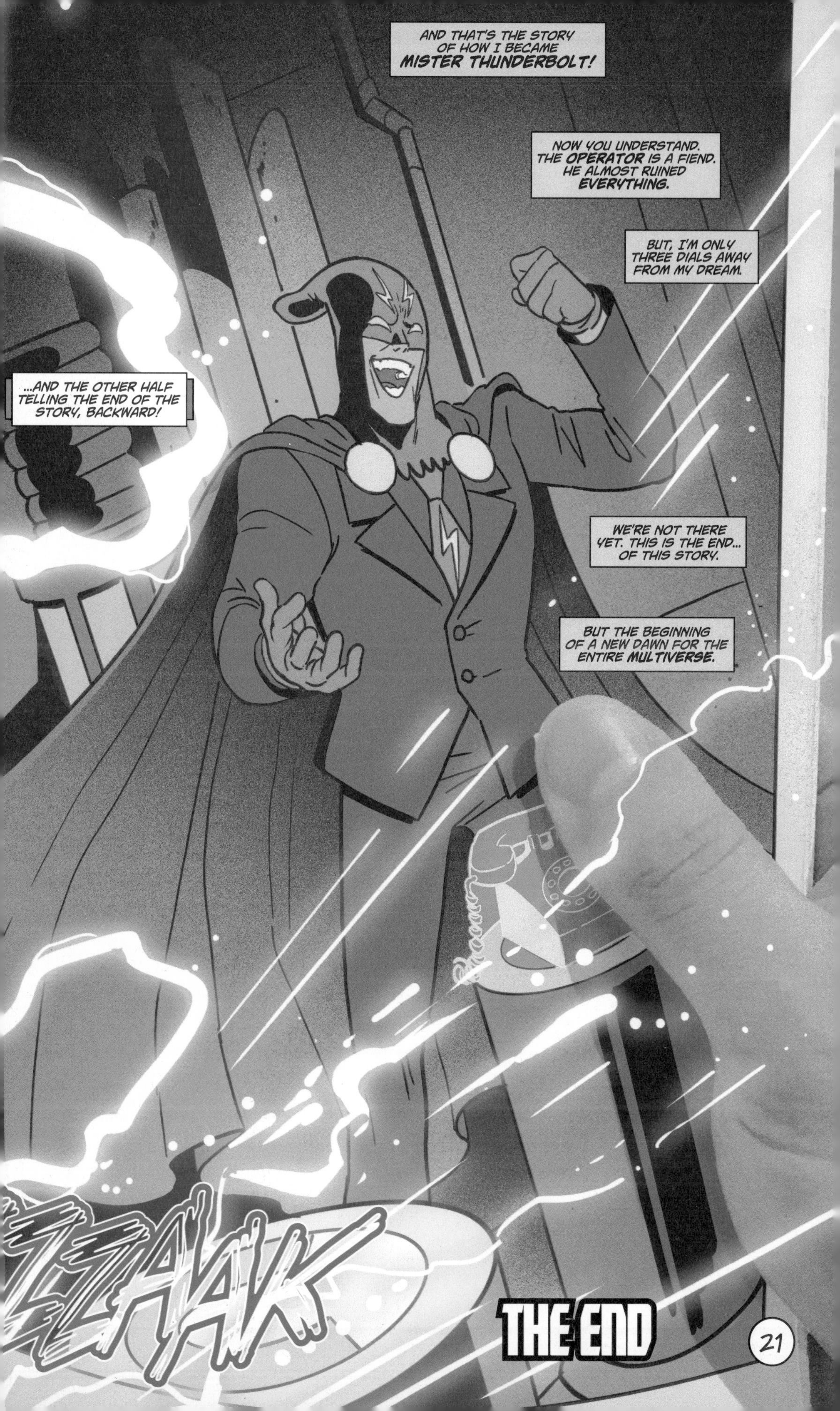
AND THAT'S THE STORY OF HOW I BECAME MISTER THUNDERBOLT!
...AND THE OTHER HALF TELLING THE END OF THE STORY, BACKWARD!
NOW YOU UNDERSTAND. THE OPERATOR IS A FIEND. HE ALMOST RUINED EVERYTHING.
BUT, I'M ONLY THREE DIALS AWAY FROM MY DREAM.
WE'RE NOT THERE YET. THIS IS THE END... OF THIS STORY.
BUT THE BEGINNING OF A NEW DAWN FOR THE ENTIRE MULTIVERSE.
ZZAAK
THE END

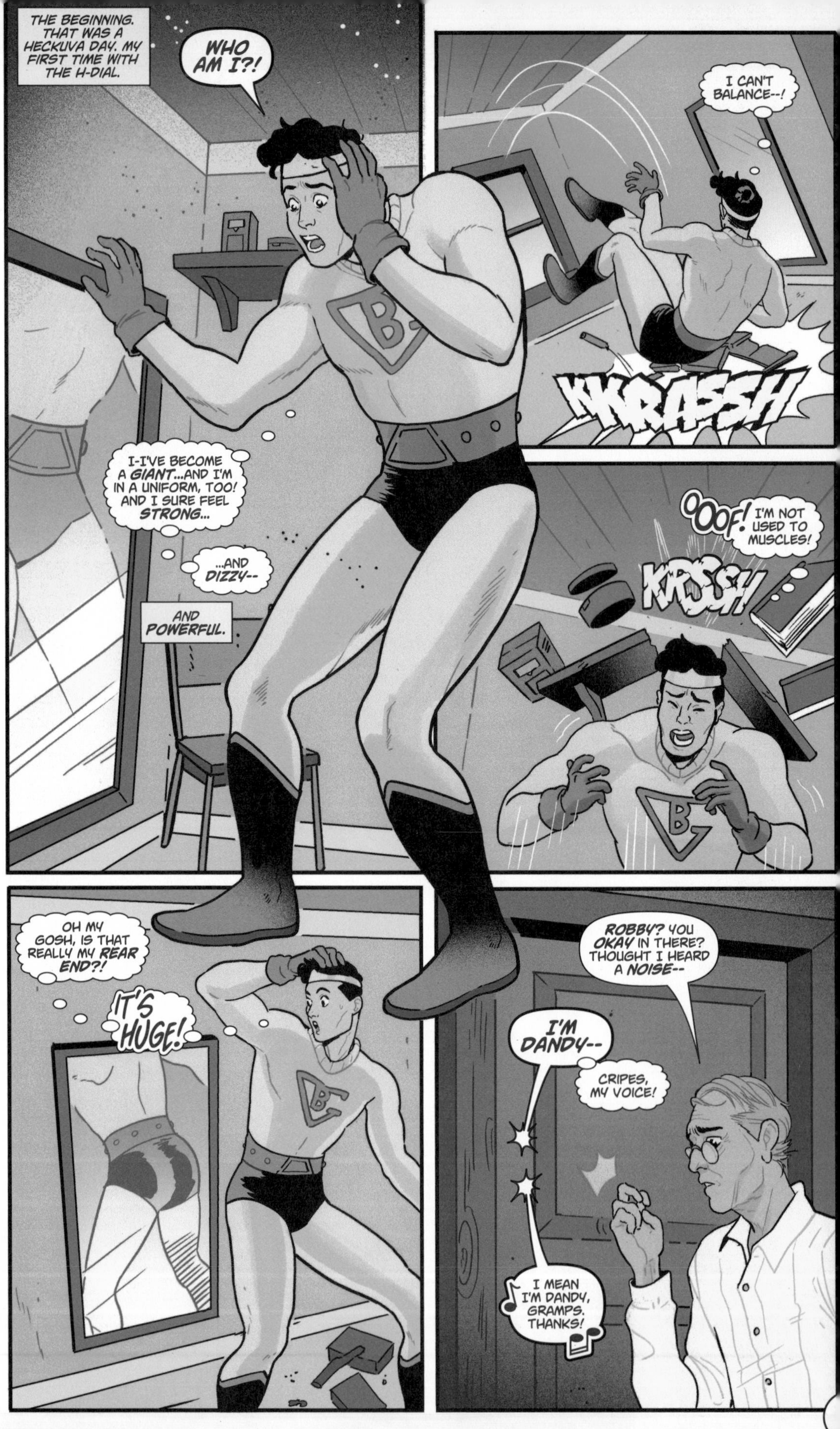
THE BEGINNING. THAT WAS A HECKUVA DAY. MY FIRST TIME WITH THE H-DIAL.
WHO AM I?!
I-I'VE BECOME A GIANT...AND I'M IN A UNIFORM, TOO! AND I SURE FEEL STRONG...
...AND DIZZY--
AND POWERFUL.
I CAN'T BALANCE--!
KKRASSH
OOOF! I'M NOT USED TO MUSCLES!
KRSSH
OH MY GOSH, IS THAT REALLY MY REAR END?!
IT'S HUGE!
ROBBY? YOU OKAY IN THERE? THOUGHT I HEARD A NOISE--
I'M DANDY--
CRIPES, MY VOICE!
I MEAN I'M DANDY, GRAMPS. THANKS!

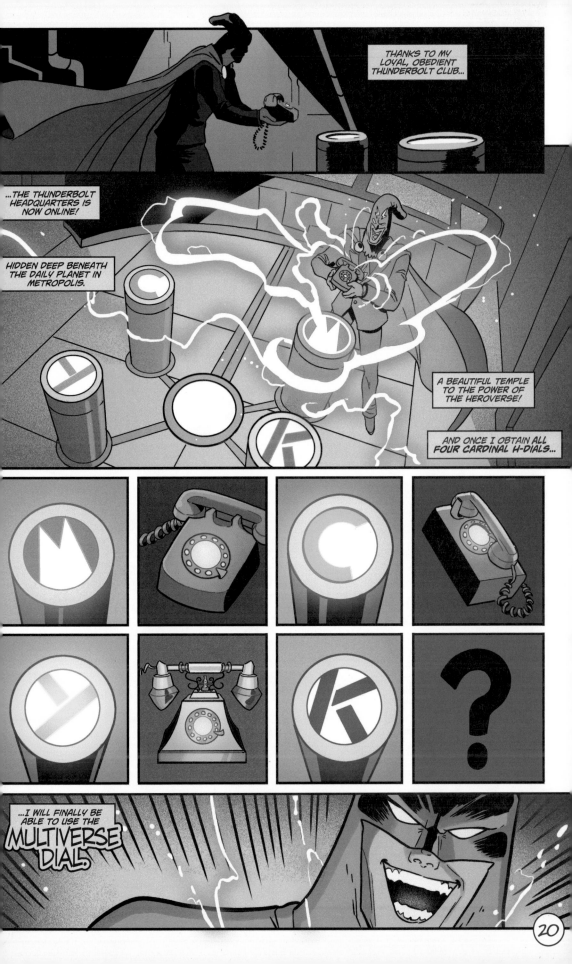

THANKS TO MY LOYAL, OBEDIENT THUNDERBOLT CLUB...

...THE THUNDERBOLT HEADQUARTERS IS NOW ONLINE!

HIDDEN DEEP BENEATH THE DAILY PLANET IN METROPOLIS.

A BEAUTIFUL TEMPLE TO THE POWER OF THE HEROVERSE!

AND ONCE I OBTAIN ALL FOUR CARDINAL H-DIALS...

...I WILL FINALLY BE ABLE TO USE THE MULTIVERSE DIAL.

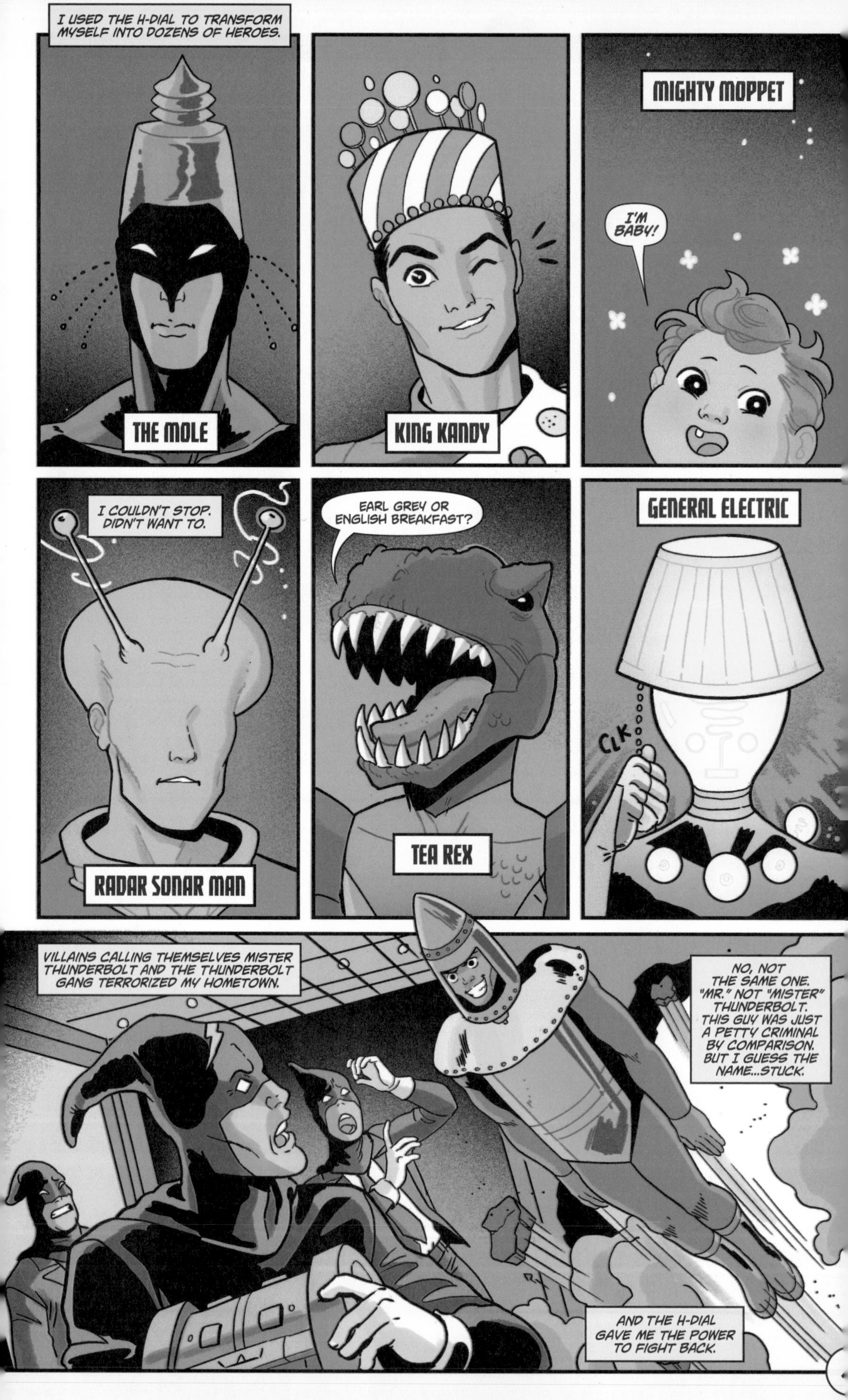
I USED THE H-DIAL TO TRANSFORM MYSELF INTO DOZENS OF HEROES.
THE MOLE
KING KANDY
MIGHTY MOPPET
I'M BABY!
I COULDN'T STOP. DIDN'T WANT TO.
RADAR SONAR MAN
EARL GREY OR ENGLISH BREAKFAST?
TEA REX
GENERAL ELECTRIC
CLK
VILLAINS CALLING THEMSELVES MISTER THUNDERBOLT AND THE THUNDERBOLT GANG TERRORIZED MY HOMETOWN.
NO, NOT THE SAME ONE. "MR." NOT "MISTER" THUNDERBOLT. THIS GUY WAS JUST A PETTY CRIMINAL BY COMPARISON. BUT I GUESS THE NAME...STUCK.
AND THE H-DIAL GAVE ME THE POWER TO FIGHT BACK.

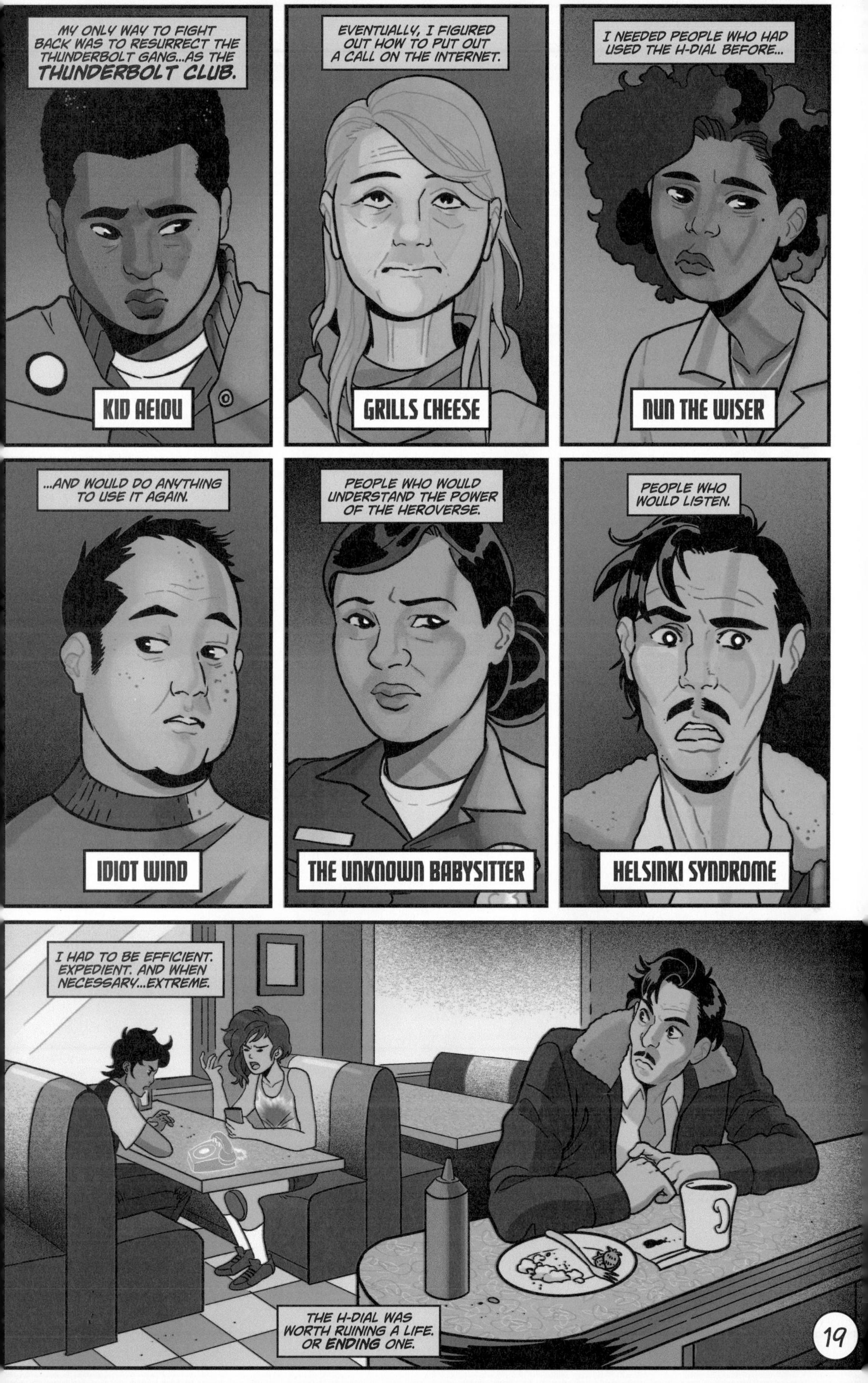
MY ONLY WAY TO FIGHT BACK WAS TO RESURRECT THE THUNDERBOLT GANG...AS THE THUNDERBOLT CLUB.
KID AEIOU
EVENTUALLY, I FIGURED OUT HOW TO PUT OUT A CALL ON THE INTERNET.
GRILLS CHEESE
I NEEDED PEOPLE WHO HAD USED THE H-DIAL BEFORE...
NUN THE WISER
...AND WOULD DO ANYTHING TO USE IT AGAIN.
IDIOT WIND
PEOPLE WHO WOULD UNDERSTAND THE POWER OF THE HEROVERSE.
THE UNKNOWN BABYSITTER
PEOPLE WHO WOULD LISTEN.
HELSINKI SYNDROME
I HAD TO BE EFFICIENT. EXPEDIENT. AND WHEN NECESSARY...EXTREME.
THE H-DIAL WAS WORTH RUINING A LIFE. OR ENDING ONE.

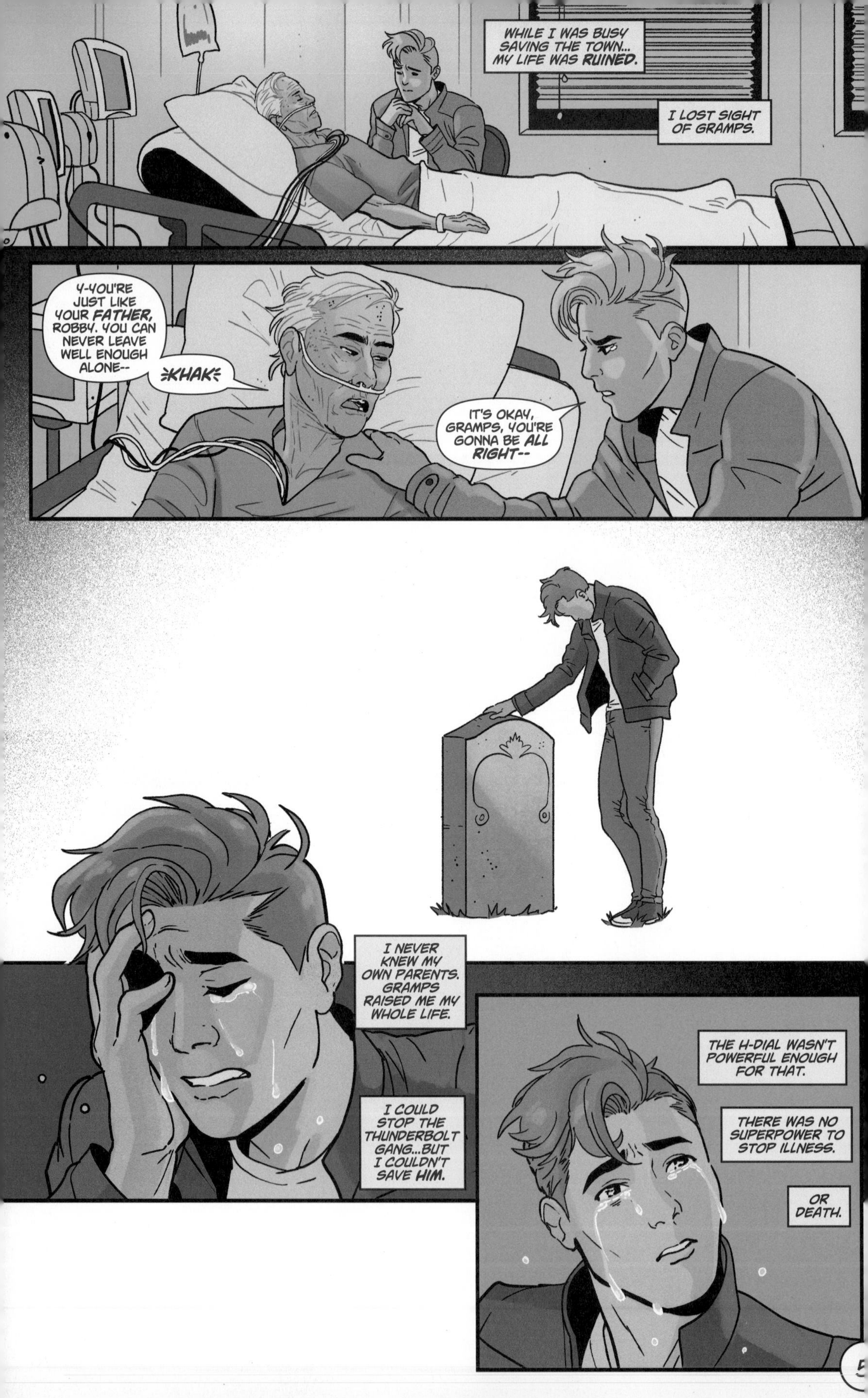
WHILE I WAS BUSY SAVING THE TOWN... MY LIFE WAS RUINED.
I LOST SIGHT OF GRAMPS.
Y-YOU'RE JUST LIKE YOUR FATHER, ROBBY. YOU CAN NEVER LEAVE WELL ENOUGH ALONE--
KHAK
IT'S OKAY, GRAMPS, YOU'RE GONNA BE ALL RIGHT--
I NEVER KNEW MY OWN PARENTS. GRAMPS RAISED ME MY WHOLE LIFE.
I COULD STOP THE THUNDERBOLT GANG...BUT I COULDN'T SAVE HIM.
THE H-DIAL WASN'T POWERFUL ENOUGH FOR THAT.
THERE WAS NO SUPERPOWER TO STOP ILLNESS.
OR DEATH.

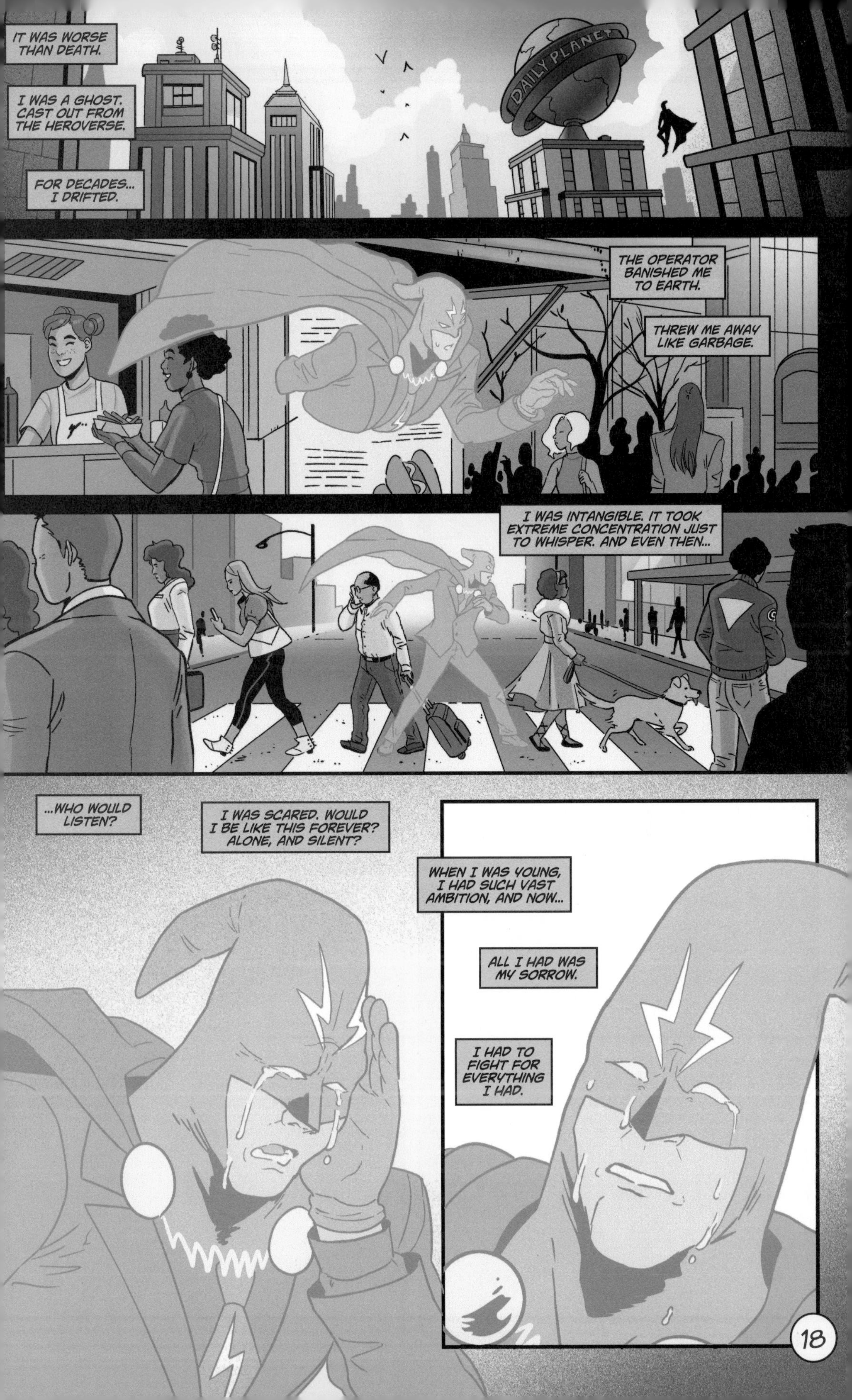
IT WAS WORSE THAN DEATH.
I WAS A GHOST. CAST OUT FROM THE HEROVERSE.
FOR DECADES... I DRIFTED.
DAILY PLANET
THE OPERATOR BANISHED ME TO EARTH.
THREW ME AWAY LIKE GARBAGE.
I WAS INTANGIBLE. IT TOOK EXTREME CONCENTRATION JUST TO WHISPER. AND EVEN THEN...
...WHO WOULD LISTEN?
I WAS SCARED. WOULD I BE LIKE THIS FOREVER? ALONE, AND SILENT?
WHEN I WAS YOUNG, I HAD SUCH VAST AMBITION, AND NOW...
ALL I HAD WAS MY SORROW.
I HAD TO FIGHT FOR EVERYTHING I HAD.

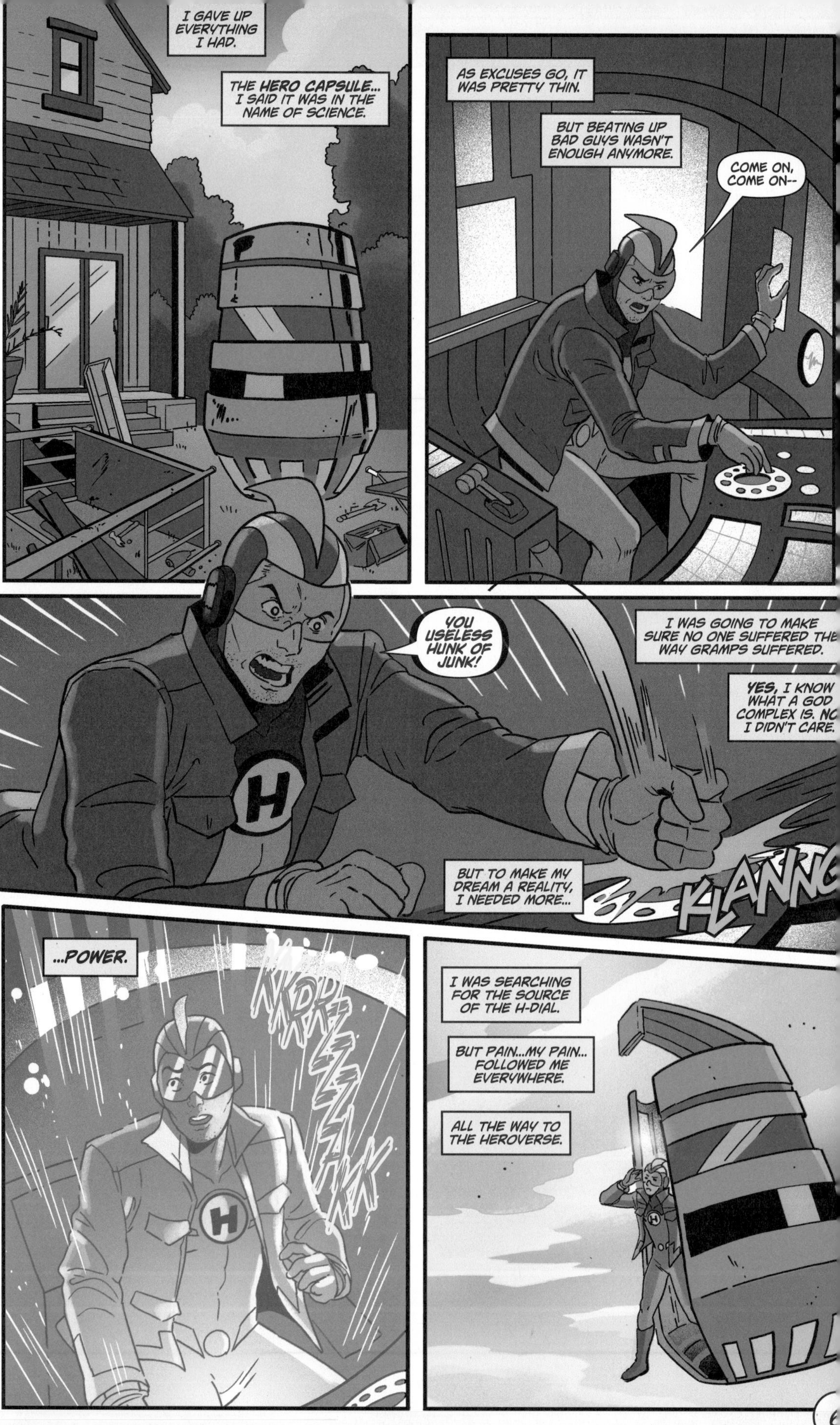
I GAVE UP EVERYTHING I HAD.
THE HERO CAPSULE... I SAID IT WAS IN THE NAME OF SCIENCE.
AS EXCUSES GO, IT WAS PRETTY THIN.
BUT BEATING UP BAD GUYS WASN'T ENOUGH ANYMORE.
COME ON, COME ON--
YOU USELESS HUNK OF JUNK!
I WAS GOING TO MAKE SURE NO ONE SUFFERED THE WAY GRAMPS SUFFERED.
YES, I KNOW WHAT A GOD COMPLEX IS. NO I DIDN'T CARE.
BUT TO MAKE MY DREAM A REALITY, I NEEDED MORE...
KLANNG
...POWER.
I WAS SEARCHING FOR THE SOURCE OF THE H-DIAL.
BUT PAIN...MY PAIN... FOLLOWED ME EVERYWHERE.
ALL THE WAY TO THE HEROVERSE.

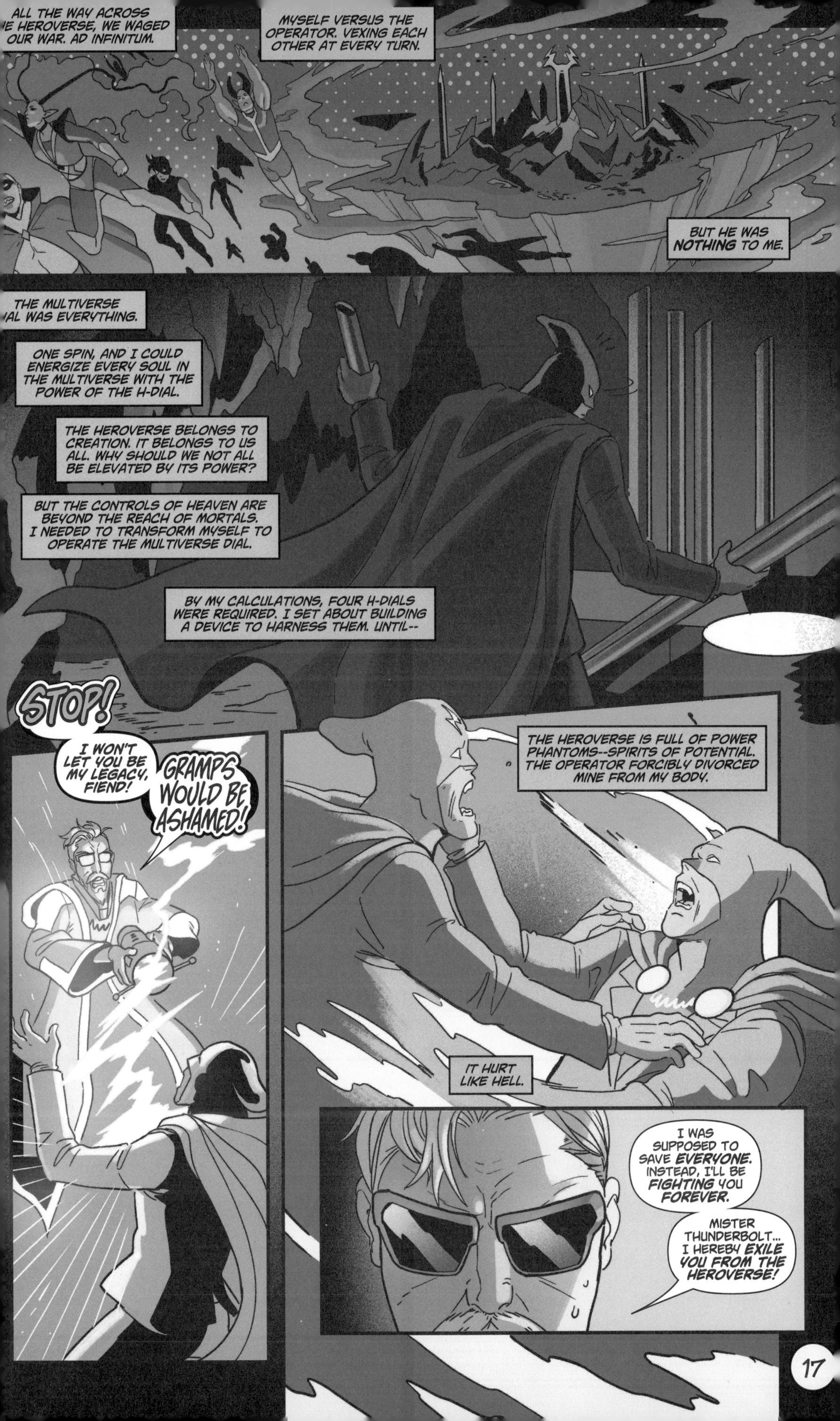
ALL THE WAY ACROSS THE HEROVERSE, WE WAGED OUR WAR. AD INFINITUM.
MYSELF VERSUS THE OPERATOR. VEXING EACH OTHER AT EVERY TURN.
BUT HE WAS NOTHING TO ME.
THE MULTIVERSE DIAL WAS EVERYTHING.
ONE SPIN, AND I COULD ENERGIZE EVERY SOUL IN THE MULTIVERSE WITH THE POWER OF THE H-DIAL.
THE HEROVERSE BELONGS TO CREATION. IT BELONGS TO US ALL. WHY SHOULD WE NOT ALL BE ELEVATED BY ITS POWER?
BUT THE CONTROLS OF HEAVEN ARE BEYOND THE REACH OF MORTALS. I NEEDED TO TRANSFORM MYSELF TO OPERATE THE MULTIVERSE DIAL.
BY MY CALCULATIONS, FOUR H-DIALS WERE REQUIRED. I SET ABOUT BUILDING A DEVICE TO HARNESS THEM. UNTIL--
STOP!
I WON'T LET YOU BE MY LEGACY, FIEND!
GRAMPS WOULD BE ASHAMED!
THE HEROVERSE IS FULL OF POWER PHANTOMS--SPIRITS OF POTENTIAL. THE OPERATOR FORCIBLY DIVORCED MINE FROM MY BODY.
IT HURT LIKE HELL.
I WAS SUPPOSED TO SAVE EVERYONE. INSTEAD, I'LL BE FIGHTING YOU FOREVER.
MISTER THUNDERBOLT... I HEREBY EXILE YOU FROM THE HEROVERSE!

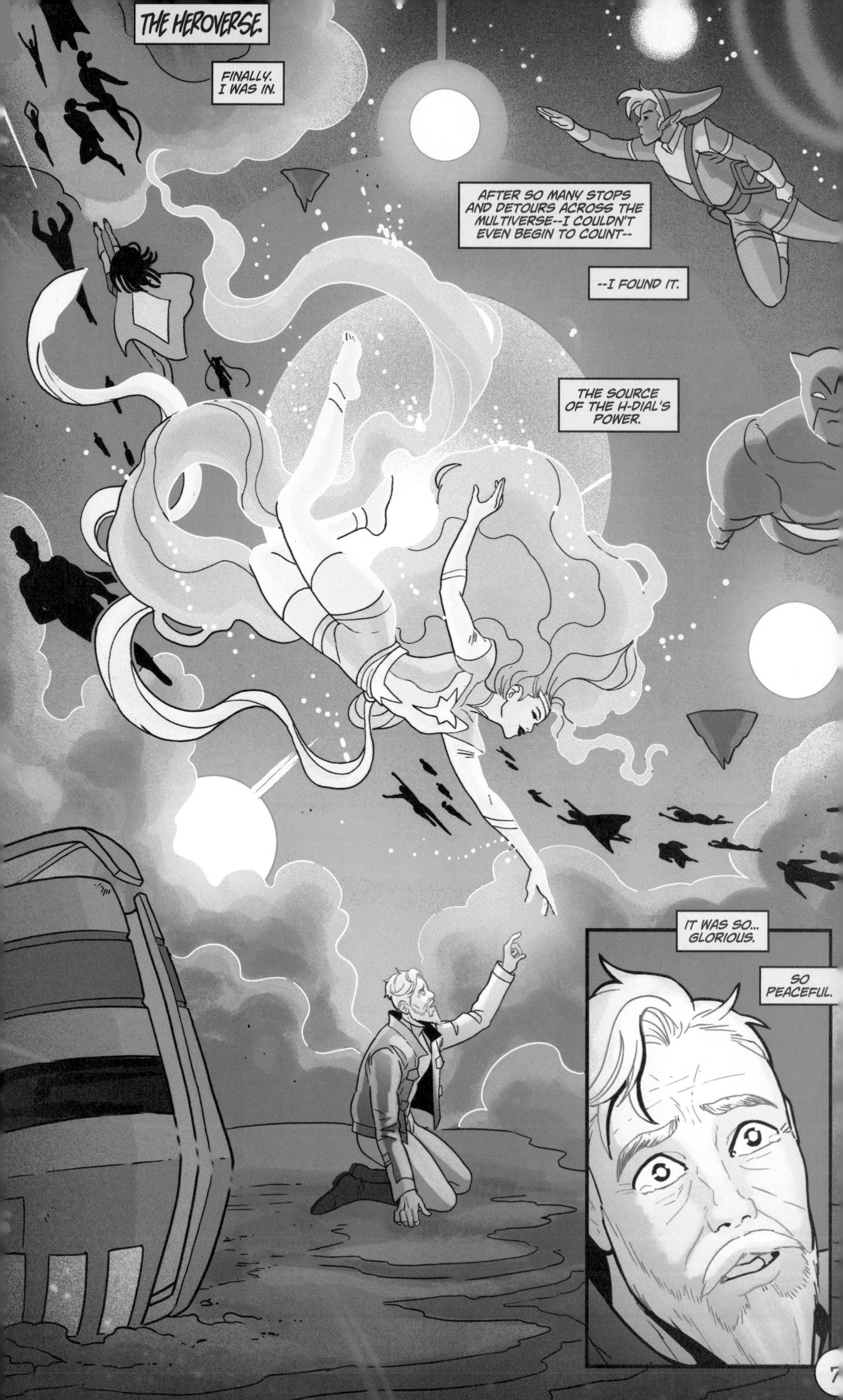
THE HEROVERSE.
FINALLY. I WAS IN.
AFTER SO MANY STOPS AND DETOURS ACROSS THE MULTIVERSE--I COULDN'T EVEN BEGIN TO COUNT--
--I FOUND IT.
THE SOURCE OF THE H-DIAL'S POWER.
IT WAS SO... GLORIOUS.
SO PEACEFUL.

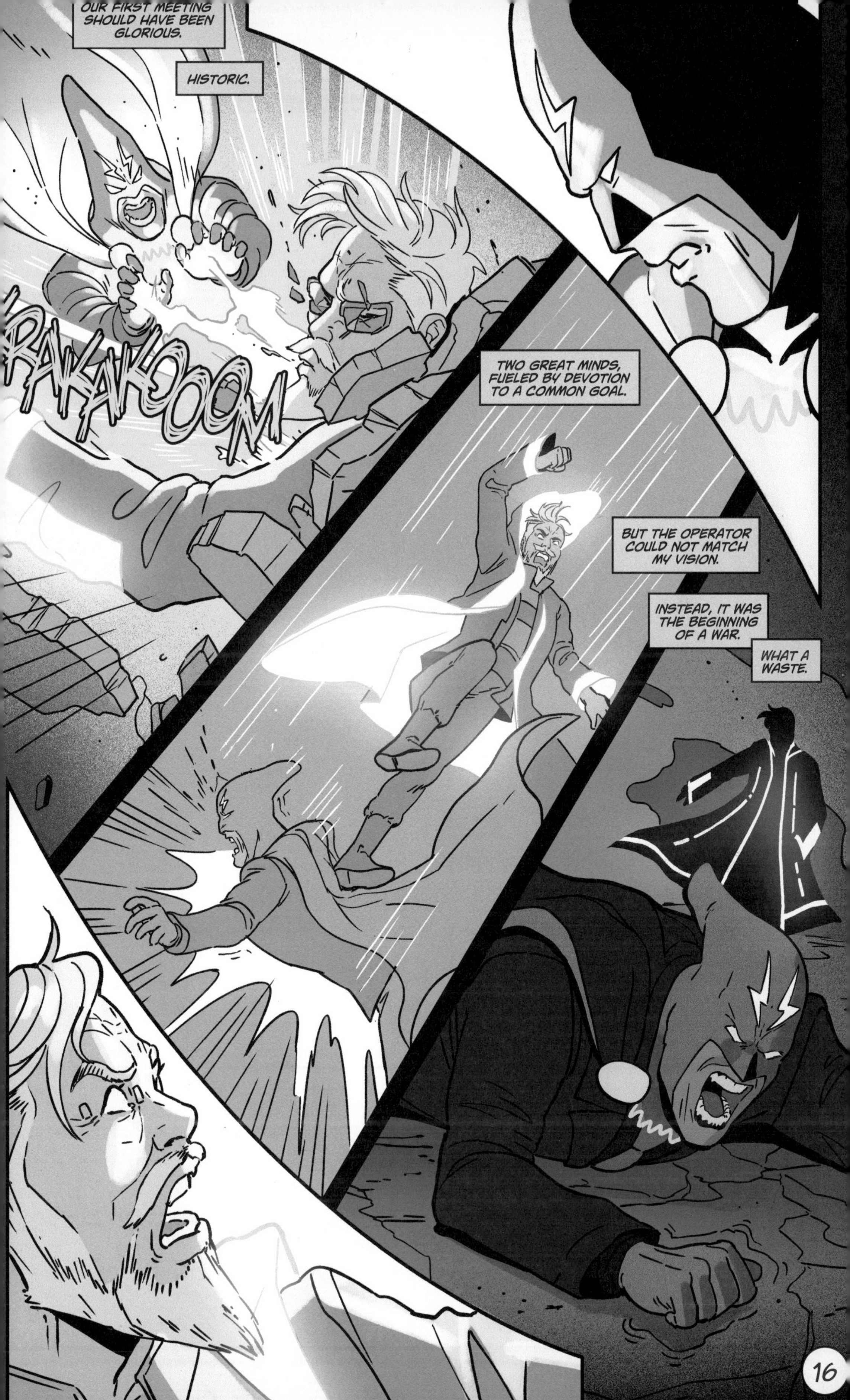

OUR FIRST MEETING SHOULD HAVE BEEN GLORIOUS.
HISTORIC.
KRAKAKOOOM
TWO GREAT MINDS, FUELED BY DEVOTION TO A COMMON GOAL.
BUT THE OPERATOR COULD NOT MATCH MY VISION.
INSTEAD, IT WAS THE BEGINNING OF A WAR.
WHAT A WASTE.

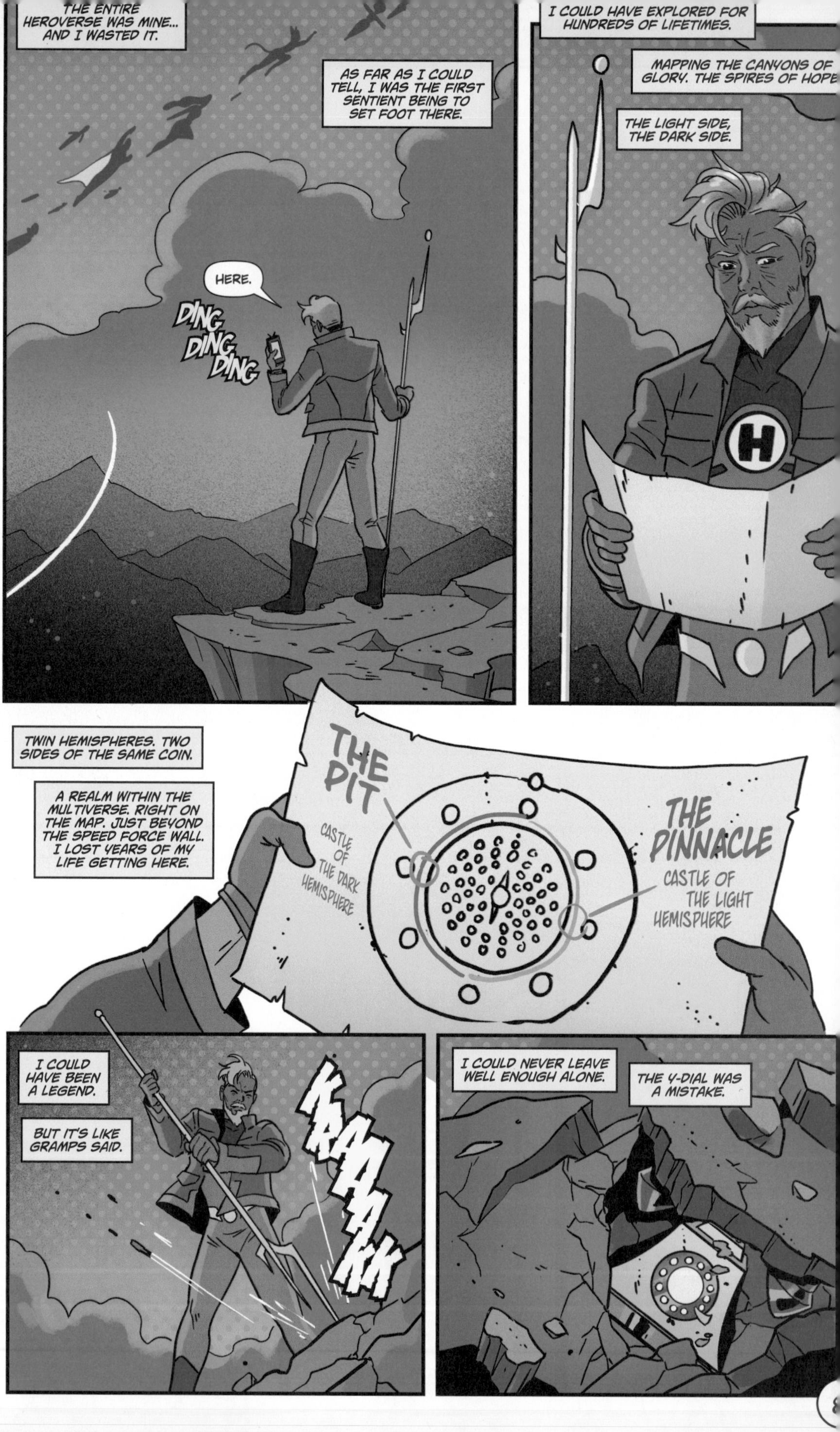
THE ENTIRE HEROVERSE WAS MINE... AND I WASTED IT.
AS FAR AS I COULD TELL, I WAS THE FIRST SENTIENT BEING TO SET FOOT THERE.
HERE.
DING DING DING
I COULD HAVE EXPLORED FOR HUNDREDS OF LIFETIMES.
MAPPING THE CANYONS OF GLORY. THE SPIRES OF HOPE
THE LIGHT SIDE, THE DARK SIDE.
TWIN HEMISPHERES. TWO SIDES OF THE SAME COIN.
A REALM WITHIN THE MULTIVERSE. RIGHT ON THE MAP. JUST BEYOND THE SPEED FORCE WALL. I LOST YEARS OF MY LIFE GETTING HERE.
THE PIT
CASTLE OF THE DARK HEMISPHERE
THE PINNACLE
CASTLE OF THE LIGHT HEMISPHERE
I COULD HAVE BEEN A LEGEND.
BUT IT'S LIKE GRAMPS SAID.
KRAAAKK
I COULD NEVER LEAVE WELL ENOUGH ALONE.
THE Y-DIAL WAS A MISTAKE.

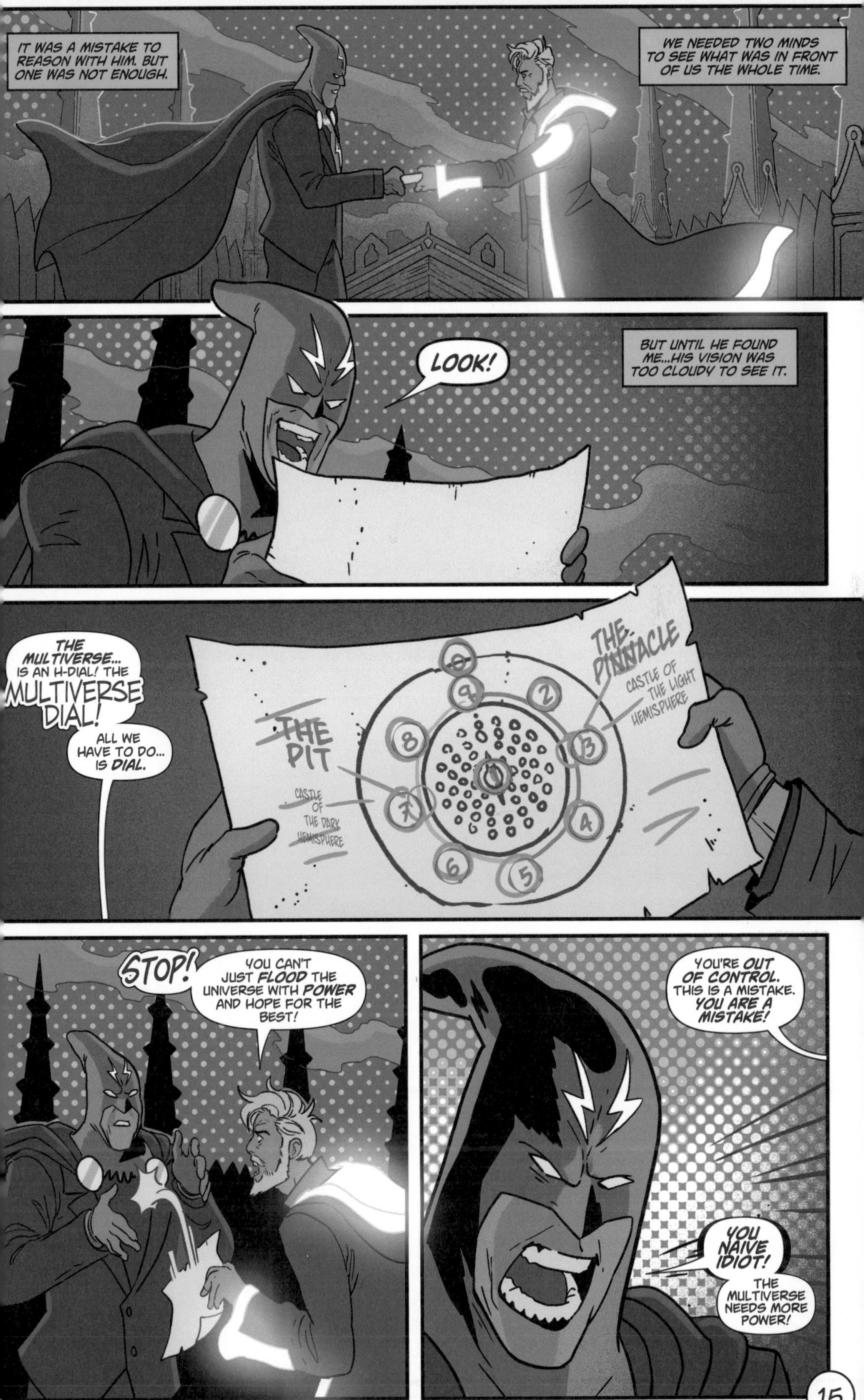

IT WAS A MISTAKE TO REASON WITH HIM. BUT ONE WAS NOT ENOUGH.
WE NEEDED TWO MINDS TO SEE WHAT WAS IN FRONT OF US THE WHOLE TIME.
LOOK!
BUT UNTIL HE FOUND ME...HIS VISION WAS TOO CLOUDY TO SEE IT.
THE MULTIVERSE... IS AN H-DIAL! THE MULTIVERSE DIAL!
ALL WE HAVE TO DO... IS DIAL.
THE PIT
CASTLE OF THE DARK HEMISPHERE
THE PINNACLE
CASTLE OF THE LIGHT HEMISPHERE
STOP!
YOU CAN'T JUST FLOOD THE UNIVERSE WITH POWER AND HOPE FOR THE BEST!
YOU'RE OUT OF CONTROL. THIS IS A MISTAKE. YOU ARE A MISTAKE!
YOU NAIVE IDIOT!
THE MULTIVERSE NEEDS MORE POWER!

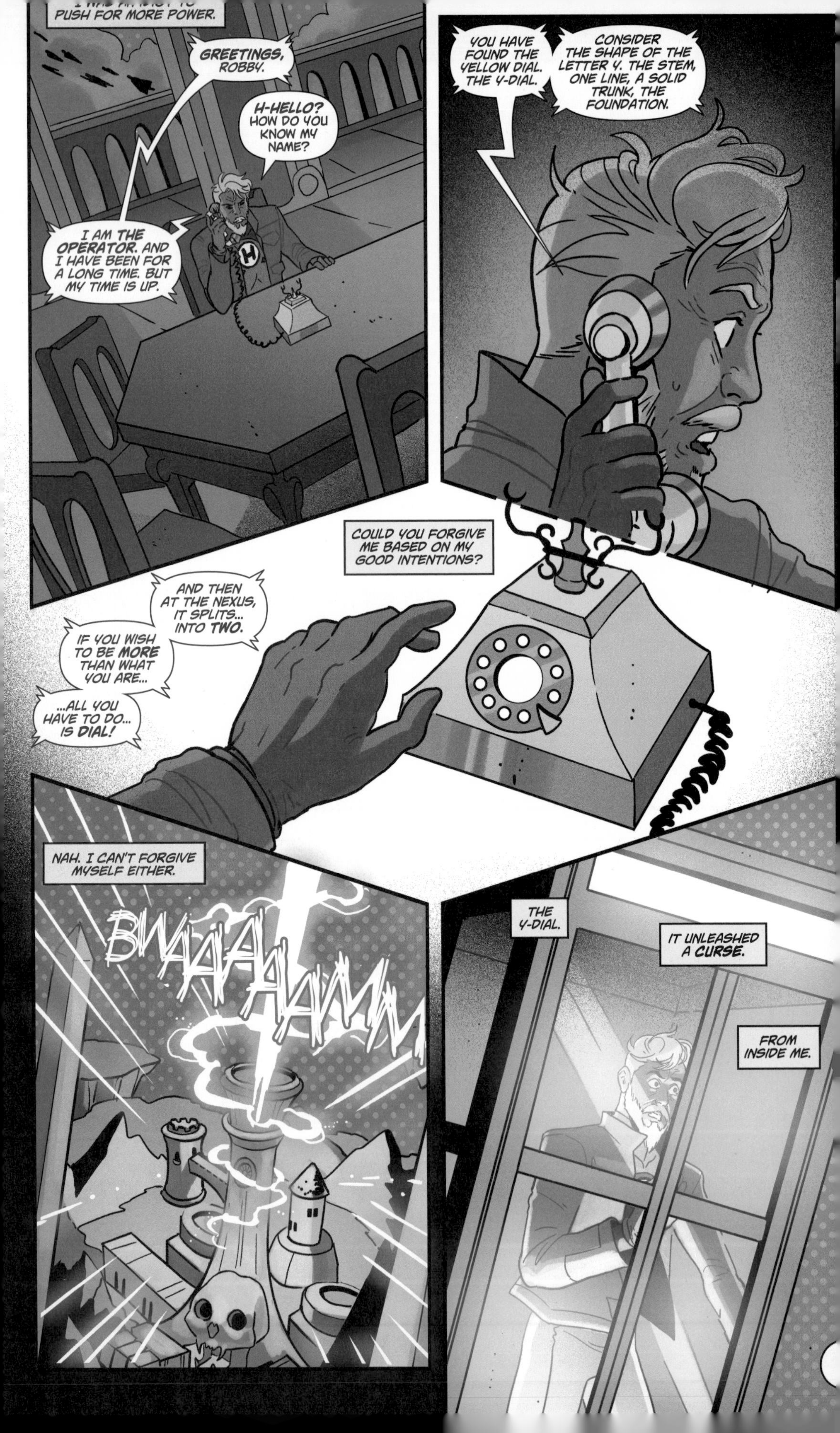
PUSH FOR MORE POWER.
GREETINGS, ROBBY.
H-HELLO? HOW DO YOU KNOW MY NAME?
I AM THE OPERATOR. AND I HAVE BEEN FOR A LONG TIME. BUT MY TIME IS UP.
YOU HAVE FOUND THE YELLOW DIAL. THE Y-DIAL.
CONSIDER THE SHAPE OF THE LETTER Y. THE STEM, ONE LINE, A SOLID TRUNK, THE FOUNDATION.
COULD YOU FORGIVE ME BASED ON MY GOOD INTENTIONS?
AND THEN AT THE NEXUS, IT SPLITS... INTO TWO.
IF YOU WISH TO BE MORE THAN WHAT YOU ARE...
...ALL YOU HAVE TO DO... IS DIAL!
NAH. I CAN'T FORGIVE MYSELF EITHER.
BWAAAAAAMM
THE Y-DIAL.
IT UNLEASHED A CURSE.
FROM INSIDE ME.

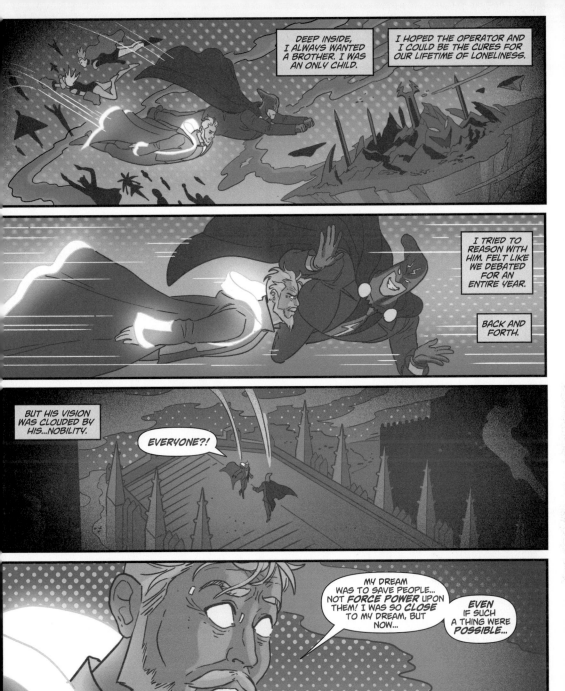

DEEP INSIDE, I ALWAYS WANTED A BROTHER. I WAS AN ONLY CHILD.

I HOPED THE OPERATOR AND I COULD BE THE CURES FOR OUR LIFETIME OF LONELINESS.

I TRIED TO REASON WITH HIM. FELT LIKE WE DEBATED FOR AN ENTIRE YEAR.

BACK AND FORTH.

BUT HIS VISION WAS CLOUDED BY HIS...NOBILITY.

EVERYONE?!

MY DREAM WAS TO SAVE PEOPLE... NOT *FORCE POWER* UPON THEM! I WAS SO *CLOSE* TO MY DREAM, BUT NOW...

EVEN IF SUCH A THING WERE *POSSIBLE*...

DON'T YOU UNDERSTAND? WE WILL USE THE H-DIAL TO GIVE EVERYONE IN THE MULTIVERSE SUPERPOWERS!

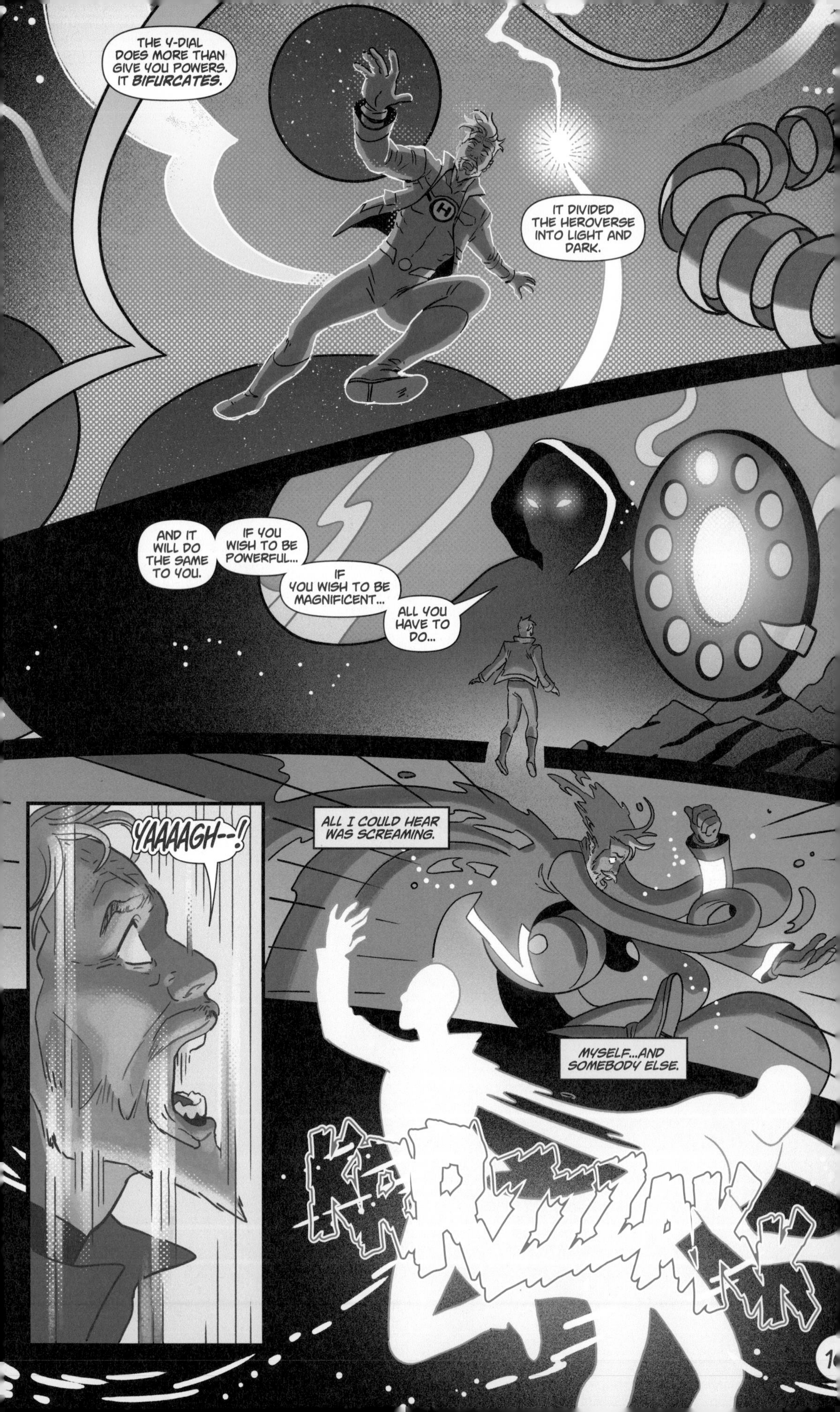
THE Y-DIAL DOES MORE THAN GIVE YOU POWERS. IT *BIFURCATES*.
IT DIVIDED THE HEROVERSE INTO LIGHT AND DARK.
AND IT WILL DO THE SAME TO YOU.
IF YOU WISH TO BE POWERFUL...
IF YOU WISH TO BE MAGNIFICENT...
ALL YOU HAVE TO DO...
YAAAAGH--!
ALL I COULD HEAR WAS SCREAMING.
MYSELF...AND SOMEBODY ELSE.
KRZZZAKK

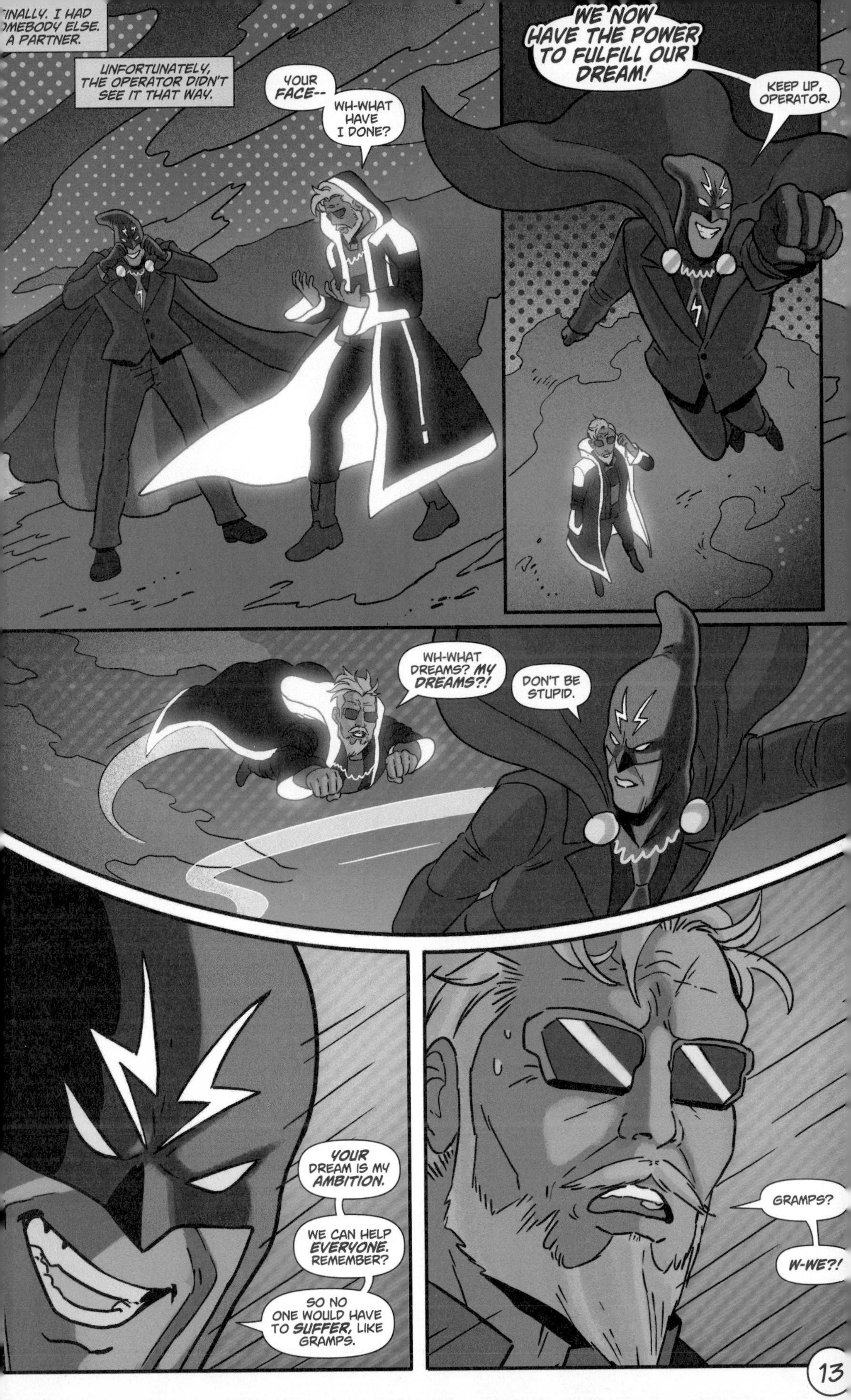

FINALLY. I HAD SOMEBODY ELSE. A PARTNER.
UNFORTUNATELY, THE OPERATOR DIDN'T SEE IT THAT WAY.
YOUR FACE--
WH-WHAT HAVE I DONE?
WE NOW HAVE THE POWER TO FULFILL OUR DREAM!
KEEP UP, OPERATOR.
WH-WHAT DREAMS? MY DREAMS?!
DON'T BE STUPID.
YOUR DREAM IS MY AMBITION.
WE CAN HELP EVERYONE. REMEMBER?
SO NO ONE WOULD HAVE TO SUFFER, LIKE GRAMPS.
GRAMPS?
W-WE?!

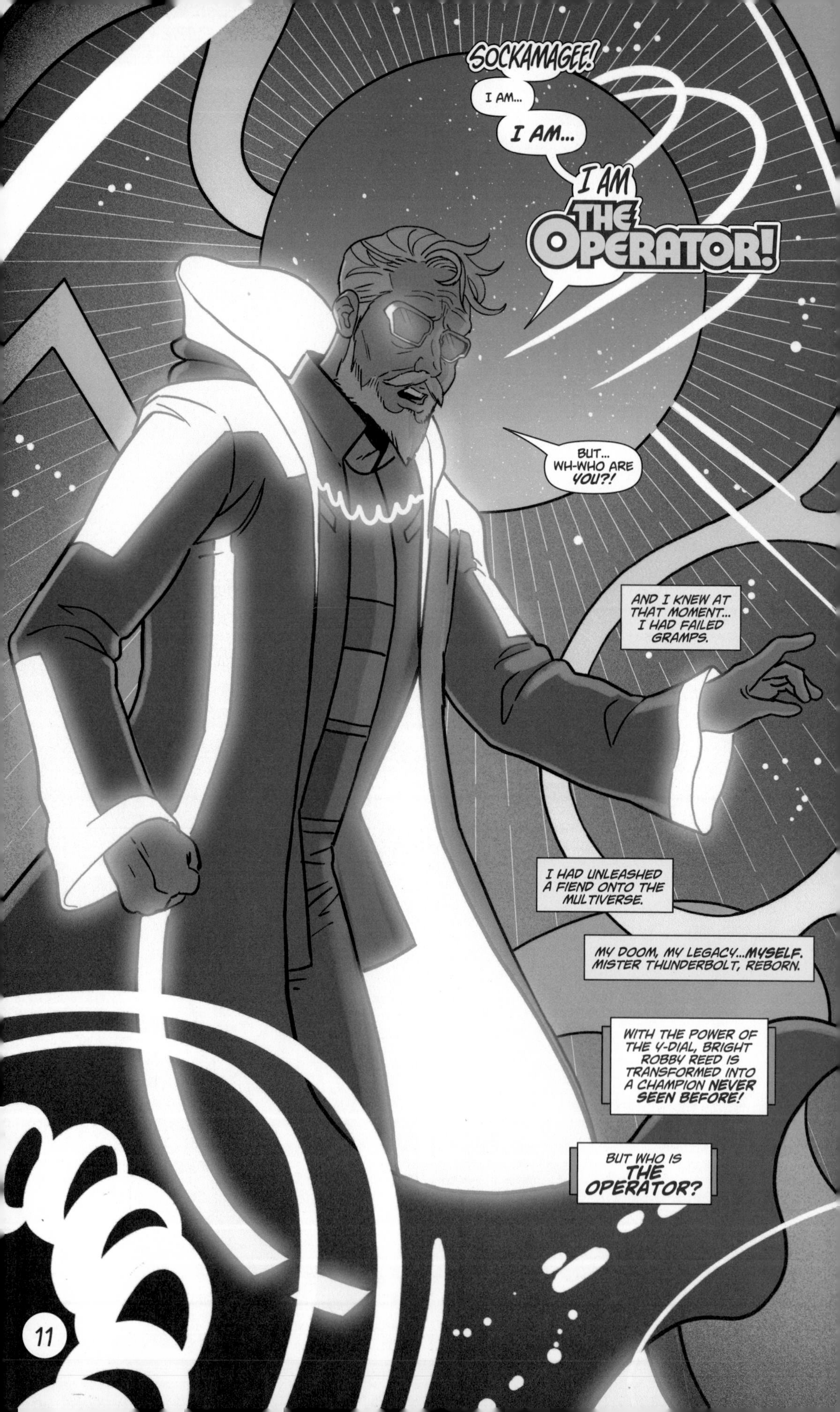
SOCKAMAGEE!
I AM...
I AM...
I AM THE OPERATOR!
BUT... WH-WHO ARE YOU?!
AND I KNEW AT THAT MOMENT... I HAD FAILED GRAMPS.
I HAD UNLEASHED A FIEND ONTO THE MULTIVERSE.
MY DOOM, MY LEGACY...MYSELF. MISTER THUNDERBOLT, REBORN.
WITH THE POWER OF THE Y-DIAL, BRIGHT ROBBY REED IS TRANSFORMED INTO A CHAMPION NEVER SEEN BEFORE!
BUT WHO IS THE OPERATOR?

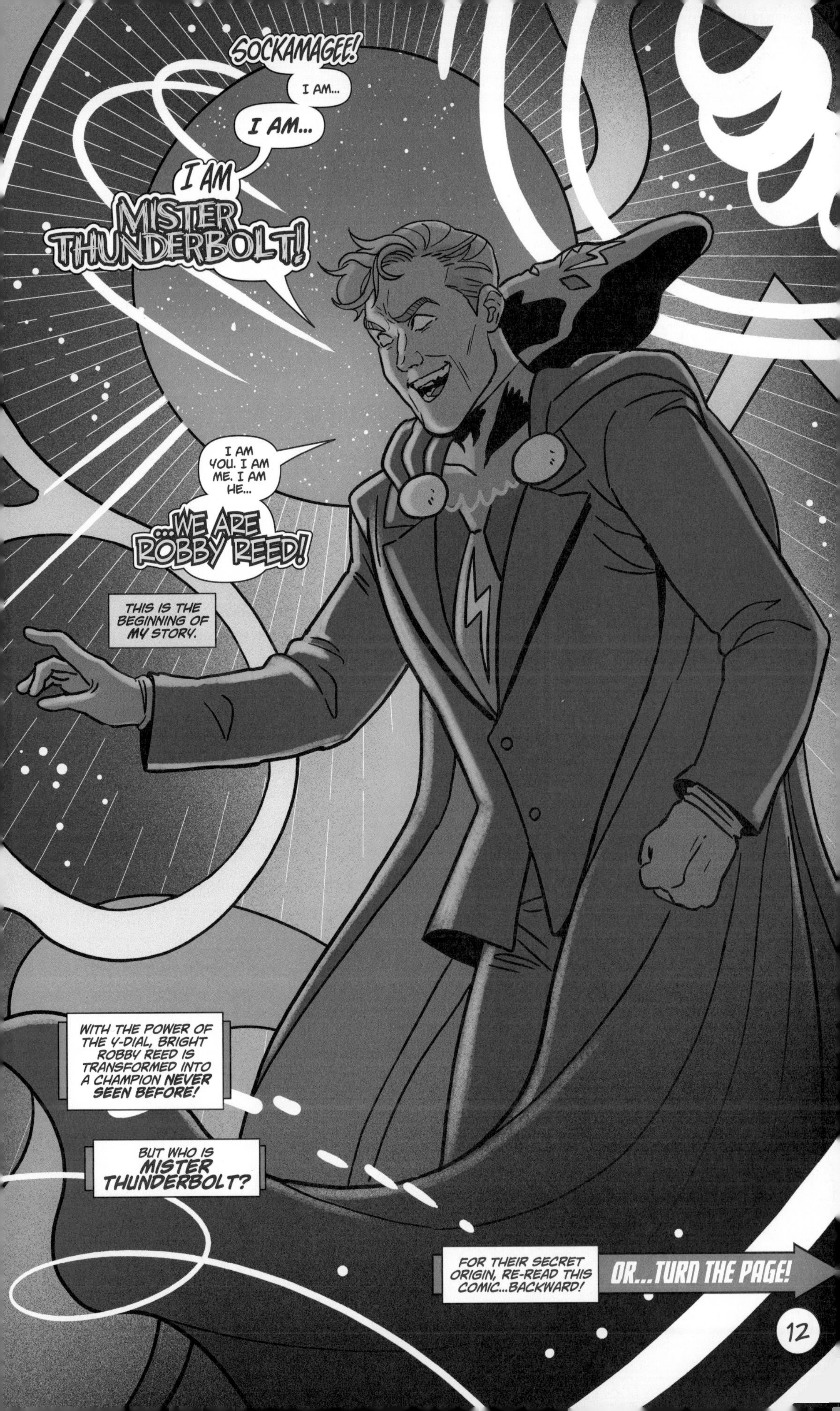
SOCKAMAGEE!
I AM...
I AM...
I AM MISTER THUNDERBOLT!
I AM YOU. I AM ME. I AM HE...
...WE ARE ROBBY REED!
THIS IS THE BEGINNING OF MY STORY.
WITH THE POWER OF THE Y-DIAL, BRIGHT ROBBY REED IS TRANSFORMED INTO A CHAMPION NEVER SEEN BEFORE!
BUT WHO IS MISTER THUNDERBOLT?
FOR THEIR SECRET ORIGIN, RE-READ THIS COMIC...BACKWARD!
OR...TURN THE PAGE!

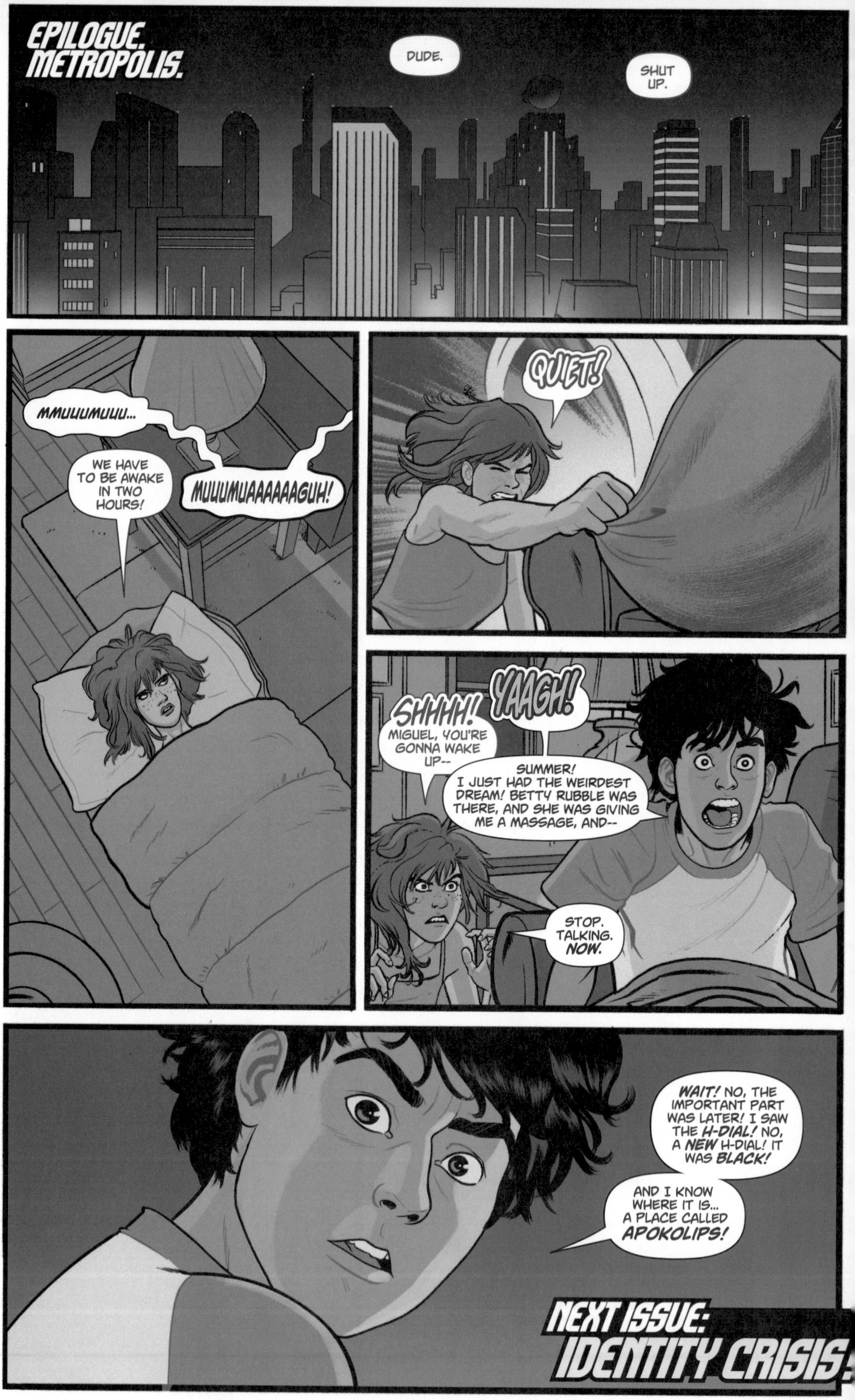
EPILOGUE. METROPOLIS.
DUDE.
SHUT UP.
MMUUUMUUU...
MUUUMUAAAAAAGUH!
WE HAVE TO BE AWAKE IN TWO HOURS!
QUIET!
SHHHH! MIGUEL, YOU'RE GONNA WAKE UP--
YAAGH!
SUMMER! I JUST HAD THE WEIRDEST DREAM! BETTY RUBBLE WAS THERE, AND SHE WAS GIVING ME A MASSAGE, AND--
STOP. TALKING. NOW.
WAIT! NO, THE IMPORTANT PART WAS LATER! I SAW THE H-DIAL! NO, A NEW H-DIAL! IT WAS BLACK!
AND I KNOW WHERE IT IS... A PLACE CALLED APOKOLIPS!
NEXT ISSUE: IDENTITY CRISIS!

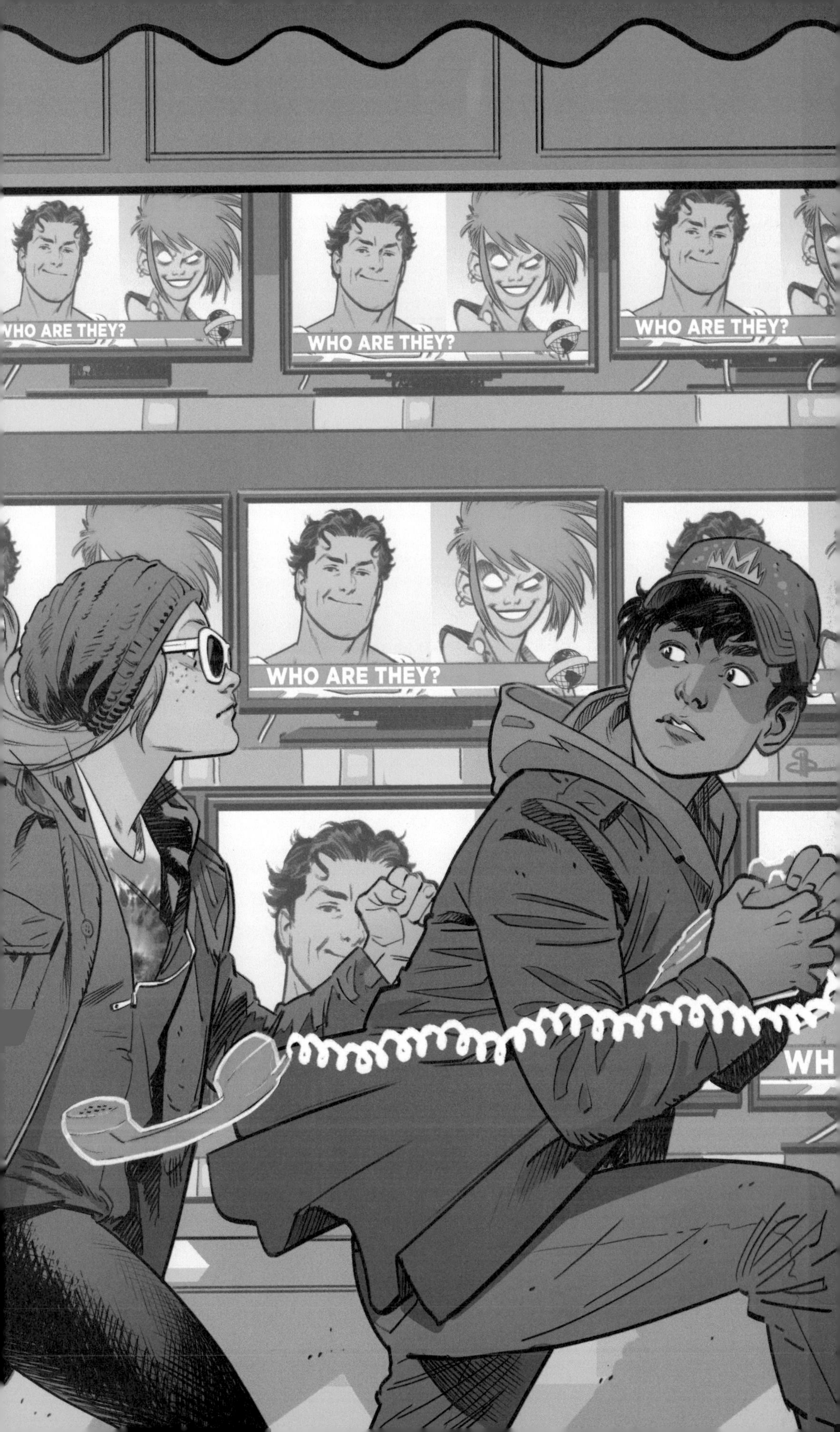
WHO ARE THEY?
WHO ARE THEY?
WHO ARE THEY?
WHO ARE THEY?

HUSTLE BUDDIES

art by
JOE QUINONES
colors by
JORDAN GIBSON
cover art by
EVAN "DOC" SHANER

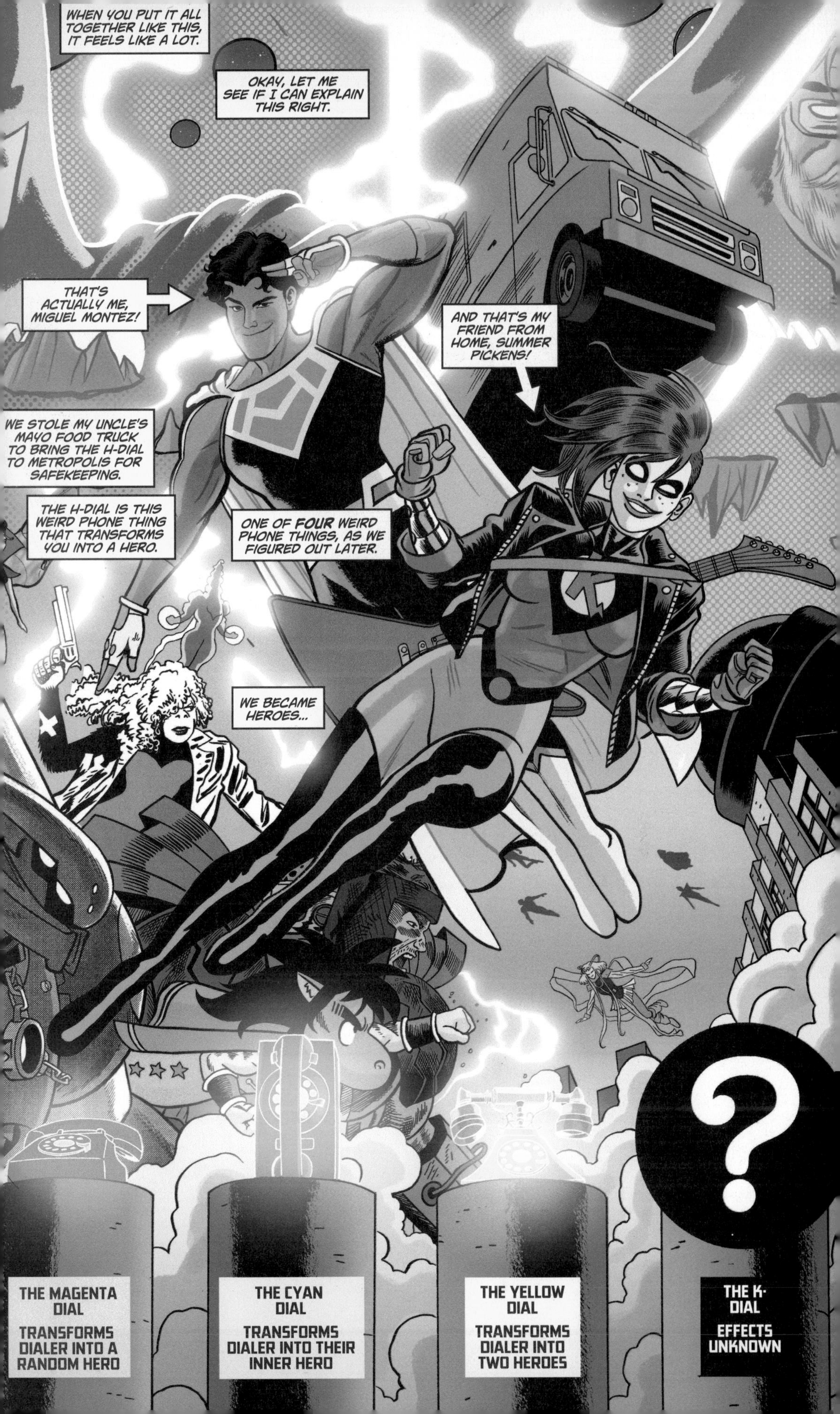
WHEN YOU PUT IT ALL TOGETHER LIKE THIS, IT FEELS LIKE A LOT.
OKAY, LET ME SEE IF I CAN EXPLAIN THIS RIGHT.
THAT'S ACTUALLY ME, MIGUEL MONTEZ!
AND THAT'S MY FRIEND FROM HOME, SUMMER PICKENS!
WE STOLE MY UNCLE'S MAYO FOOD TRUCK TO BRING THE H-DIAL TO METROPOLIS FOR SAFEKEEPING.
THE H-DIAL IS THIS WEIRD PHONE THING THAT TRANSFORMS YOU INTO A HERO.
ONE OF FOUR WEIRD PHONE THINGS, AS WE FIGURED OUT LATER.
WE BECAME HEROES...
THE MAGENTA DIAL
TRANSFORMS DIALER INTO A RANDOM HERO
THE CYAN DIAL
TRANSFORMS DIALER INTO THEIR INNER HERO
THE YELLOW DIAL
TRANSFORMS DIALER INTO TWO HEROES
THE K-DIAL
EFFECTS UNKNOWN

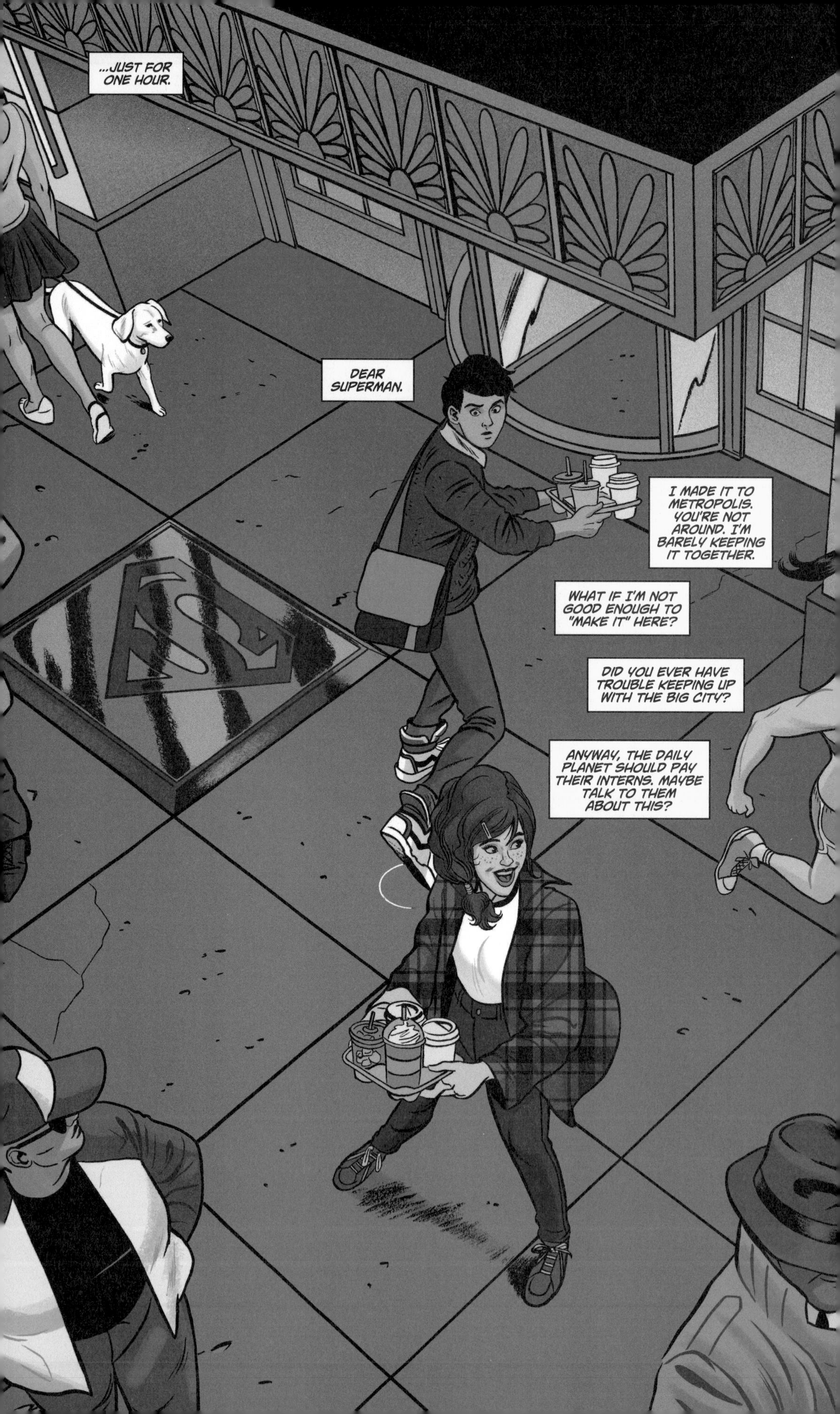
...JUST FOR ONE HOUR.
DEAR SUPERMAN.
I MADE IT TO METROPOLIS. YOU'RE NOT AROUND. I'M BARELY KEEPING IT TOGETHER.
WHAT IF I'M NOT GOOD ENOUGH TO "MAKE IT" HERE?
DID YOU EVER HAVE TROUBLE KEEPING UP WITH THE BIG CITY?
ANYWAY, THE DAILY PLANET SHOULD PAY THEIR INTERNS. MAYBE TALK TO THEM ABOUT THIS?

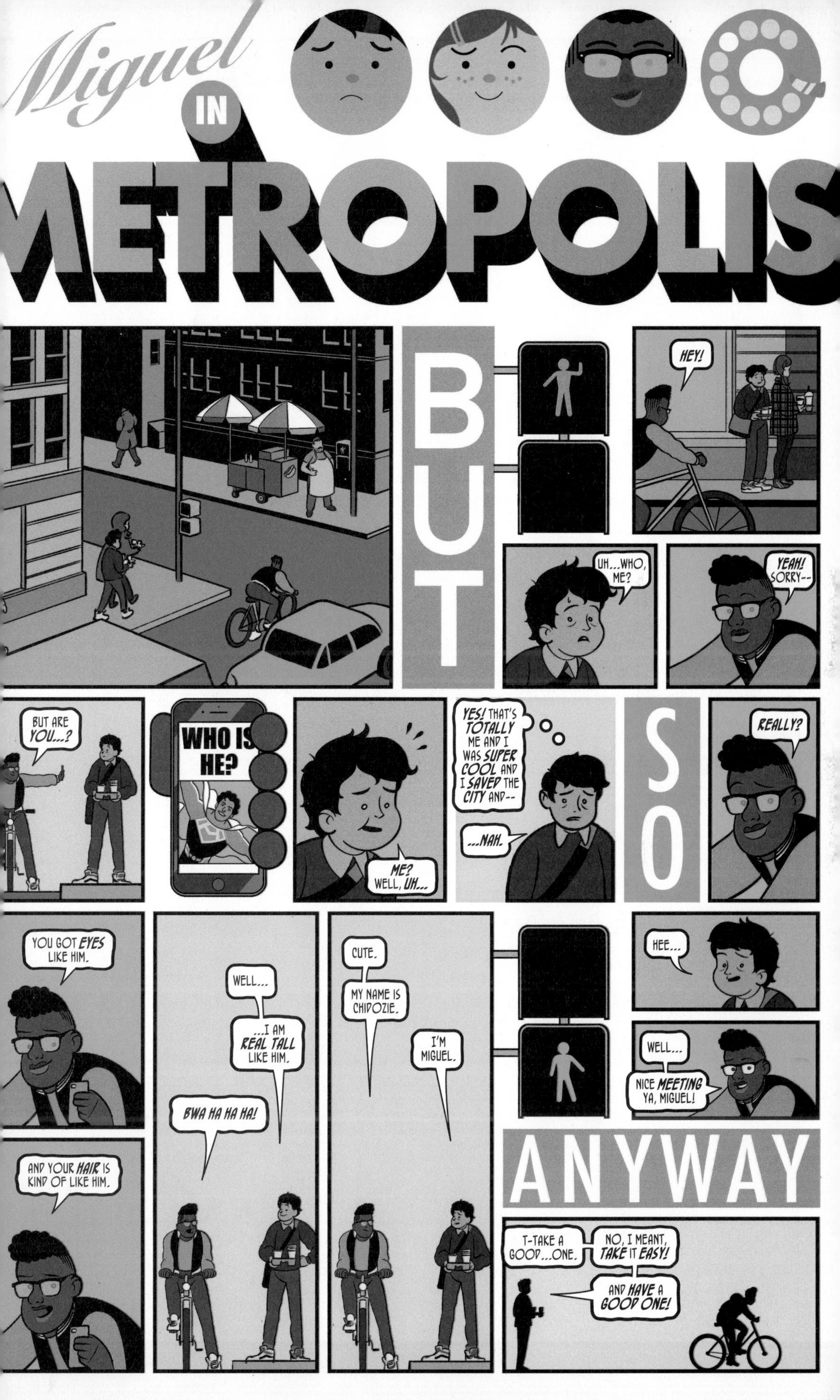
Miguel IN METROPOLIS
BUT
HEY!
UH...WHO, ME?
YEAH! SORRY--
BUT ARE YOU...?
WHO IS HE?
ME? WELL, UH...
YES! THAT'S TOTALLY ME AND I WAS SUPER COOL AND I SAVED THE CITY AND--
...NAH.
SO
REALLY?
YOU GOT EYES LIKE HIM.
AND YOUR HAIR IS KIND OF LIKE HIM.
WELL...
...I AM REAL TALL LIKE HIM.
BWA HA HA HA!
CUTE.
MY NAME IS CHIDOZIE.
I'M MIGUEL.
HEE...
WELL...
NICE MEETING YA, MIGUEL!
ANYWAY
T-TAKE A GOOD...ONE.
NO, I MEANT, TAKE IT EASY!
AND HAVE A GOOD ONE!

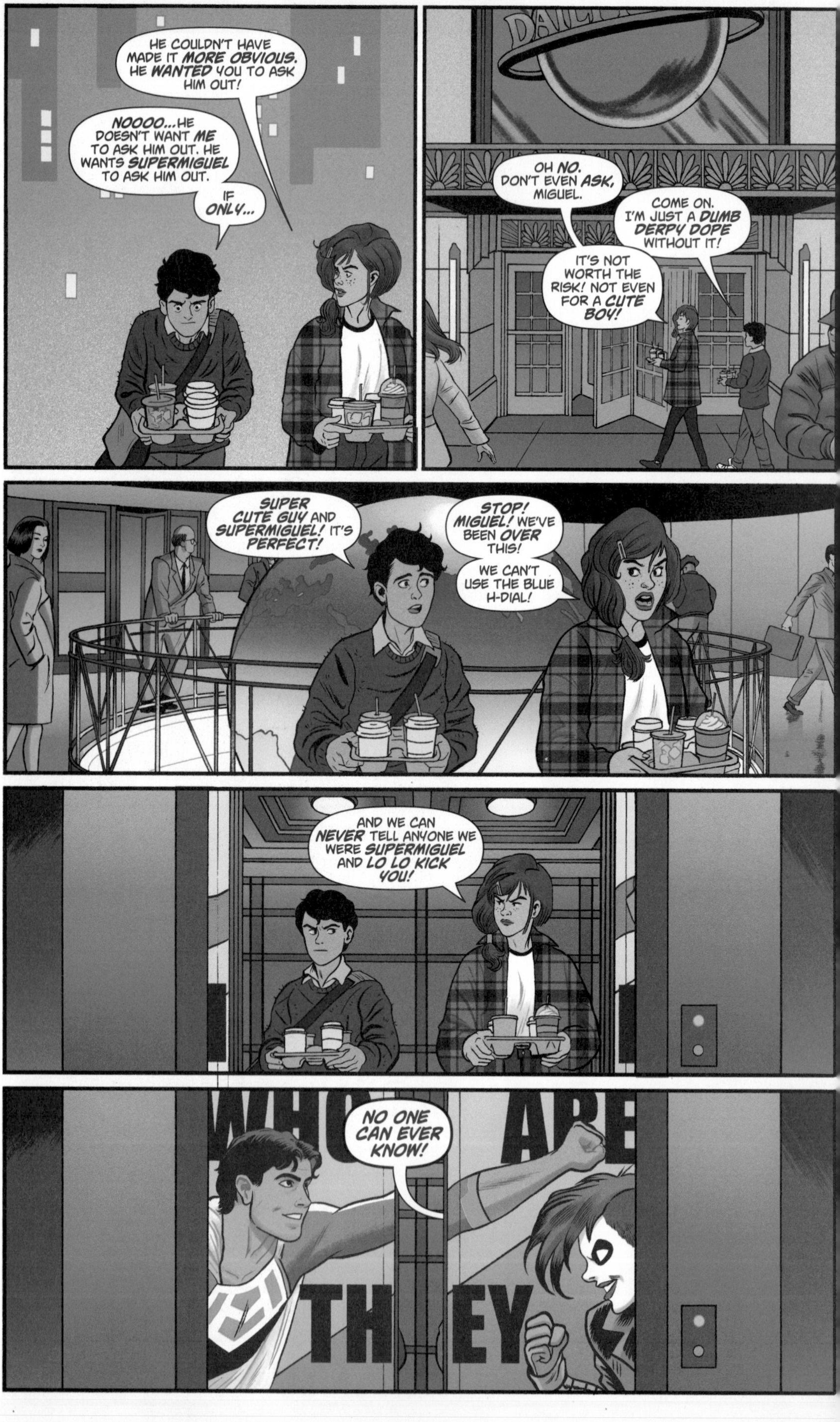
HE COULDN'T HAVE MADE IT MORE OBVIOUS. HE WANTED YOU TO ASK HIM OUT!
NOOOO...HE DOESN'T WANT ME TO ASK HIM OUT. HE WANTS SUPERMIGUEL TO ASK HIM OUT.
IF ONLY...
OH NO. DON'T EVEN ASK, MIGUEL.
COME ON. I'M JUST A DUMB DERPY DOPE WITHOUT IT!
IT'S NOT WORTH THE RISK! NOT EVEN FOR A CUTE BOY!
SUPER CUTE GUY AND SUPERMIGUEL! IT'S PERFECT!
STOP! MIGUEL! WE'VE BEEN OVER THIS!
WE CAN'T USE THE BLUE H-DIAL!
AND WE CAN NEVER TELL ANYONE WE WERE SUPERMIGUEL AND LO LO KICK YOU!
NO ONE CAN EVER KNOW!

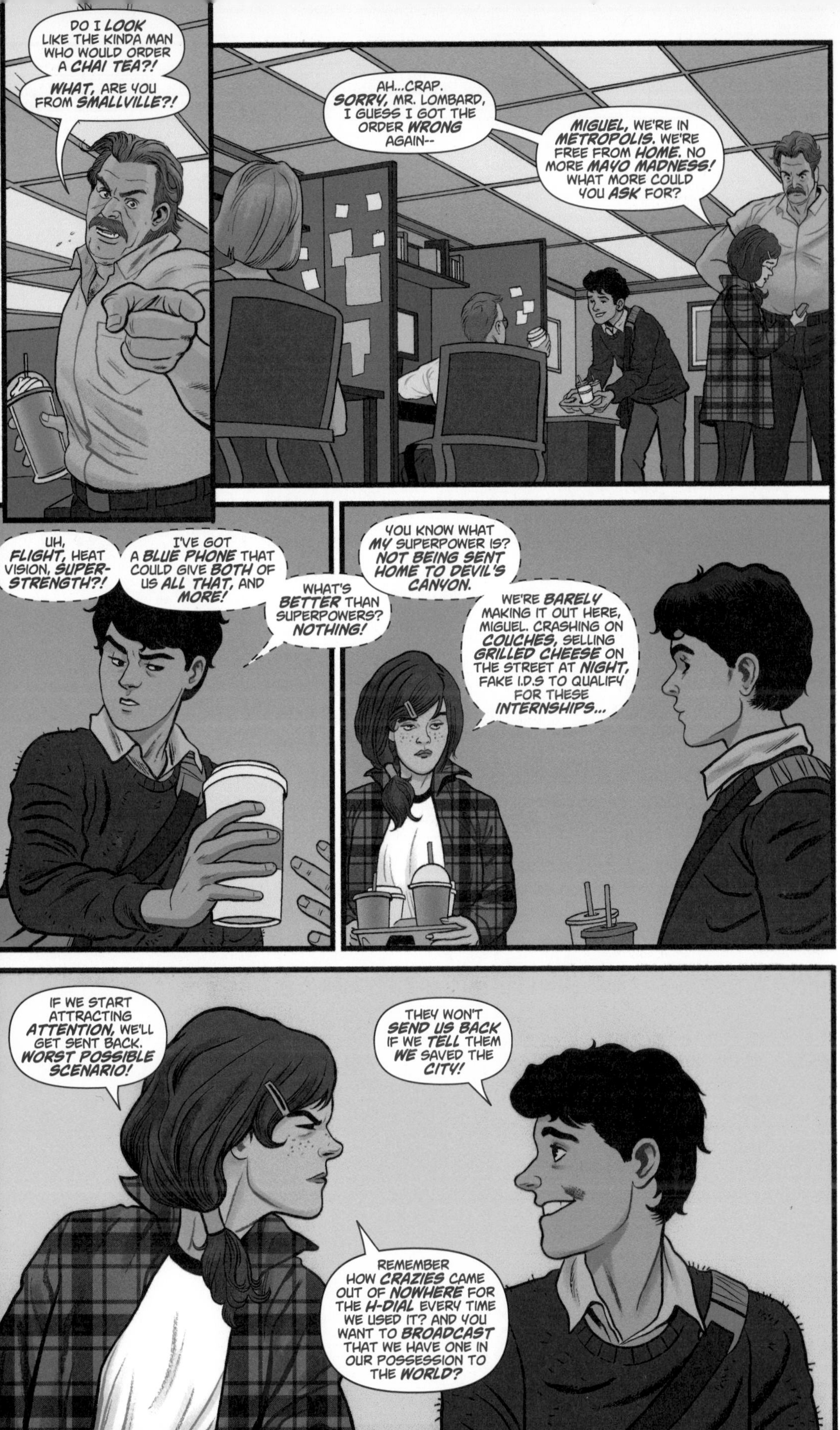
DO I LOOK LIKE THE KINDA MAN WHO WOULD ORDER A CHAI TEA?!
WHAT, ARE YOU FROM SMALLVILLE?!
AH...CRAP. SORRY, MR. LOMBARD, I GUESS I GOT THE ORDER WRONG AGAIN--
MIGUEL, WE'RE IN METROPOLIS. WE'RE FREE FROM HOME. NO MORE MAYO MADNESS! WHAT MORE COULD YOU ASK FOR?
UH, FLIGHT, HEAT VISION, SUPER-STRENGTH?!
I'VE GOT A BLUE PHONE THAT COULD GIVE BOTH OF US ALL THAT, AND MORE!
WHAT'S BETTER THAN SUPERPOWERS? NOTHING!
YOU KNOW WHAT MY SUPERPOWER IS? NOT BEING SENT HOME TO DEVIL'S CANYON.
WE'RE BARELY MAKING IT OUT HERE, MIGUEL. CRASHING ON COUCHES, SELLING GRILLED CHEESE ON THE STREET AT NIGHT, FAKE I.D.S TO QUALIFY FOR THESE INTERNSHIPS...
IF WE START ATTRACTING ATTENTION, WE'LL GET SENT BACK. WORST POSSIBLE SCENARIO!
THEY WON'T SEND US BACK IF WE TELL THEM WE SAVED THE CITY!
REMEMBER HOW CRAZIES CAME OUT OF NOWHERE FOR THE H-DIAL EVERY TIME WE USED IT? AND YOU WANT TO BROADCAST THAT WE HAVE ONE IN OUR POSSESSION TO THE WORLD?

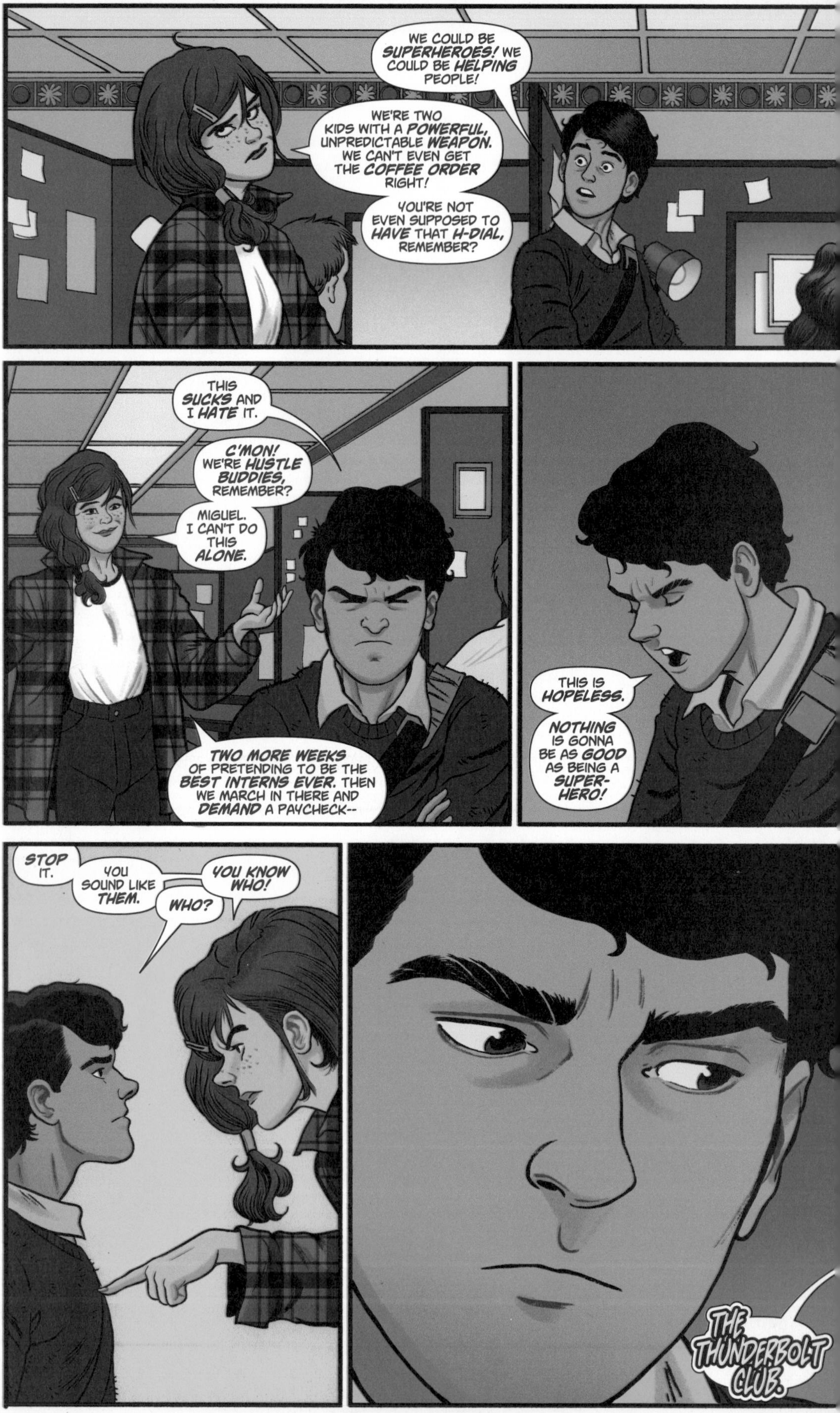
WE COULD BE SUPERHEROES! WE COULD BE HELPING PEOPLE!
WE'RE TWO KIDS WITH A POWERFUL, UNPREDICTABLE WEAPON. WE CAN'T EVEN GET THE COFFEE ORDER RIGHT!
YOU'RE NOT EVEN SUPPOSED TO HAVE THAT H-DIAL, REMEMBER?
THIS SUCKS AND I HATE IT.
C'MON! WE'RE HUSTLE BUDDIES, REMEMBER?
MIGUEL. I CAN'T DO THIS ALONE.
TWO MORE WEEKS OF PRETENDING TO BE THE BEST INTERNS EVER. THEN WE MARCH IN THERE AND DEMAND A PAYCHECK--
THIS IS HOPELESS.
NOTHING IS GONNA BE AS GOOD AS BEING A SUPER-HERO!
STOP IT.
YOU SOUND LIKE THEM.
WHO?
YOU KNOW WHO!
THE THUNDERBOLT CLUB.

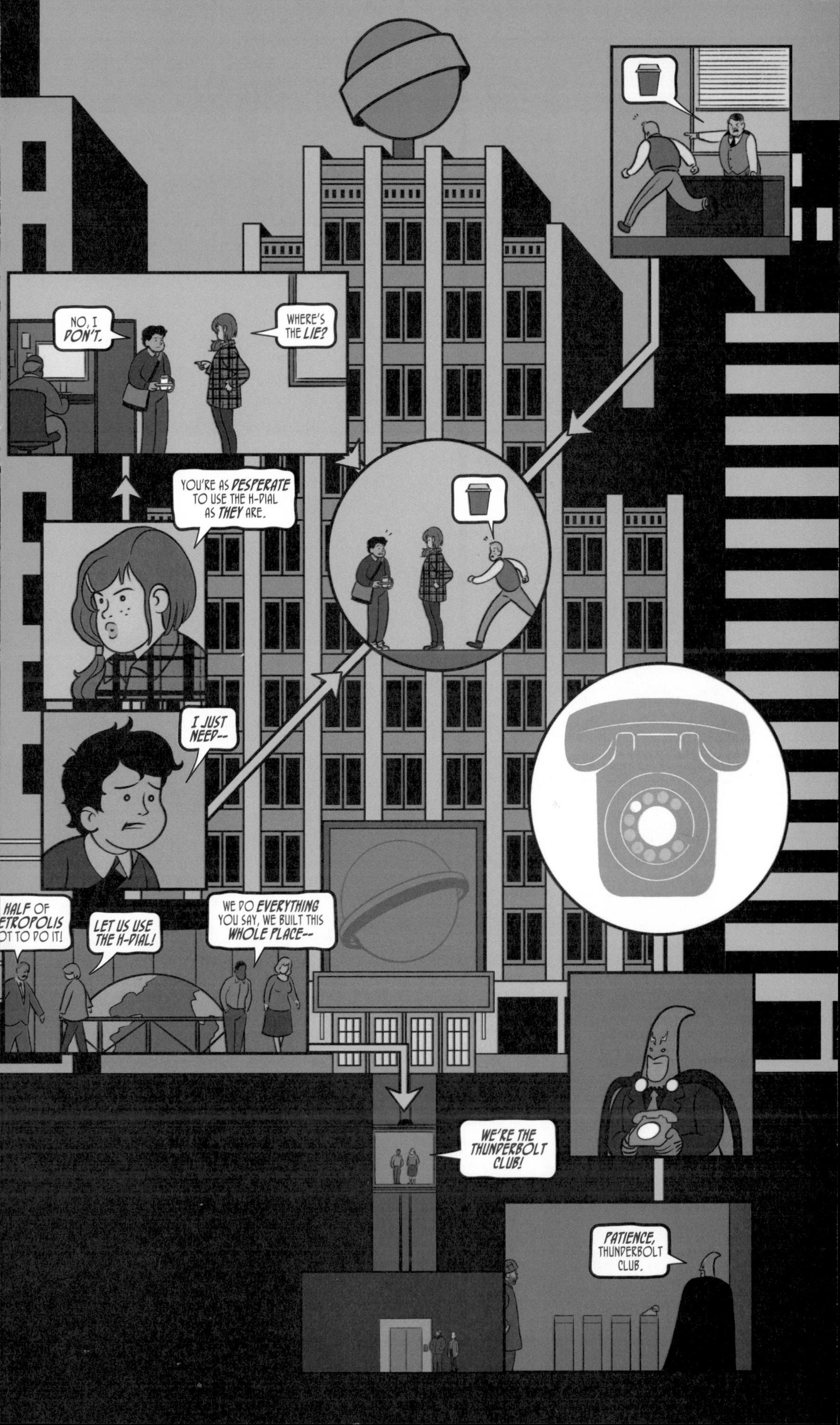

NO, I DON'T.
WHERE'S THE LIE?
YOU'RE AS DESPERATE TO USE THE H-DIAL AS THEY ARE.
I JUST NEED--
HALF OF ETROPOLIS OT TO DO IT!
LET US USE THE H-DIAL!
WE DO EVERYTHING YOU SAY, WE BUILT THIS WHOLE PLACE--
WE'RE THE THUNDERBOLT CLUB!
PATIENCE, THUNDERBOLT CLUB.

I KNOW I HAVE BEEN *PROMISING* YOU THE POWER OF THE *HEROVERSE* FOR QUITE SOME TIME, *I KNOW.* LET'S PLAY A *GAME* INSTEAD.

WHAT WOULD YOU DO...TO SAVE *FOUR HUNDRED THOUSAND* PEOPLE?

UM, WHAT? I JUST WANNA USE THE *DIAL* AGAIN--

THE *GREEN LANTERN CORPS* PATROL *3,600 SECTORS* IN OUR UNIVERSE. EACH ONE WITH AN AVERAGE OF *FIFTEEN BILLION* SENTIENT LIFE-FORMS.

THAT'S A TOTAL OF *54 TRILLION* LIVES.

BUT WE ARE *ONE* PART OF A *MULTIVERSE.* MANY *EARTHS,* MANY *SECTORS...MANY, MANY* MORE *LIVES.*

MULTIPLY THAT NUMBER BY *52 UNIVERSES,* AND YOU GET *2.8 QUADRILLION* LIVES.

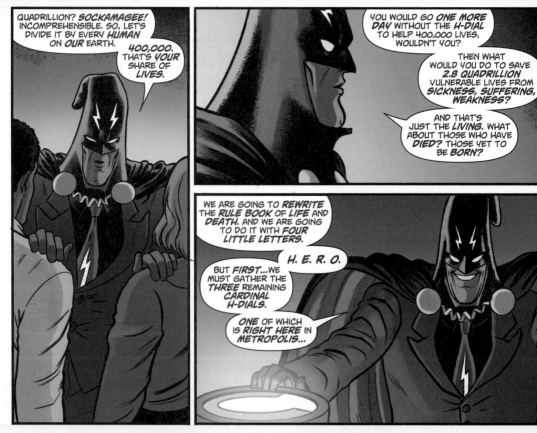

QUADRILLION? *SOCKAMAGEE!* INCOMPREHENSIBLE. SO, LET'S DIVIDE IT BY EVERY *HUMAN* ON *OUR* EARTH.

400,000. THAT'S *YOUR* SHARE OF LIVES.

YOU WOULD GO *ONE MORE DAY* WITHOUT THE *H-DIAL* TO HELP 400,000 LIVES, WOULDN'T YOU?

THEN WHAT WOULD YOU DO TO SAVE *2.8 QUADRILLION* VULNERABLE LIVES FROM *SICKNESS, SUFFERING, WEAKNESS?*

AND THAT'S JUST THE *LIVING.* WHAT ABOUT THOSE WHO HAVE *DIED?* THOSE YET TO BE *BORN?*

WE ARE GOING TO *REWRITE* THE *RULE BOOK* OF LIFE AND *DEATH.* AND WE ARE GOING TO DO IT WITH *FOUR LITTLE LETTERS.*

H. E. R. O.

BUT *FIRST...WE* MUST GATHER THE *THREE* REMAINING *CARDINAL H-DIALS.*

ONE OF WHICH IS *RIGHT HERE* IN *METROPOLIS...*

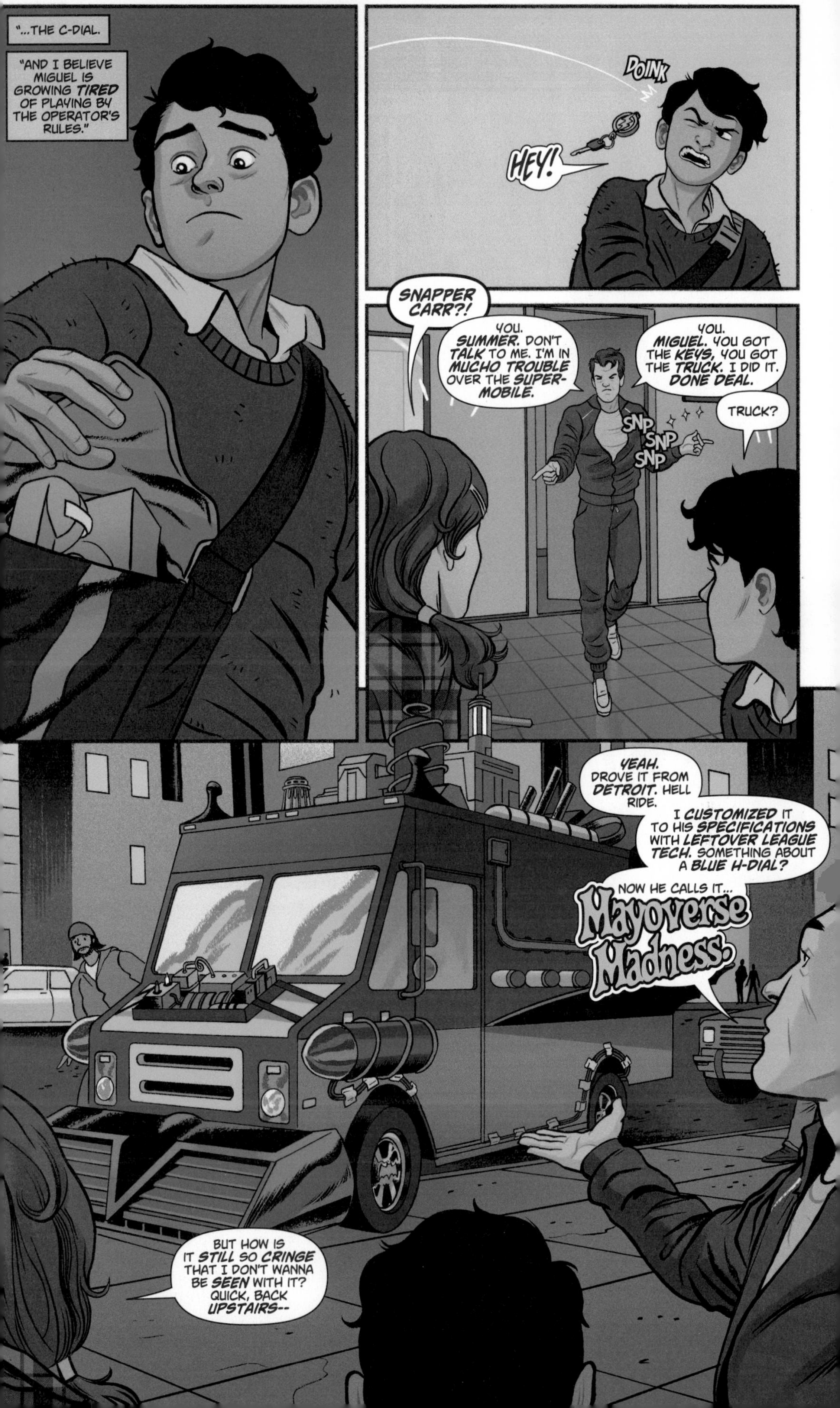
"...THE C-DIAL.
"AND I BELIEVE MIGUEL IS GROWING TIRED OF PLAYING BY THE OPERATOR'S RULES."
DOINK
HEY!
SNAPPER CARR?!
YOU. SUMMER. DON'T TALK TO ME. I'M IN MUCHO TROUBLE OVER THE SUPER-MOBILE.
YOU. MIGUEL. YOU GOT THE KEYS, YOU GOT THE TRUCK. I DID IT. DONE DEAL.
SNP SNP SNP
TRUCK?
YEAH. DROVE IT FROM DETROIT. HELL RIDE.
I CUSTOMIZED IT TO HIS SPECIFICATIONS WITH LEFTOVER LEAGUE TECH. SOMETHING ABOUT A BLUE H-DIAL?
NOW HE CALLS IT...
Mayoverse Madness.
BUT HOW IS IT STILL SO CRINGE THAT I DON'T WANNA BE SEEN WITH IT? QUICK, BACK UPSTAIRS--

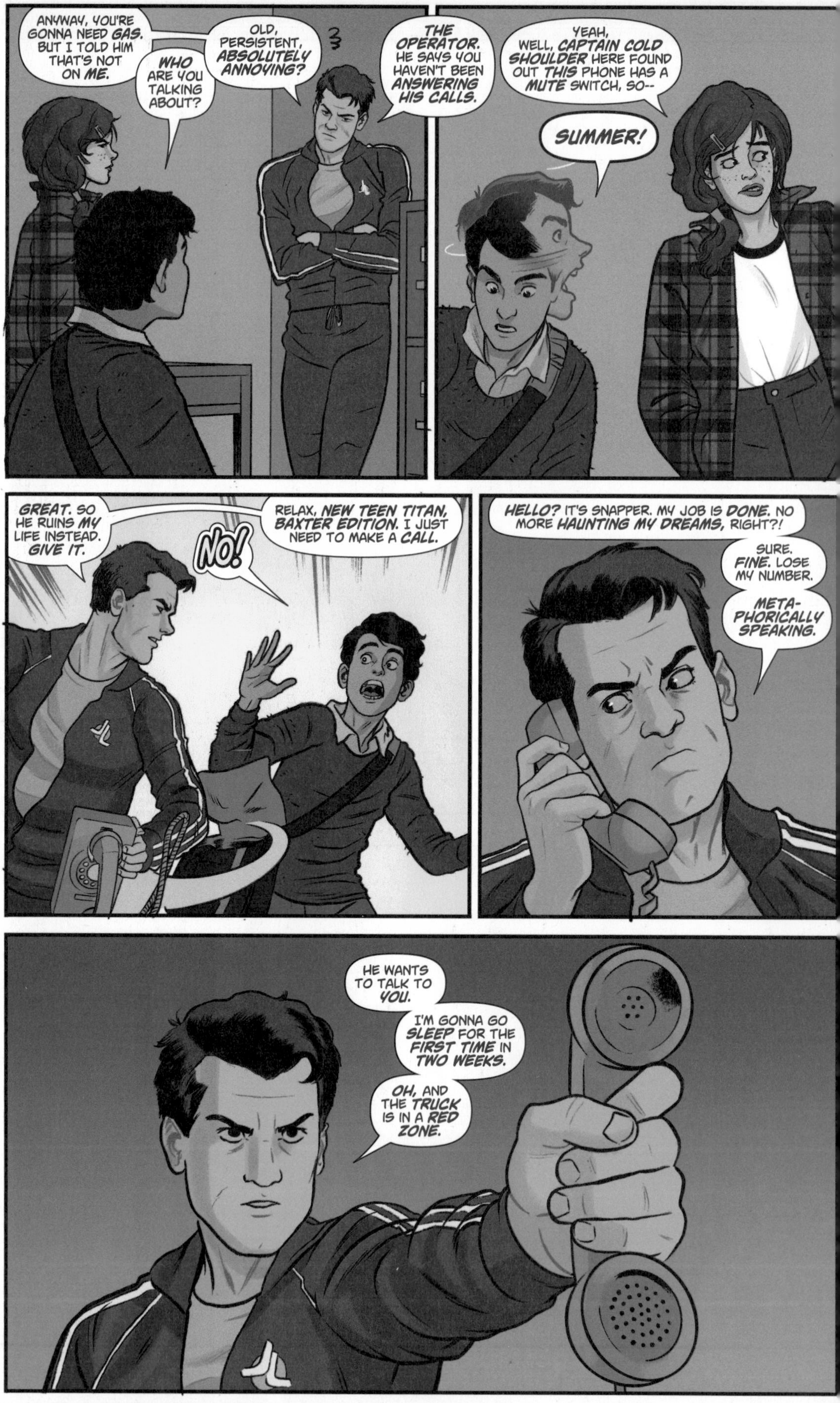
ANYWAY, YOU'RE GONNA NEED GAS. BUT I TOLD HIM THAT'S NOT ON ME.
WHO ARE YOU TALKING ABOUT?
OLD, PERSISTENT, ABSOLUTELY ANNOYING?
THE OPERATOR. HE SAYS YOU HAVEN'T BEEN ANSWERING HIS CALLS.
YEAH, WELL, CAPTAIN COLD SHOULDER HERE FOUND OUT THIS PHONE HAS A MUTE SWITCH, SO--
SUMMER!
GREAT. SO HE RUINS MY LIFE INSTEAD. GIVE IT.
RELAX, NEW TEEN TITAN, BAXTER EDITION. I JUST NEED TO MAKE A CALL.
NO!
HELLO? IT'S SNAPPER. MY JOB IS DONE. NO MORE HAUNTING MY DREAMS, RIGHT?!
SURE. FINE. LOSE MY NUMBER.
META-PHORICALLY SPEAKING.
HE WANTS TO TALK TO YOU.
I'M GONNA GO SLEEP FOR THE FIRST TIME IN TWO WEEKS.
OH, AND THE TRUCK IS IN A RED ZONE.

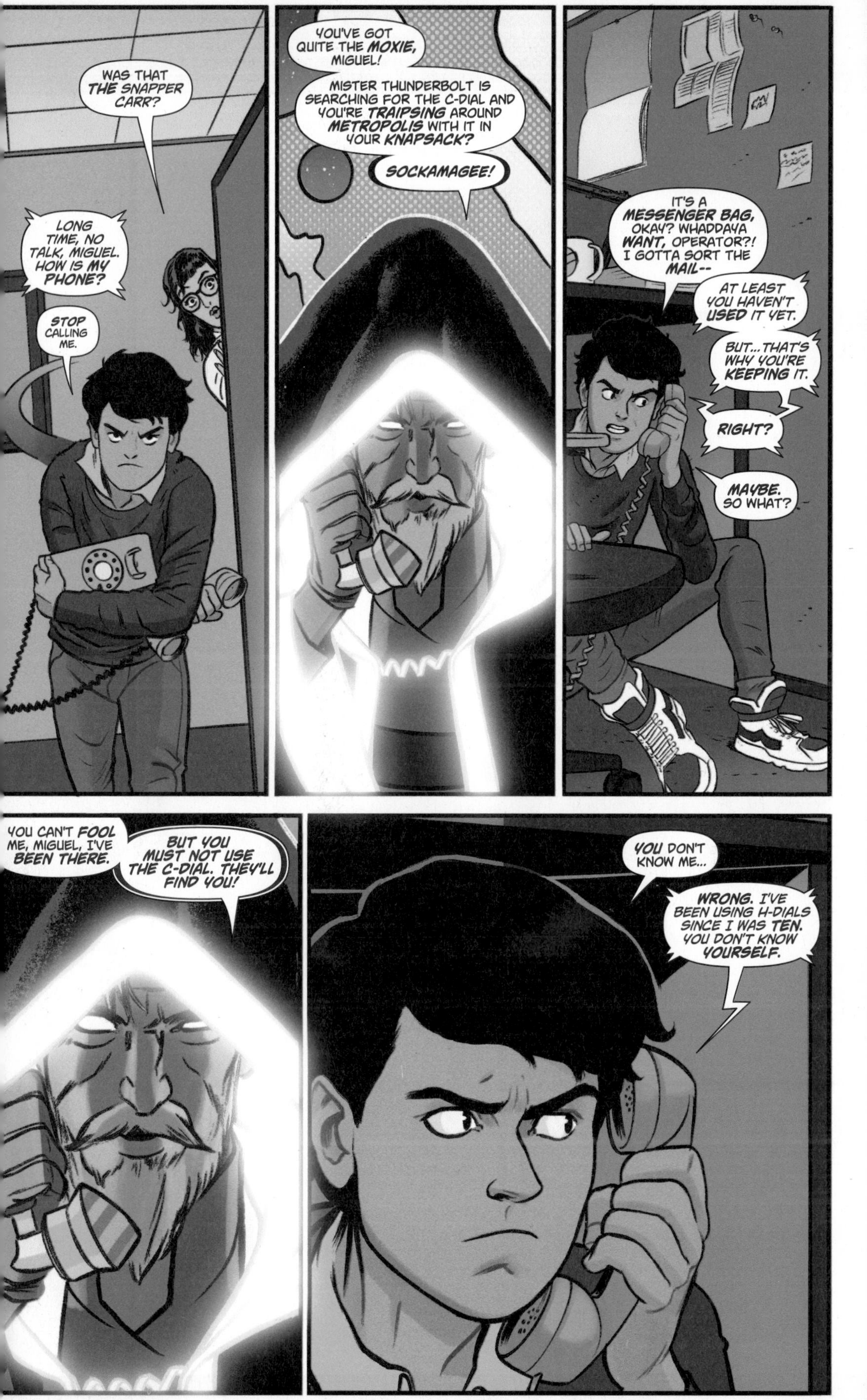
WAS THAT THE SNAPPER CARR?
LONG TIME, NO TALK, MIGUEL. HOW IS MY PHONE?
STOP CALLING ME.
YOU'VE GOT QUITE THE MOXIE, MIGUEL!
MISTER THUNDERBOLT IS SEARCHING FOR THE C-DIAL AND YOU'RE TRAIPSING AROUND METROPOLIS WITH IT IN YOUR KNAPSACK?
SOCKAMAGEE!
IT'S A MESSENGER BAG, OKAY? WHADDAYA WANT, OPERATOR?! I GOTTA SORT THE MAIL--
AT LEAST YOU HAVEN'T USED IT YET.
BUT... THAT'S WHY YOU'RE KEEPING IT.
RIGHT?
MAYBE. SO WHAT?
YOU CAN'T FOOL ME, MIGUEL, I'VE BEEN THERE.
BUT YOU MUST NOT USE THE C-DIAL. THEY'LL FIND YOU!
YOU DON'T KNOW ME...
WRONG. I'VE BEEN USING H-DIALS SINCE I WAS TEN. YOU DON'T KNOW YOURSELF.

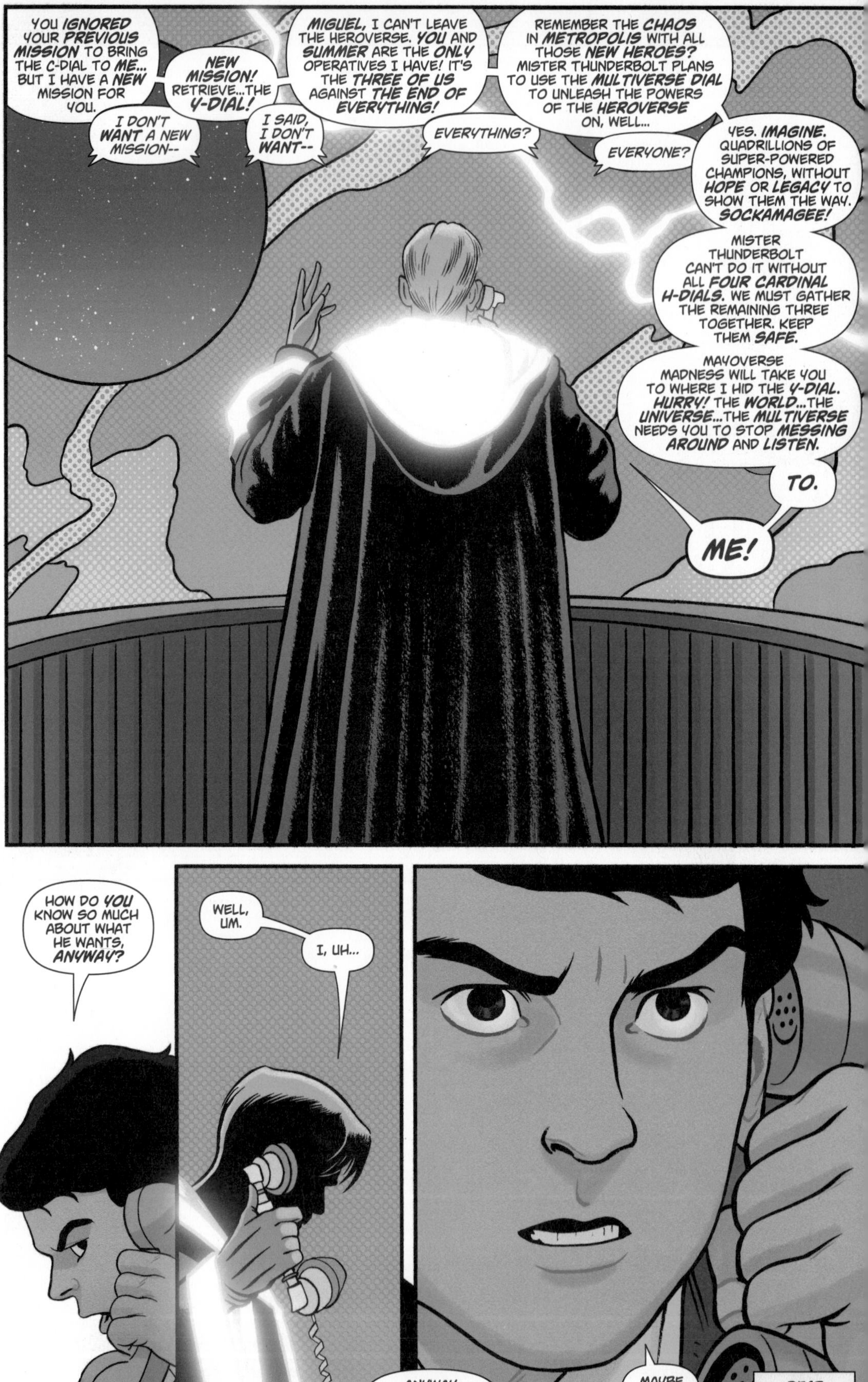
YOU IGNORED YOUR PREVIOUS MISSION TO BRING THE C-DIAL TO ME... BUT I HAVE A NEW MISSION FOR YOU.
I DON'T WANT A NEW MISSION--
NEW MISSION! RETRIEVE...THE Y-DIAL!
I SAID, I DON'T WANT--
MIGUEL, I CAN'T LEAVE THE HEROVERSE. YOU AND SUMMER ARE THE ONLY OPERATIVES I HAVE! IT'S THE THREE OF US AGAINST THE END OF EVERYTHING!
EVERYTHING?
REMEMBER THE CHAOS IN METROPOLIS WITH ALL THOSE NEW HEROES? MISTER THUNDERBOLT PLANS TO USE THE MULTIVERSE DIAL TO UNLEASH THE POWERS OF THE HEROVERSE ON, WELL...
EVERYONE?
YES. IMAGINE. QUADRILLIONS OF SUPER-POWERED CHAMPIONS, WITHOUT HOPE OR LEGACY TO SHOW THEM THE WAY. SOCKAMAGEE!
MISTER THUNDERBOLT CAN'T DO IT WITHOUT ALL FOUR CARDINAL H-DIALS. WE MUST GATHER THE REMAINING THREE TOGETHER. KEEP THEM SAFE.
MAYOVERSE MADNESS WILL TAKE YOU TO WHERE I HID THE Y-DIAL. HURRY! THE WORLD...THE UNIVERSE...THE MULTIVERSE NEEDS YOU TO STOP MESSING AROUND AND LISTEN.
TO.
ME!
HOW DO YOU KNOW SO MUCH ABOUT WHAT HE WANTS, ANYWAY?
WELL, UM.
I, UH...
ANYWAY, GIVING EVERYONE POWERS DOESN'T SEEM SO BAD, YOU KNOW?
MAYBE THEY DON'T NEED A BABYSITTER AFTER ALL.
MAYBE I DON'T, EITHER.
DEAR SUPERMAN.

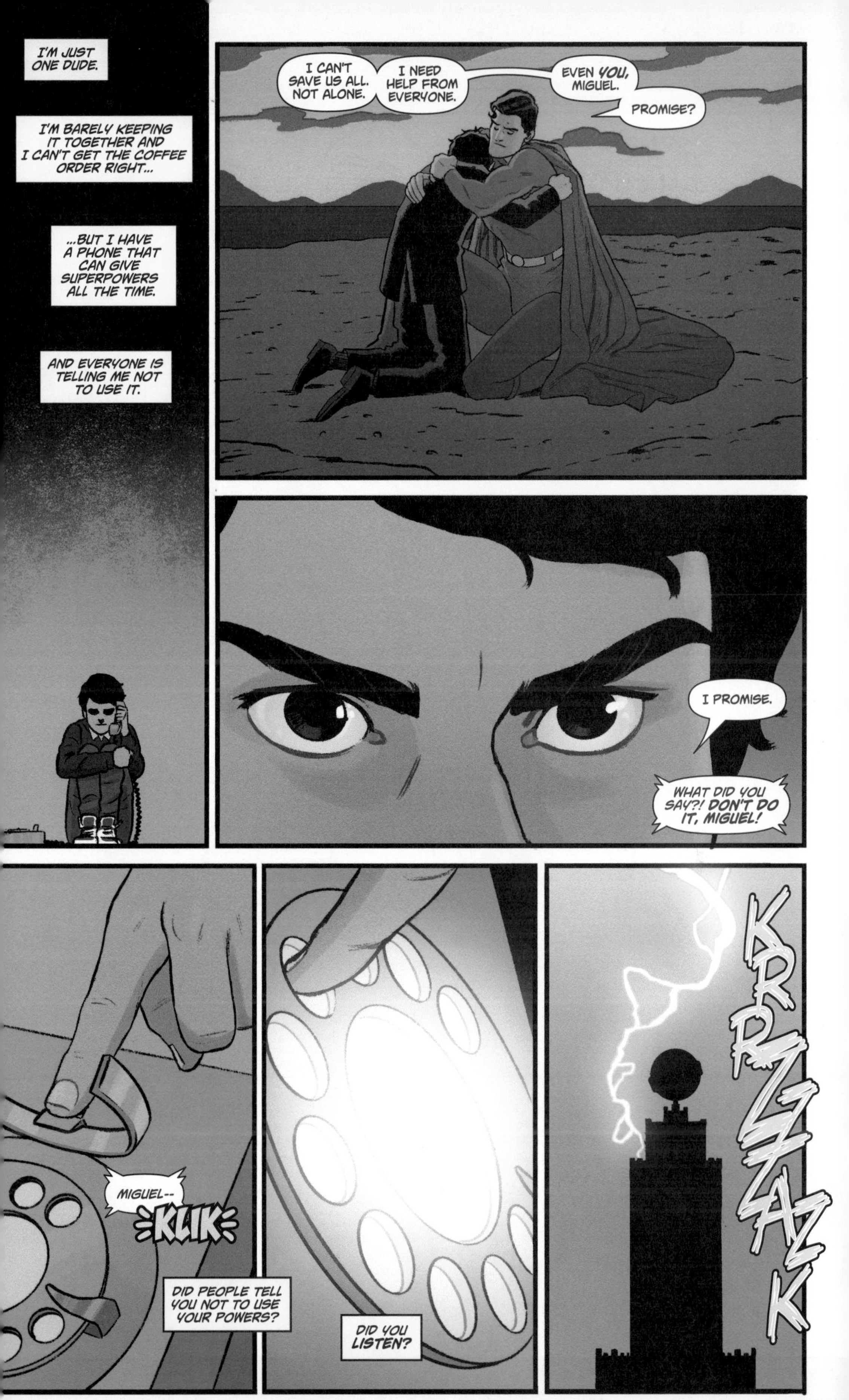
I'M JUST ONE DUDE.
I'M BARELY KEEPING IT TOGETHER AND I CAN'T GET THE COFFEE ORDER RIGHT...
...BUT I HAVE A PHONE THAT CAN GIVE SUPERPOWERS ALL THE TIME.
AND EVERYONE IS TELLING ME NOT TO USE IT.
I CAN'T SAVE US ALL. NOT ALONE.
I NEED HELP FROM EVERYONE.
EVEN YOU, MIGUEL.
PROMISE?
I PROMISE.
WHAT DID YOU SAY?! DON'T DO IT, MIGUEL!
MIGUEL--
KLIK
DID PEOPLE TELL YOU NOT TO USE YOUR POWERS?
DID YOU LISTEN?
KRRZZZAK

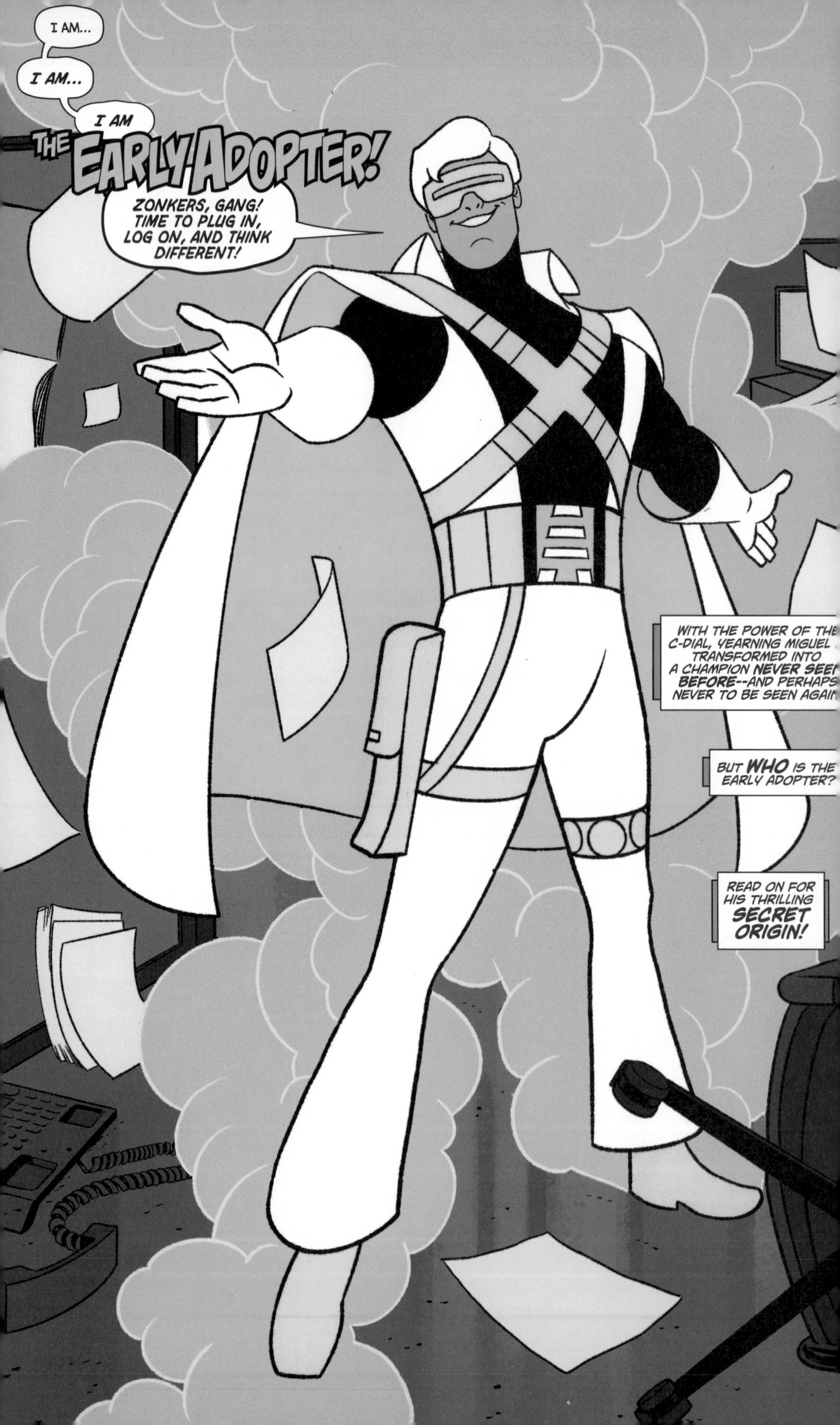
I AM...
I AM...
I AM
THE EARLY ADOPTER!
ZONKERS, GANG! TIME TO PLUG IN, LOG ON, AND THINK DIFFERENT!
WITH THE POWER OF THE C-DIAL, YEARNING MIGUEL TRANSFORMED INTO A CHAMPION NEVER SEEN BEFORE--AND PERHAPS NEVER TO BE SEEN AGAIN
BUT WHO IS THE EARLY ADOPTER?
READ ON FOR HIS THRILLING SECRET ORIGIN!

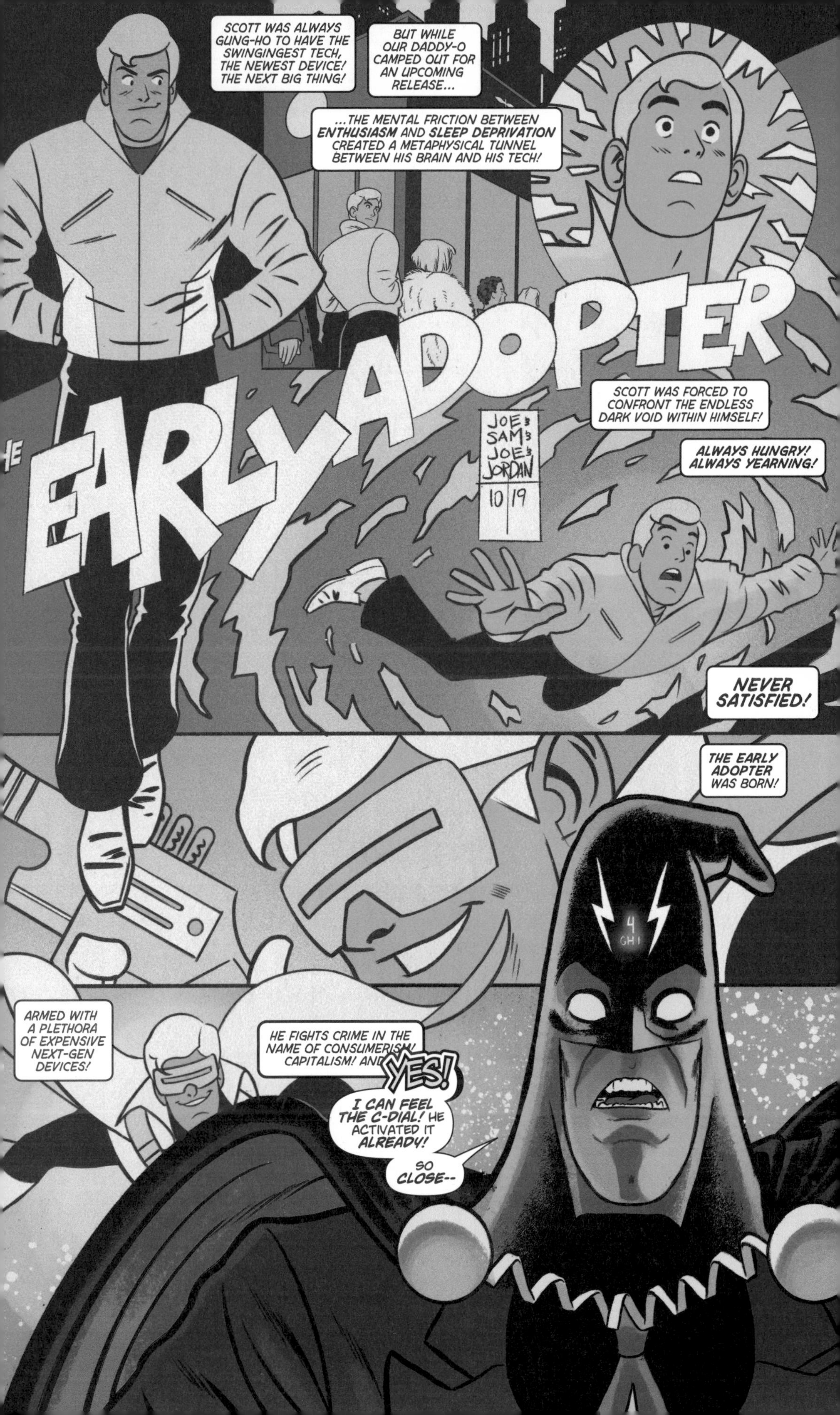
SCOTT WAS ALWAYS GUNG-HO TO HAVE THE SWINGINGEST TECH, THE NEWEST DEVICE! THE NEXT BIG THING!
BUT WHILE OUR DADDY-O CAMPED OUT FOR AN UPCOMING RELEASE...
...THE MENTAL FRICTION BETWEEN ENTHUSIASM AND SLEEP DEPRIVATION CREATED A METAPHYSICAL TUNNEL BETWEEN HIS BRAIN AND HIS TECH!
EARLY ADOPTER
JOE & SAM & JOE & JORDAN
10 19
SCOTT WAS FORCED TO CONFRONT THE ENDLESS DARK VOID WITHIN HIMSELF!
ALWAYS HUNGRY! ALWAYS YEARNING!
NEVER SATISFIED!
THE EARLY ADOPTER WAS BORN!
ARMED WITH A PLETHORA OF EXPENSIVE NEXT-GEN DEVICES!
HE FIGHTS CRIME IN THE NAME OF CONSUMERISM! CAPITALISM! AND
YES!
I CAN FEEL THE C-DIAL! HE ACTIVATED IT ALREADY!
SO CLOSE--

The EARLY ADOPTER

AND THAT'S THE SECRET ORIGIN OF *ME, THE EARLY ADOPTER!*

THE *NEWEST* HERO ON THE *METROPOLIS* SCENE!

AND, UH, I *GU...* I'LL ANSWER *QUESTIONS*

OKAY, I'LL *BITE.* WHAT ARE YOUR *POWERS?*

I'M GLAD YOU *ASKED!* LET ME *DEMONSTRATE.*

THIS IS THE *DARK WEB*--IT SHOOTS A *NET* TO ENSNARE ANY BAD GUYS WHO--

♪

AH...THAT ONE MUST STILL BE IN *BETA.* WORKING OUT THE *KINKS!* HEH HEH!

THIS DEVICE IS THE *PRIVACY SUCKERBERG*--IT WILL SHOW ME *EVERYWHERE* A CRIMINAL HAS *BEEN*--

UH--

HAW HAW!

HE'S AN EARLY *DUMB-ASS!*

YOU'RE A BRAYING JACKASS, STEVE LOMBARD!

FACE THE POWER OF THE *UNSUBSCRIBE BUTTON!*

IS THAT... *"KISS FROM A ROSE"?*

POW

BRAYING JACKASS?!

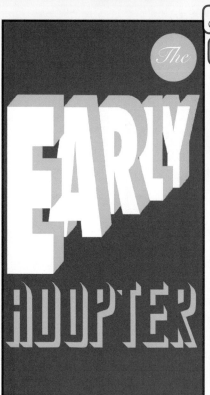

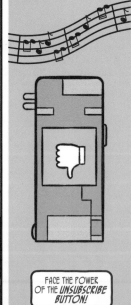

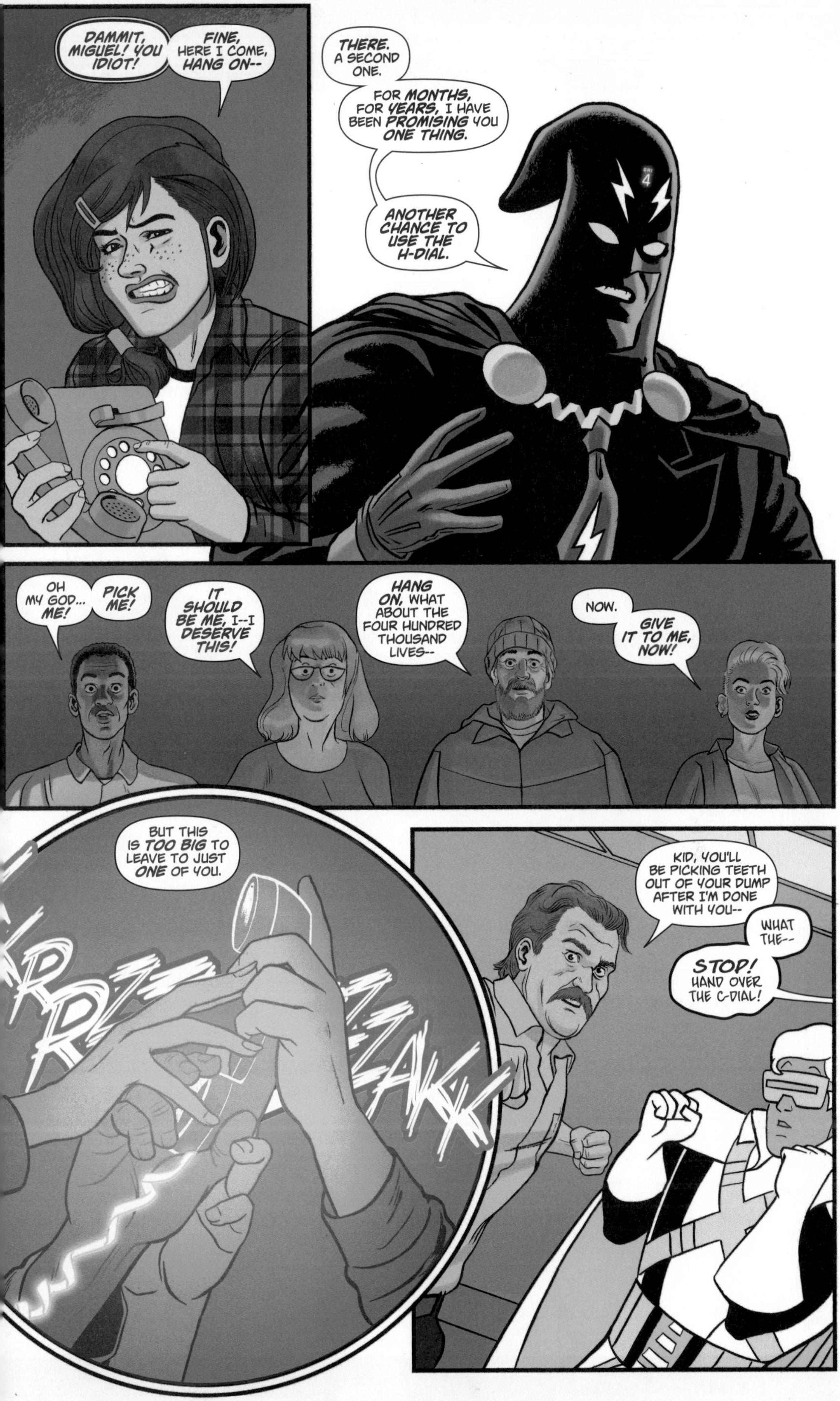
DAMMIT, MIGUEL! YOU IDIOT!
FINE, HERE I COME, HANG ON--
THERE. A SECOND ONE.
FOR MONTHS, FOR YEARS, I HAVE BEEN PROMISING YOU ONE THING.
ANOTHER CHANCE TO USE THE H-DIAL.
OH MY GOD... ME!
PICK ME!
IT SHOULD BE ME, I--I DESERVE THIS!
HANG ON, WHAT ABOUT THE FOUR HUNDRED THOUSAND LIVES--
NOW.
GIVE IT TO ME, NOW!
BUT THIS IS TOO BIG TO LEAVE TO JUST ONE OF YOU.
KID, YOU'LL BE PICKING TEETH OUT OF YOUR DUMP AFTER I'M DONE WITH YOU--
WHAT THE--
STOP! HAND OVER THE C-DIAL!

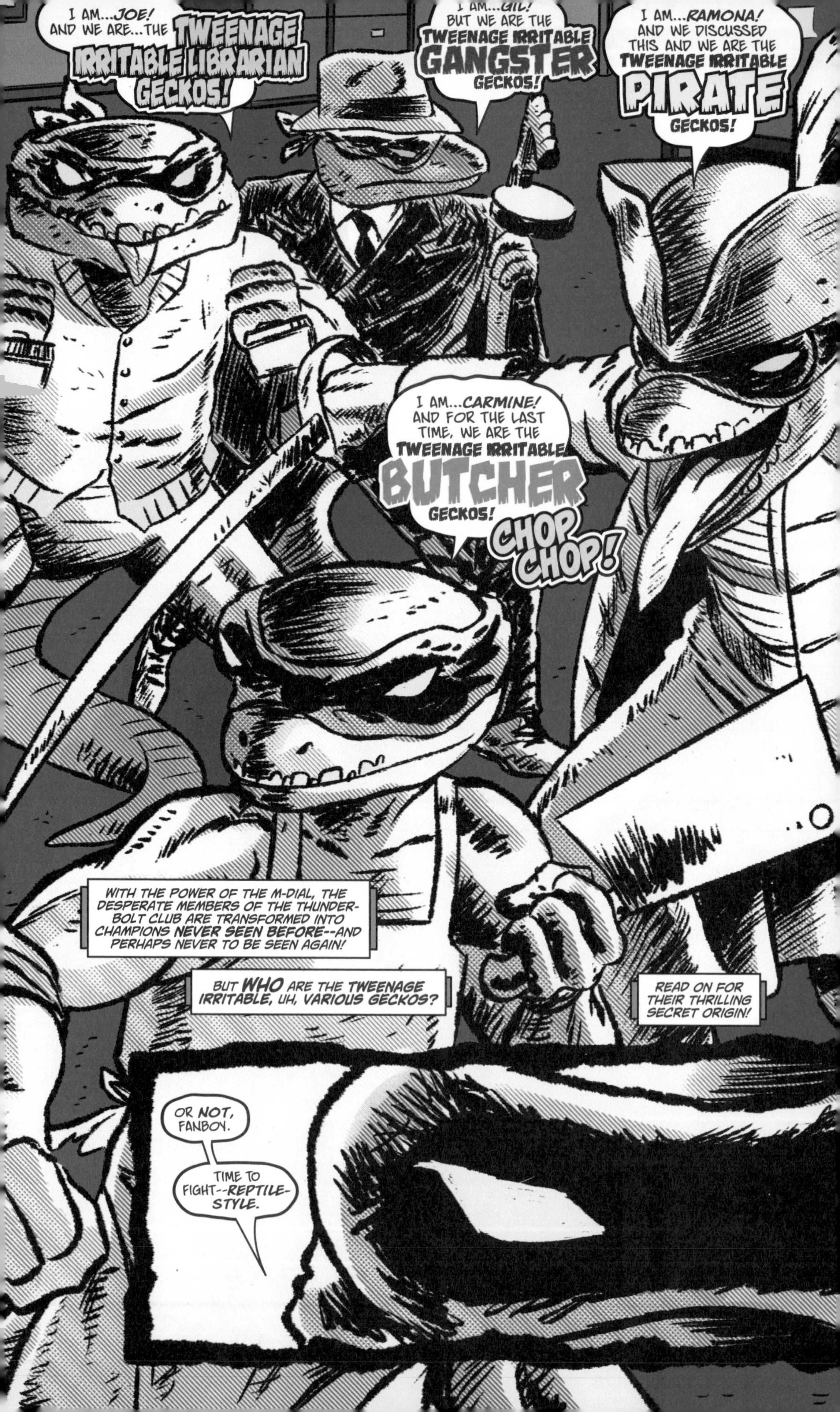

I AM...JOE! AND WE ARE...THE TWEENAGE IRRITABLE LIBRARIAN GECKOS!
I AM...GIL! BUT WE ARE THE TWEENAGE IRRITABLE GANGSTER GECKOS!
I AM...RAMONA! AND WE DISCUSSED THIS AND WE ARE THE TWEENAGE IRRITABLE PIRATE GECKOS!
I AM...CARMINE! AND FOR THE LAST TIME, WE ARE THE TWEENAGE IRRITABLE BUTCHER GECKOS!
CHOP CHOP!
WITH THE POWER OF THE M-DIAL, THE DESPERATE MEMBERS OF THE THUNDER-BOLT CLUB ARE TRANSFORMED INTO CHAMPIONS NEVER SEEN BEFORE--AND PERHAPS NEVER TO BE SEEN AGAIN!
BUT WHO ARE THE TWEENAGE IRRITABLE, UH, VARIOUS GECKOS?
READ ON FOR THEIR THRILLING SECRET ORIGIN!
OR NOT, FANBOY.
TIME TO FIGHT--REPTILE-STYLE.

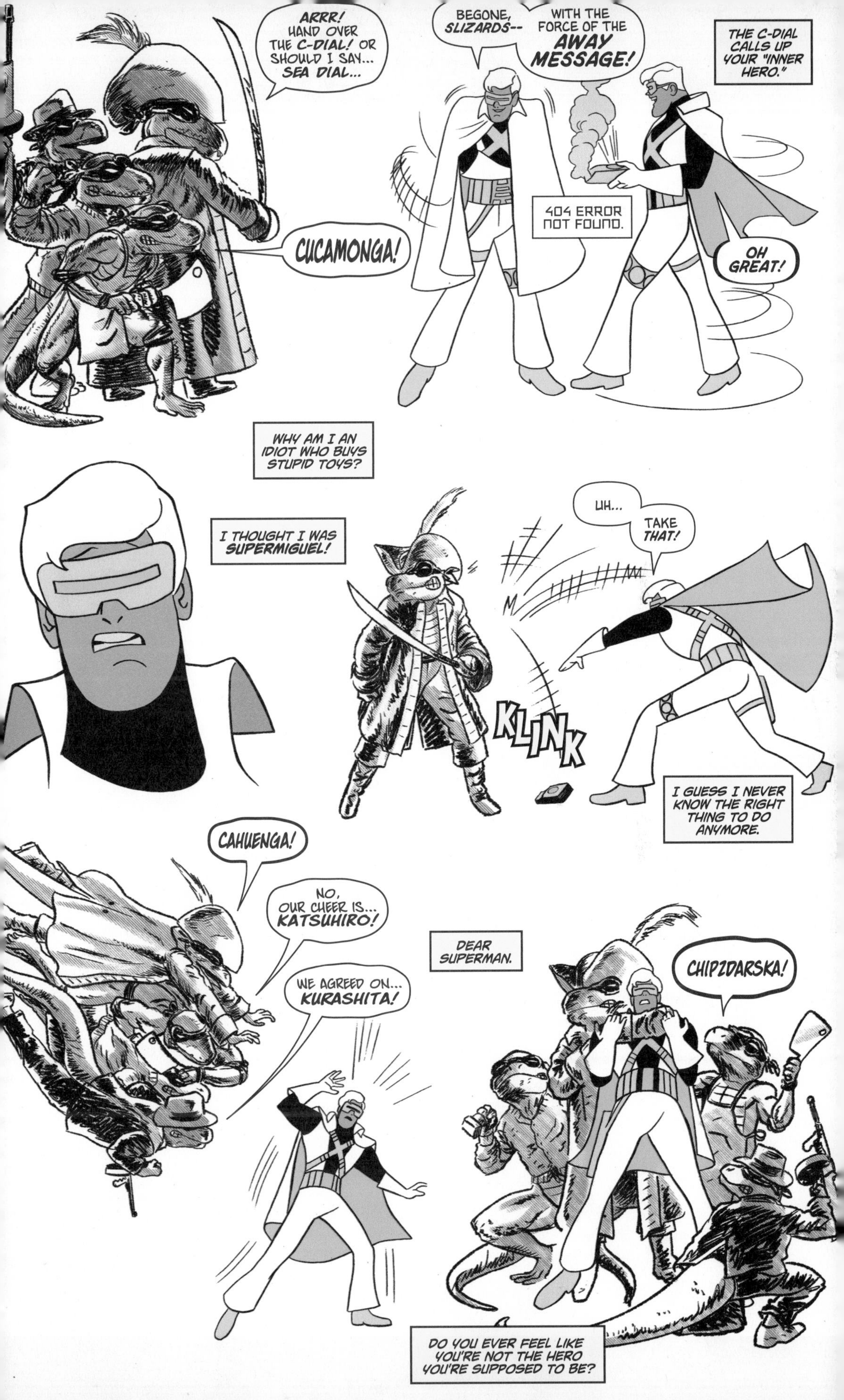
ARRR! HAND OVER THE C-DIAL! OR SHOULD I SAY... SEA DIAL...
CUCAMONGA!
BEGONE, SLIZARDS--
WITH THE FORCE OF THE AWAY MESSAGE!
THE C-DIAL CALLS UP YOUR "INNER HERO."
404 ERROR NOT FOUND.
OH GREAT!
WHY AM I AN IDIOT WHO BUYS STUPID TOYS?
I THOUGHT I WAS SUPERMIGUEL!
UH...
TAKE THAT!
KLINK
I GUESS I NEVER KNOW THE RIGHT THING TO DO ANYMORE.
CAHUENGA!
NO, OUR CHEER IS... KATSUHIRO!
WE AGREED ON... KURASHITA!
DEAR SUPERMAN.
CHIPZDARSKA!
DO YOU EVER FEEL LIKE YOU'RE NOT THE HERO YOU'RE SUPPOSED TO BE?

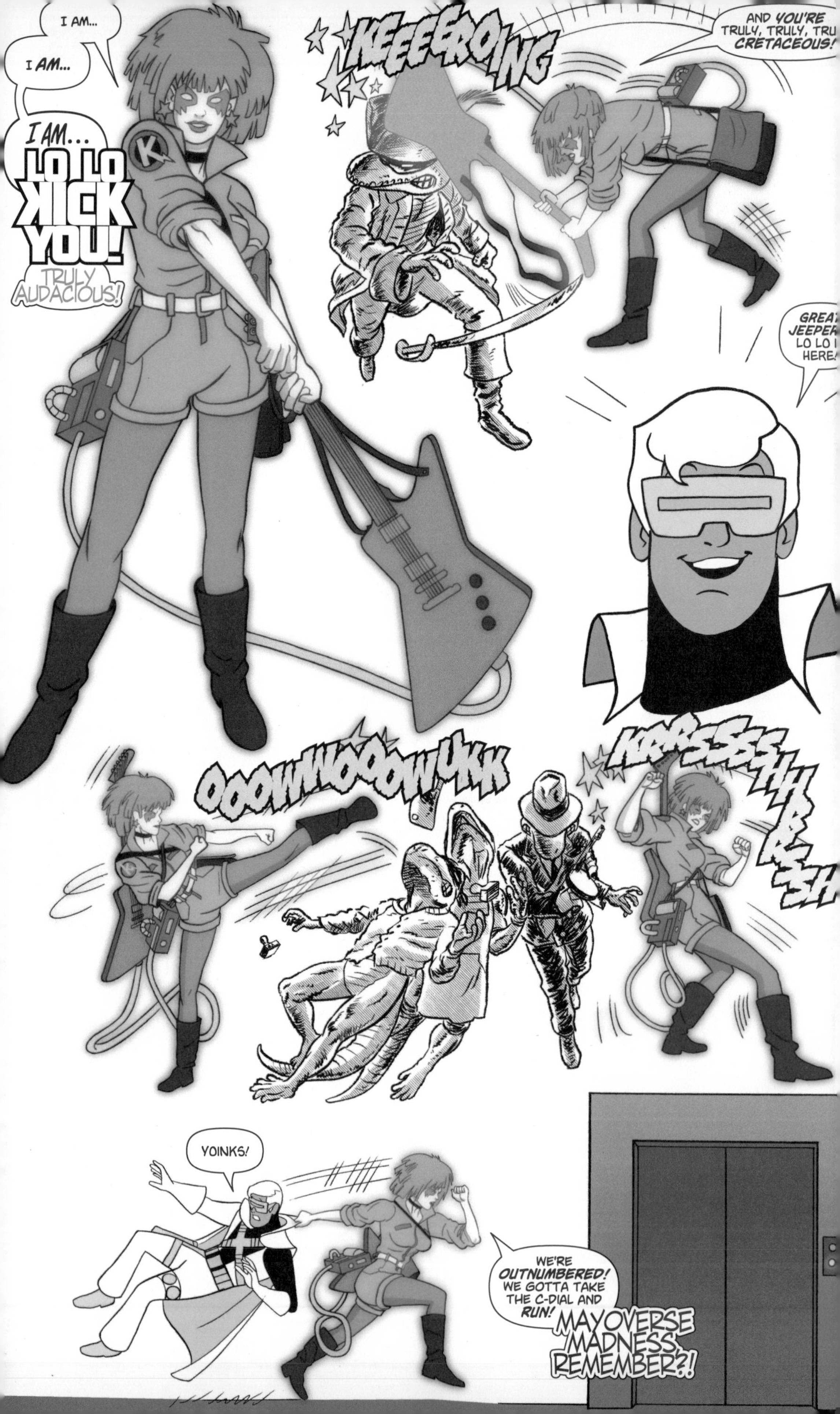
I AM...
I AM...
I AM... LO LO KICK YOU!
TRULY AUDACIOUS!
KEEEEROING
AND YOU'RE TRULY, TRULY, TRU CRETACEOUS!
GREA JEEPER LO LO I HERE
OOOWWOOOWUKK
KRRSSSSHHRRSSH
YOINKS!
WE'RE OUTNUMBERED! WE GOTTA TAKE THE C-DIAL AND RUN!
MAYOVERSE MADNESS, REMEMBER?!

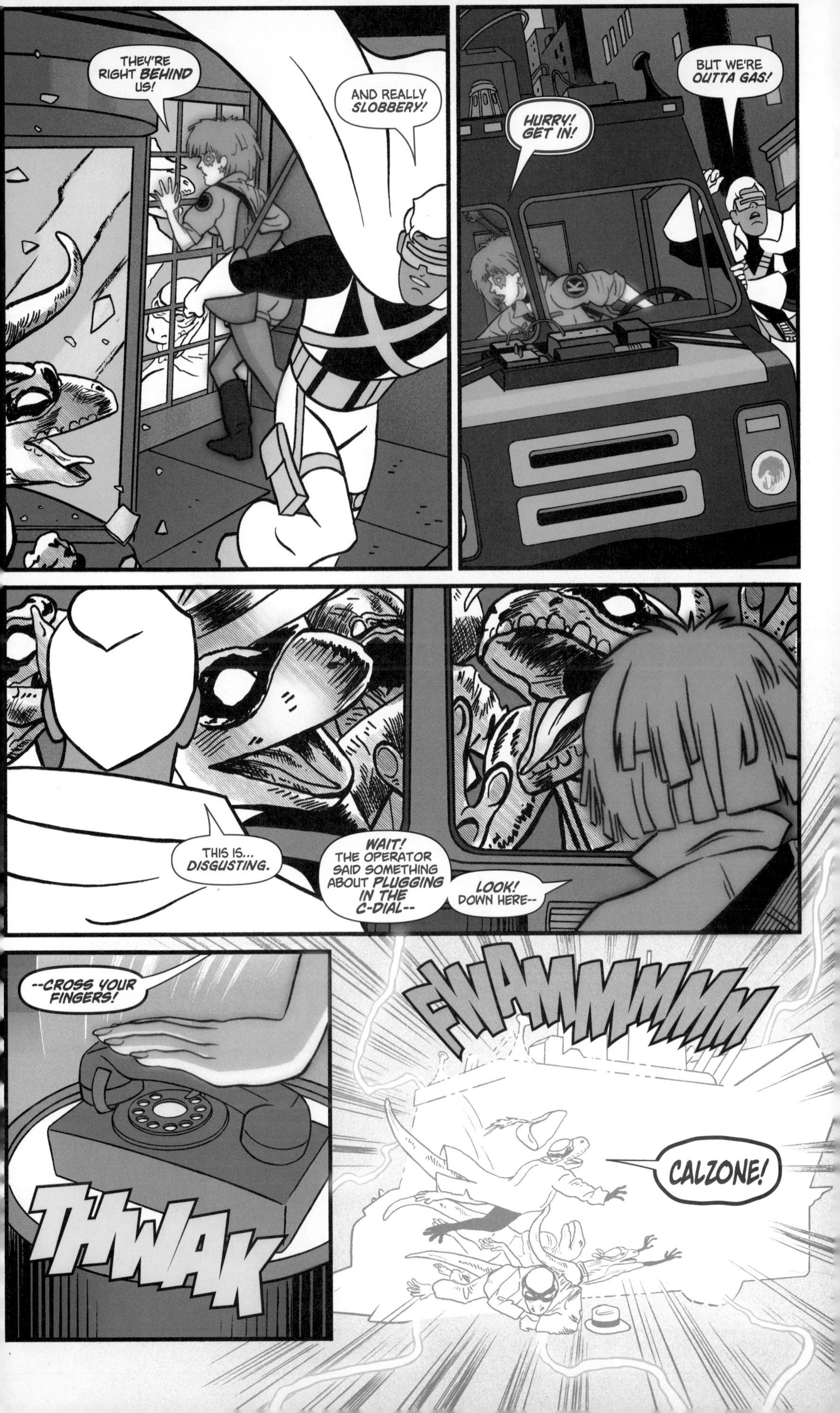

THEY'RE RIGHT BEHIND US!
AND REALLY SLOBBERY!
HURRY! GET IN!
BUT WE'RE OUTTA GAS!
THIS IS... DISGUSTING.
WAIT! THE OPERATOR SAID SOMETHING ABOUT PLUGGING IN THE C-DIAL--
LOOK! DOWN HERE--
--CROSS YOUR FINGERS!
THWAK
FWAMMMMMM
CALZONE!

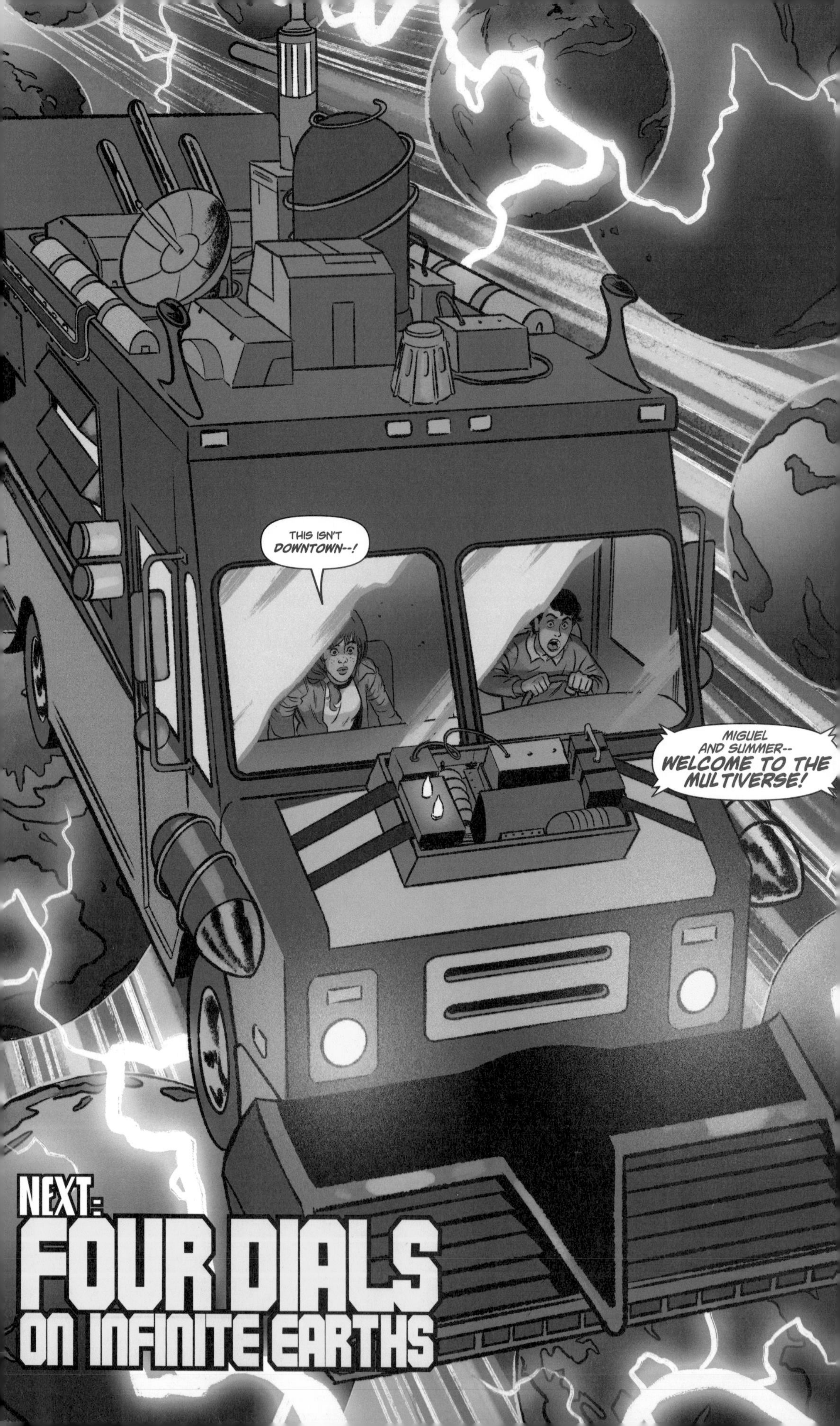
THIS ISN'T DOWNTOWN--!
MIGUEL AND SUMMER-- WELCOME TO THE MULTIVERSE!
NEXT:
FOUR DIALS ON INFINITE EARTHS

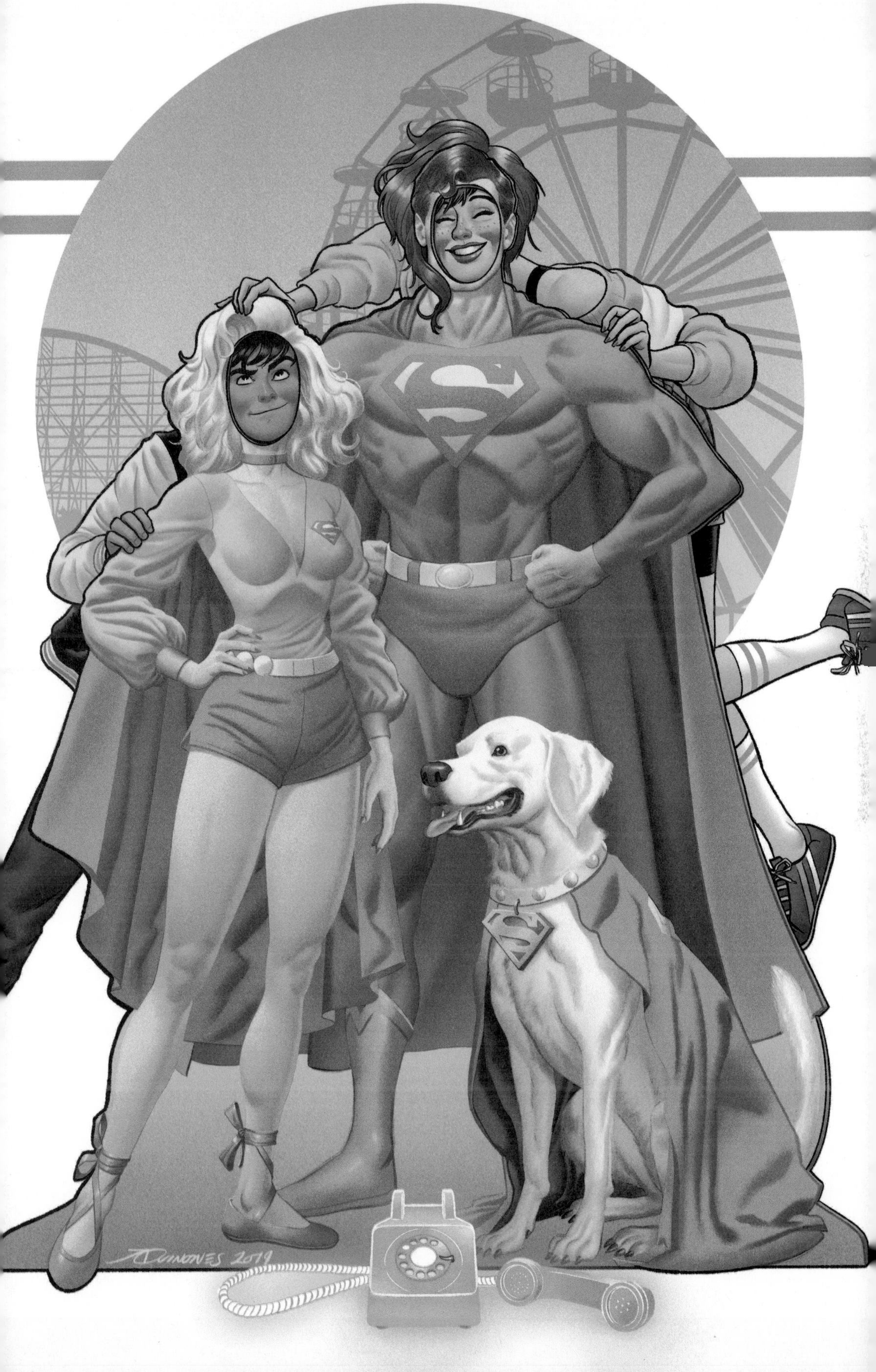

MIGUEL AND SUMMER TRAVEL THE MULTIVERSE

art by
JOE QUINONES

colors by
JORDAN GIBSON

cover art by
JOE QUINONES

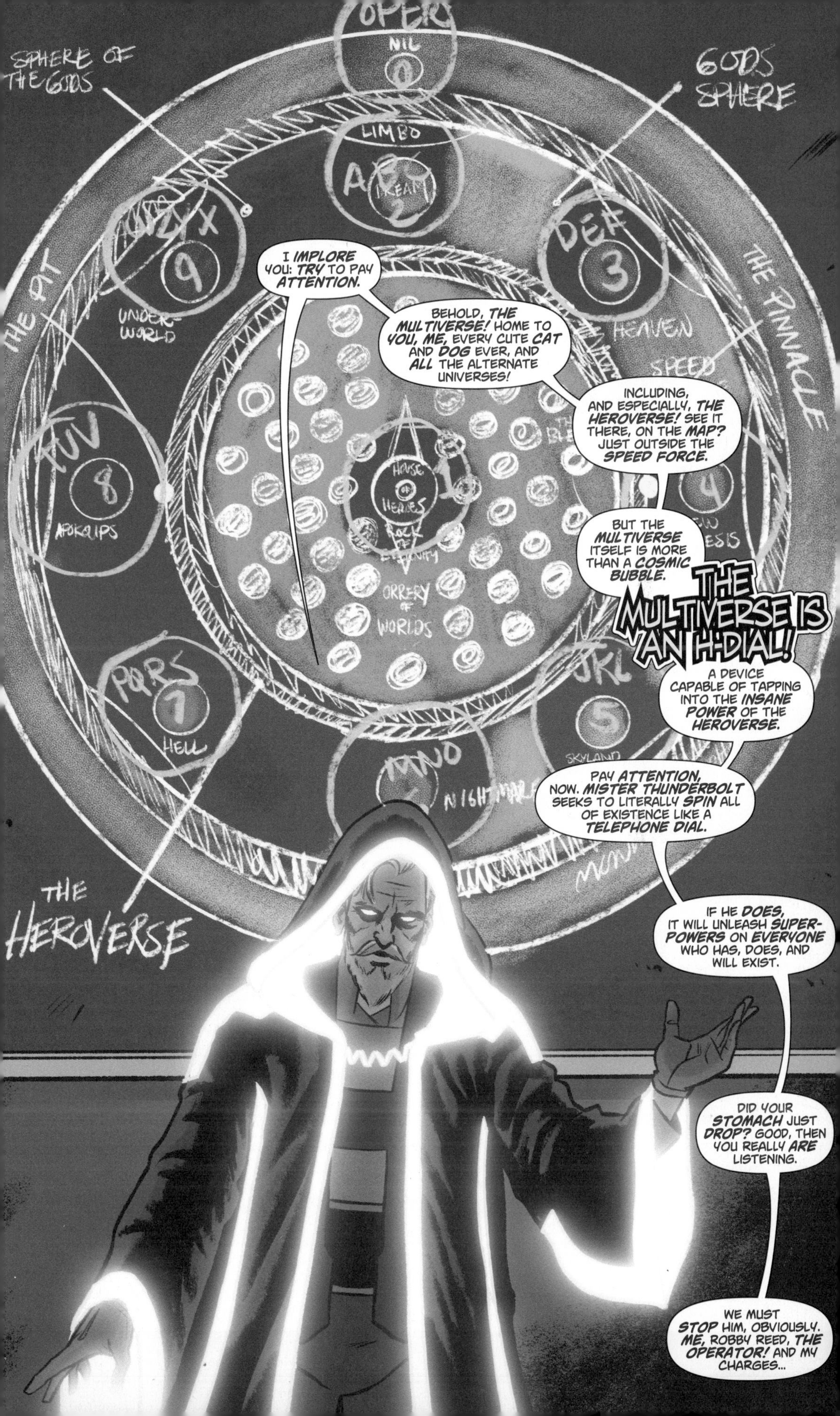
SPHERE OF THE GODS
GODS SPHERE
NIL
LIMBO
HEAVEN
SPEED
THE PINNACLE
THE PIT
UNDER-WORLD
APOKOLIPS
HELL
SKYLAND
NIGHTMARE
ORRERY OF WORLDS
THE HEROVERSE
I IMPLORE YOU: TRY TO PAY ATTENTION.
BEHOLD, THE MULTIVERSE! HOME TO YOU, ME, EVERY CUTE CAT AND DOG EVER, AND ALL THE ALTERNATE UNIVERSES!
INCLUDING, AND ESPECIALLY, THE HEROVERSE! SEE IT THERE, ON THE MAP? JUST OUTSIDE THE SPEED FORCE.
BUT THE MULTIVERSE ITSELF IS MORE THAN A COSMIC BUBBLE.
THE MULTIVERSE IS AN H-DIAL!
A DEVICE CAPABLE OF TAPPING INTO THE INSANE POWER OF THE HEROVERSE.
PAY ATTENTION, NOW. MISTER THUNDERBOLT SEEKS TO LITERALLY SPIN ALL OF EXISTENCE LIKE A TELEPHONE DIAL.
IF HE DOES, IT WILL UNLEASH SUPER-POWERS ON EVERYONE WHO HAS, DOES, AND WILL EXIST.
DID YOUR STOMACH JUST DROP? GOOD, THEN YOU REALLY ARE LISTENING.
WE MUST STOP HIM, OBVIOUSLY. ME, ROBBY REED, THE OPERATOR! AND MY CHARGES...

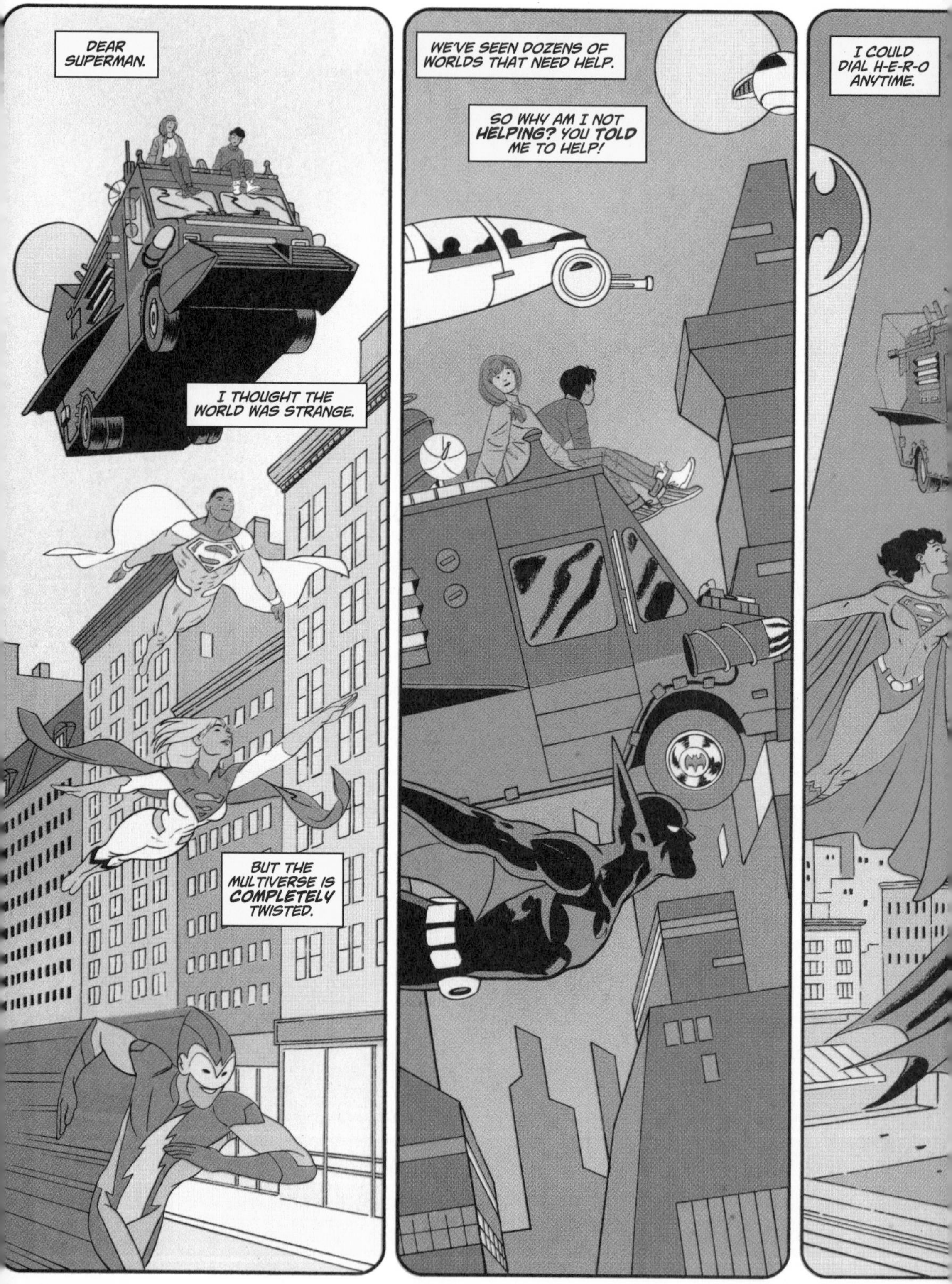
DEAR SUPERMAN.
I THOUGHT THE WORLD WAS STRANGE.
BUT THE MULTIVERSE IS COMPLETELY TWISTED.
WE'VE SEEN DOZENS OF WORLDS THAT NEED HELP.
SO WHY AM I NOT HELPING? YOU TOLD ME TO HELP!
I COULD DIAL H-E-R-O ANYTIME.

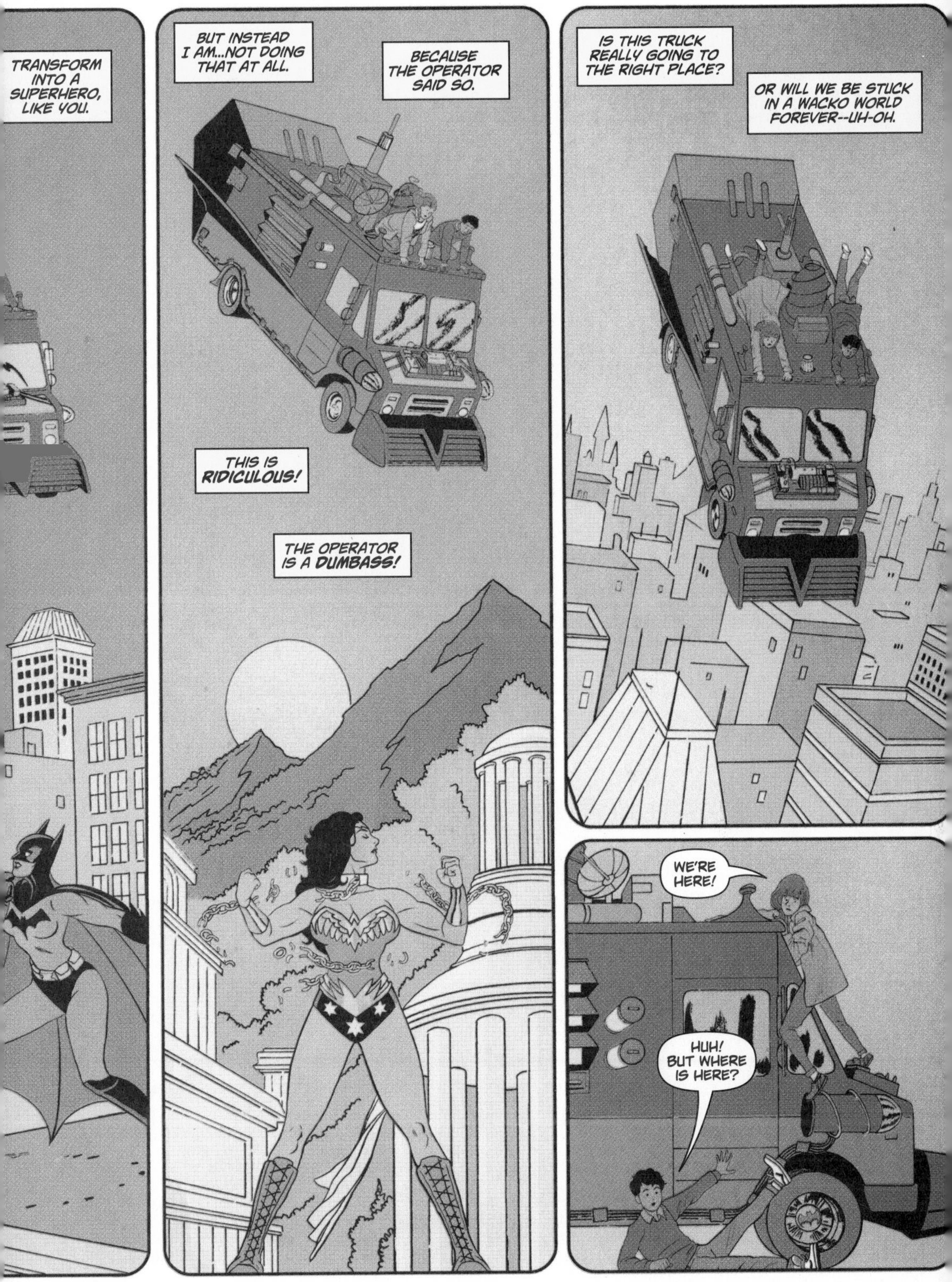
TRANSFORM INTO A SUPERHERO, LIKE YOU.
BUT INSTEAD I AM...NOT DOING THAT AT ALL.
BECAUSE THE OPERATOR SAID SO.
THIS IS RIDICULOUS!
THE OPERATOR IS A DUMBASS!
IS THIS TRUCK REALLY GOING TO THE RIGHT PLACE?
OR WILL WE BE STUCK IN A WACKO WORLD FOREVER--UH-OH.
WE'RE HERE!
HUH! BUT WHERE IS HERE?

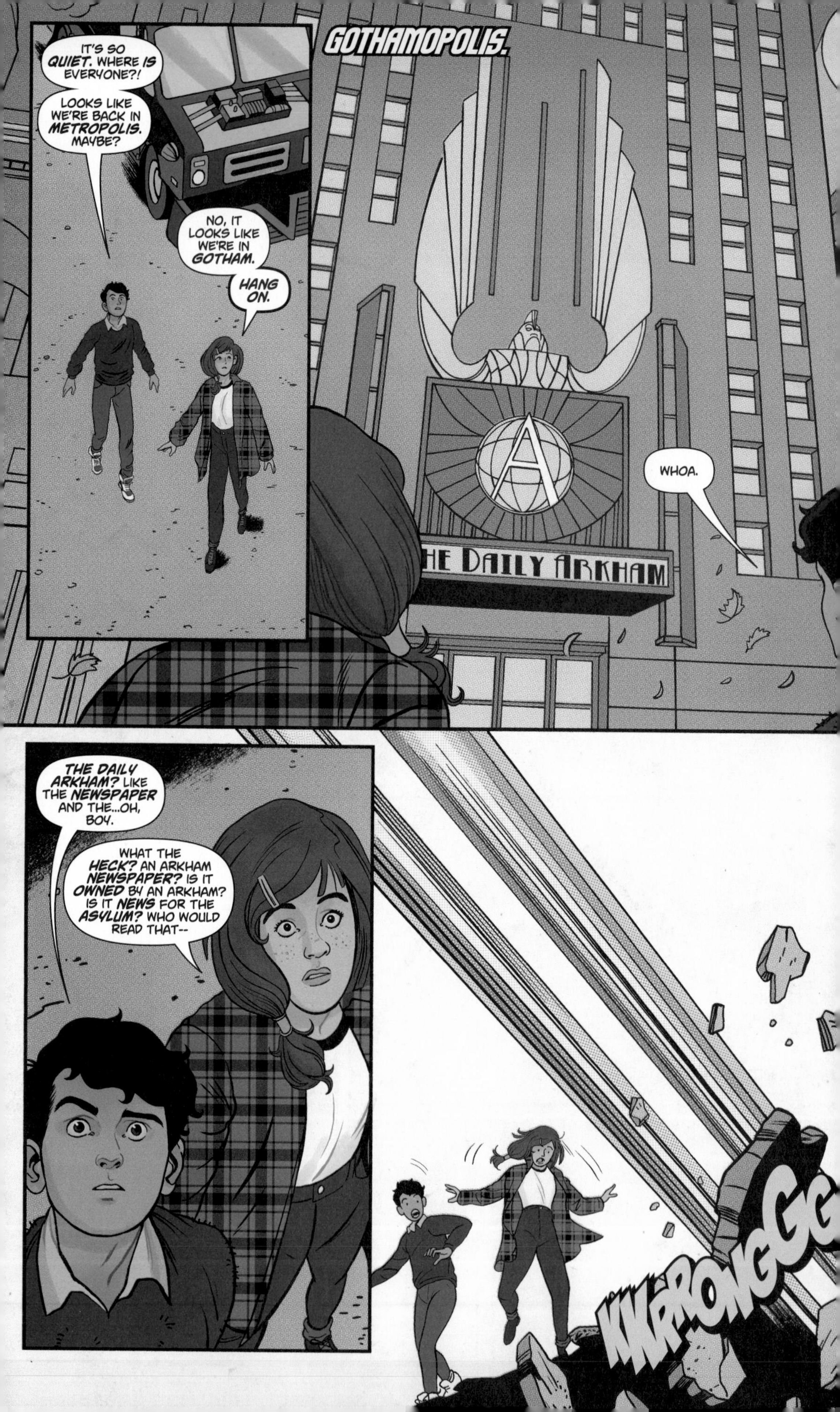
GOTHAMOPOLIS.
IT'S SO QUIET. WHERE IS EVERYONE?!
LOOKS LIKE WE'RE BACK IN METROPOLIS. MAYBE?
NO, IT LOOKS LIKE WE'RE IN GOTHAM.
HANG ON.
HE DAILY ARKHAM
WHOA.
THE DAILY ARKHAM? LIKE THE NEWSPAPER AND THE...OH, BOY.
WHAT THE HECK? AN ARKHAM NEWSPAPER? IS IT OWNED BY AN ARKHAM? IS IT NEWS FOR THE ASYLUM? WHO WOULD READ THAT--
KKKRONGGG

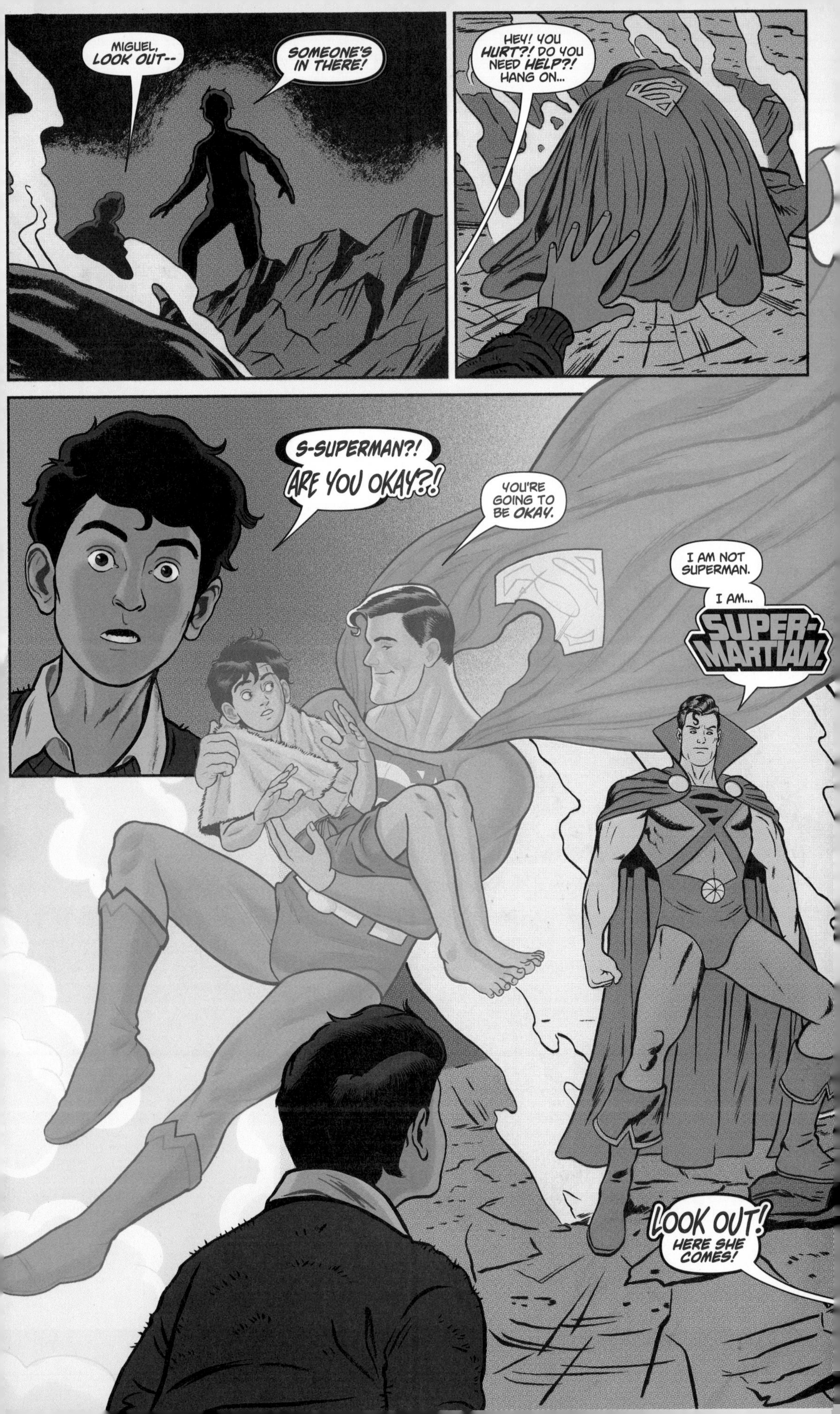
MIGUEL, LOOK OUT--
SOMEONE'S IN THERE!
HEY! YOU HURT?! DO YOU NEED HELP?! HANG ON...
S-SUPERMAN?! ARE YOU OKAY?!
YOU'RE GOING TO BE OKAY.
I AM NOT SUPERMAN.
I AM...
SUPER-MARTIAN.
LOOK OUT! HERE SHE COMES!

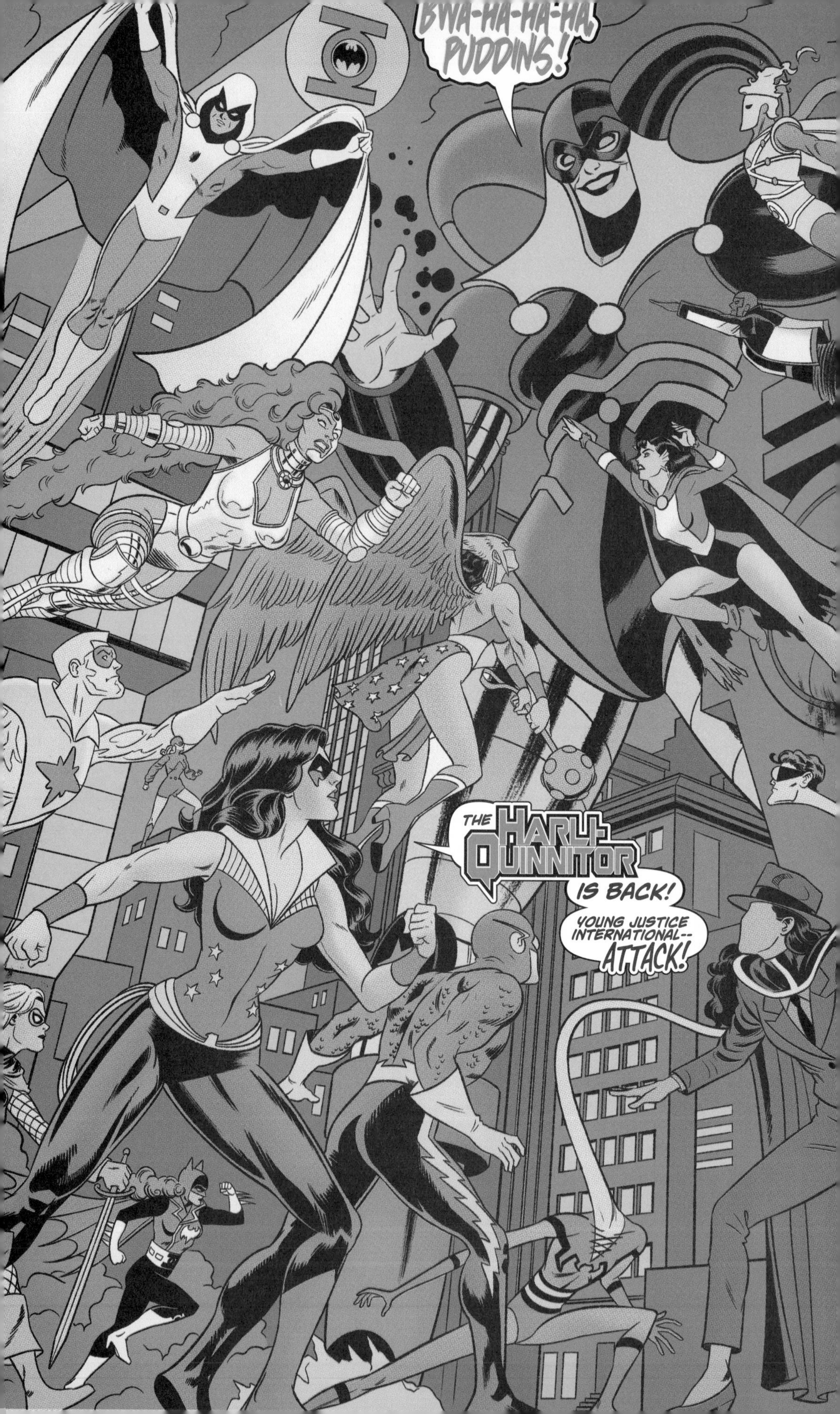
BWA-HA-HA-HA, PUDDINS!
THE HARLI-QUINNITOR IS BACK!
YOUNG JUSTICE INTERNATIONAL-- ATTACK!

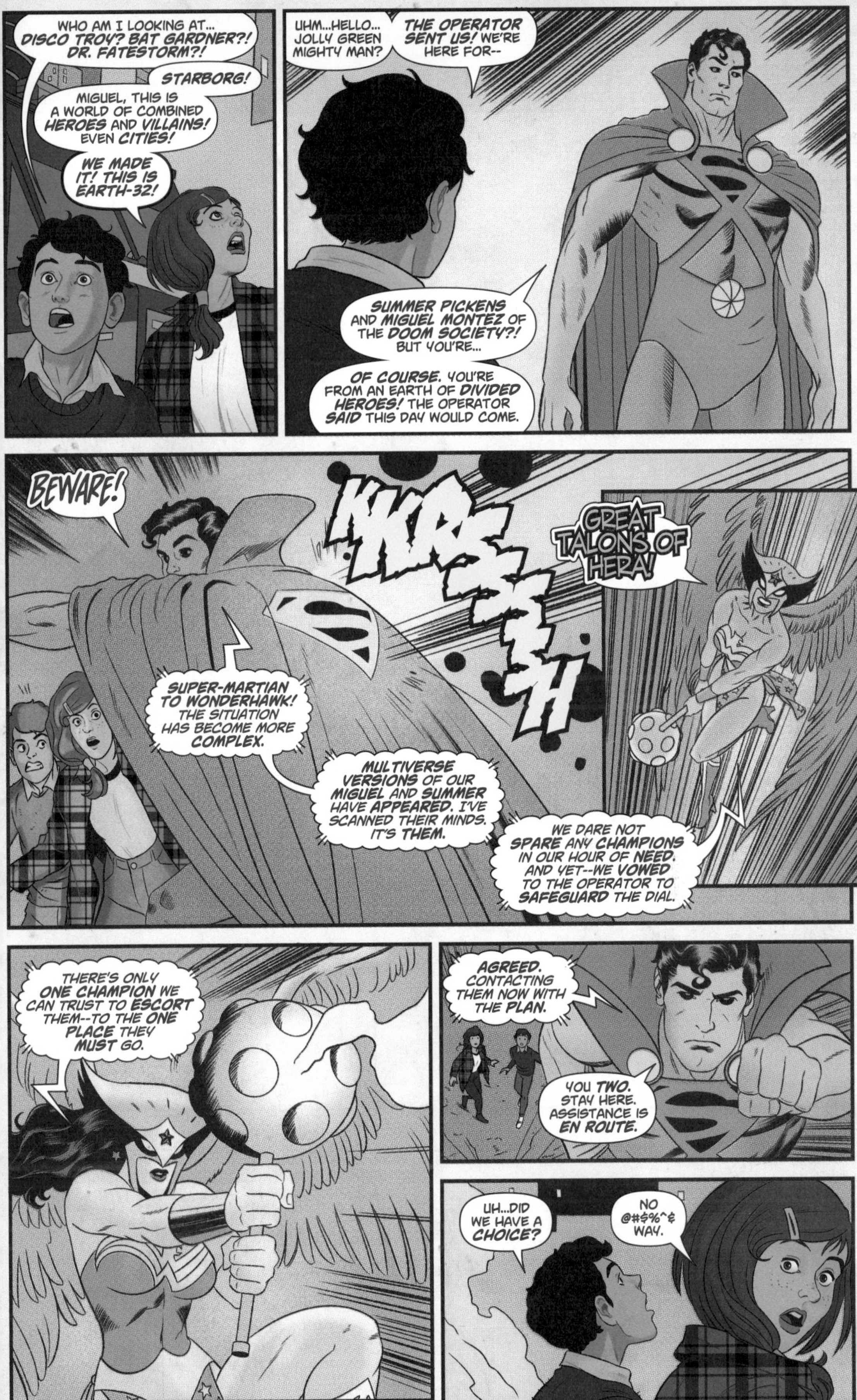
WHO AM I LOOKING AT... DISCO TROY? BAT GARDNER?! DR. FATESTORM?!
STARBORG!
MIGUEL, THIS IS A WORLD OF COMBINED HEROES AND VILLAINS! EVEN CITIES!
WE MADE IT! THIS IS EARTH-32!
UHM...HELLO... JOLLY GREEN MIGHTY MAN?
THE OPERATOR SENT US! WE'RE HERE FOR--
SUMMER PICKENS AND MIGUEL MONTEZ OF THE DOOM SOCIETY?! BUT YOU'RE...
OF COURSE. YOU'RE FROM AN EARTH OF DIVIDED HEROES! THE OPERATOR SAID THIS DAY WOULD COME.
BEWARE!
KKRSSSHH
GREAT TALONS OF HERA!
SUPER-MARTIAN TO WONDERHAWK! THE SITUATION HAS BECOME MORE COMPLEX.
MULTIVERSE VERSIONS OF OUR MIGUEL AND SUMMER HAVE APPEARED. I'VE SCANNED THEIR MINDS. IT'S THEM.
WE DARE NOT SPARE ANY CHAMPIONS IN OUR HOUR OF NEED. AND YET--WE VOWED TO THE OPERATOR TO SAFEGUARD THE DIAL.
THERE'S ONLY ONE CHAMPION WE CAN TRUST TO ESCORT THEM--TO THE ONE PLACE THEY MUST GO.
AGREED. CONTACTING THEM NOW WITH THE PLAN.
YOU TWO. STAY HERE. ASSISTANCE IS EN ROUTE.
UH...DID WE HAVE A CHOICE?
NO @#$%^& WAY.

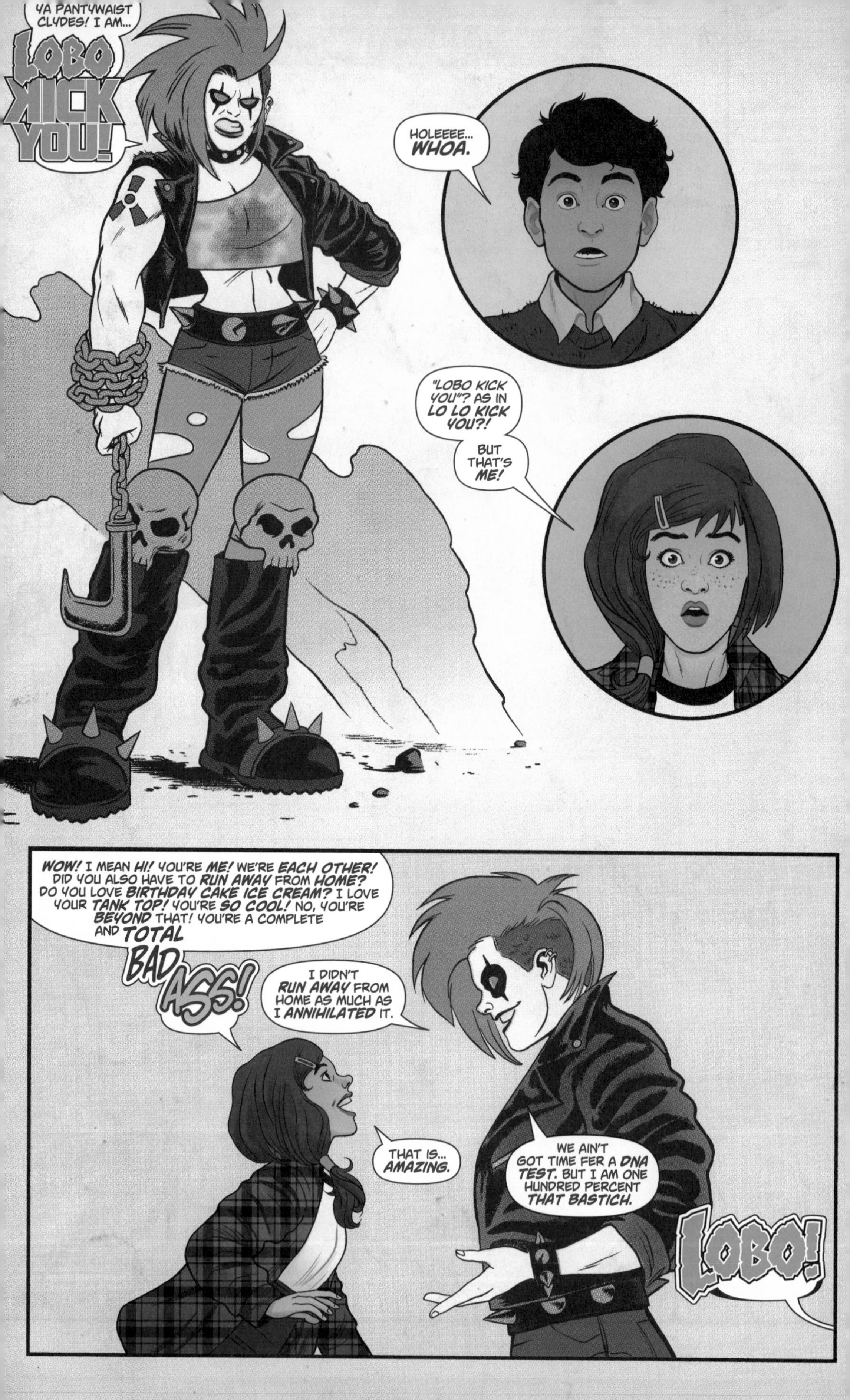
YA PANTYWAIST CLYDES! I AM...
LOBO KICK YOU!
HOLEEEE... WHOA.
"LOBO KICK YOU"? AS IN LO LO KICK YOU?!
BUT THAT'S ME!
WOW! I MEAN HI! YOU'RE ME! WE'RE EACH OTHER! DID YOU ALSO HAVE TO RUN AWAY FROM HOME? DO YOU LOVE BIRTHDAY CAKE ICE CREAM? I LOVE YOUR TANK TOP! YOU'RE SO COOL! NO, YOU'RE BEYOND THAT! YOU'RE A COMPLETE AND TOTAL
BAD ASS!
I DIDN'T RUN AWAY FROM HOME AS MUCH AS I ANNIHILATED IT.
THAT IS... AMAZING.
WE AIN'T GOT TIME FER A DNA TEST. BUT I AM ONE HUNDRED PERCENT THAT BASTICH.
LOBO!

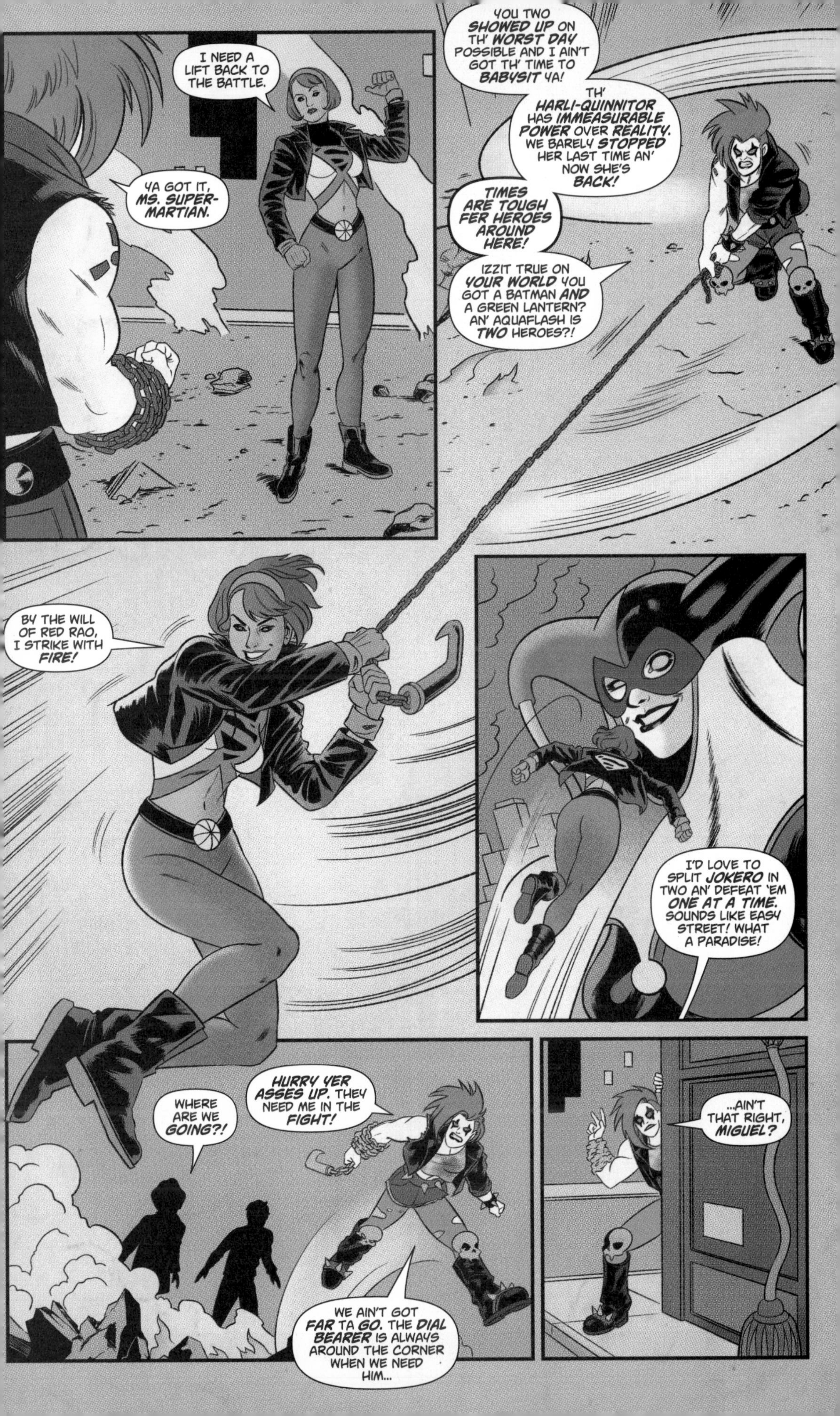
I NEED A LIFT BACK TO THE BATTLE.
YA GOT IT, MS. SUPER-MARTIAN.
YOU TWO SHOWED UP ON TH' WORST DAY POSSIBLE AND I AIN'T GOT TH' TIME TO BABYSIT YA!
TH' HARLI-QUINNITOR HAS IMMEASURABLE POWER OVER REALITY. WE BARELY STOPPED HER LAST TIME AN' NOW SHE'S BACK!
TIMES ARE TOUGH FER HEROES AROUND HERE!
IZZIT TRUE ON YOUR WORLD YOU GOT A BATMAN AND A GREEN LANTERN? AN' AQUAFLASH IS TWO HEROES?!
BY THE WILL OF RED RAO, I STRIKE WITH FIRE!
I'D LOVE TO SPLIT JOKERO IN TWO AN' DEFEAT 'EM ONE AT A TIME. SOUNDS LIKE EASY STREET! WHAT A PARADISE!
WHERE ARE WE GOING?!
HURRY YER ASSES UP. THEY NEED ME IN THE FIGHT!
WE AIN'T GOT FAR TA GO. THE DIAL BEARER IS ALWAYS AROUND THE CORNER WHEN WE NEED HIM...
...AIN'T THAT RIGHT, MIGUEL?

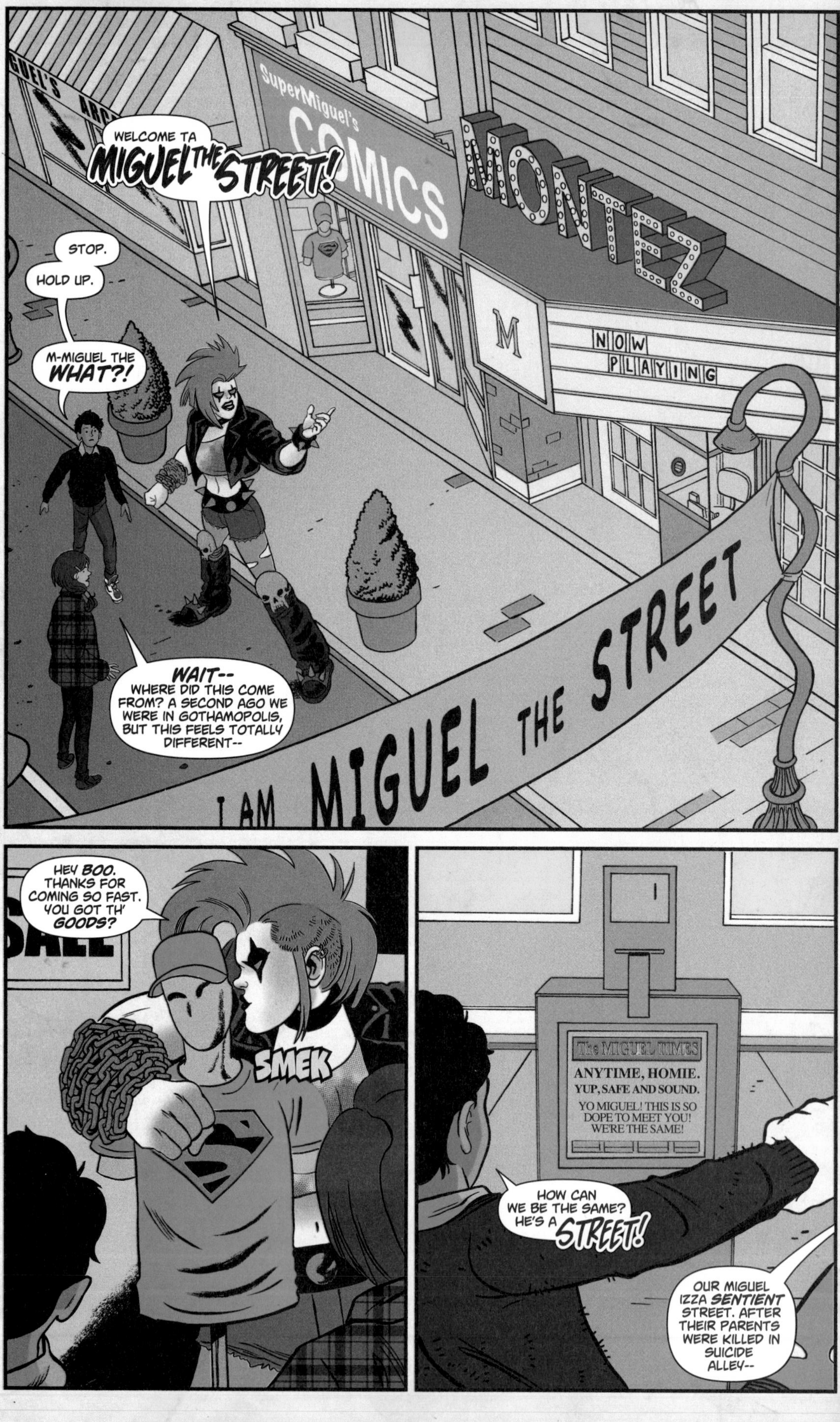

MIGUEL'S ARC
SuperMiguel's COMICS
MONTEZ
M
NOW PLAYING
WELCOME TA MIGUEL THE STREET!
STOP.
HOLD UP.
M-MIGUEL THE WHAT?!
WAIT-- WHERE DID THIS COME FROM? A SECOND AGO WE WERE IN GOTHAMOPOLIS, BUT THIS FEELS TOTALLY DIFFERENT--
I AM MIGUEL THE STREET
HEY BOO. THANKS FOR COMING SO FAST. YOU GOT TH' GOODS?
SMEK
The MIGUEL TIMES
ANYTIME, HOMIE.
YUP, SAFE AND SOUND.
YO MIGUEL! THIS IS SO DOPE TO MEET YOU! WE'RE THE SAME!
HOW CAN WE BE THE SAME? HE'S A STREET!
OUR MIGUEL IZZA SENTIENT STREET. AFTER THEIR PARENTS WERE KILLED IN SUICIDE ALLEY--

I CANNOT SAVE US ALL.

NOT ALONE.

I NEED ASSISTANCE FROM ALL.

EVEN *YOU*, MIGUEL.

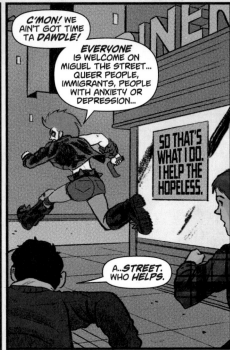

C'MON! WE AIN'T GOT TIME TA *DAWDLE!*

EVERYONE IS WELCOME ON MIGUEL THE STREET... QUEER PEOPLE, IMMIGRANTS, PEOPLE WITH ANXIETY OR DEPRESSION...

SO THAT'S WHAT I DO. I HELP THE HOPELESS.

A...STREET. WHO *HELPS.*

AN' MIGUEL CAN TELEPORT. SO *WONDERHAWK* THOUGHT THEY WERE THE *SAFEST GUARDIAN*...FOR THE *DIAL.*

IN THE H-VAULT!

C'MON, BOO, POP THE LOCK! HOW DO WE GET IN?!

LOOK-- INSTRUCTIONS!

"A RIDDLE ONLY A TRUE MIGUEL OF THE MULTIVERSE CAN SOLVE.

"WHY DID YOU PUKE IN FRONT OF THE WHOLE CLASS IN SECOND GRADE?"

Heh.

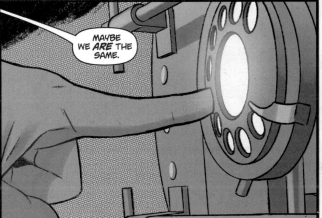

MAYBE WE *ARE* THE SAME.

M — MNO 6

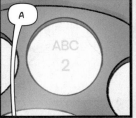

A — ABC 2

Y — WXYZ 9

O — MNO 6

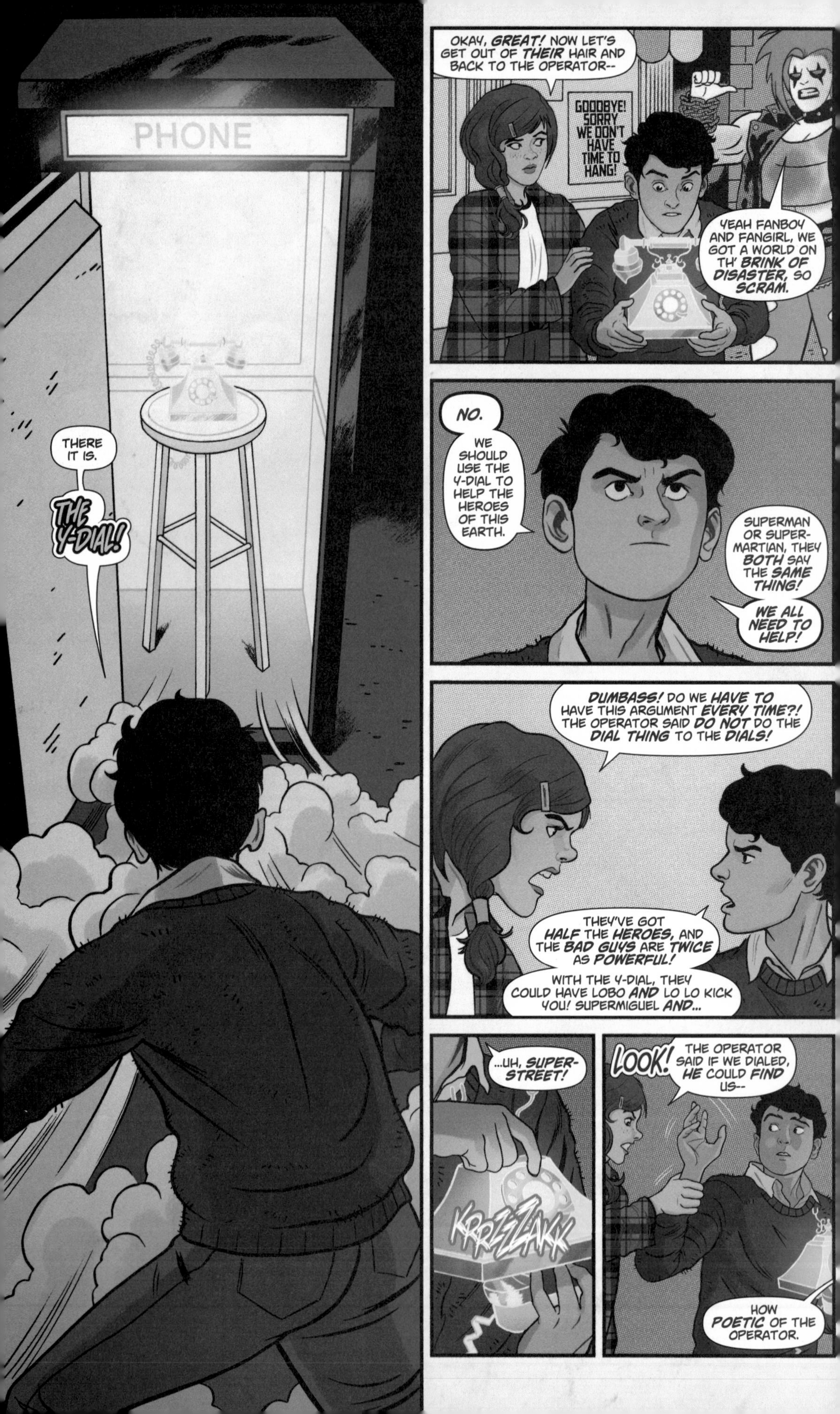
PHONE
THERE IT IS.
THE Y-DIAL!
OKAY, GREAT! NOW LET'S GET OUT OF THEIR HAIR AND BACK TO THE OPERATOR--
GOODBYE! SORRY WE DON'T HAVE TIME TO HANG!
YEAH FANBOY AND FANGIRL, WE GOT A WORLD ON TH' BRINK OF DISASTER, SO SCRAM.
NO.
WE SHOULD USE THE Y-DIAL TO HELP THE HEROES OF THIS EARTH.
SUPERMAN OR SUPER-MARTIAN, THEY BOTH SAY THE SAME THING!
WE ALL NEED TO HELP!
DUMBASS! DO WE HAVE TO HAVE THIS ARGUMENT EVERY TIME?! THE OPERATOR SAID DO NOT DO THE DIAL THING TO THE DIALS!
THEY'VE GOT HALF THE HEROES, AND THE BAD GUYS ARE TWICE AS POWERFUL!
WITH THE Y-DIAL, THEY COULD HAVE LOBO AND LO LO KICK YOU! SUPERMIGUEL AND...
...UH, SUPER-STREET!
KRRZZAKK
LOOK! THE OPERATOR SAID IF WE DIALED, HE COULD FIND US--
HOW POETIC OF THE OPERATOR.

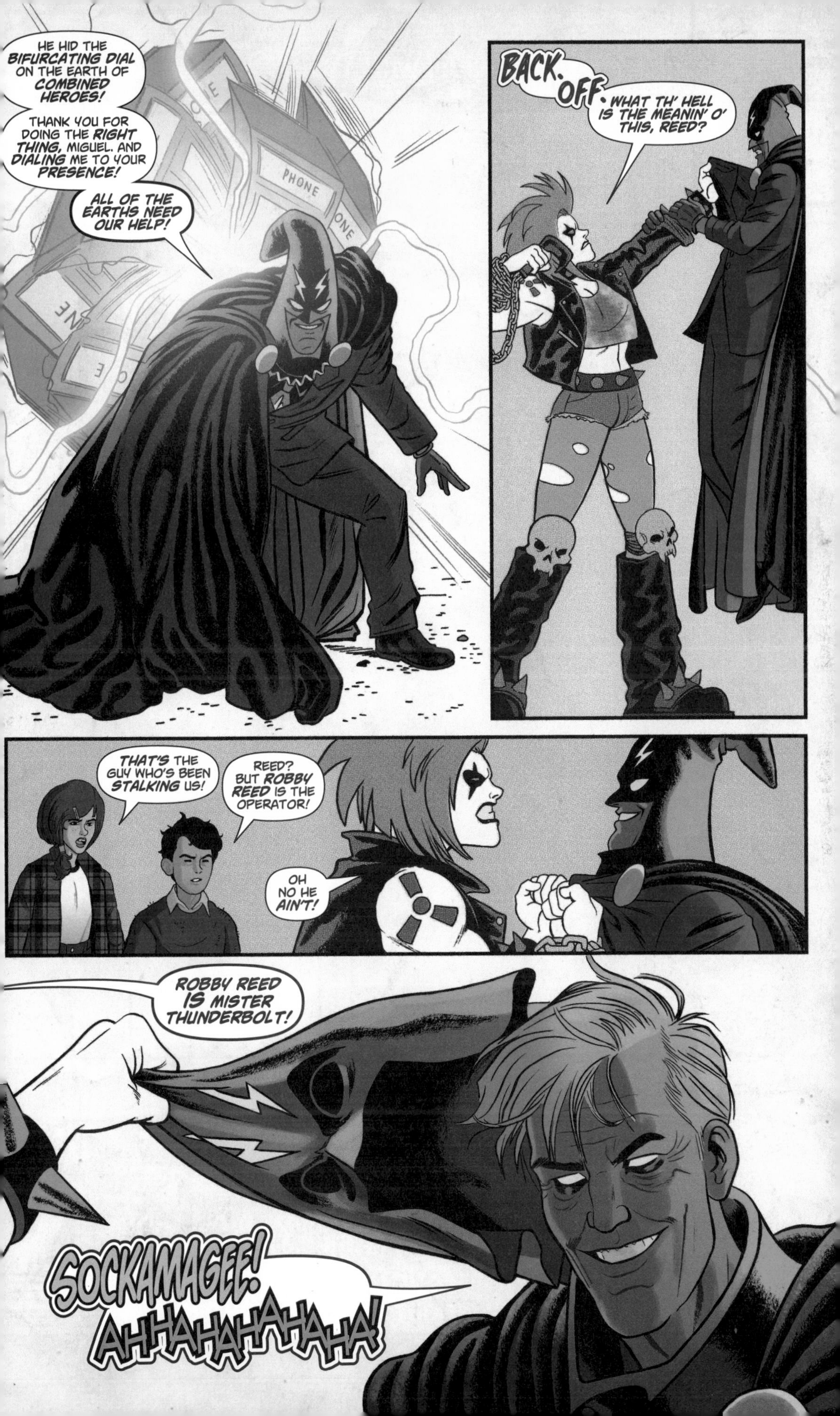
HE HID THE BIFURCATING DIAL ON THE EARTH OF COMBINED HEROES!
THANK YOU FOR DOING THE RIGHT THING, MIGUEL. AND DIALING ME TO YOUR PRESENCE!
ALL OF THE EARTHS NEED OUR HELP!
BACK. OFF.
WHAT TH' HELL IS THE MEANIN' O' THIS, REED?
THAT'S THE GUY WHO'S BEEN STALKING US!
REED? BUT ROBBY REED IS THE OPERATOR!
OH NO HE AIN'T!
ROBBY REED IS MISTER THUNDERBOLT!
SOCKAMAGEE! AHHAHAHAHAHA!

WHAT IS THE CONNECTION BETWEEN THE OPERATOR AND MISTER THUNDERBOLT?

HERE WE GO WITH ANOTHER RIDICULOUS DIAL H FOLD-IN!

The Operator and Mister Thunderbolt often seem like opposites! One has been helping Miguel and Summer, while the other has been hunting them! One watches over the Heroverse, the other leads the villainous Thunderbolt Club. How can these total opposites have any connection? To find out what their relationship is, fold page in as shown.

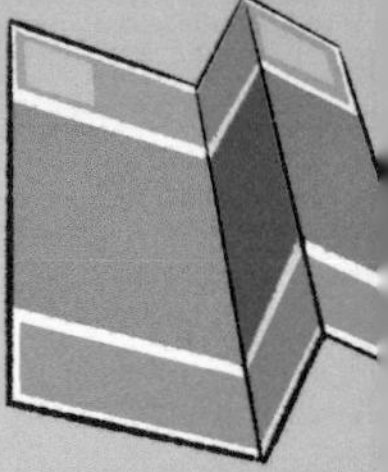

FOLD PAGE OVER LIKE TH

A

FOLD PAGE OVER LEFT

B FOLD BACK SO "A" MEETS "B"

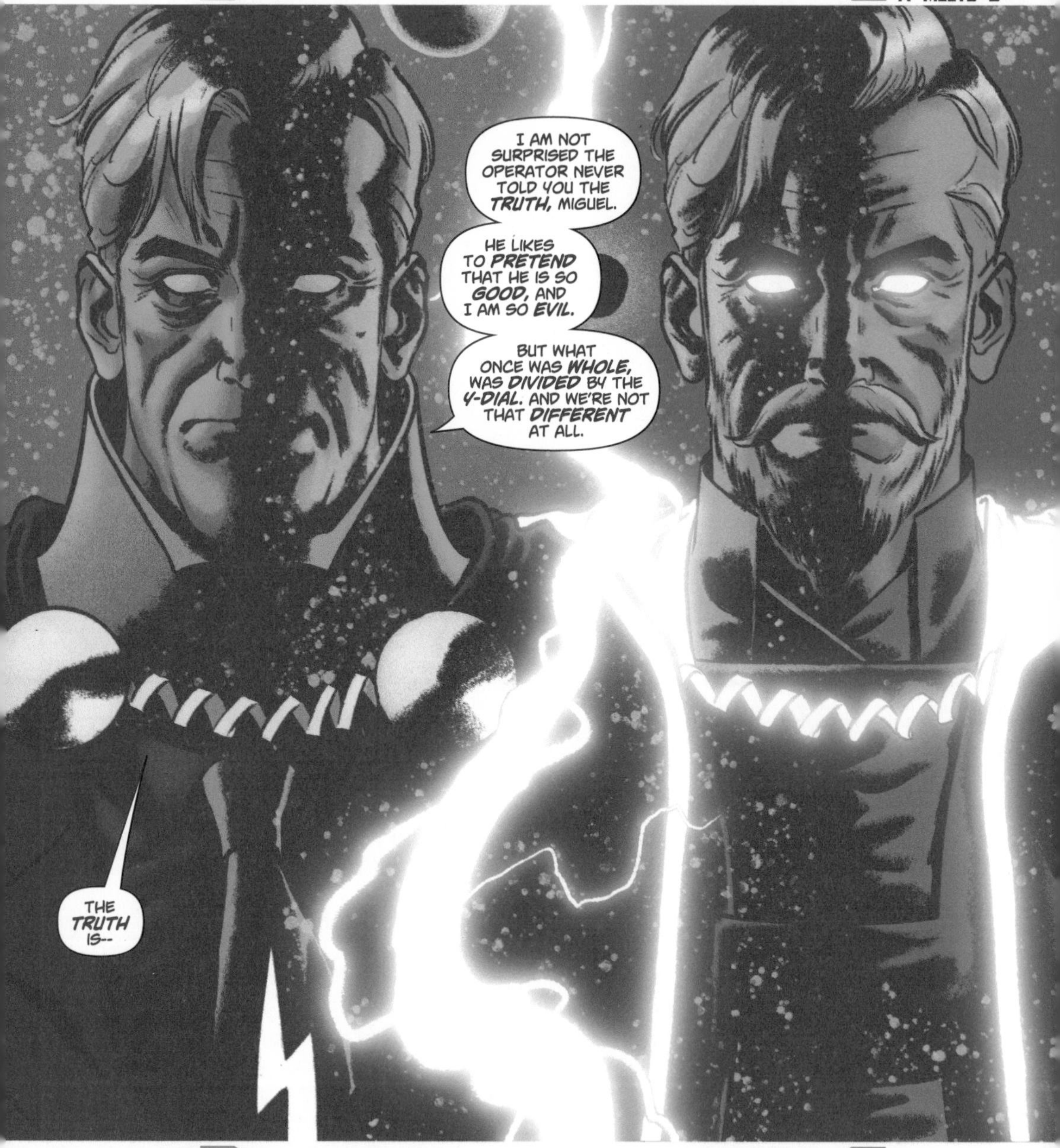

I AM NOT SURPRISED THE OPERATOR NEVER TOLD YOU THE TRUTH, MIGUEL.
HE LIKES TO PRETEND THAT HE IS SO GOOD, AND I AM SO EVIL.
BUT WHAT ONCE WAS WHOLE, WAS DIVIDED BY THE Y-DIAL. AND WE'RE NOT THAT DIFFERENT AT ALL.
THE TRUTH IS--

A B

WITH THE H-DIAL IT CAN BE HARD TO ADHERE
BY OUTMODED IDEAS OF IDENTITY WORN SMOOTH
ROLES CAN SHIFT AND LEAVE YOU CRABBY
REACH FOR NEW INSIGHT AND BE ENLIGHTENED

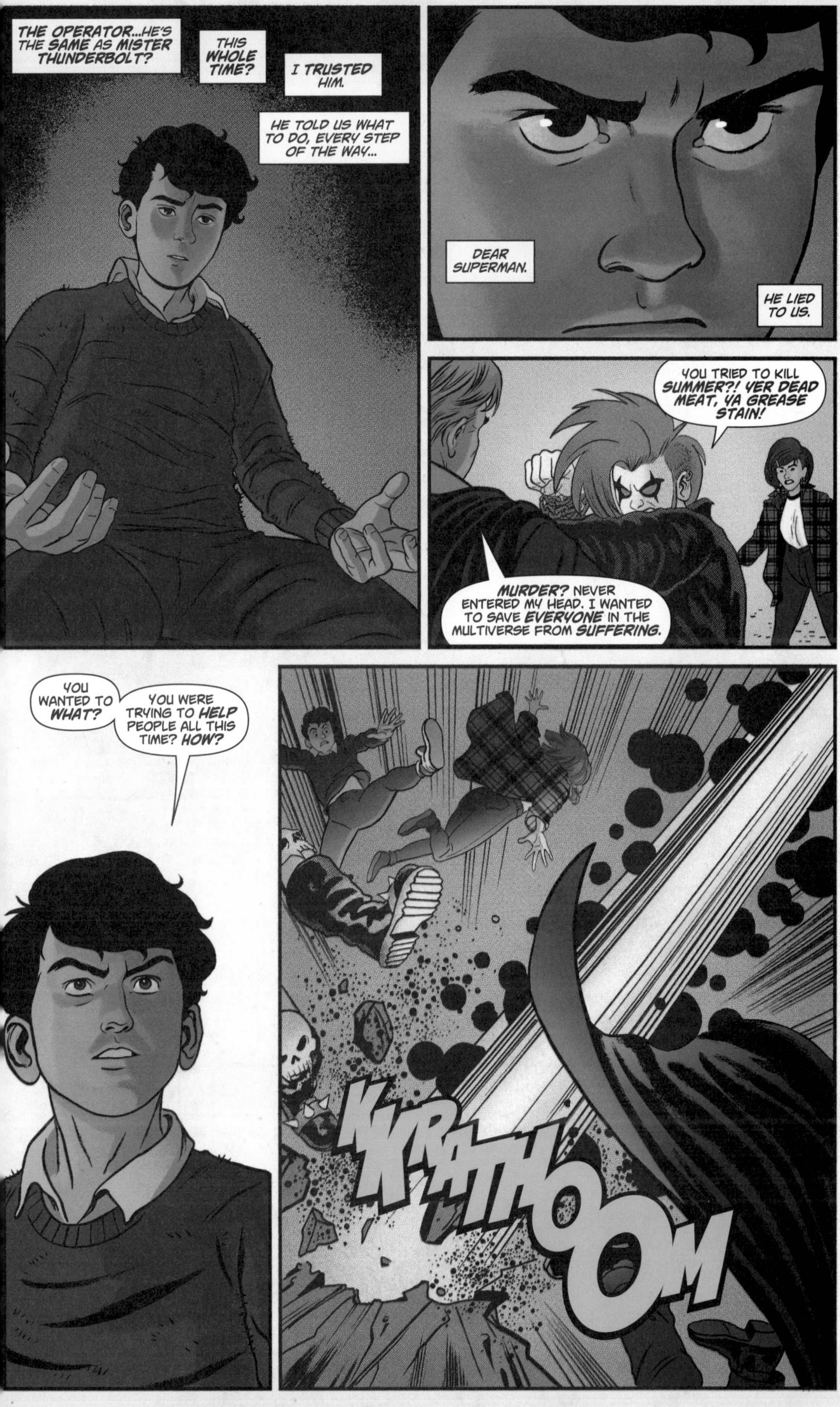
THE OPERATOR...HE'S THE SAME AS MISTER THUNDERBOLT?
THIS WHOLE TIME?
I TRUSTED HIM.
HE TOLD US WHAT TO DO, EVERY STEP OF THE WAY...
DEAR SUPERMAN.
HE LIED TO US.
YOU TRIED TO KILL SUMMER?! YER DEAD MEAT, YA GREASE STAIN!
MURDER? NEVER ENTERED MY HEAD. I WANTED TO SAVE EVERYONE IN THE MULTIVERSE FROM SUFFERING.
YOU WANTED TO WHAT?
YOU WERE TRYING TO HELP PEOPLE ALL THIS TIME? HOW?
KKRATHOOOM

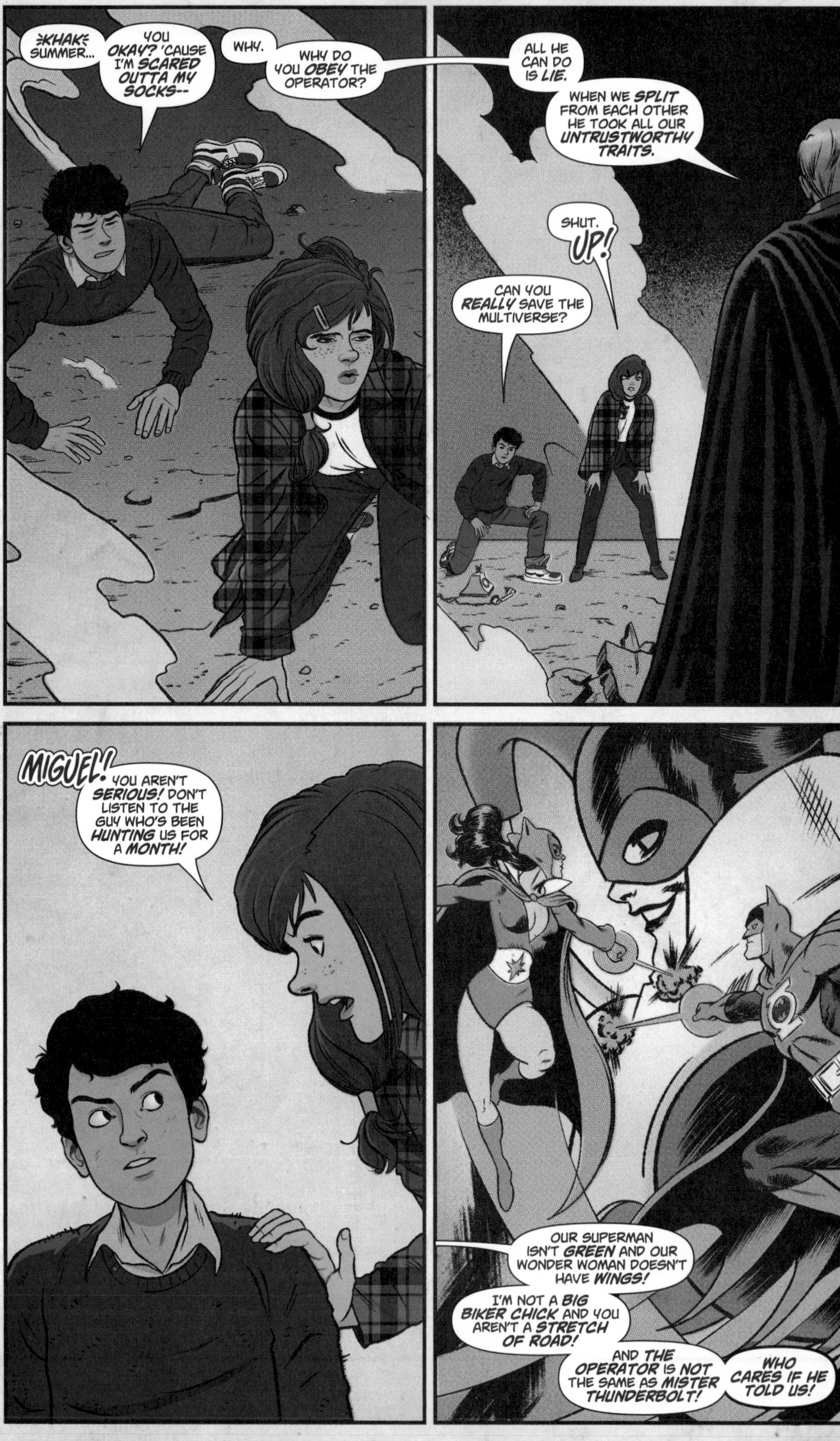

KHAK SUMMER...
YOU OKAY? 'CAUSE I'M SCARED OUTTA MY SOCKS--
WHY.
WHY DO YOU OBEY THE OPERATOR?
ALL HE CAN DO IS LIE.
WHEN WE SPLIT FROM EACH OTHER HE TOOK ALL OUR UNTRUSTWORTHY TRAITS.
SHUT. UP!
CAN YOU REALLY SAVE THE MULTIVERSE?
MIGUEL!
YOU AREN'T SERIOUS! DON'T LISTEN TO THE GUY WHO'S BEEN HUNTING US FOR A MONTH!
OUR SUPERMAN ISN'T GREEN AND OUR WONDER WOMAN DOESN'T HAVE WINGS!
I'M NOT A BIG BIKER CHICK AND YOU AREN'T A STRETCH OF ROAD!
AND THE OPERATOR IS NOT THE SAME AS MISTER THUNDERBOLT!
WHO CARES IF HE TOLD US!

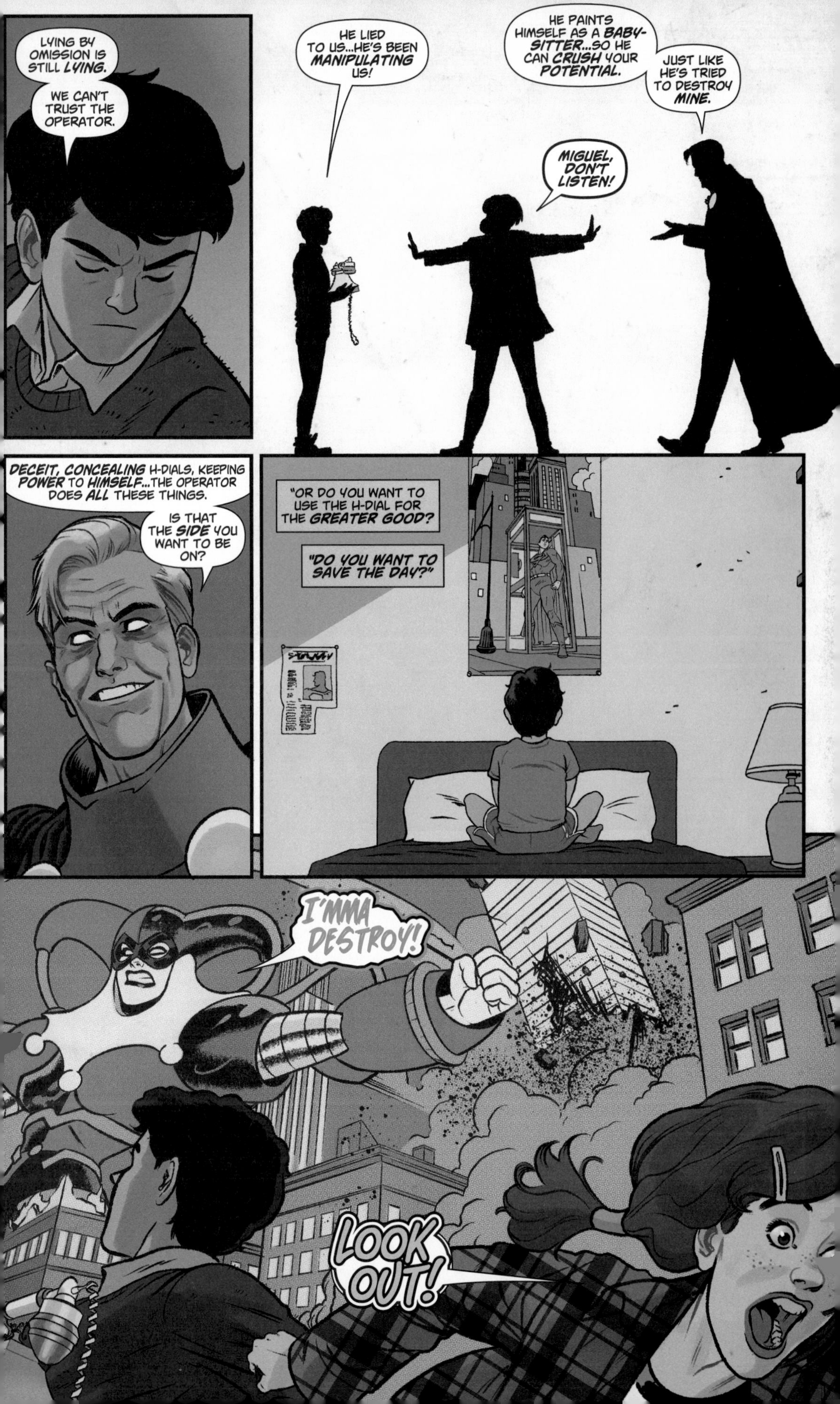

LYING BY OMISSION IS STILL LYING.
WE CAN'T TRUST THE OPERATOR.
HE LIED TO US...HE'S BEEN MANIPULATING US!
HE PAINTS HIMSELF AS A BABY-SITTER...SO HE CAN CRUSH YOUR POTENTIAL.
JUST LIKE HE'S TRIED TO DESTROY MINE.
MIGUEL, DON'T LISTEN!
DECEIT, CONCEALING H-DIALS, KEEPING POWER TO HIMSELF...THE OPERATOR DOES ALL THESE THINGS.
IS THAT THE SIDE YOU WANT TO BE ON?
"OR DO YOU WANT TO USE THE H-DIAL FOR THE GREATER GOOD?
"DO YOU WANT TO SAVE THE DAY?"
I'MMA DESTROY!
LOOK OUT!

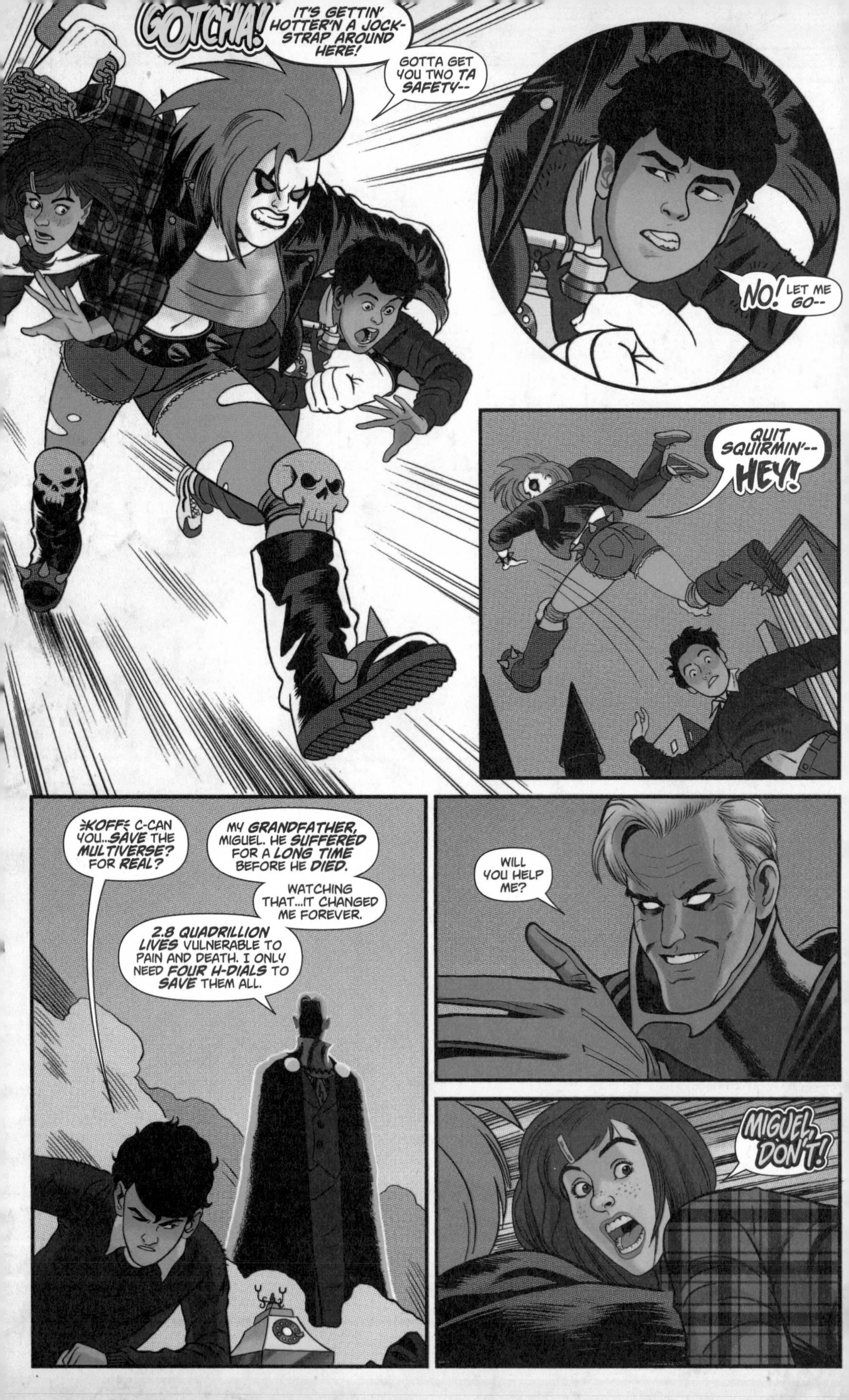
GOTCHA!
IT'S GETTIN' HOTTER'N A JOCK-STRAP AROUND HERE!
GOTTA GET YOU TWO TA SAFETY--
NO! LET ME GO--
QUIT SQUIRMIN'-- HEY!
KOFF C-CAN YOU...SAVE THE MULTIVERSE? FOR REAL?
MY GRANDFATHER, MIGUEL. HE SUFFERED FOR A LONG TIME BEFORE HE DIED.
WATCHING THAT...IT CHANGED ME FOREVER.
2.8 QUADRILLION LIVES VULNERABLE TO PAIN AND DEATH. I ONLY NEED FOUR H-DIALS TO SAVE THEM ALL.
WILL YOU HELP ME?
MIGUEL, DON'T!

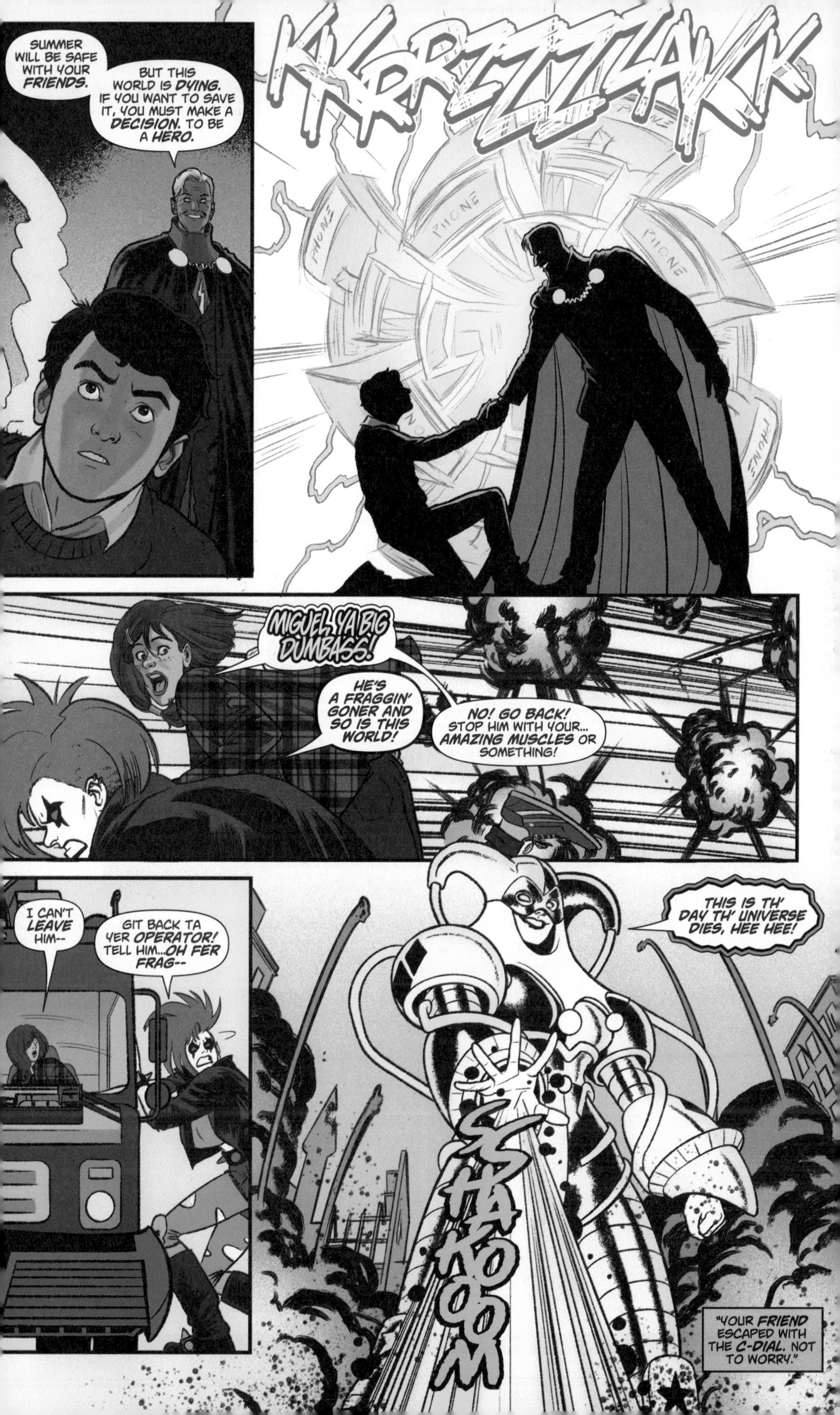
SUMMER WILL BE SAFE WITH YOUR FRIENDS.
BUT THIS WORLD IS DYING. IF YOU WANT TO SAVE IT, YOU MUST MAKE A DECISION. TO BE A HERO.
KKKRRZZZZZAKKK
PHONE
MIGUEL, YA BIG DUMBASS!
HE'S A FRAGGIN' GONER AND SO IS THIS WORLD!
NO! GO BACK! STOP HIM WITH YOUR... AMAZING MUSCLES OR SOMETHING!
I CAN'T LEAVE HIM--
GIT BACK TA YER OPERATOR! TELL HIM...OH FER FRAG--
THIS IS TH' DAY TH' UNIVERSE DIES, HEE HEE!
SSHAKOOOM
"YOUR FRIEND ESCAPED WITH THE C-DIAL. NOT TO WORRY."

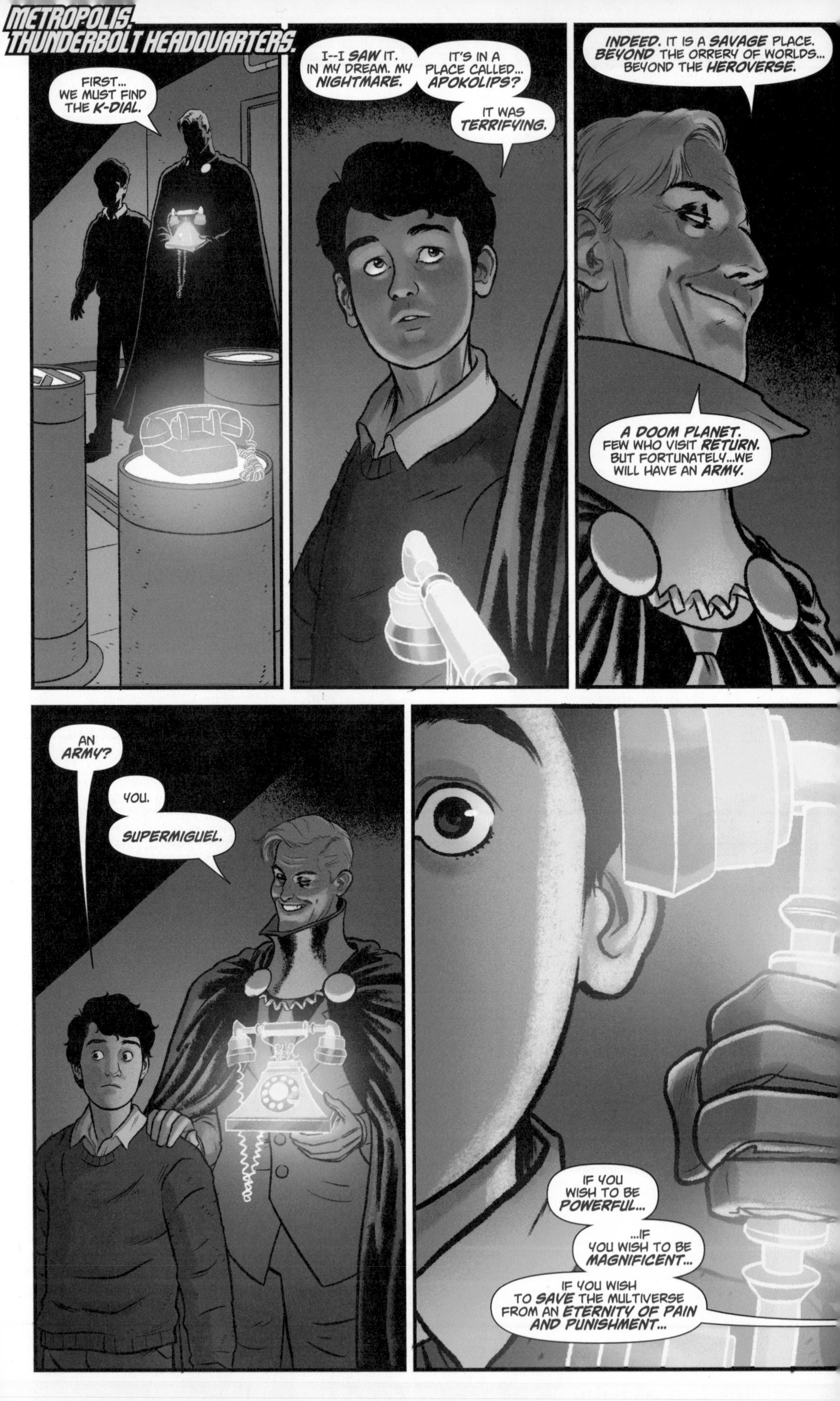
METROPOLIS. THUNDERBOLT HEADQUARTERS.
FIRST... WE MUST FIND THE K-DIAL.
I--I SAW IT. IN MY DREAM. MY NIGHTMARE.
IT'S IN A PLACE CALLED... APOKOLIPS?
IT WAS TERRIFYING.
INDEED. IT IS A SAVAGE PLACE. BEYOND THE ORRERY OF WORLDS... BEYOND THE HEROVERSE.
A DOOM PLANET. FEW WHO VISIT RETURN. BUT FORTUNATELY...WE WILL HAVE AN ARMY.
AN ARMY?
YOU.
SUPERMIGUEL.
IF YOU WISH TO BE POWERFUL...
...IF YOU WISH TO BE MAGNIFICENT...
IF YOU WISH TO SAVE THE MULTIVERSE FROM AN ETERNITY OF PAIN AND PUNISHMENT...

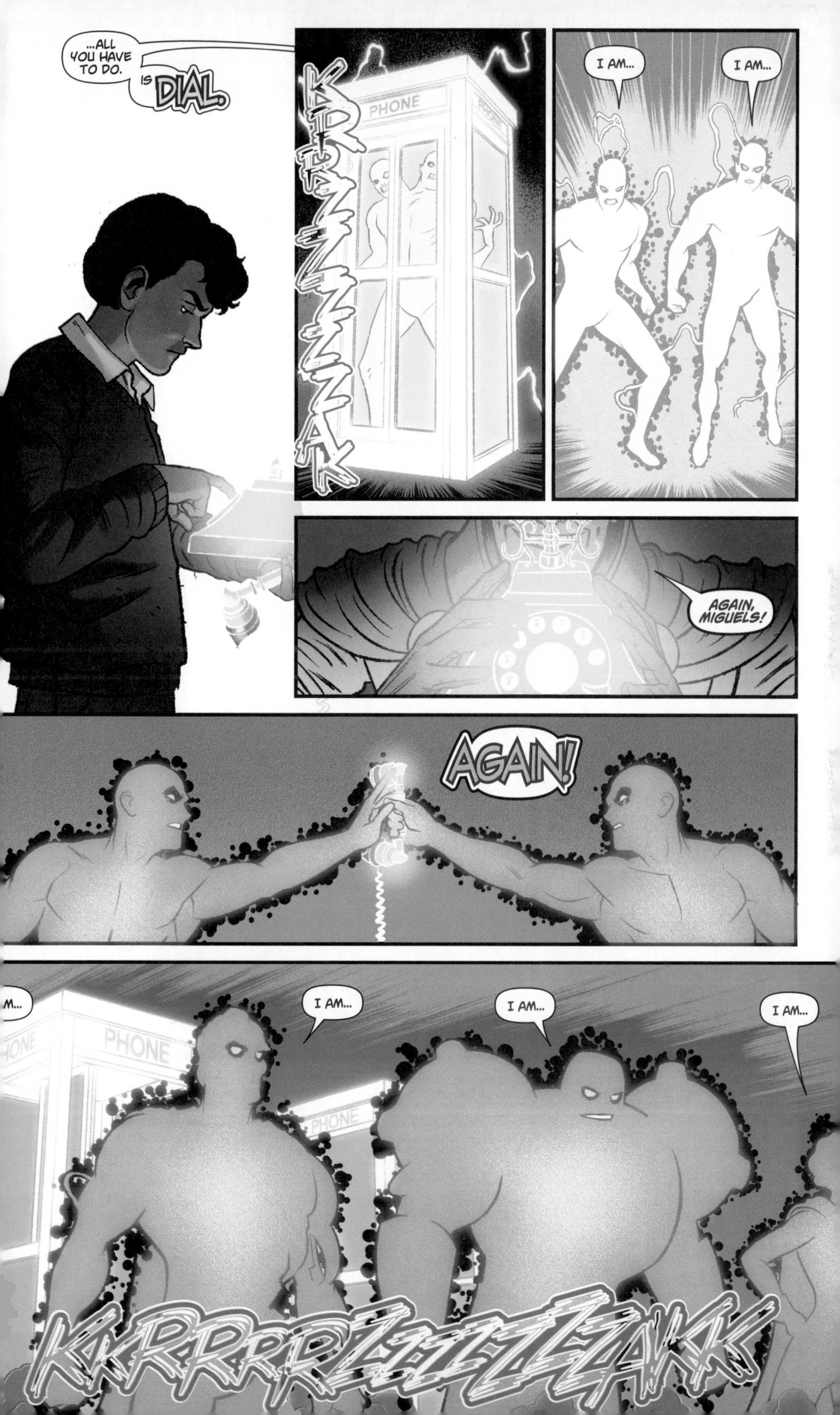

...ALL YOU HAVE TO DO.
IS DIAL.
KRRZZZZZAK
I AM...
I AM...
AGAIN, MIGUELS!
AGAIN!
...M...
I AM...
I AM...
I AM...
KRRRRRZZZZZAKK

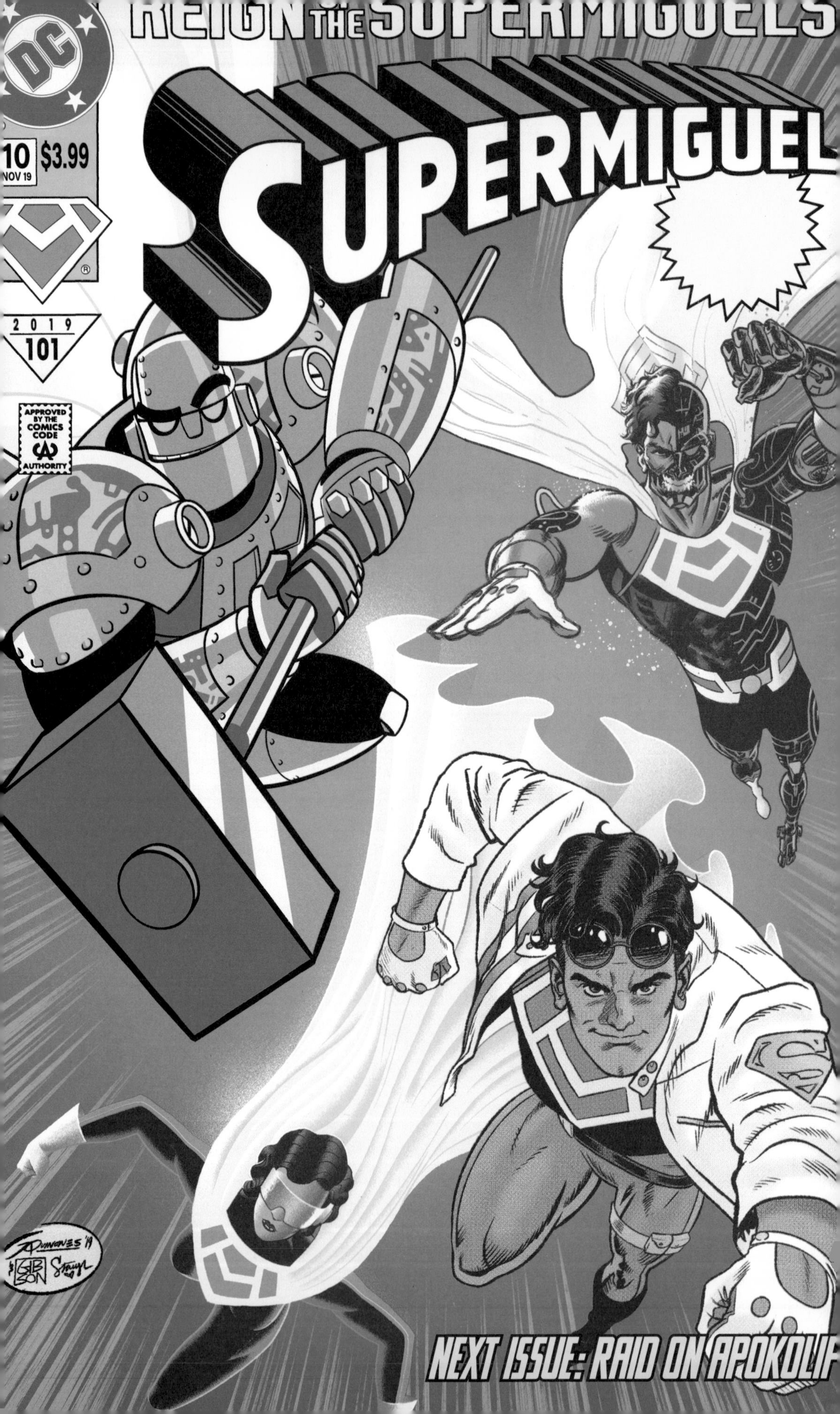

REIGN OF THE SUPERMIGUELS
DC
10 $3.99
NOV 19
SUPERMIGUEL
2019
101
APPROVED BY THE COMICS CODE AUTHORITY
NEXT ISSUE: RAID ON APOKOLIPS

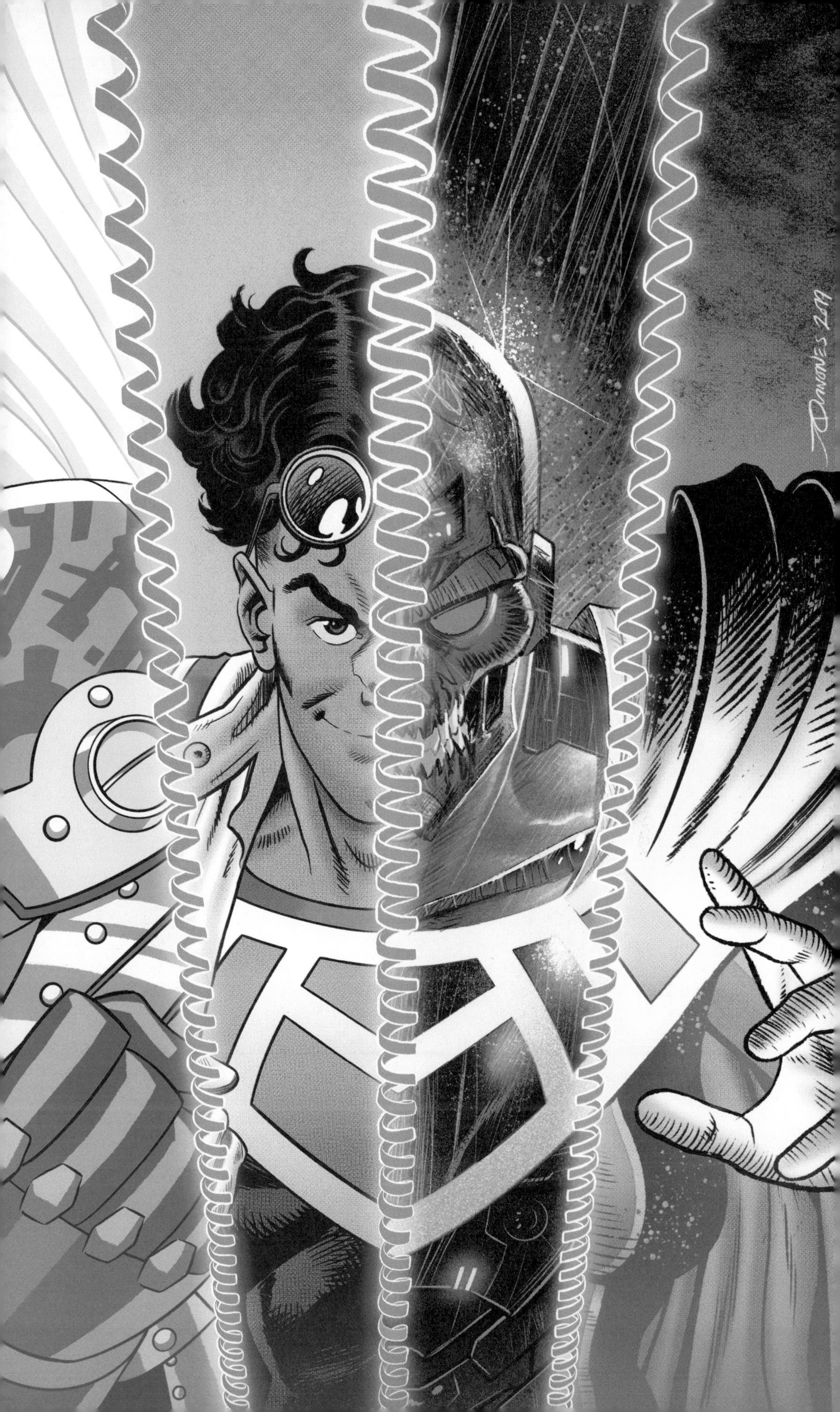

DEAR DAD

art by
JOE QUINONES
colors by
JORDAN GIBSON
cover art by
JOE QUINONES

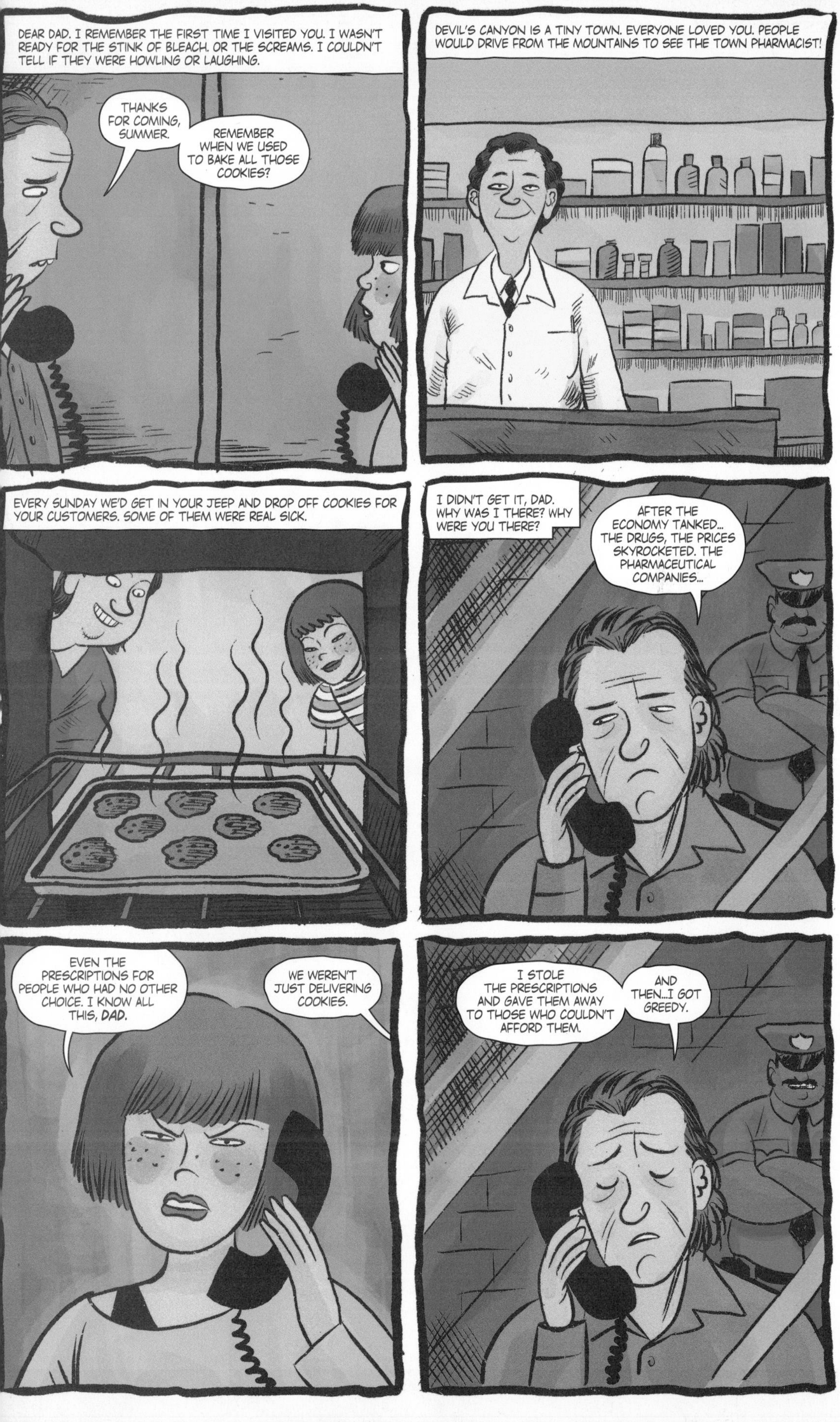
DEAR DAD. I REMEMBER THE FIRST TIME I VISITED YOU. I WASN'T READY FOR THE STINK OF BLEACH. OR THE SCREAMS. I COULDN'T TELL IF THEY WERE HOWLING OR LAUGHING.
THANKS FOR COMING, SUMMER.
REMEMBER WHEN WE USED TO BAKE ALL THOSE COOKIES?
DEVIL'S CANYON IS A TINY TOWN. EVERYONE LOVED YOU. PEOPLE WOULD DRIVE FROM THE MOUNTAINS TO SEE THE TOWN PHARMACIST!
EVERY SUNDAY WE'D GET IN YOUR JEEP AND DROP OFF COOKIES FOR YOUR CUSTOMERS. SOME OF THEM WERE REAL SICK.
I DIDN'T GET IT, DAD. WHY WAS I THERE? WHY WERE YOU THERE?
AFTER THE ECONOMY TANKED... THE DRUGS, THE PRICES SKYROCKETED. THE PHARMACEUTICAL COMPANIES...
EVEN THE PRESCRIPTIONS FOR PEOPLE WHO HAD NO OTHER CHOICE. I KNOW ALL THIS, **DAD.**
WE WEREN'T JUST DELIVERING COOKIES.
I STOLE THE PRESCRIPTIONS AND GAVE THEM AWAY TO THOSE WHO COULDN'T AFFORD THEM.
AND THEN...I GOT GREEDY.

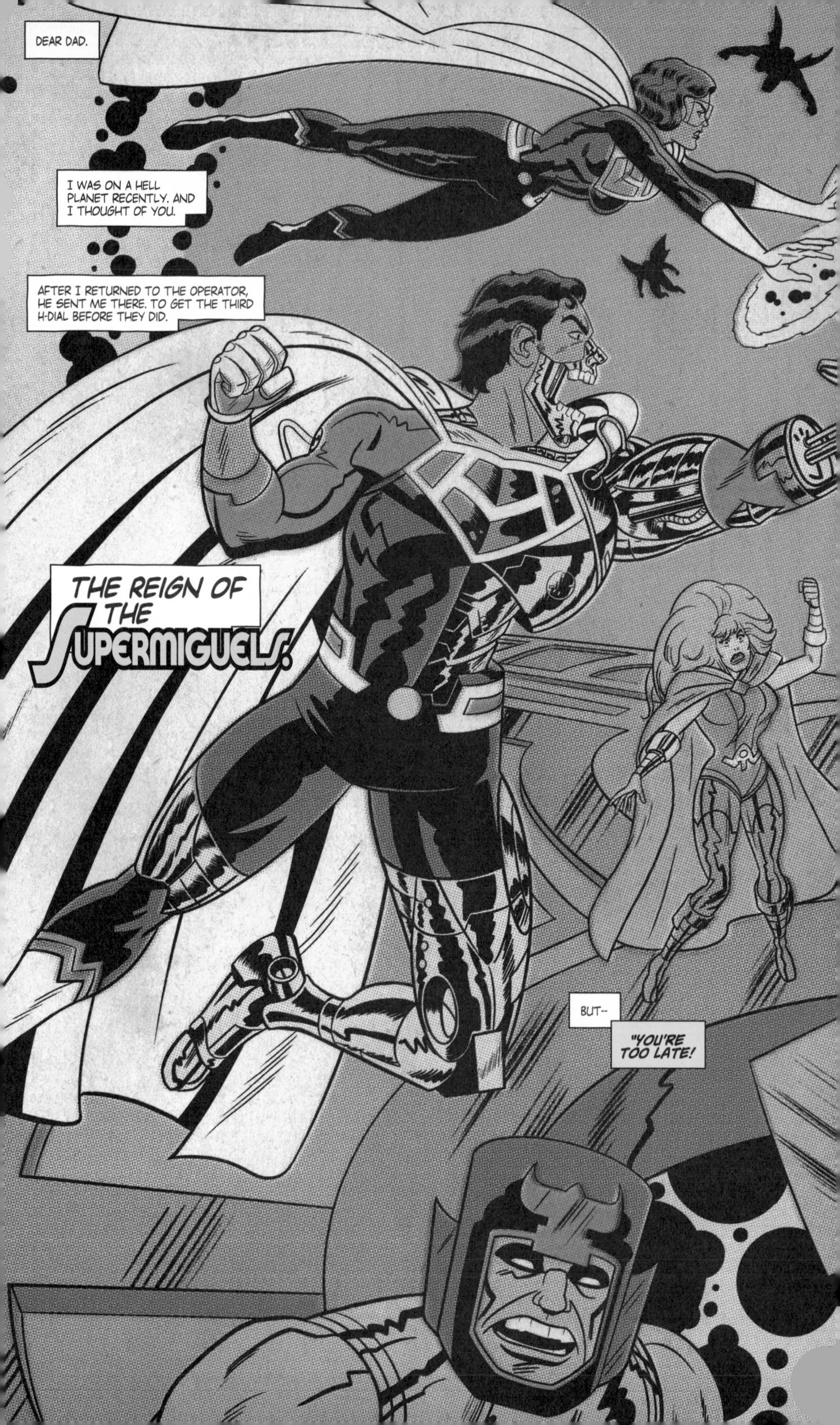
DEAR DAD.
I WAS ON A HELL PLANET RECENTLY. AND I THOUGHT OF YOU.
AFTER I RETURNED TO THE OPERATOR, HE SENT ME THERE. TO GET THE THIRD H-DIAL BEFORE THEY DID.
THE REIGN OF THE SUPERMIGUELS!
BUT--
"YOU'RE TOO LATE!

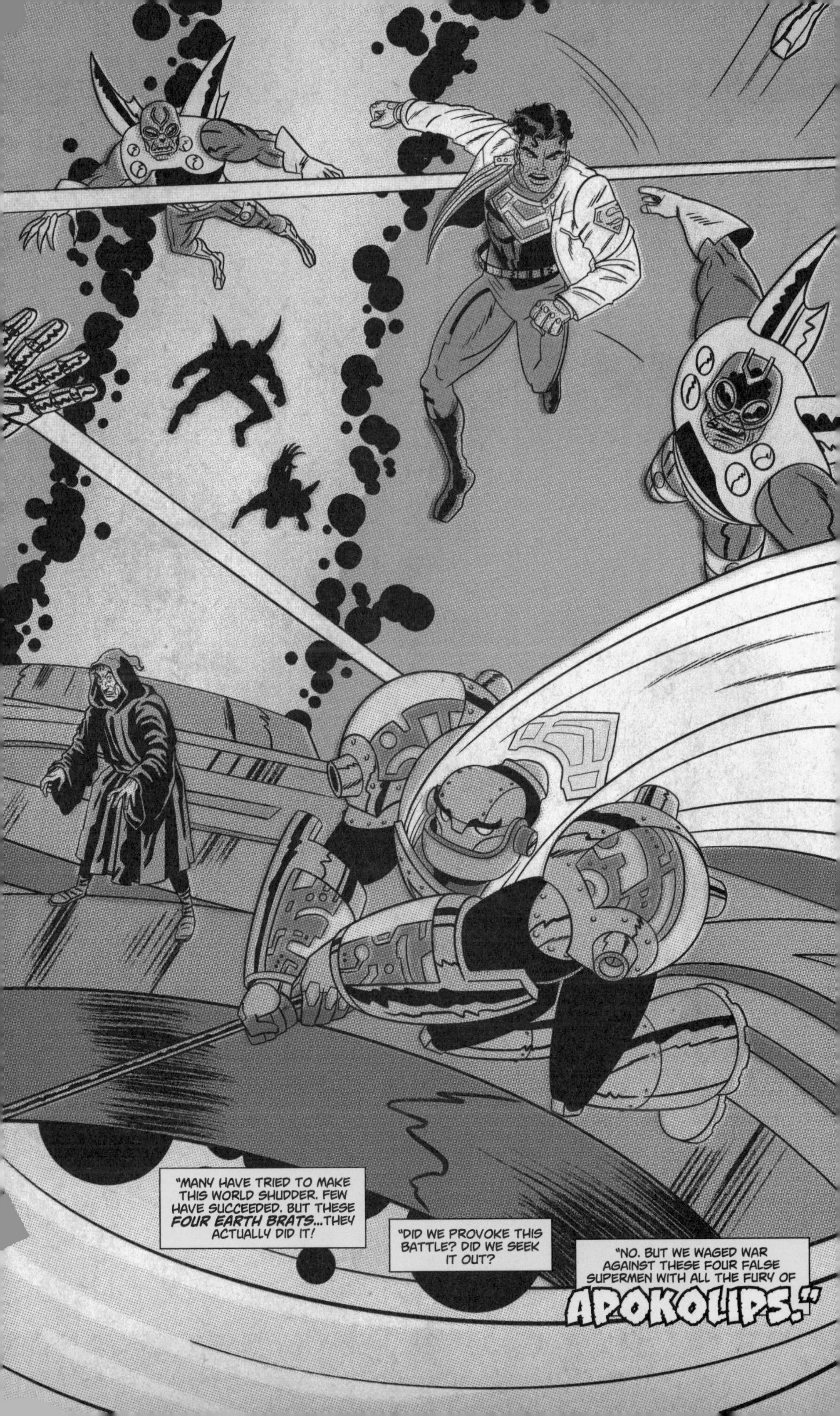
"MANY HAVE TRIED TO MAKE THIS WORLD SHUDDER. FEW HAVE SUCCEEDED. BUT THESE FOUR EARTH BRATS...THEY ACTUALLY DID IT!
"DID WE PROVOKE THIS BATTLE? DID WE SEEK IT OUT?
"NO. BUT WE WAGED WAR AGAINST THESE FOUR FALSE SUPERMEN WITH ALL THE FURY OF
APOKOLIPS."

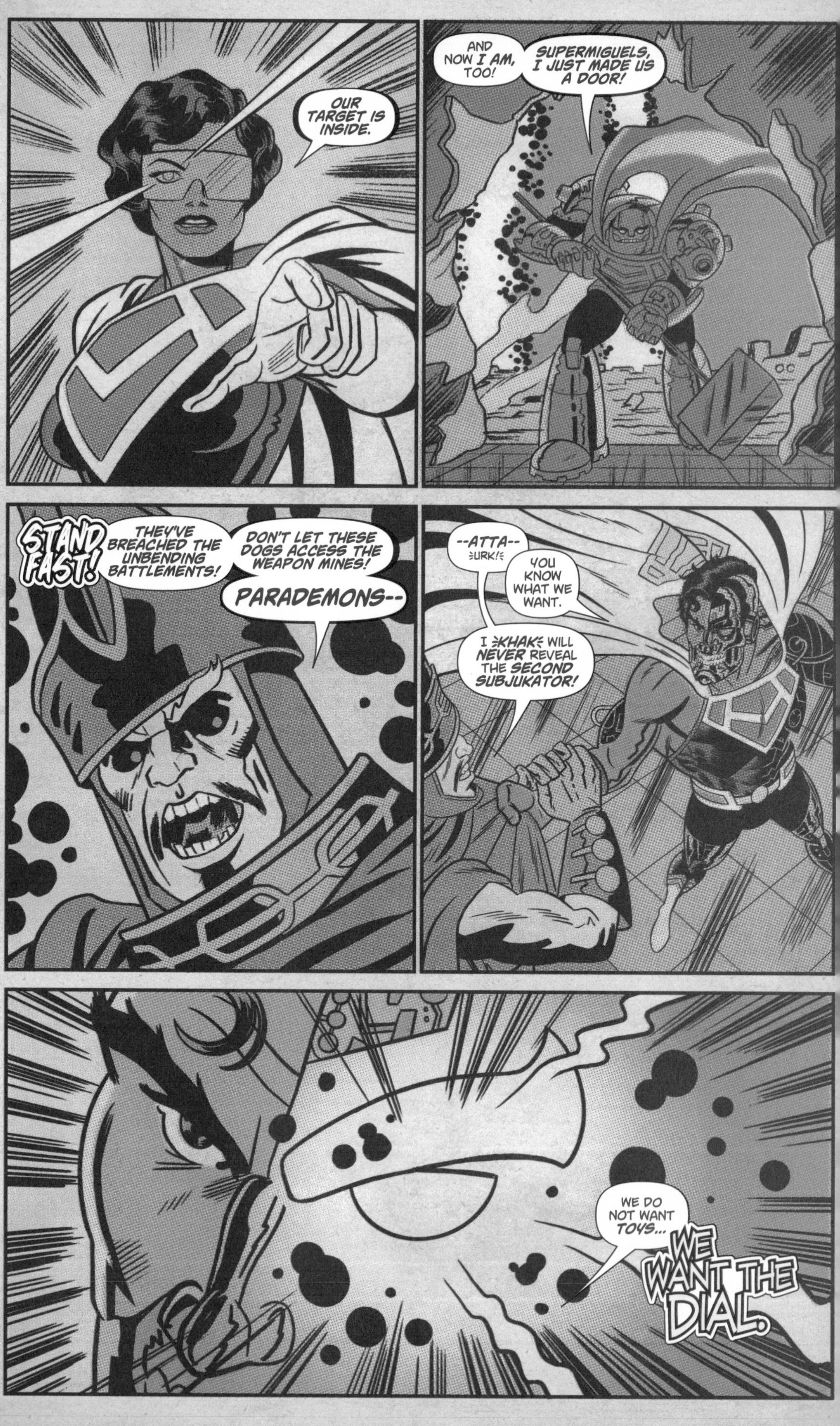
OUR TARGET IS INSIDE.
AND NOW I AM, TOO!
SUPERMIGUELS, I JUST MADE US A DOOR!
STAND FAST!
THEY'VE BREACHED THE UNBENDING BATTLEMENTS!
DON'T LET THESE DOGS ACCESS THE WEAPON MINES!
PARADEMONS--
--ATTA-- URK!
YOU KNOW WHAT WE WANT.
I KHAK WILL NEVER REVEAL THE SECOND SUBJUKATOR!
WE DO NOT WANT TOYS...
WE WANT THE DIAL.

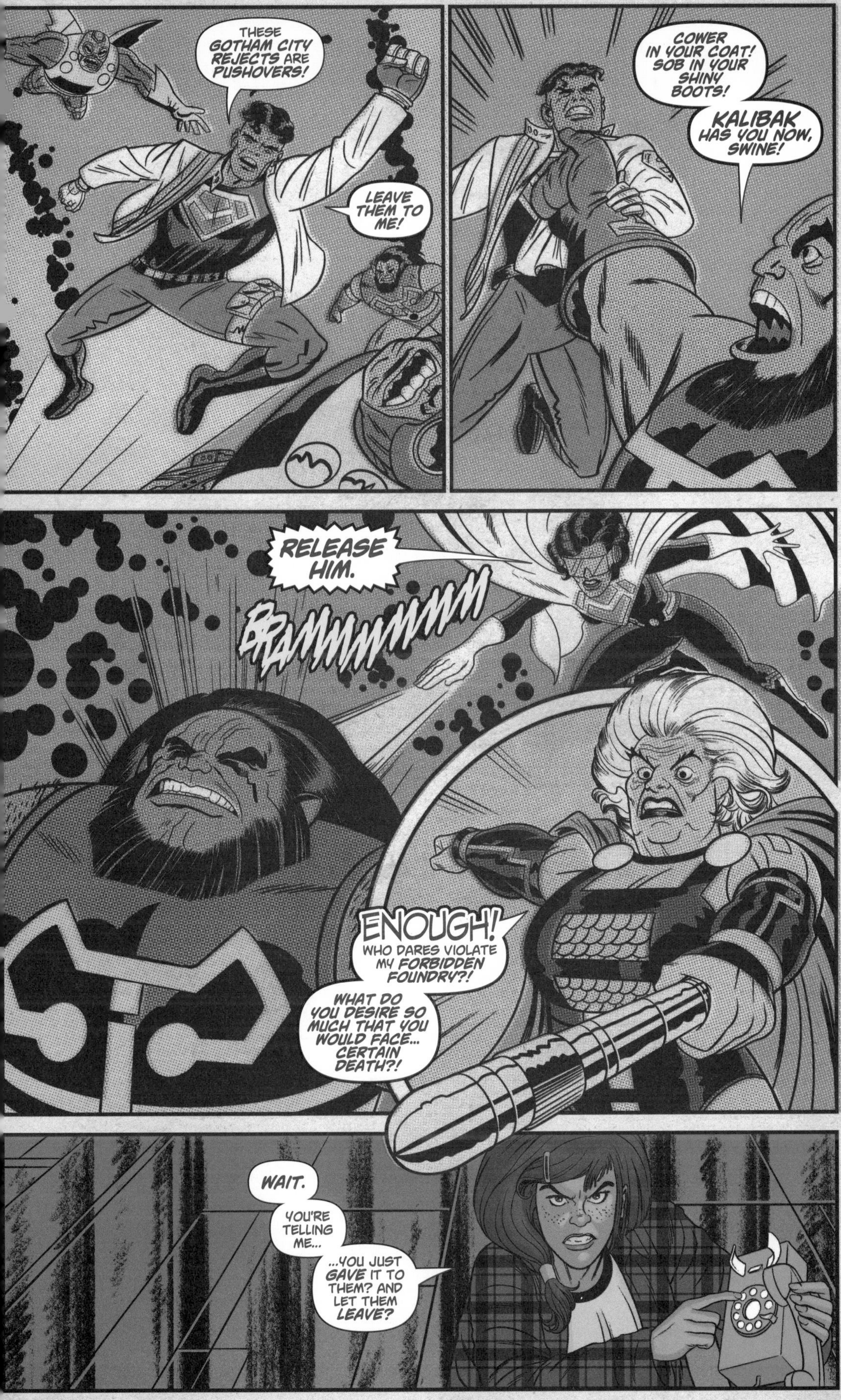
THESE GOTHAM CITY REJECTS ARE PUSHOVERS!
LEAVE THEM TO ME!
COWER IN YOUR COAT! SOB IN YOUR SHINY BOOTS!
KALIBAK HAS YOU NOW, SWINE!
RELEASE HIM.
BRAMMMMMM
ENOUGH! WHO DARES VIOLATE MY FORBIDDEN FOUNDRY?!
WHAT DO YOU DESIRE SO MUCH THAT YOU WOULD FACE... CERTAIN DEATH?!
WAIT.
YOU'RE TELLING ME...
...YOU JUST GAVE IT TO THEM? AND LET THEM LEAVE?

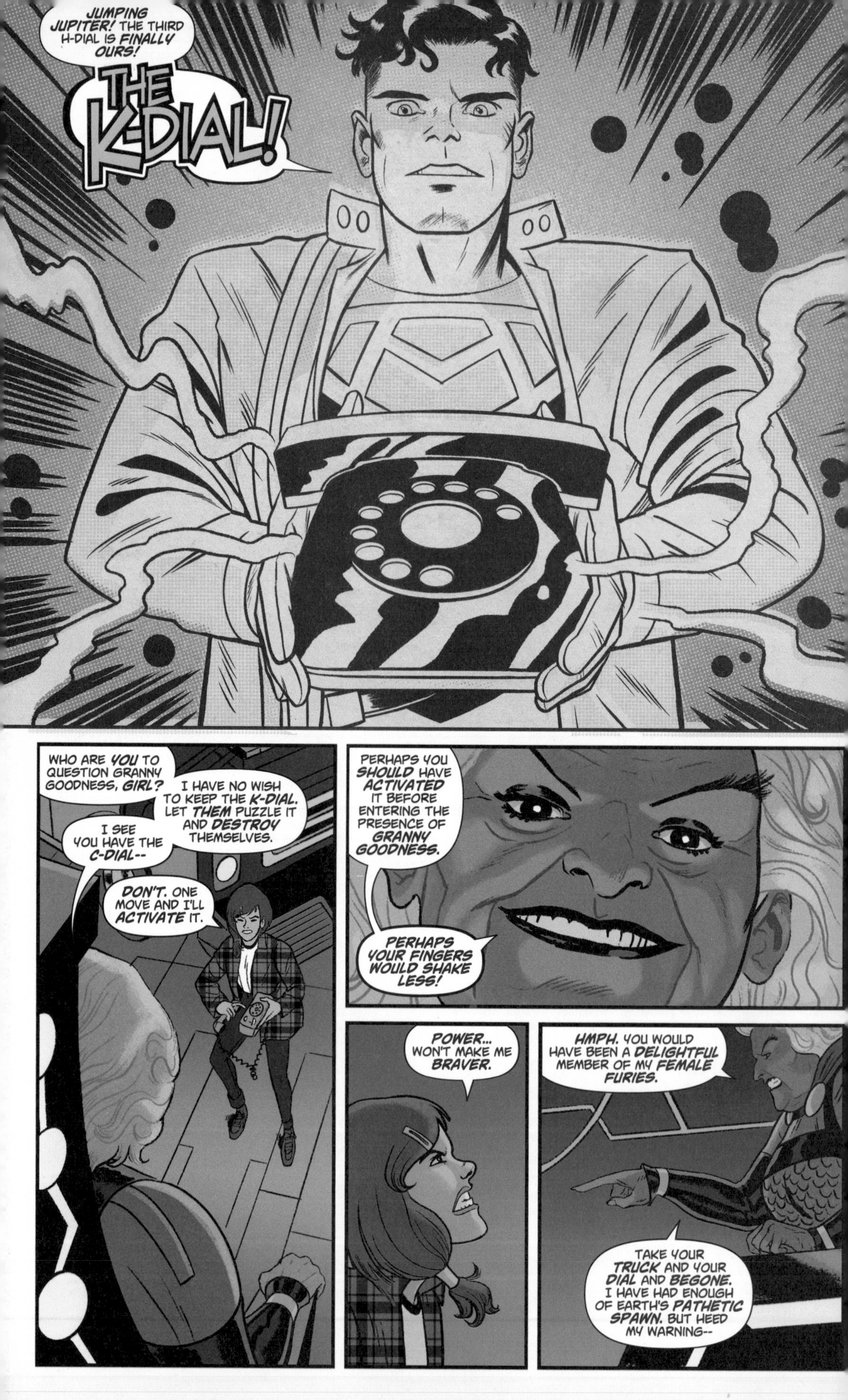

JUMPING JUPITER! THE THIRD H-DIAL IS FINALLY OURS!
THE K-DIAL!
WHO ARE YOU TO QUESTION GRANNY GOODNESS, GIRL?
I HAVE NO WISH TO KEEP THE K-DIAL. LET THEM PUZZLE IT AND DESTROY THEMSELVES.
I SEE YOU HAVE THE C-DIAL--
DON'T. ONE MOVE AND I'LL ACTIVATE IT.
PERHAPS YOU SHOULD HAVE ACTIVATED IT BEFORE ENTERING THE PRESENCE OF GRANNY GOODNESS.
PERHAPS YOUR FINGERS WOULD SHAKE LESS!
POWER... WON'T MAKE ME BRAVER.
HMPH. YOU WOULD HAVE BEEN A DELIGHTFUL MEMBER OF MY FEMALE FURIES.
TAKE YOUR TRUCK AND YOUR DIAL AND BEGONE. I HAVE HAD ENOUGH OF EARTH'S PATHETIC SPAWN. BUT HEED MY WARNING--

THE K-DIAL *is a* CURSE!

HEY, KIDS,
Create your own K-DIAL!

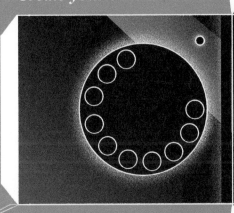

✂ *Cut along the outer lines.*

Fold along the inner lines and white tabs.

FOR *DECADES*, MY CANNIEST WAR SCIENTISTS HAVE *STUDIED* IT! THE MOST *LOATHSOME, ODIOUS, WARRIORS* IN ALL OF APOKOLIPS HAVE *DIALED* ITS *DAMNED DIGITS!* NONE HAVE RETURNED ALIVE!

IT IS A GATEWAY TO *ANGUISH,* A PIT OF *OBLIVION!*

AND YOU... *EARTH CHILDREN.* YOU MILK-MUSCLED *GUTTERSNIPES.* THE K-DIAL IS MY *GIFT* TO *YOU.*

SCREW YOUR *COURAGE* TO THE STICKING PLACE, IF YOU *CAN!* IT WILL MAKE *NO DIFFERENCE.*

THE K-DIAL WILL *DEVOUR YOUR SOULS!*

AHAHAHAHAHA!

"THAT'S WHAT SHE SAID."

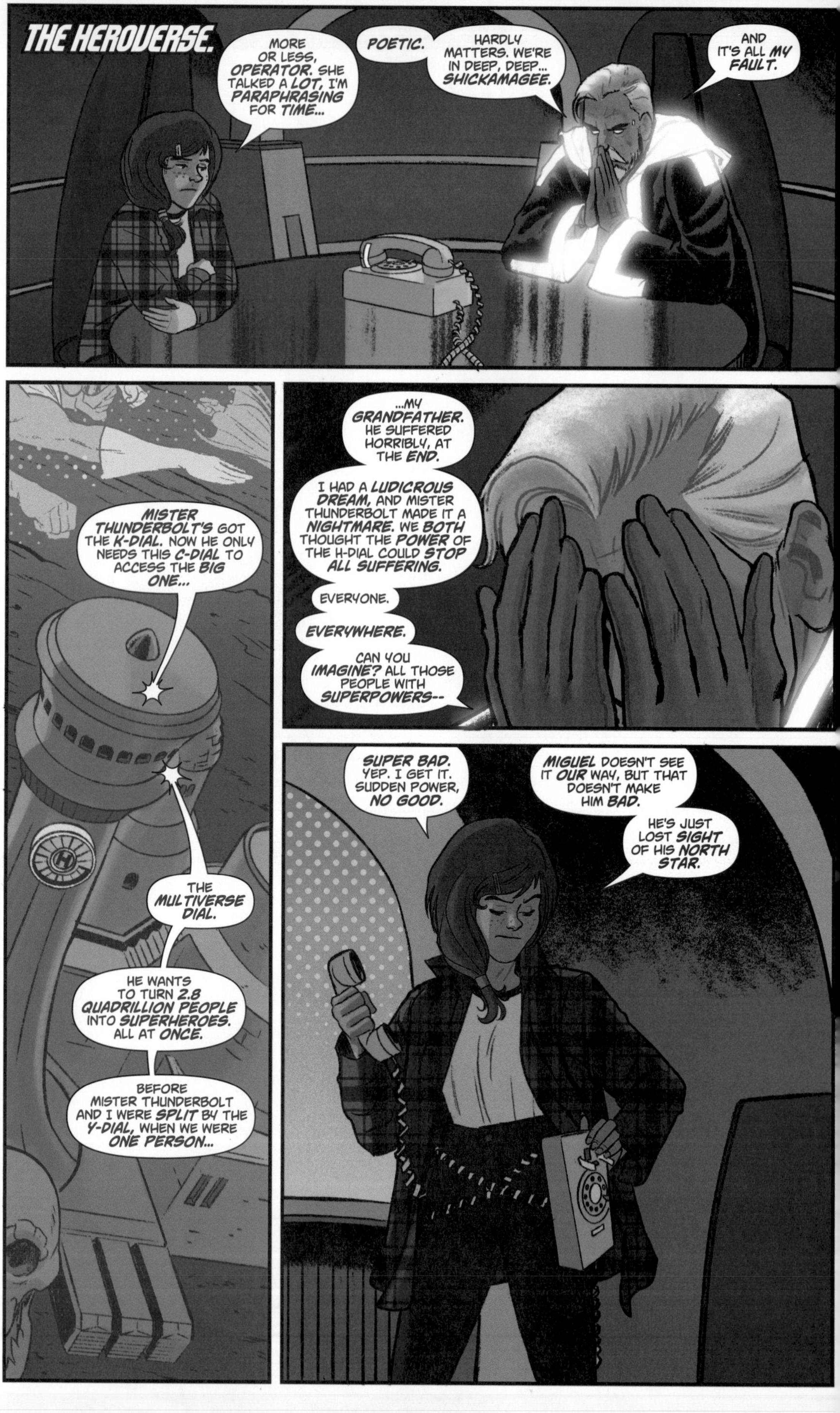

THE HEROVERSE.
MORE OR LESS, OPERATOR. SHE TALKED A LOT, I'M PARAPHRASING FOR TIME...
POETIC.
HARDLY MATTERS. WE'RE IN DEEP, DEEP... SHICKAMAGEE.
AND IT'S ALL MY FAULT.
MISTER THUNDERBOLT'S GOT THE K-DIAL. NOW HE ONLY NEEDS THIS C-DIAL TO ACCESS THE BIG ONE...
THE MULTIVERSE DIAL.
HE WANTS TO TURN 2.8 QUADRILLION PEOPLE INTO SUPERHEROES. ALL AT ONCE.
BEFORE MISTER THUNDERBOLT AND I WERE SPLIT BY THE Y-DIAL, WHEN WE WERE ONE PERSON...
...MY GRANDFATHER. HE SUFFERED HORRIBLY, AT THE END.
I HAD A LUDICROUS DREAM, AND MISTER THUNDERBOLT MADE IT A NIGHTMARE. WE BOTH THOUGHT THE POWER OF THE H-DIAL COULD STOP ALL SUFFERING.
EVERYONE.
EVERYWHERE.
CAN YOU IMAGINE? ALL THOSE PEOPLE WITH SUPERPOWERS--
SUPER BAD. YEP. I GET IT. SUDDEN POWER, NO GOOD.
MIGUEL DOESN'T SEE IT OUR WAY, BUT THAT DOESN'T MAKE HIM BAD.
HE'S JUST LOST SIGHT OF HIS NORTH STAR.

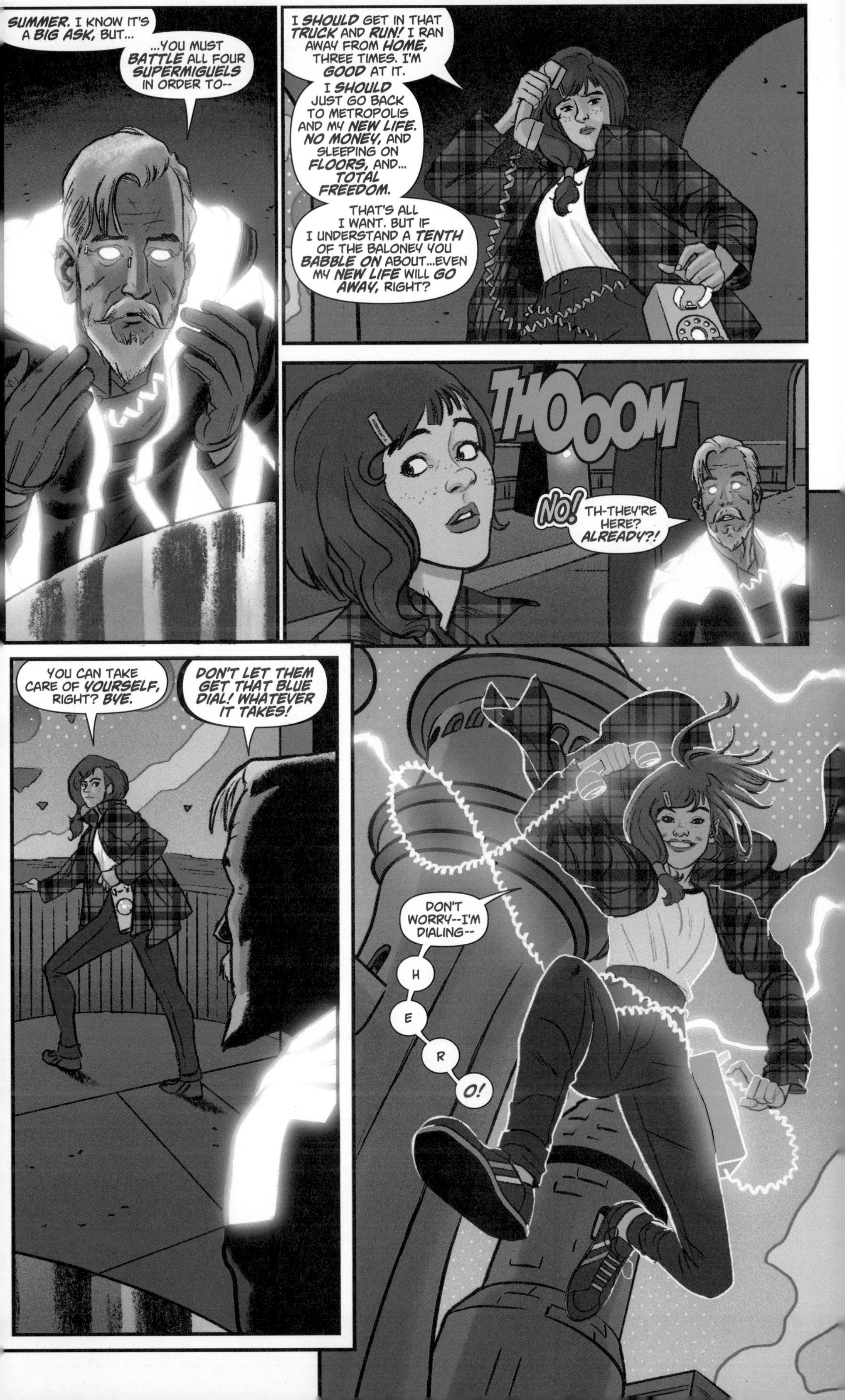
SUMMER. I KNOW IT'S A BIG ASK, BUT...
...YOU MUST BATTLE ALL FOUR SUPERMIGUELS IN ORDER TO--
I SHOULD GET IN THAT TRUCK AND RUN! I RAN AWAY FROM HOME, THREE TIMES. I'M GOOD AT IT.
I SHOULD JUST GO BACK TO METROPOLIS AND MY NEW LIFE. NO MONEY, AND SLEEPING ON FLOORS, AND... TOTAL FREEDOM.
THAT'S ALL I WANT. BUT IF I UNDERSTAND A TENTH OF THE BALONEY YOU BABBLE ON ABOUT...EVEN MY NEW LIFE WILL GO AWAY, RIGHT?
THOOOM
NO!
TH-THEY'RE HERE? ALREADY?!
YOU CAN TAKE CARE OF YOURSELF, RIGHT? BYE.
DON'T LET THEM GET THAT BLUE DIAL! WHATEVER IT TAKES!
DON'T WORRY--I'M DIALING--
H
E
R
O!

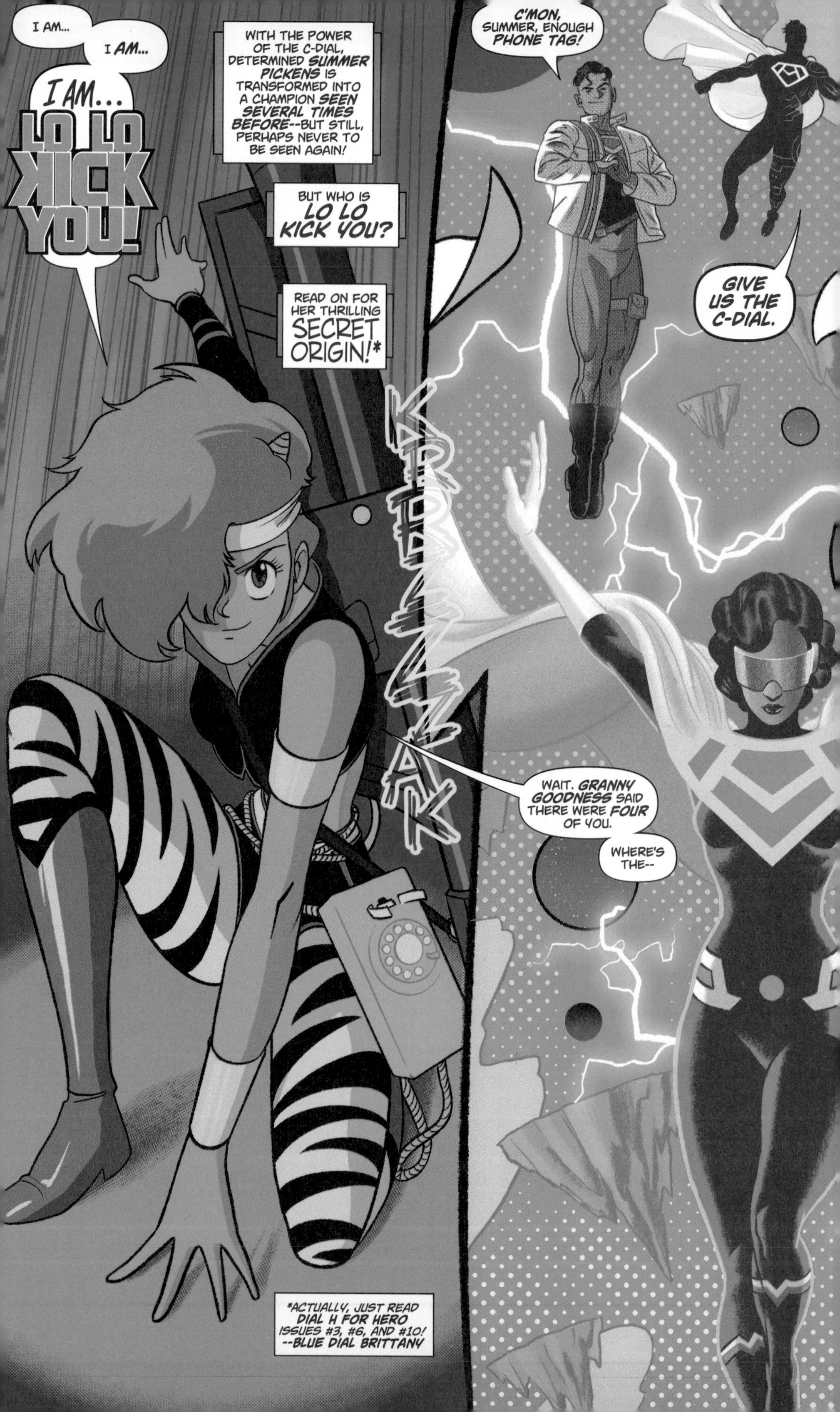

I AM...
I AM...
I AM... LO LO KICK YOU!
WITH THE POWER OF THE C-DIAL, DETERMINED SUMMER PICKENS IS TRANSFORMED INTO A CHAMPION SEEN SEVERAL TIMES BEFORE--BUT STILL, PERHAPS NEVER TO BE SEEN AGAIN!
BUT WHO IS LO LO KICK YOU?
READ ON FOR HER THRILLING SECRET ORIGIN!*
*ACTUALLY, JUST READ DIAL H FOR HERO ISSUES #3, #6, AND #10! --BLUE DIAL BRITTANY
C'MON, SUMMER, ENOUGH PHONE TAG!
GIVE US THE C-DIAL.
WAIT. GRANNY GOODNESS SAID THERE WERE FOUR OF YOU.
WHERE'S THE--

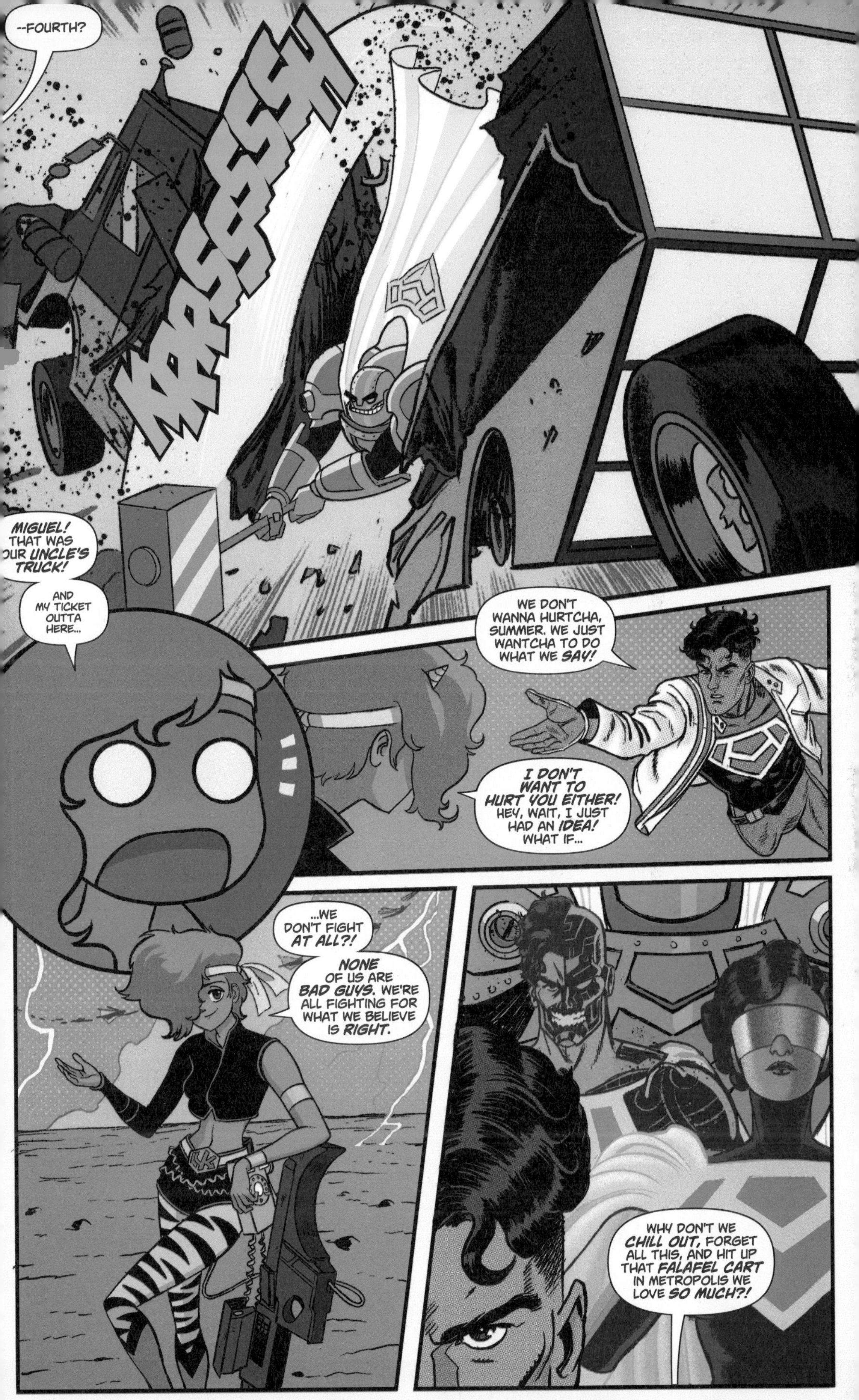
--FOURTH?
KRRSSSSH
MIGUEL! THAT WAS OUR UNCLE'S TRUCK!
AND MY TICKET OUTTA HERE...
WE DON'T WANNA HURTCHA, SUMMER. WE JUST WANTCHA TO DO WHAT WE SAY!
I DON'T WANT TO HURT YOU EITHER! HEY, WAIT, I JUST HAD AN IDEA! WHAT IF...
...WE DON'T FIGHT AT ALL?!
NONE OF US ARE BAD GUYS. WE'RE ALL FIGHTING FOR WHAT WE BELIEVE IS RIGHT.
WHY DON'T WE CHILL OUT, FORGET ALL THIS, AND HIT UP THAT FALAFEL CART IN METROPOLIS WE LOVE SO MUCH?!

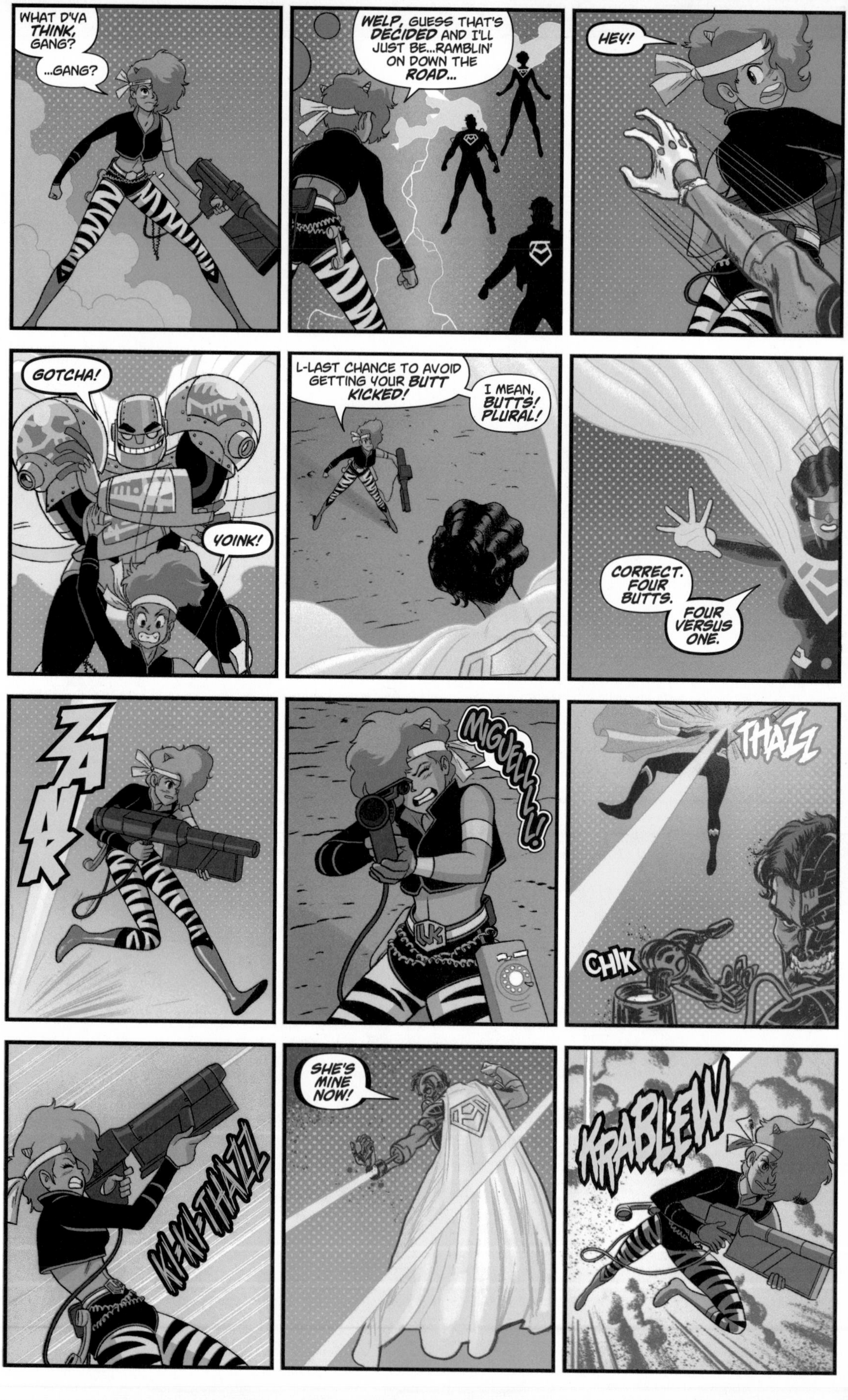
WHAT D'YA THINK, GANG?
...GANG?
WELP, GUESS THAT'S DECIDED AND I'LL JUST BE...RAMBLIN' ON DOWN THE ROAD...
HEY!
GOTCHA!
YOINK!
L-LAST CHANCE TO AVOID GETTING YOUR BUTT KICKED!
I MEAN, BUTTS! PLURAL!
CORRECT. FOUR BUTTS.
FOUR VERSUS ONE.
ZANK
MIGUELLLLL!
THAZZ
CHIK
KEKKTHAZZ
SHE'S MINE NOW!
KRABLEW

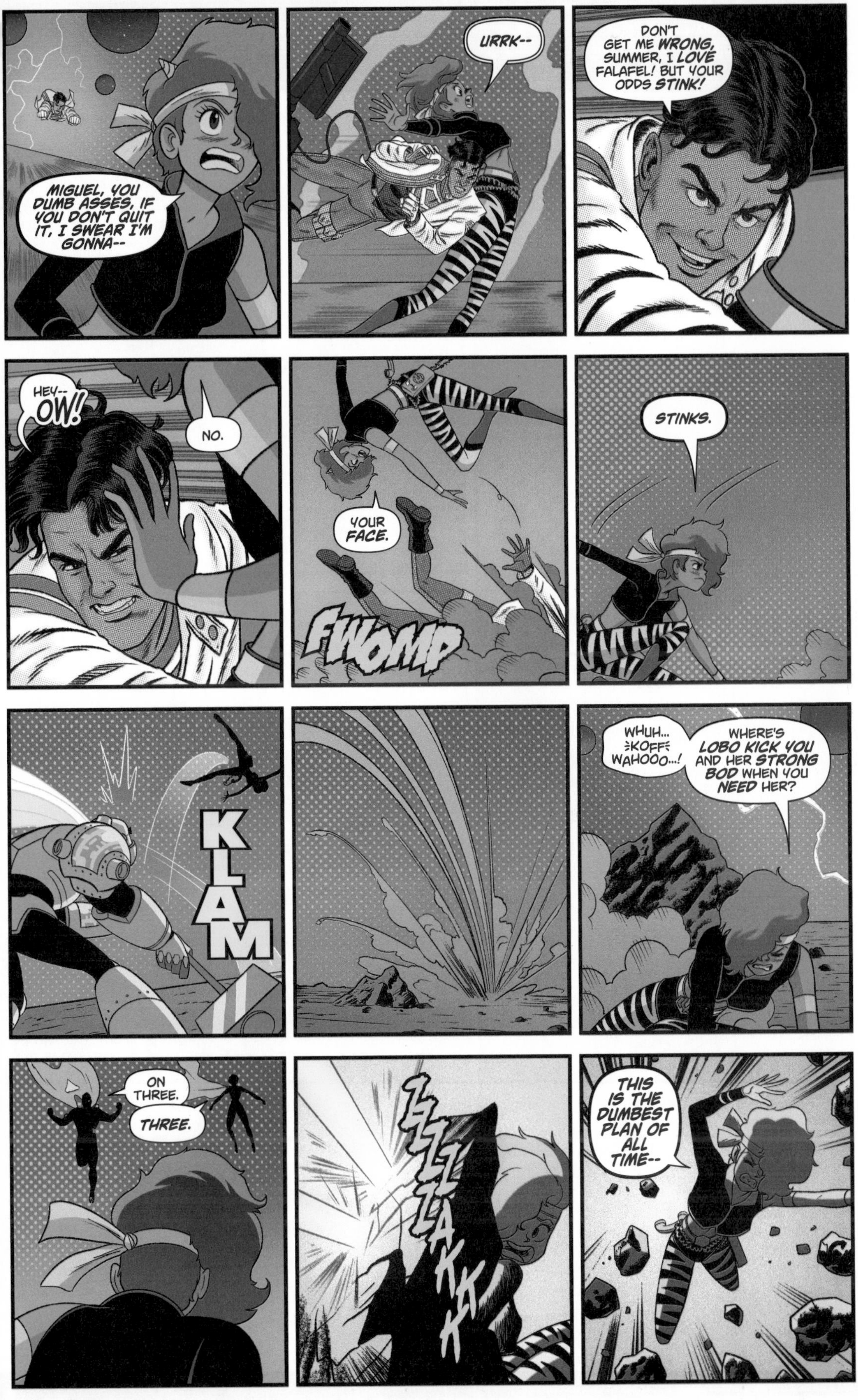
MIGUEL, YOU DUMB ASSES, IF YOU DON'T QUIT IT, I SWEAR I'M GONNA--
URRK--
DON'T GET ME WRONG, SUMMER, I LOVE FALAFEL! BUT YOUR ODDS STINK!
HEY-- OW!
NO.
YOUR FACE.
FWOMP
STINKS.
KLAM
WHUH... KOFF WAHOOO...!
WHERE'S LOBO KICK YOU AND HER STRONG BOD WHEN YOU NEED HER?
ON THREE.
THREE.
ZZZZAKKK
THIS IS THE DUMBEST PLAN OF ALL TIME--

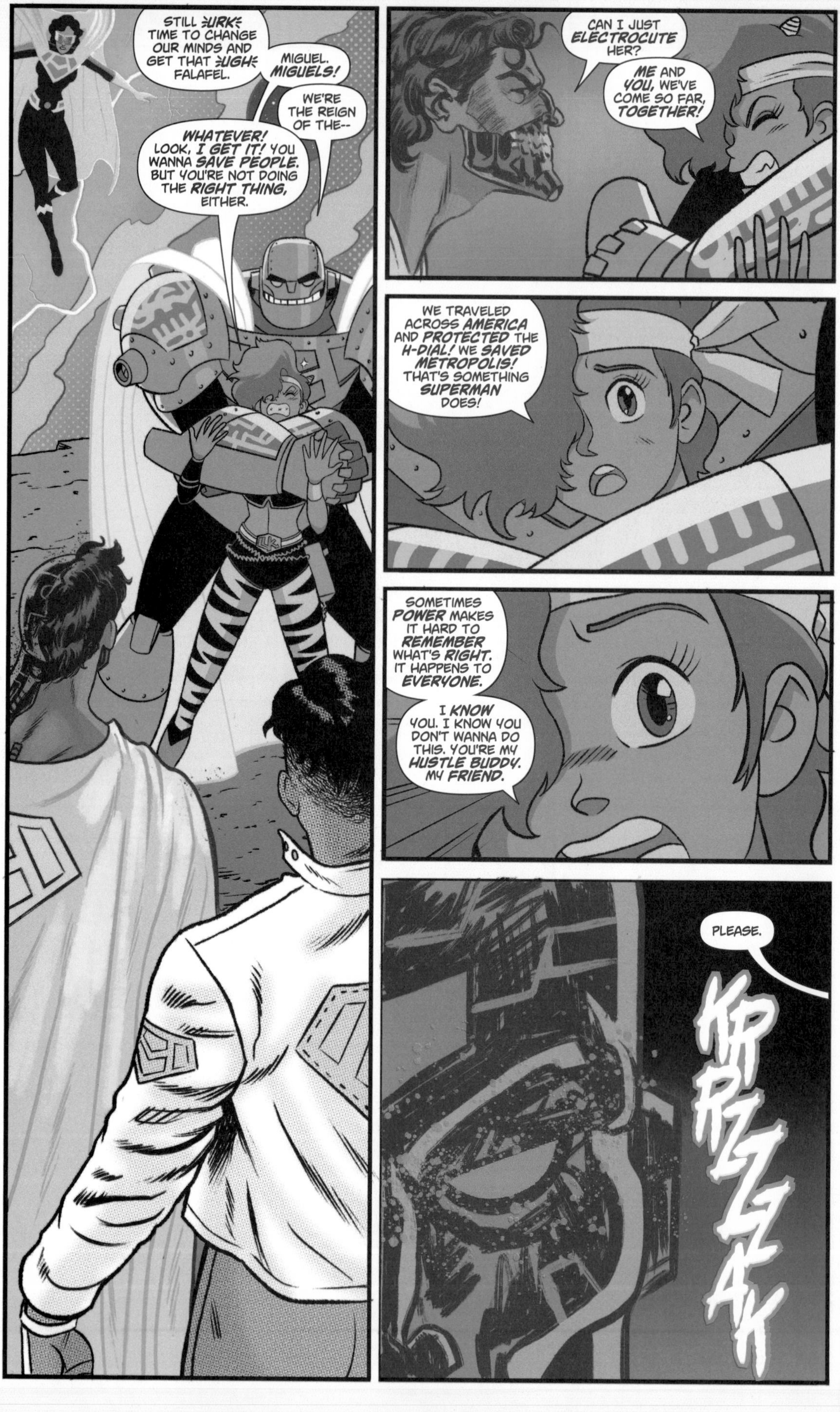
STILL ≷URK≶ TIME TO CHANGE OUR MINDS AND GET THAT ≷UGH≶ FALAFEL.
MIGUEL. MIGUELS!
WE'RE THE REIGN OF THE--
WHATEVER! LOOK, I GET IT! YOU WANNA SAVE PEOPLE. BUT YOU'RE NOT DOING THE RIGHT THING, EITHER.
CAN I JUST ELECTROCUTE HER?
ME AND YOU, WE'VE COME SO FAR, TOGETHER!
WE TRAVELED ACROSS AMERICA AND PROTECTED THE H-DIAL! WE SAVED METROPOLIS! THAT'S SOMETHING SUPERMAN DOES!
SOMETIMES POWER MAKES IT HARD TO REMEMBER WHAT'S RIGHT. IT HAPPENS TO EVERYONE.
I KNOW YOU. I KNOW YOU DON'T WANNA DO THIS. YOU'RE MY HUSTLE BUDDY. MY FRIEND.
PLEASE.
KRRZZAK

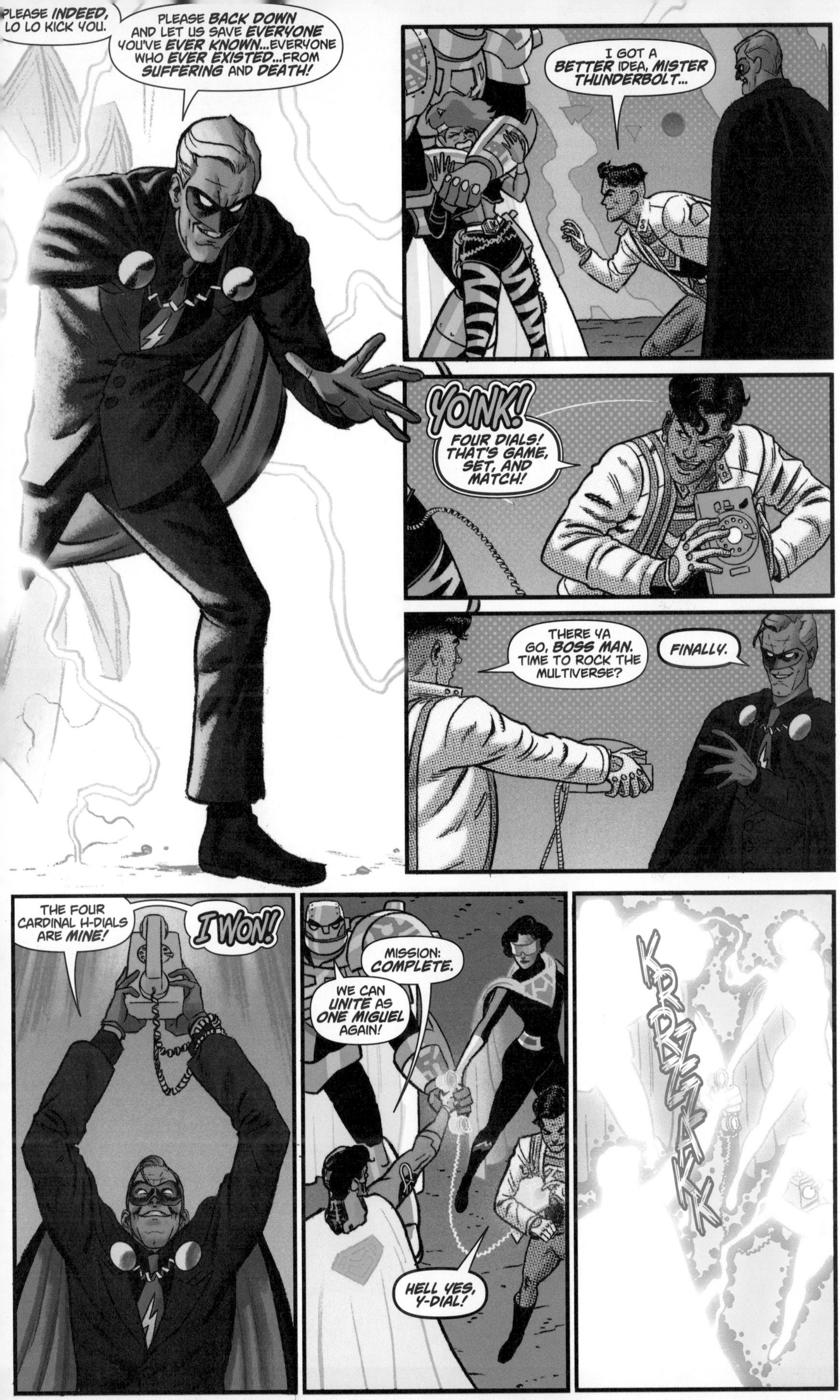
PLEASE INDEED, LO LO KICK YOU.
PLEASE BACK DOWN AND LET US SAVE EVERYONE YOU'VE EVER KNOWN...EVERYONE WHO EVER EXISTED...FROM SUFFERING AND DEATH!
I GOT A BETTER IDEA, MISTER THUNDERBOLT...
YOINK!
FOUR DIALS! THAT'S GAME, SET, AND MATCH!
THERE YA GO, BOSS MAN. TIME TO ROCK THE MULTIVERSE?
FINALLY.
THE FOUR CARDINAL H-DIALS ARE MINE!
I WON!
MISSION: COMPLETE.
WE CAN UNITE AS ONE MIGUEL AGAIN!
HELL YES, Y-DIAL!
KRDZZAKK

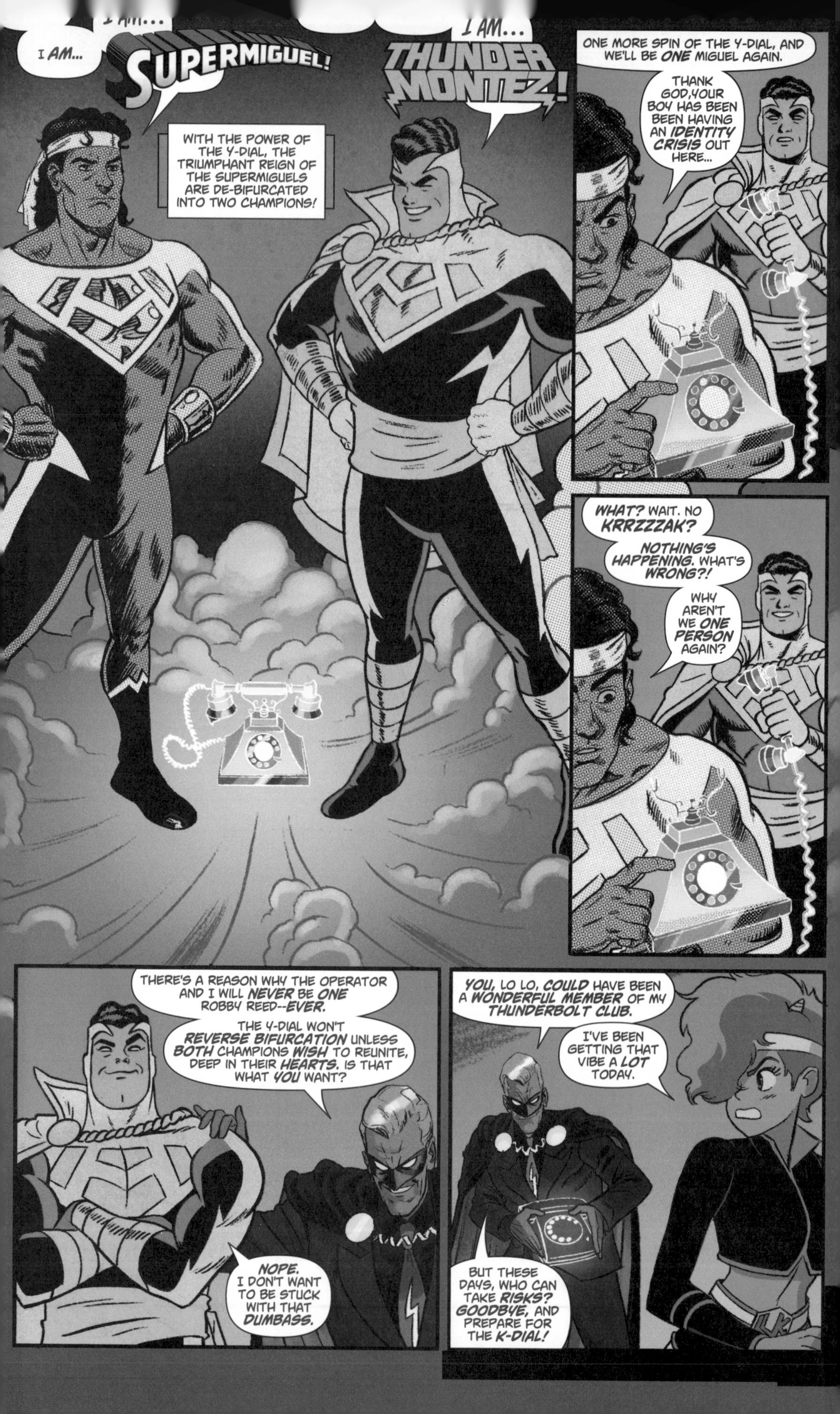

I AM...
SUPERMIGUEL!
I AM...
THUNDER MONTEZ!
WITH THE POWER OF THE Y-DIAL, THE TRIUMPHANT REIGN OF THE SUPERMIGUELS ARE DE-BIFURCATED INTO TWO CHAMPIONS!
ONE MORE SPIN OF THE Y-DIAL, AND WE'LL BE ONE MIGUEL AGAIN.
THANK GOD,YOUR BOY HAS BEEN BEEN HAVING AN IDENTITY CRISIS OUT HERE...
WHAT? WAIT. NO KRRZZZAK?
NOTHING'S HAPPENING. WHAT'S WRONG?!
WHY AREN'T WE ONE PERSON AGAIN?
THERE'S A REASON WHY THE OPERATOR AND I WILL NEVER BE ONE ROBBY REED--EVER.
THE Y-DIAL WON'T REVERSE BIFURCATION UNLESS BOTH CHAMPIONS WISH TO REUNITE, DEEP IN THEIR HEARTS. IS THAT WHAT YOU WANT?
NOPE. I DON'T WANT TO BE STUCK WITH THAT DUMBASS.
YOU, LO LO, COULD HAVE BEEN A WONDERFUL MEMBER OF MY THUNDERBOLT CLUB.
I'VE BEEN GETTING THAT VIBE A LOT TODAY.
BUT THESE DAYS, WHO CAN TAKE RISKS? GOODBYE, AND PREPARE FOR THE K-DIAL!

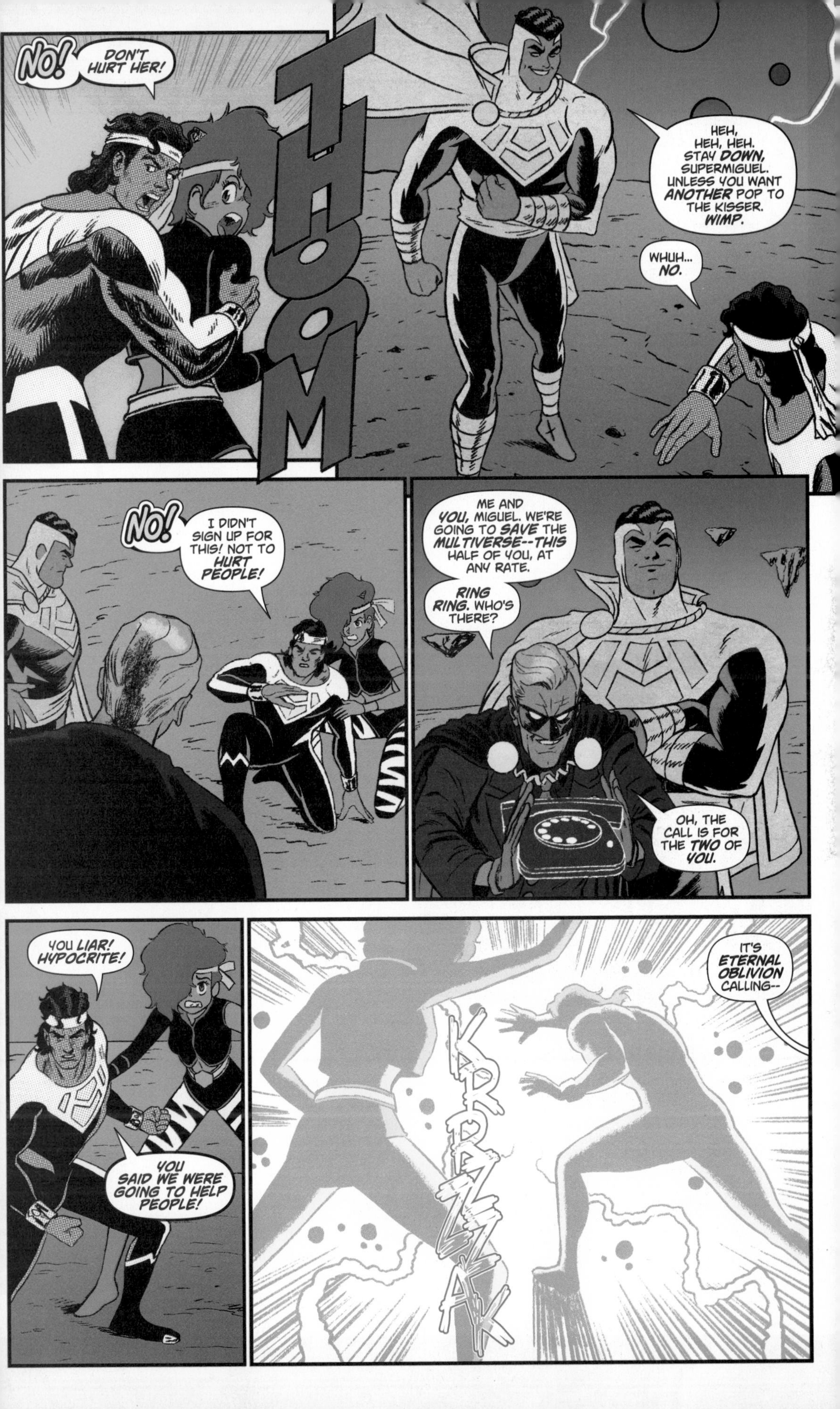
NO!
DON'T HURT HER!
THOOM
HEH, HEH, HEH. STAY DOWN, SUPERMIGUEL. UNLESS YOU WANT ANOTHER POP TO THE KISSER. WIMP.
WHUH... NO.
NO!
I DIDN'T SIGN UP FOR THIS! NOT TO HURT PEOPLE!
ME AND YOU, MIGUEL. WE'RE GOING TO SAVE THE MULTIVERSE--THIS HALF OF YOU, AT ANY RATE.
RING RING. WHO'S THERE?
OH, THE CALL IS FOR THE TWO OF YOU.
YOU LIAR! HYPOCRITE!
YOU SAID WE WERE GOING TO HELP PEOPLE!
IT'S ETERNAL OBLIVION CALLING--
KRZZZAK

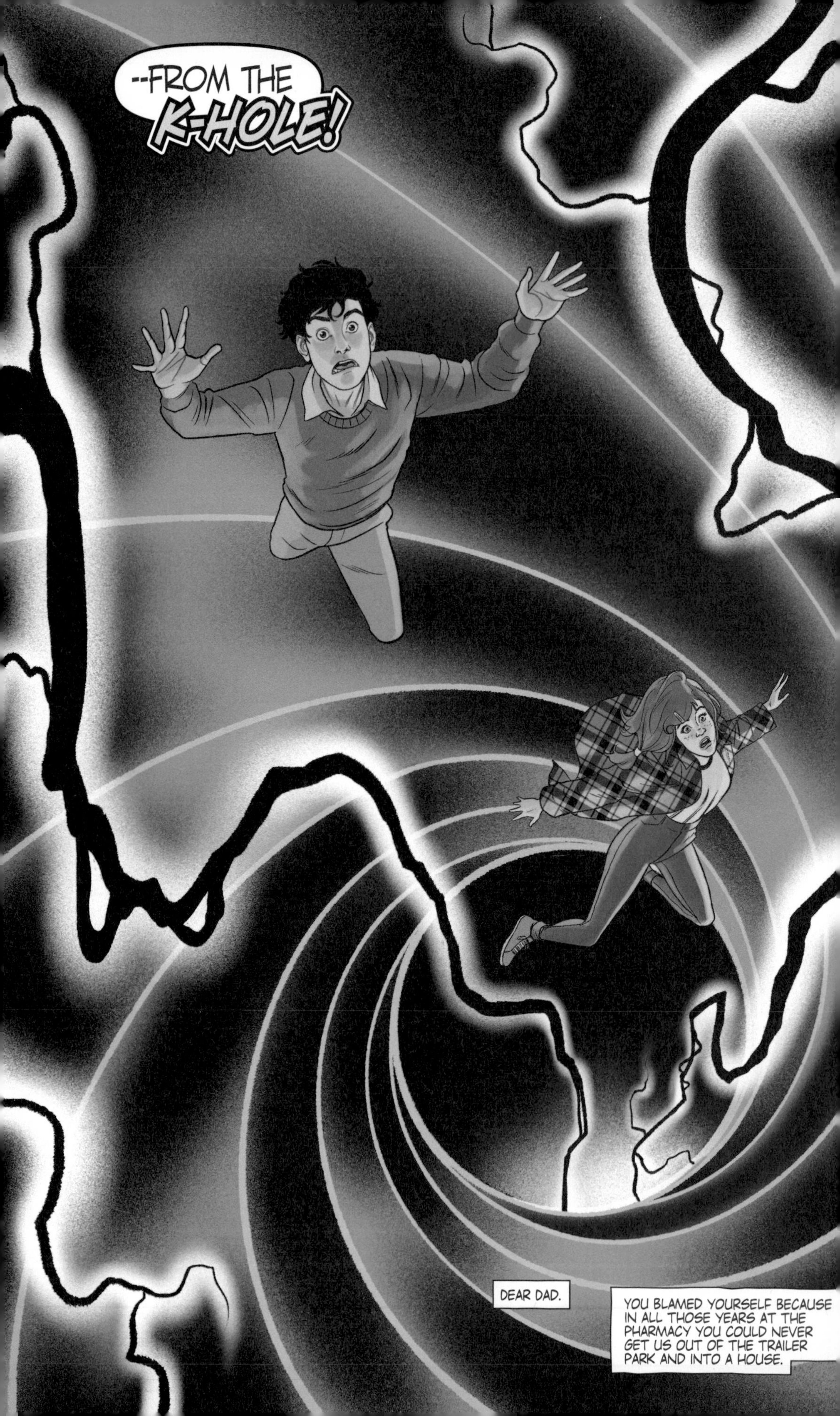
--FROM THE K-HOLE!
DEAR DAD.
YOU BLAMED YOURSELF BECAUSE IN ALL THOSE YEARS AT THE PHARMACY YOU COULD NEVER GET US OUT OF THE TRAILER PARK AND INTO A HOUSE.

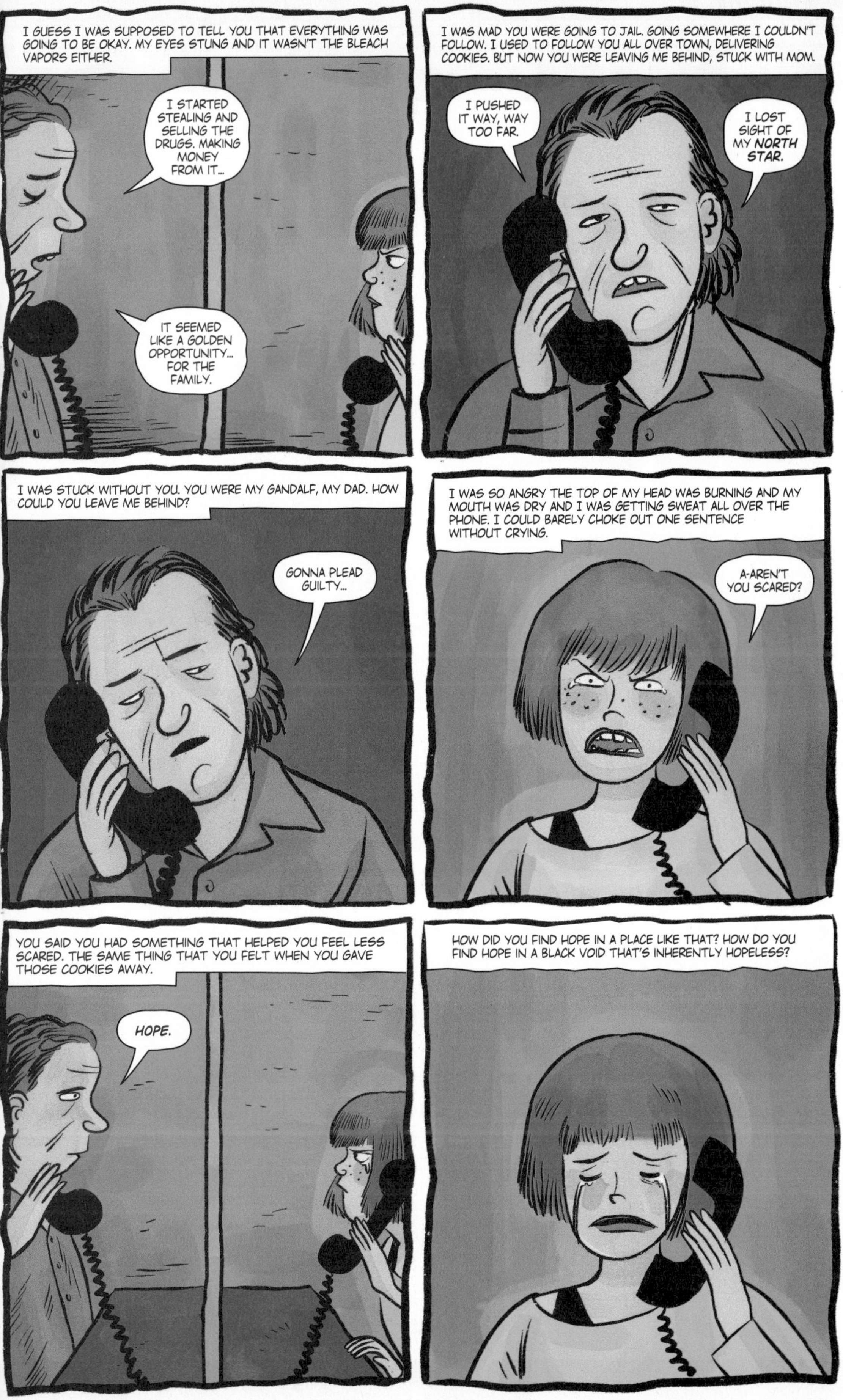

I GUESS I WAS SUPPOSED TO TELL YOU THAT EVERYTHING WAS GOING TO BE OKAY. MY EYES STUNG AND IT WASN'T THE BLEACH VAPORS EITHER.
I STARTED STEALING AND SELLING THE DRUGS. MAKING MONEY FROM IT...
IT SEEMED LIKE A GOLDEN OPPORTUNITY... FOR THE FAMILY.
I WAS MAD YOU WERE GOING TO JAIL. GOING SOMEWHERE I COULDN'T FOLLOW. I USED TO FOLLOW YOU ALL OVER TOWN, DELIVERING COOKIES. BUT NOW YOU WERE LEAVING ME BEHIND, STUCK WITH MOM.
I PUSHED IT WAY, WAY TOO FAR.
I LOST SIGHT OF MY **NORTH STAR.**
I WAS STUCK WITHOUT YOU. YOU WERE MY GANDALF, MY DAD. HOW COULD YOU LEAVE ME BEHIND?
GONNA PLEAD GUILTY...
I WAS SO ANGRY THE TOP OF MY HEAD WAS BURNING AND MY MOUTH WAS DRY AND I WAS GETTING SWEAT ALL OVER THE PHONE. I COULD BARELY CHOKE OUT ONE SENTENCE WITHOUT CRYING.
A-AREN'T YOU SCARED?
YOU SAID YOU HAD SOMETHING THAT HELPED YOU FEEL LESS SCARED. THE SAME THING THAT YOU FELT WHEN YOU GAVE THOSE COOKIES AWAY.
HOPE.
HOW DID YOU FIND HOPE IN A PLACE LIKE THAT? HOW DO YOU FIND HOPE IN A BLACK VOID THAT'S INHERENTLY HOPELESS?

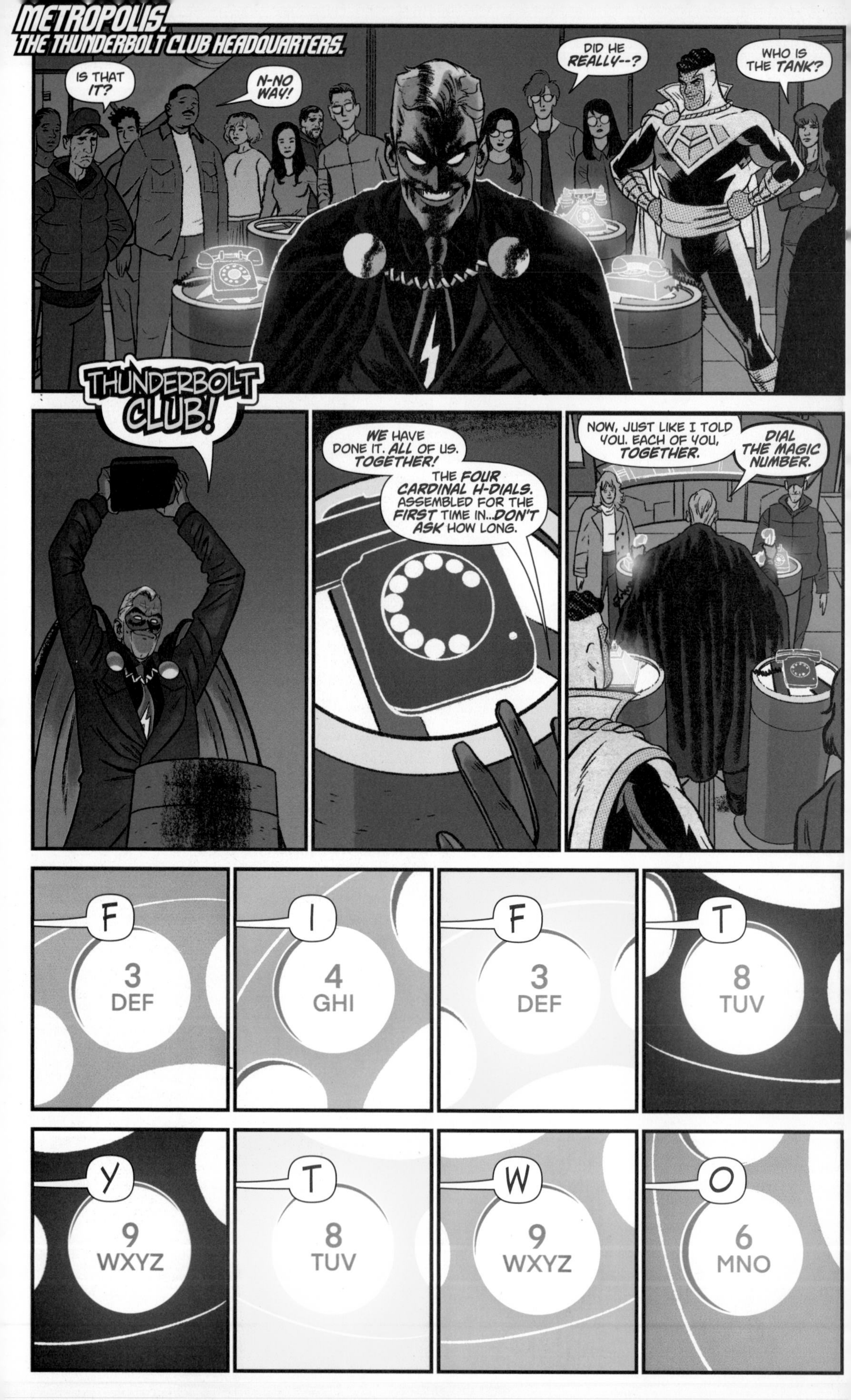
METROPOLIS.
THE THUNDERBOLT CLUB HEADQUARTERS.
IS THAT IT?
N-NO WAY!
DID HE REALLY--?
WHO IS THE TANK?
THUNDERBOLT CLUB!
WE HAVE DONE IT. ALL OF US. TOGETHER!
THE FOUR CARDINAL H-DIALS. ASSEMBLED FOR THE FIRST TIME IN...DON'T ASK HOW LONG.
NOW, JUST LIKE I TOLD YOU. EACH OF YOU, TOGETHER.
DIAL THE MAGIC NUMBER.
F
3
DEF
I
4
GHI
F
3
DEF
T
8
TUV
Y
9
WXYZ
T
8
TUV
W
9
WXYZ
O
6
MNO

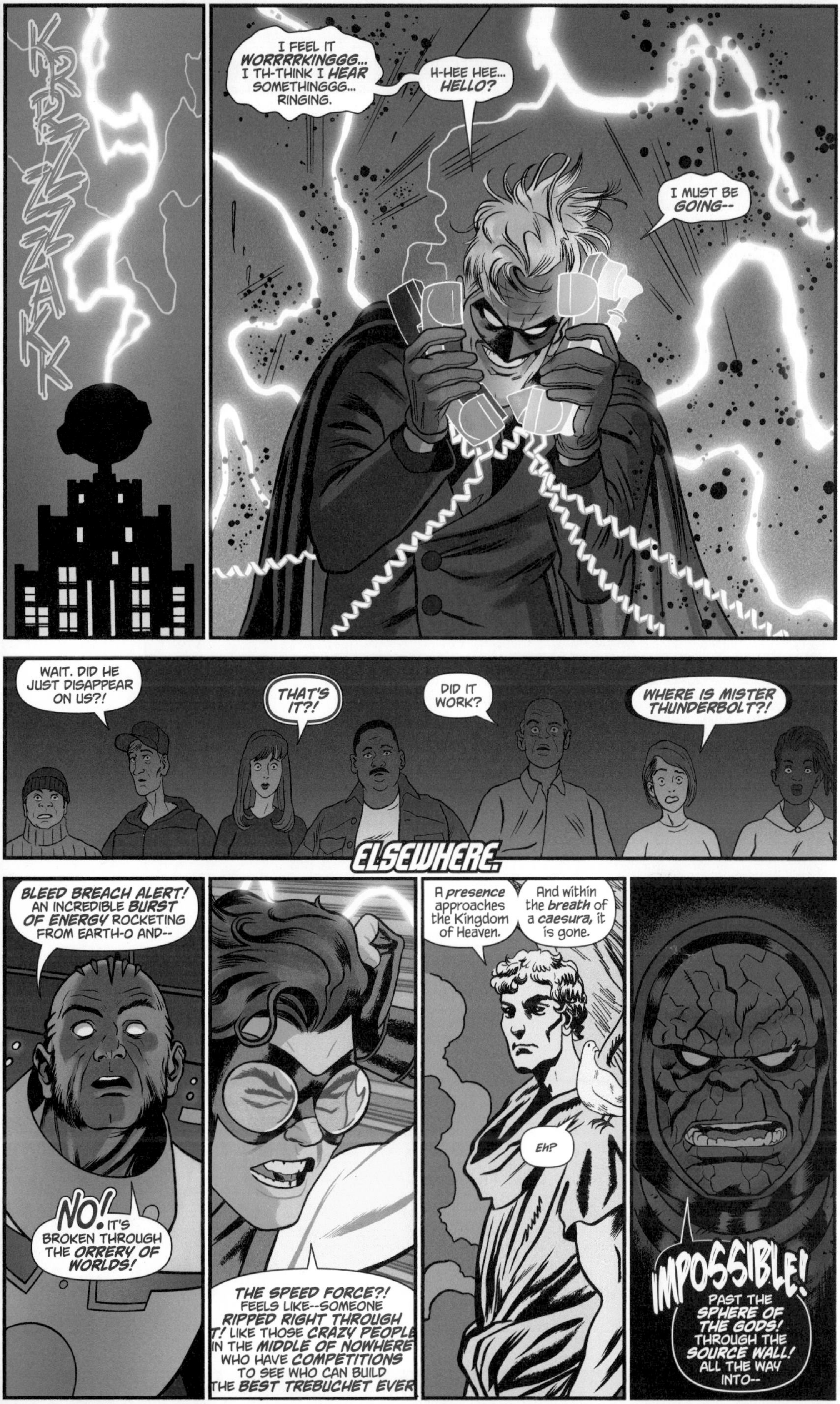
KRRZZZZAKK
I FEEL IT WORRRRKINGGG... I TH-THINK I HEAR SOMETHINGGG... RINGING.
H-HEE HEE... HELLO?
I MUST BE GOING--
WAIT. DID HE JUST DISAPPEAR ON US?!
THAT'S IT?!
DID IT WORK?
WHERE IS MISTER THUNDERBOLT?!
ELSEWHERE.
BLEED BREACH ALERT! AN INCREDIBLE BURST OF ENERGY ROCKETING FROM EARTH-0 AND--
NO! IT'S BROKEN THROUGH THE ORRERY OF WORLDS!
THE SPEED FORCE?! FEELS LIKE--SOMEONE RIPPED RIGHT THROUGH IT! LIKE THOSE CRAZY PEOPLE IN THE MIDDLE OF NOWHERE WHO HAVE COMPETITIONS TO SEE WHO CAN BUILD THE BEST TREBUCHET EVER
A presence approaches the Kingdom of Heaven.
And within the breath of a caesura, it is gone.
Eh?
IMPOSSIBLE! PAST THE SPHERE OF THE GODS! THROUGH THE SOURCE WALL! ALL THE WAY INTO--

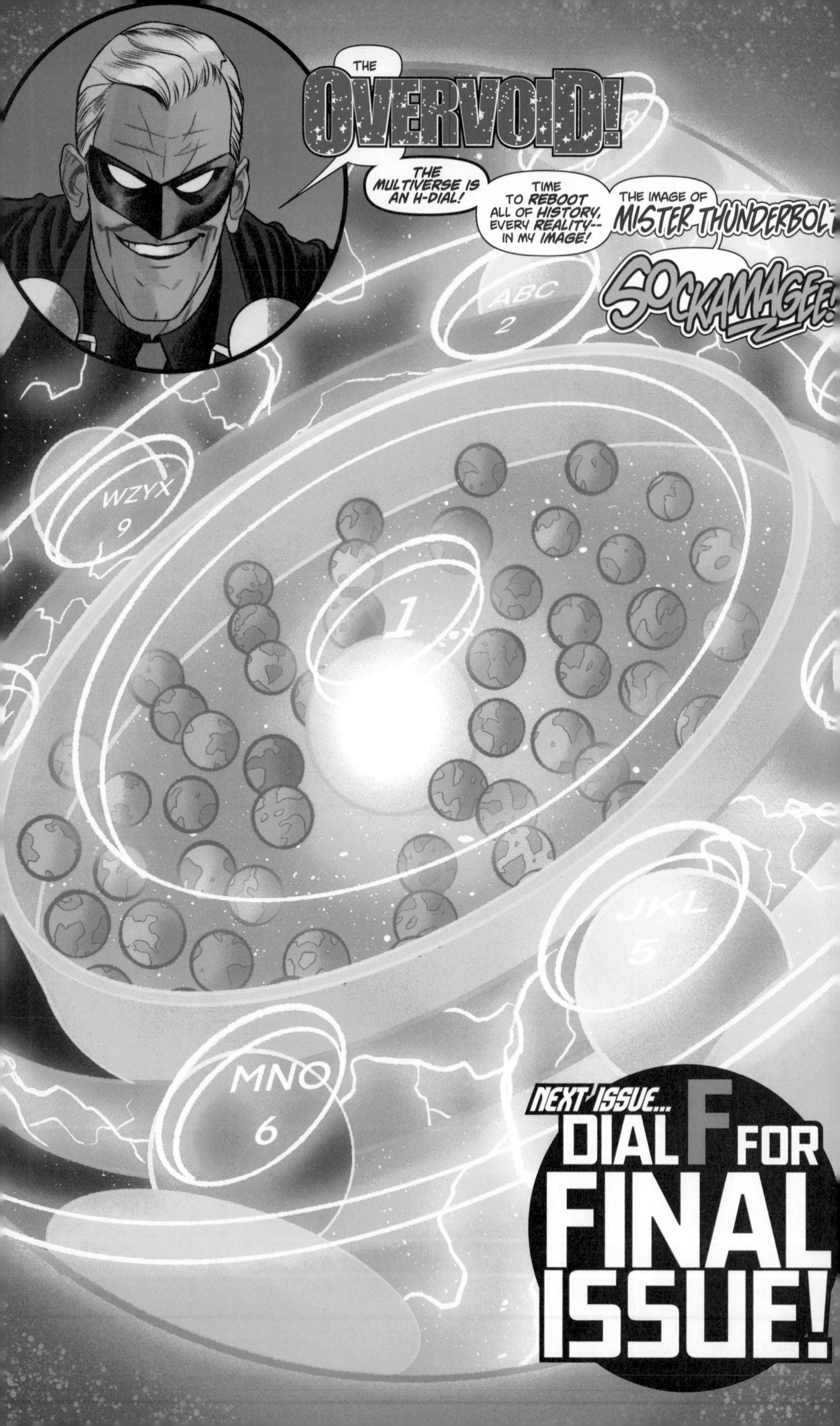

THE OVERVOID!
THE MULTIVERSE IS AN H-DIAL!
TIME TO REBOOT ALL OF HISTORY, EVERY REALITY-- IN MY IMAGE!
THE IMAGE OF MISTER THUNDERBOLT
SOCKAMAGEE!
ABC 2
WZYX 9
1
JKL 5
MNO 6
NEXT ISSUE... DIAL F FOR FINAL ISSUE!

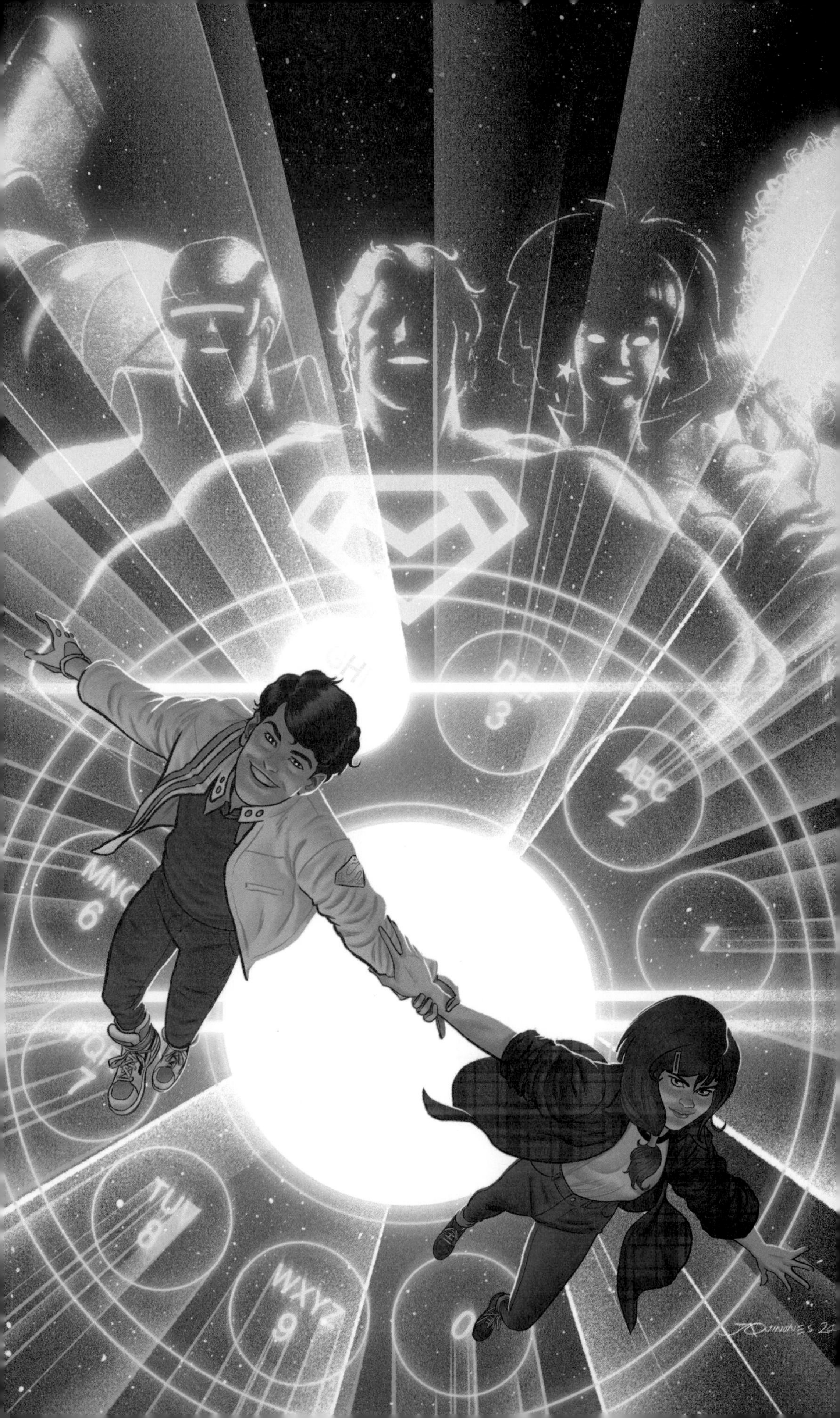
3
ABC
2
6
1
TUV
8
WXYZ
9
0

DIAL F FOR FINALE

art by
JOE QUINONES

colors by
JORDAN GIBSON and **JOE QUINONES**

cover art by
JOE QUINONES

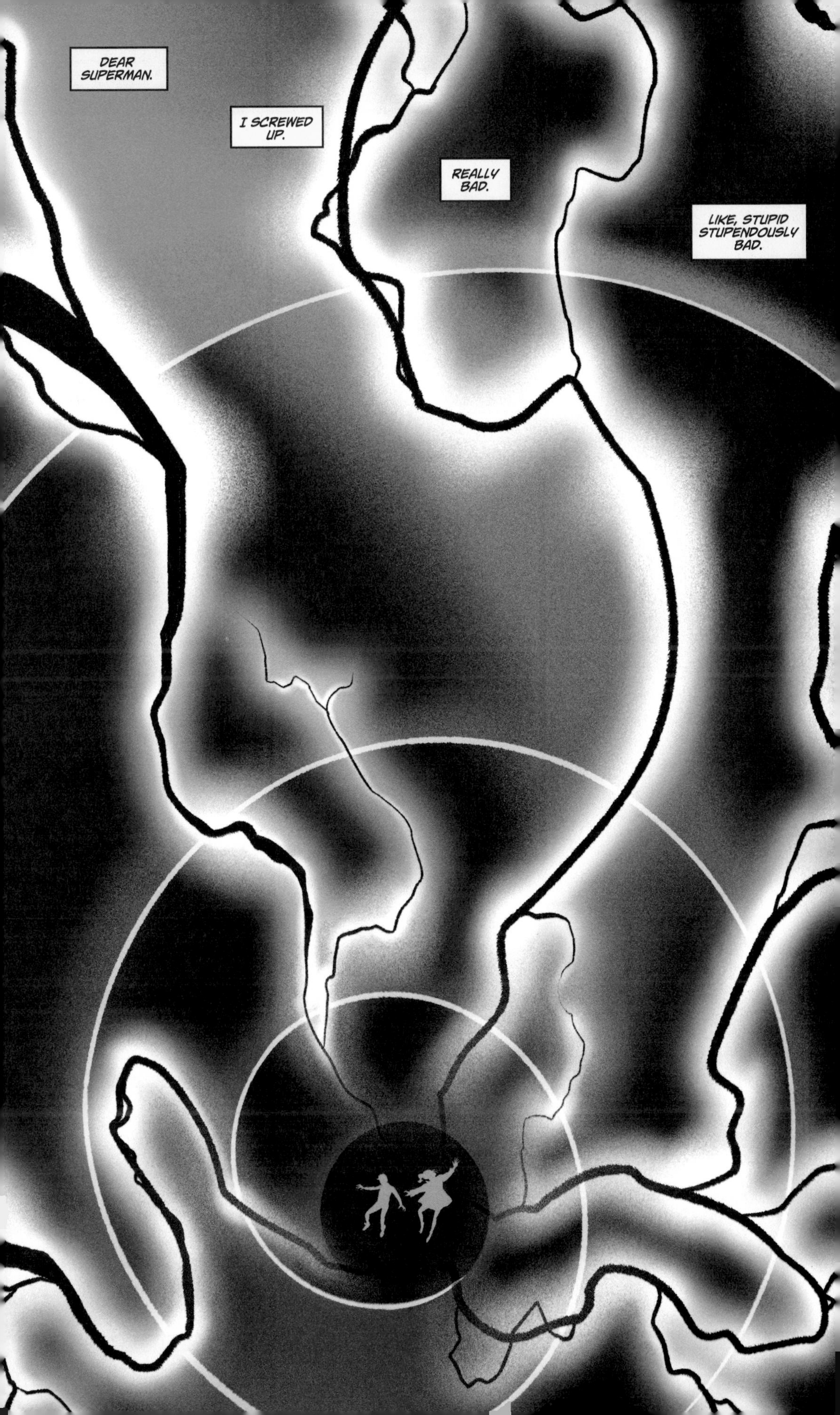
DEAR SUPERMAN.
I SCREWED UP.
REALLY BAD.
LIKE, STUPID STUPENDOUSLY BAD.

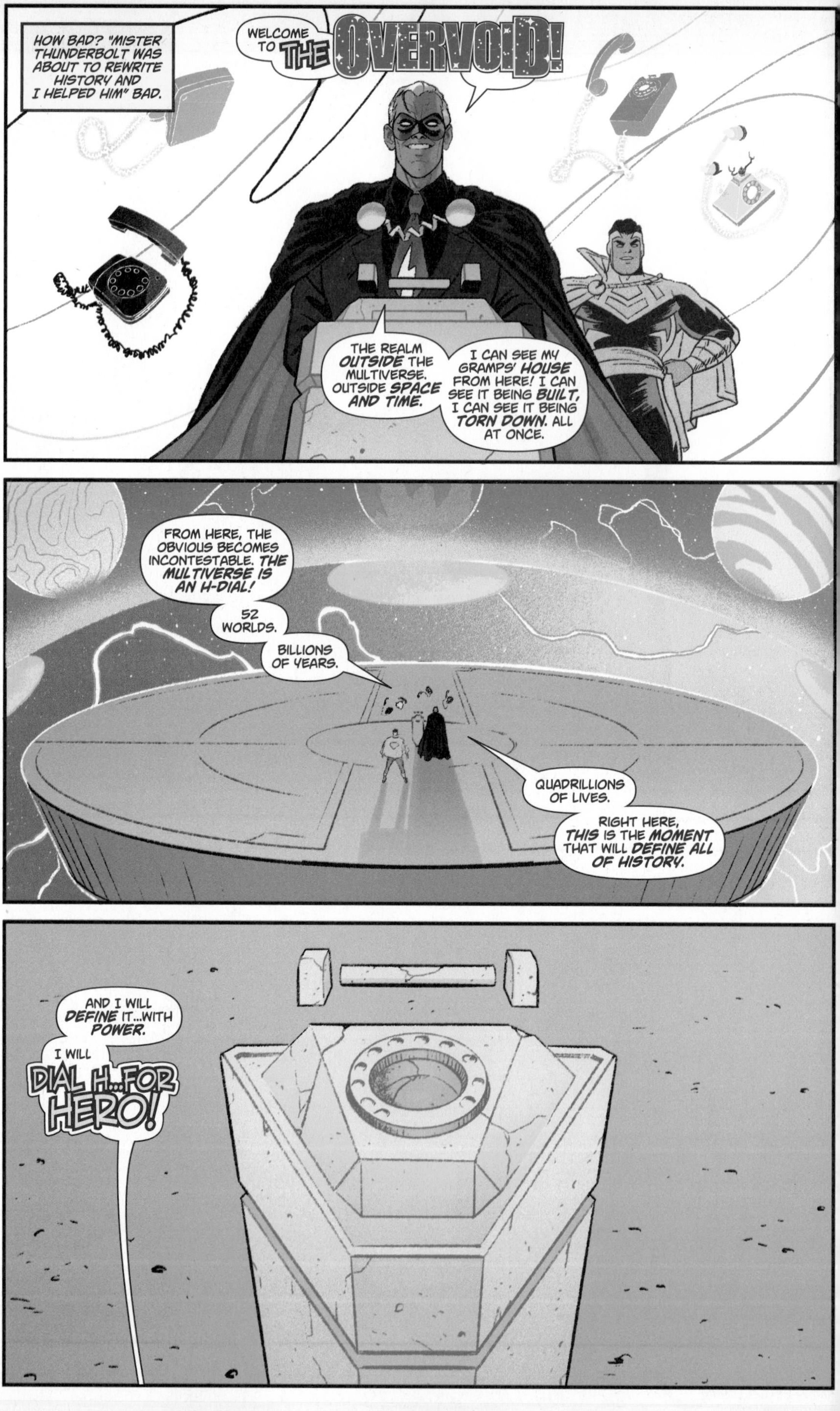

HOW BAD? "MISTER THUNDERBOLT WAS ABOUT TO REWRITE HISTORY AND I HELPED HIM" BAD.
WELCOME TO THE OVERVOID!
THE REALM OUTSIDE THE MULTIVERSE. OUTSIDE SPACE AND TIME.
I CAN SEE MY GRAMPS' HOUSE FROM HERE! I CAN SEE IT BEING BUILT, I CAN SEE IT BEING TORN DOWN. ALL AT ONCE.
FROM HERE, THE OBVIOUS BECOMES INCONTESTABLE. THE MULTIVERSE IS AN H-DIAL!
52 WORLDS.
BILLIONS OF YEARS.
QUADRILLIONS OF LIVES.
RIGHT HERE, THIS IS THE MOMENT THAT WILL DEFINE ALL OF HISTORY.
AND I WILL DEFINE IT...WITH POWER.
I WILL
DIAL H...FOR HERO!

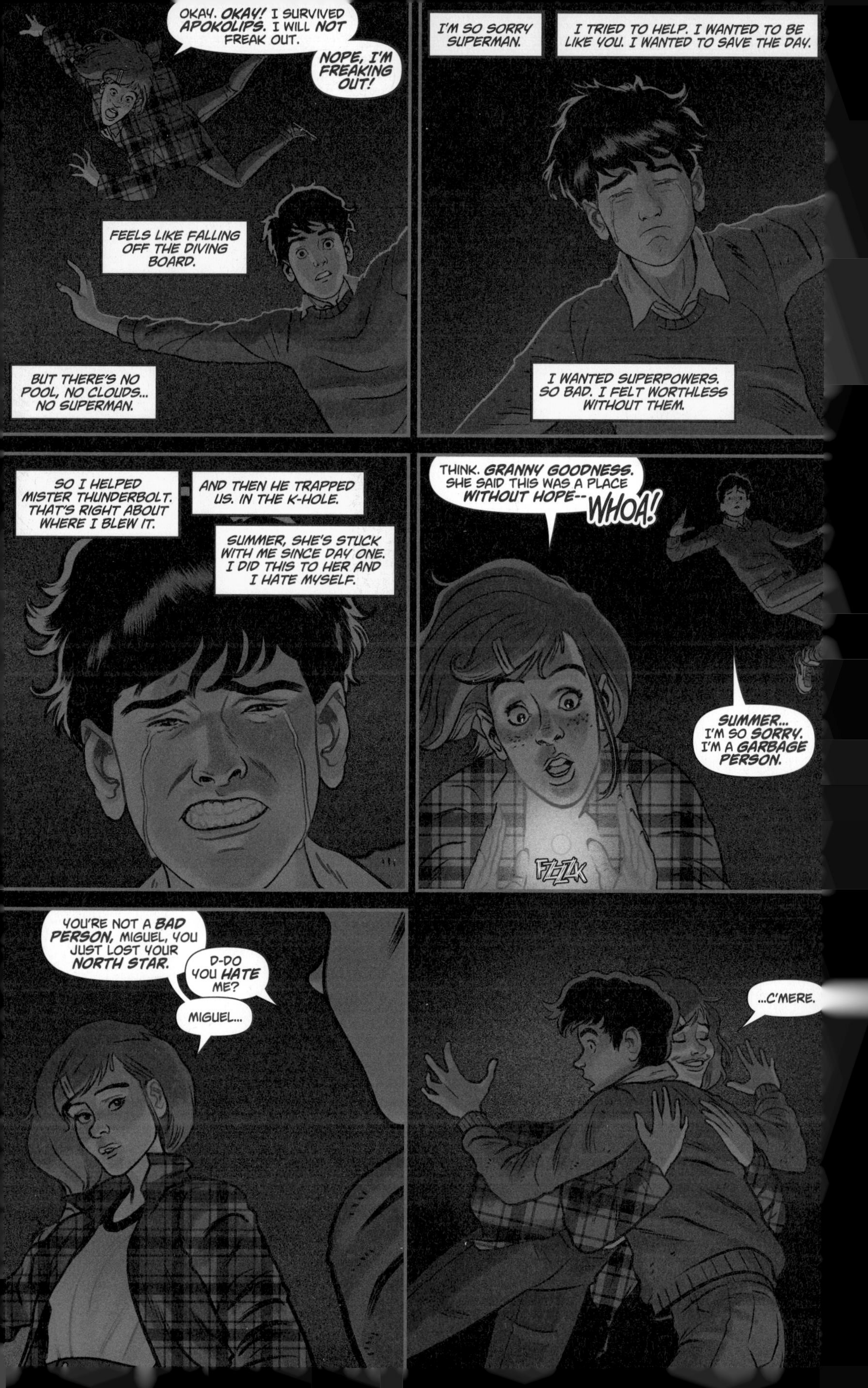
OKAY. OKAY! I SURVIVED APOKOLIPS. I WILL NOT FREAK OUT.
NOPE, I'M FREAKING OUT!
FEELS LIKE FALLING OFF THE DIVING BOARD.
BUT THERE'S NO POOL, NO CLOUDS... NO SUPERMAN.
I'M SO SORRY SUPERMAN.
I TRIED TO HELP. I WANTED TO BE LIKE YOU. I WANTED TO SAVE THE DAY.
I WANTED SUPERPOWERS. SO BAD. I FELT WORTHLESS WITHOUT THEM.
SO I HELPED MISTER THUNDERBOLT. THAT'S RIGHT ABOUT WHERE I BLEW IT.
AND THEN HE TRAPPED US. IN THE K-HOLE.
SUMMER, SHE'S STUCK WITH ME SINCE DAY ONE. I DID THIS TO HER AND I HATE MYSELF.
THINK. GRANNY GOODNESS. SHE SAID THIS WAS A PLACE WITHOUT HOPE--
WHOA!
SUMMER... I'M SO SORRY. I'M A GARBAGE PERSON.
FZZZAK
MIGUEL...
D-DO YOU HATE ME?
YOU'RE NOT A BAD PERSON, MIGUEL, YOU JUST LOST YOUR NORTH STAR.
...C'MERE.

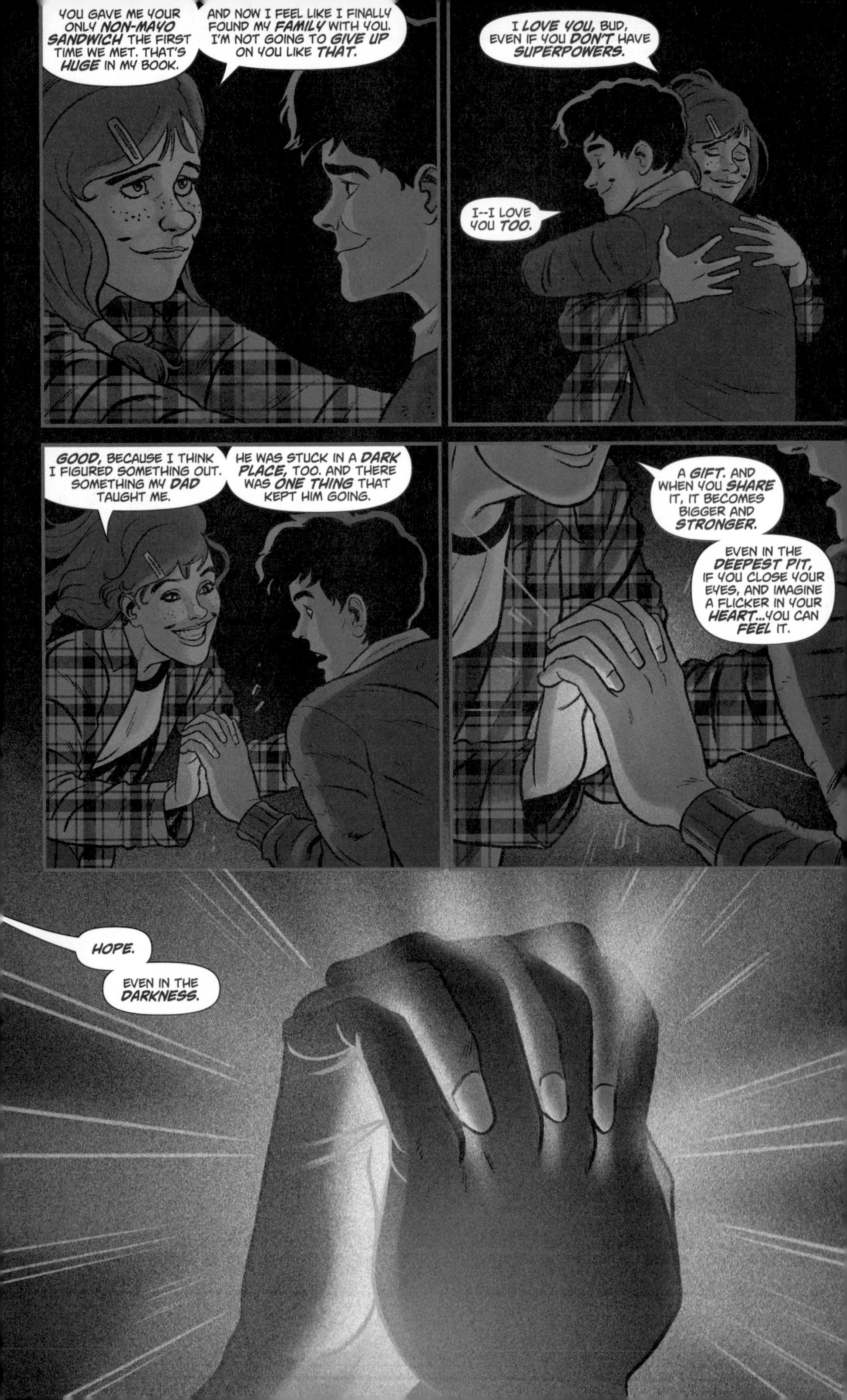
YOU GAVE ME YOUR ONLY NON-MAYO SANDWICH THE FIRST TIME WE MET. THAT'S HUGE IN MY BOOK.
AND NOW I FEEL LIKE I FINALLY FOUND MY FAMILY WITH YOU. I'M NOT GOING TO GIVE UP ON YOU LIKE THAT.
I LOVE YOU, BUD, EVEN IF YOU DON'T HAVE SUPERPOWERS.
I--I LOVE YOU TOO.
GOOD, BECAUSE I THINK I FIGURED SOMETHING OUT. SOMETHING MY DAD TAUGHT ME.
HE WAS STUCK IN A DARK PLACE, TOO. AND THERE WAS ONE THING THAT KEPT HIM GOING.
A GIFT. AND WHEN YOU SHARE IT, IT BECOMES BIGGER AND STRONGER.
EVEN IN THE DEEPEST PIT, IF YOU CLOSE YOUR EYES, AND IMAGINE A FLICKER IN YOUR HEART...YOU CAN FEEL IT.
HOPE.
EVEN IN THE DARKNESS.

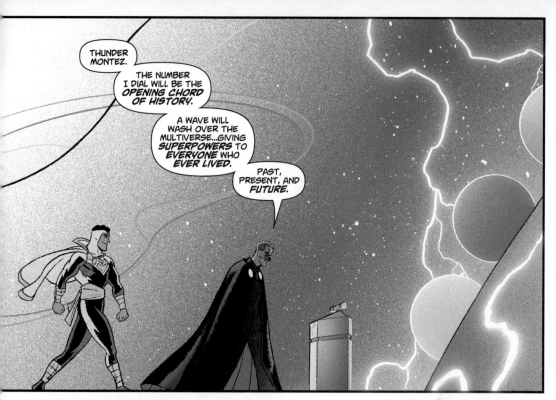

THUNDER MONTEZ.

THE NUMBER I DIAL WILL BE THE *OPENING CHORD* OF HISTORY.

A WAVE WILL WASH OVER THE MULTIVERSE...GIVING *SUPERPOWERS* TO *EVERYONE* WHO *EVER LIVED.*

PAST, PRESENT, AND *FUTURE.*

NO ONE WILL EVER FEEL *PAIN,* OR *SUFFERING...*

...NOT LIKE *GRAMPS.*

ALL I HAVE *FOUGHT* FOR. ALL THAT I HAVE *SACRIFICED.*

SO THAT *NO ONE* WILL EVER *DIE* LIKE *HIM* AGAIN.

ALL I HAVE TO DO... IS *DIAL H...FOR HERO.*

H

E

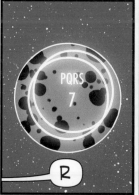

R

STOP!

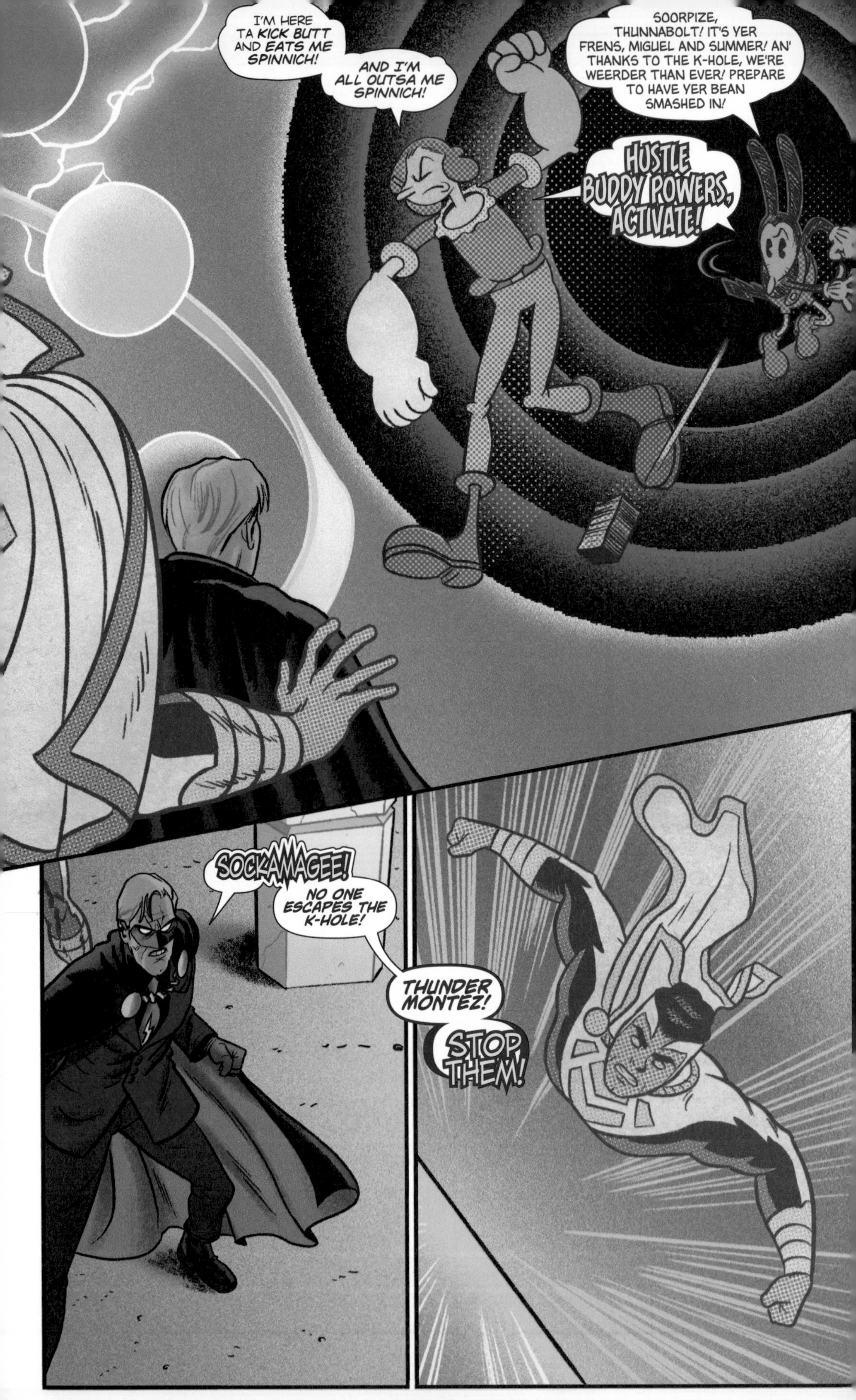
I'M HERE TA KICK BUTT AND EATS ME SPINNICH!
AND I'M ALL OUTSA ME SPINNICH!
SOORPIZE, THUNNABOLT! IT'S YER FRENS, MIGUEL AND SUMMER! AN' THANKS TO THE K-HOLE, WE'RE WEERDER THAN EVER! PREPARE TO HAVE YER BEAN SMASHED IN!
HUSTLE BUDDY POWERS, ACTIVATE!
SOCKAMAGEE!
NO ONE ESCAPES THE K-HOLE!
THUNDER MONTEZ!
STOP THEM!

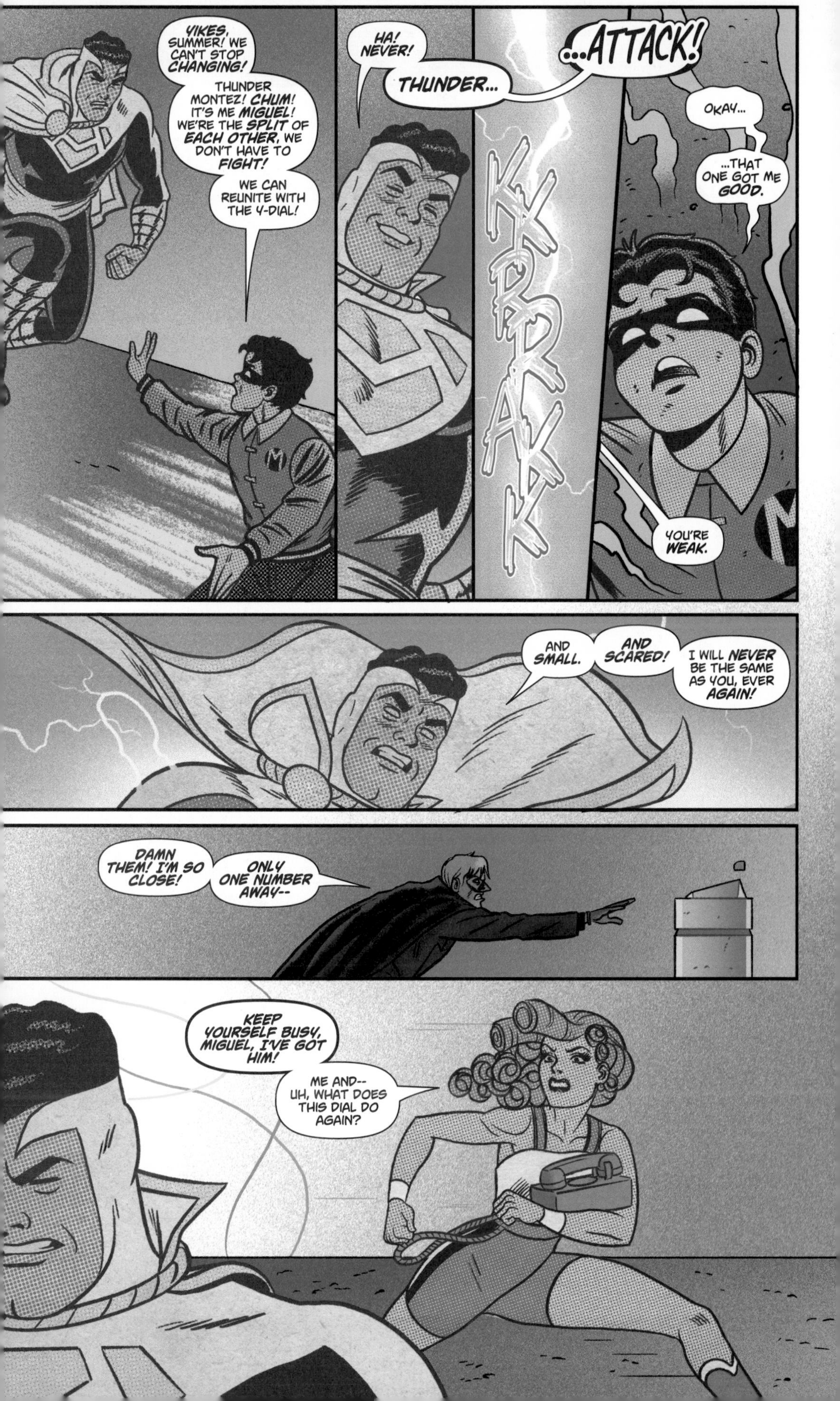
YIKES, SUMMER! WE CAN'T STOP CHANGING!
THUNDER MONTEZ! CHUM! IT'S ME MIGUEL! WE'RE THE SPLIT OF EACH OTHER, WE DON'T HAVE TO FIGHT!
WE CAN REUNITE WITH THE 4-DIAL!
HA! NEVER!
THUNDER...
...ATTACK!
KRAKAKAK
OKAY...
...THAT ONE GOT ME GOOD.
YOU'RE WEAK.
AND SMALL.
AND SCARED!
I WILL NEVER BE THE SAME AS YOU, EVER AGAIN!
DAMN THEM! I'M SO CLOSE!
ONLY ONE NUMBER AWAY--
KEEP YOURSELF BUSY, MIGUEL, I'VE GOT HIM!
ME AND-- UH, WHAT DOES THIS DIAL DO AGAIN?

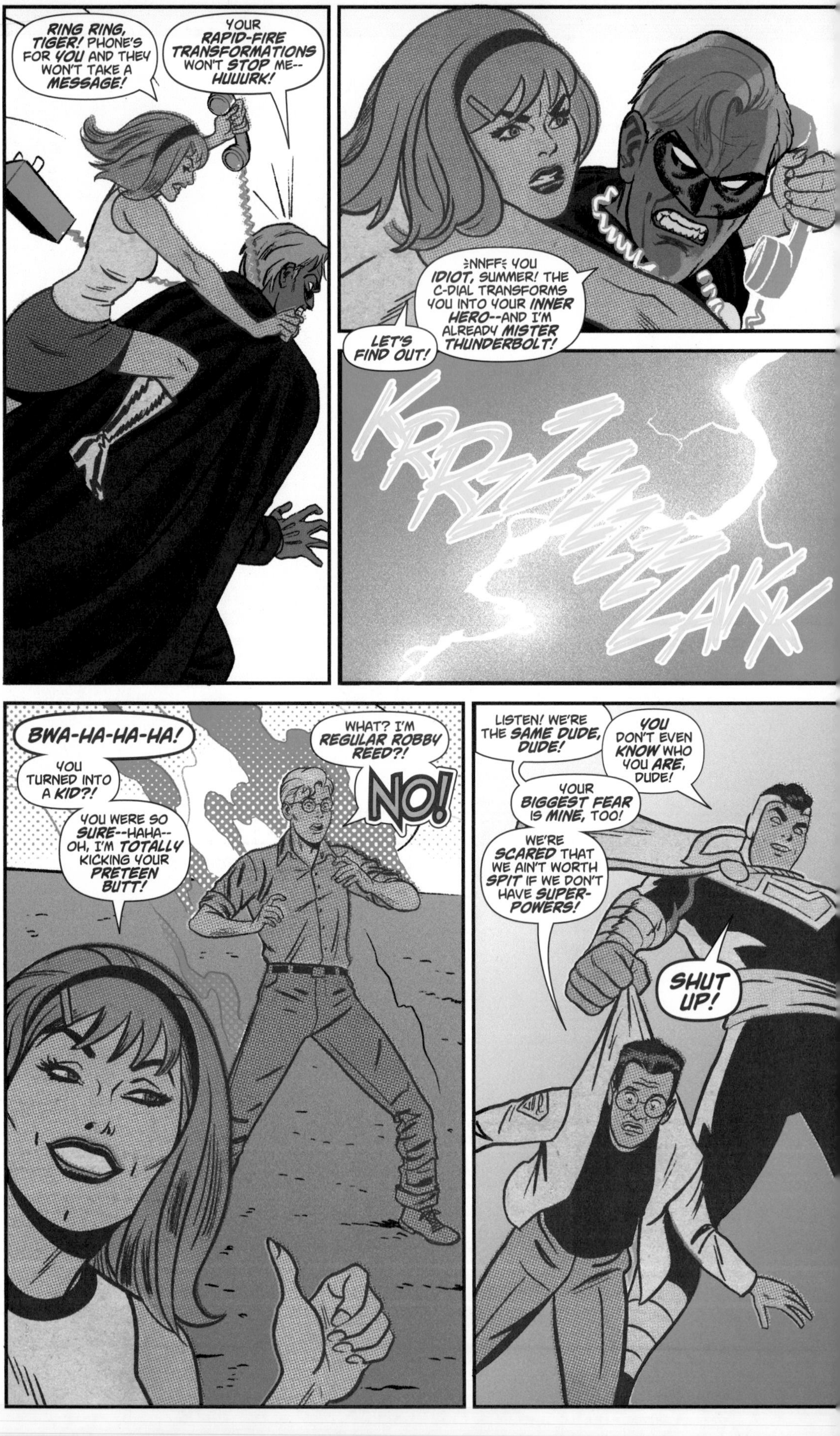

RING RING, TIGER! PHONE'S FOR YOU AND THEY WON'T TAKE A MESSAGE!
YOUR RAPID-FIRE TRANSFORMATIONS WON'T STOP ME-- HUUURK!
NNFF YOU IDIOT, SUMMER! THE C-DIAL TRANSFORMS YOU INTO YOUR INNER HERO--AND I'M ALREADY MISTER THUNDERBOLT!
LET'S FIND OUT!
KRRZZZZZZZAKK
BWA-HA-HA-HA!
YOU TURNED INTO A KID?!
YOU WERE SO SURE--HAHA-- OH, I'M TOTALLY KICKING YOUR PRETEEN BUTT!
WHAT? I'M REGULAR ROBBY REED?!
NO!
LISTEN! WE'RE THE SAME DUDE, DUDE!
YOU DON'T EVEN KNOW WHO YOU ARE, DUDE!
YOUR BIGGEST FEAR IS MINE, TOO!
WE'RE SCARED THAT WE AIN'T WORTH SPIT IF WE DON'T HAVE SUPER-POWERS!
SHUT UP!

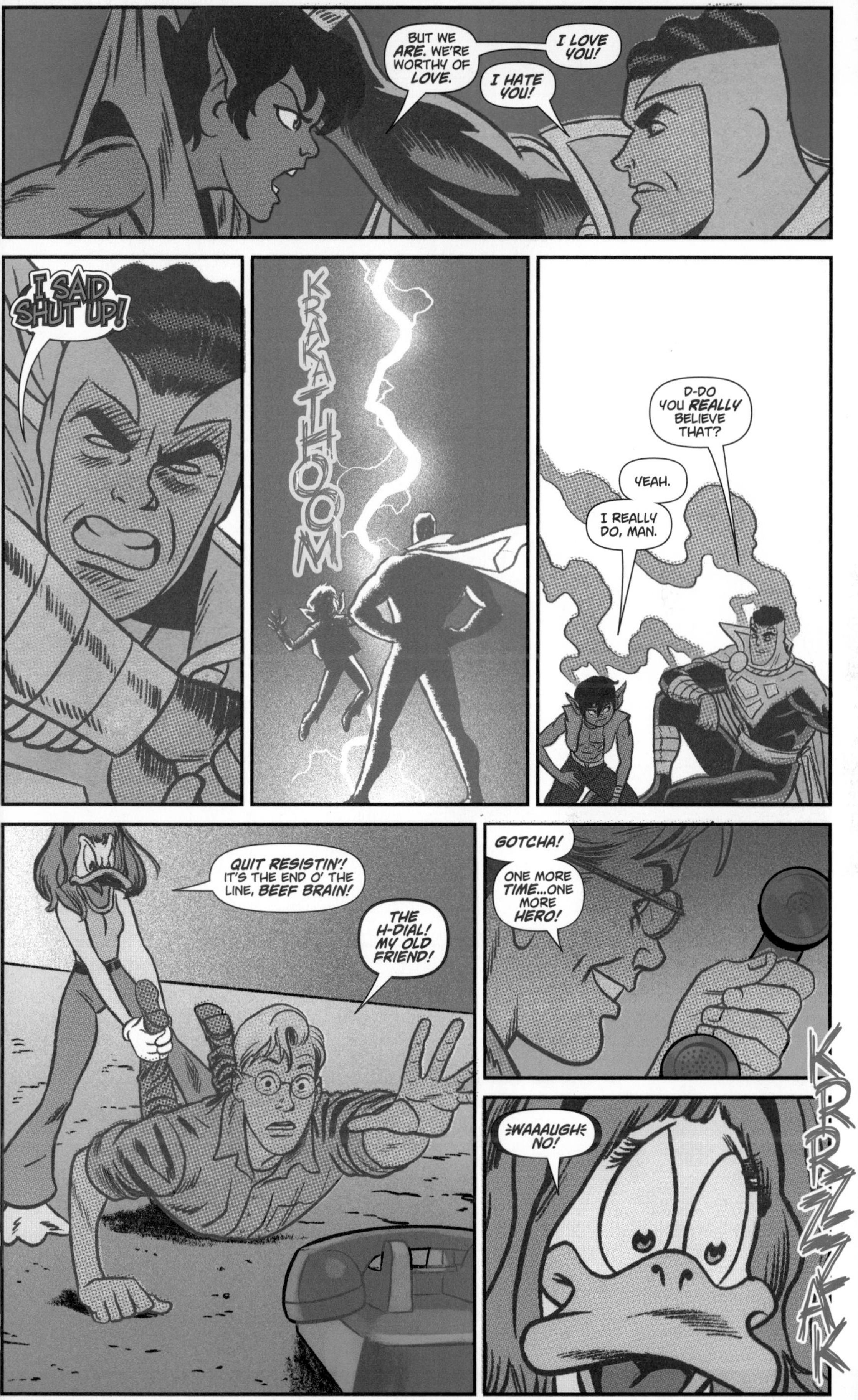

BUT WE ARE. WE'RE WORTHY OF LOVE.
I LOVE YOU!
I HATE YOU!
I SAID SHUT UP!
KRAKATHOOOM
D-DO YOU REALLY BELIEVE THAT?
YEAH.
I REALLY DO, MAN.
QUIT RESISTIN'! IT'S THE END O' THE LINE, BEEF BRAIN!
THE H-DIAL! MY OLD FRIEND!
GOTCHA!
ONE MORE TIME...ONE MORE HERO!
KRRZZAK
WAAAUGH NO!

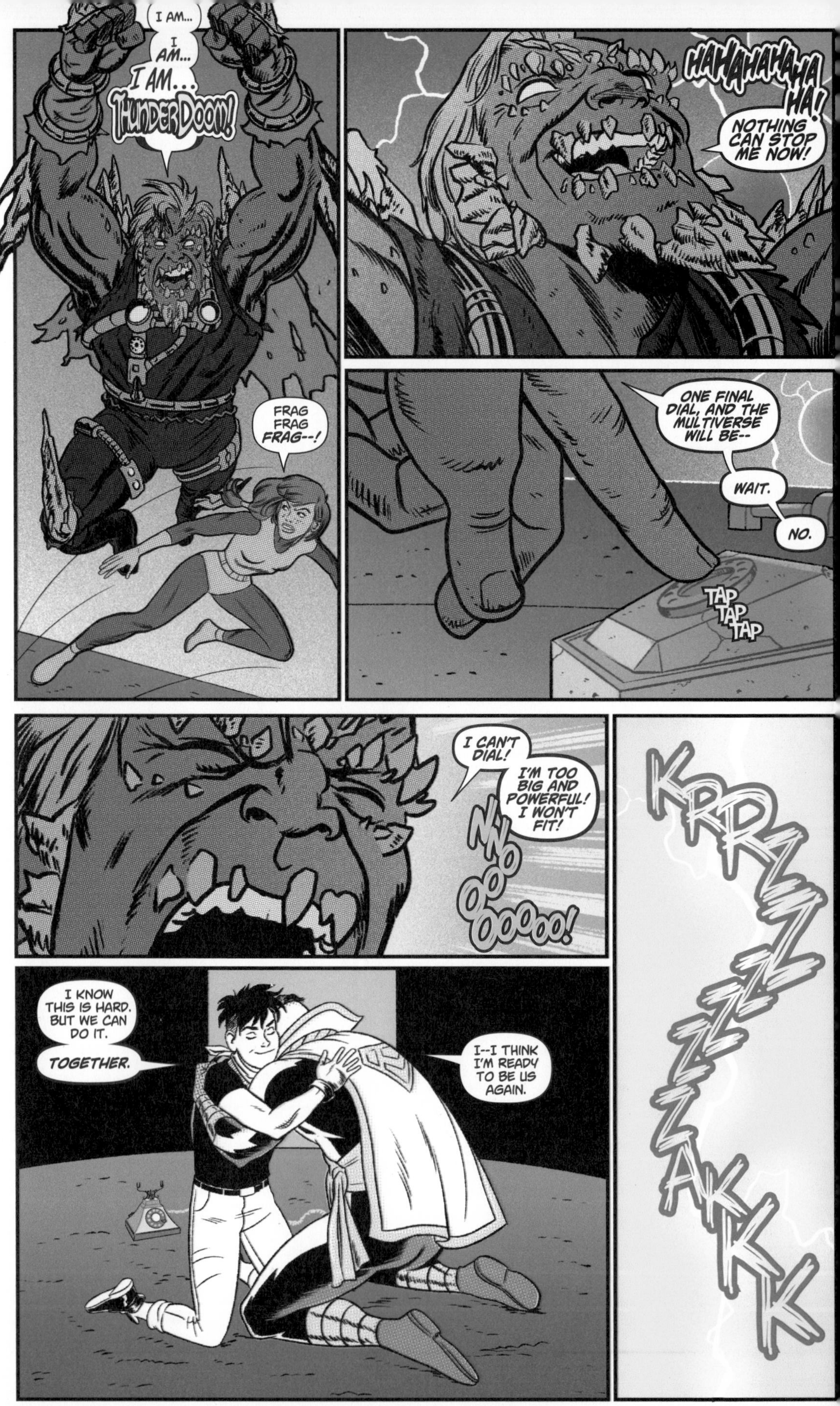
I AM...
I AM...
I AM... THUNDERDOOM!
FRAG FRAG FRAG--!
HAHAHAHAHAHA HA!
NOTHING CAN STOP ME NOW!
ONE FINAL DIAL, AND THE MULTIVERSE WILL BE--
WAIT.
NO.
TAP TAP TAP
I CAN'T DIAL!
I'M TOO BIG AND POWERFUL! I WON'T FIT!
NNOOOOOOOOO!
KRRZZZZZAKKK
I KNOW THIS IS HARD. BUT WE CAN DO IT.
TOGETHER.
I--I THINK I'M READY TO BE US AGAIN.

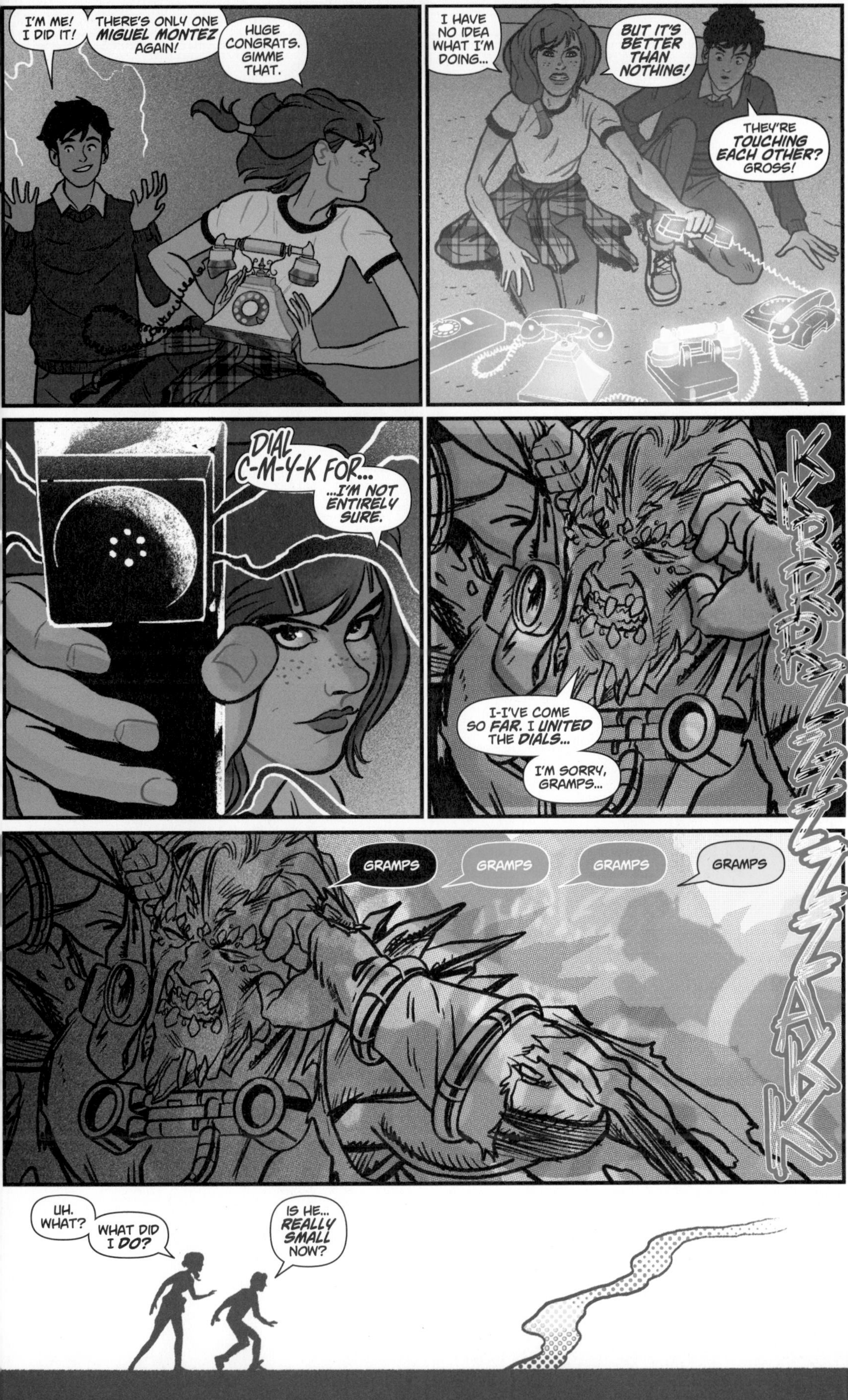
I'M ME! I DID IT!
THERE'S ONLY ONE MIGUEL MONTEZ AGAIN!
HUGE CONGRATS. GIMME THAT.
I HAVE NO IDEA WHAT I'M DOING...
BUT IT'S BETTER THAN NOTHING!
THEY'RE TOUCHING EACH OTHER? GROSS!
DIAL C-M-Y-K FOR...
...I'M NOT ENTIRELY SURE.
I-I'VE COME SO FAR. I UNITED THE DIALS...
I'M SORRY, GRAMPS...
KRRZZZZAAKK
GRAMPS
GRAMPS
GRAMPS
GRAMPS
UH. WHAT?
WHAT DID I DO?
IS HE... REALLY SMALL NOW?

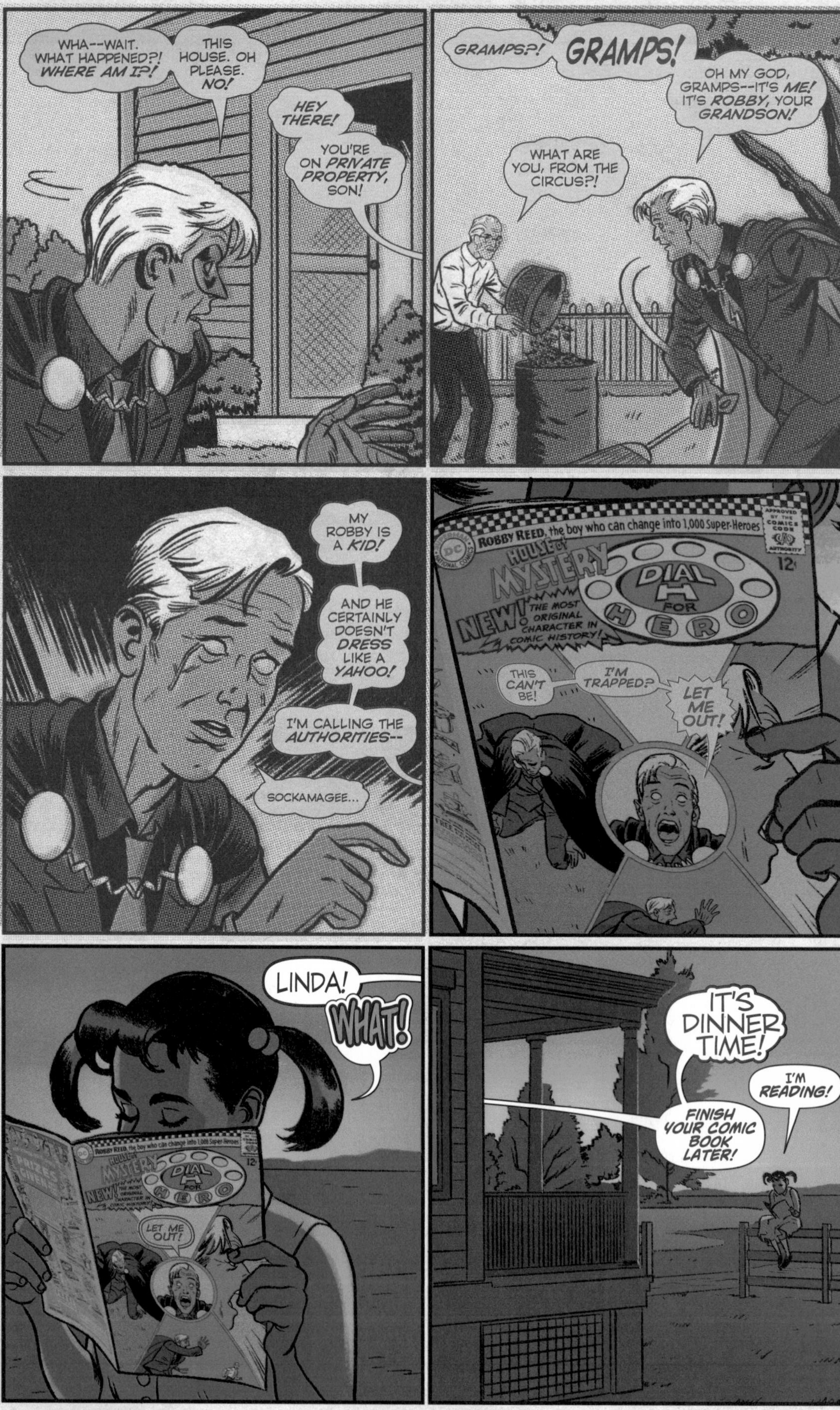
WHA--WAIT. WHAT HAPPENED?! WHERE AM I?!
THIS HOUSE. OH PLEASE. NO!
HEY THERE!
YOU'RE ON PRIVATE PROPERTY, SON!
GRAMPS?!
GRAMPS!
OH MY GOD, GRAMPS--IT'S ME! IT'S ROBBY, YOUR GRANDSON!
WHAT ARE YOU, FROM THE CIRCUS?!
MY ROBBY IS A KID!
AND HE CERTAINLY DOESN'T DRESS LIKE A YAHOO!
I'M CALLING THE AUTHORITIES--
SOCKAMAGEE...
ROBBY REED, the boy who can change into 1,000 Super-Heroes
HOUSE OF MYSTERY
DIAL H FOR HERO
NEW! THE MOST ORIGINAL CHARACTER IN COMIC HISTORY!
12¢
APPROVED BY THE COMICS CODE AUTHORITY
THIS CAN'T BE!
I'M TRAPPED?
LET ME OUT!
LINDA!
WHAT!
LET ME OUT!
IT'S DINNER TIME!
I'M READING!
FINISH YOUR COMIC BOOK LATER!

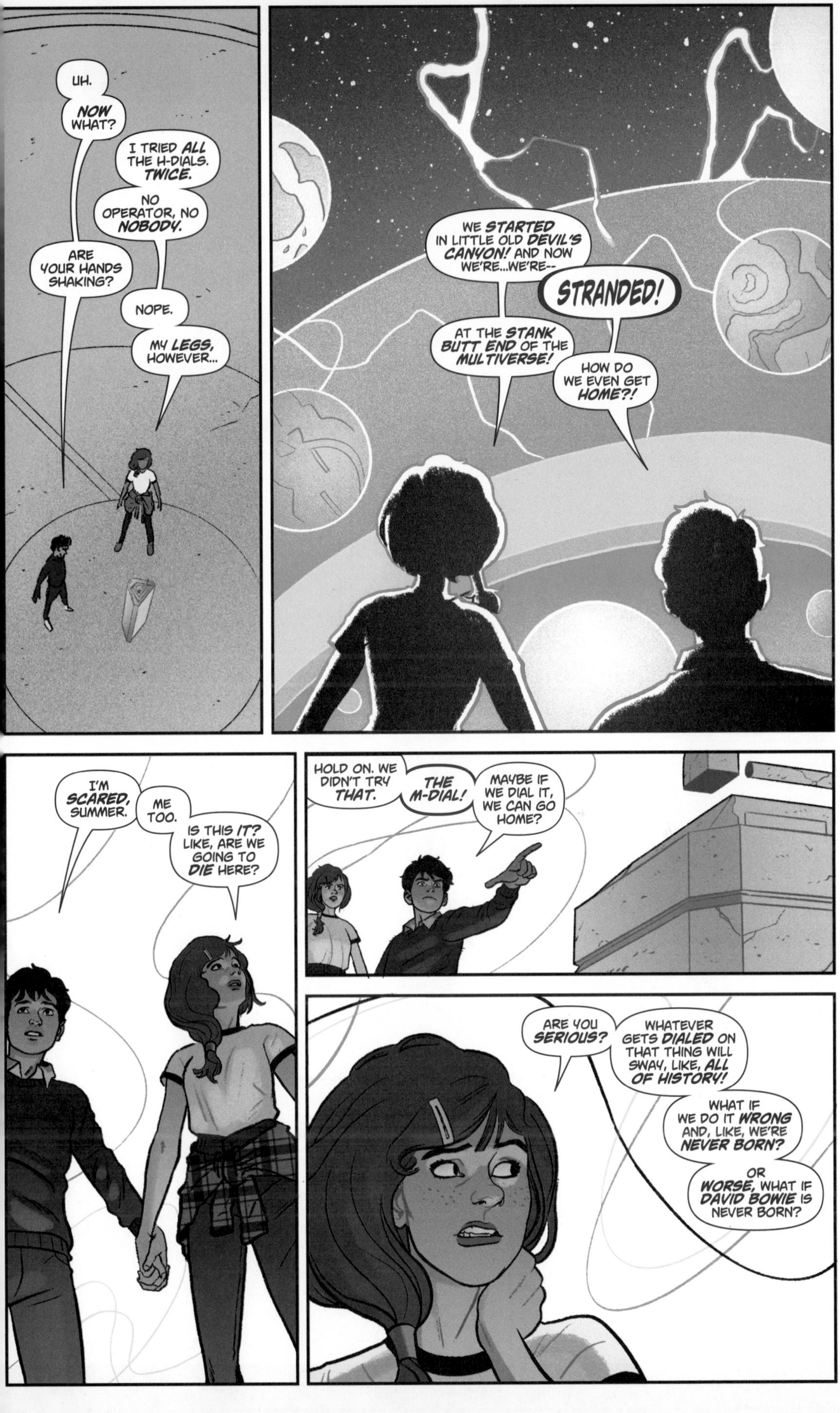
UH.
NOW WHAT?
I TRIED ALL THE H-DIALS. TWICE.
NO OPERATOR, NO NOBODY.
ARE YOUR HANDS SHAKING?
NOPE.
MY LEGS, HOWEVER...
WE STARTED IN LITTLE OLD DEVIL'S CANYON! AND NOW WE'RE...WE'RE--
STRANDED!
AT THE STANK BUTT END OF THE MULTIVERSE!
HOW DO WE EVEN GET HOME?!
I'M SCARED, SUMMER.
ME TOO.
IS THIS IT? LIKE, ARE WE GOING TO DIE HERE?
HOLD ON. WE DIDN'T TRY THAT.
THE M-DIAL!
MAYBE IF WE DIAL IT, WE CAN GO HOME?
ARE YOU SERIOUS?
WHATEVER GETS DIALED ON THAT THING WILL SWAY, LIKE, ALL OF HISTORY!
WHAT IF WE DO IT WRONG AND, LIKE, WE'RE NEVER BORN?
OR WORSE, WHAT IF DAVID BOWIE IS NEVER BORN?

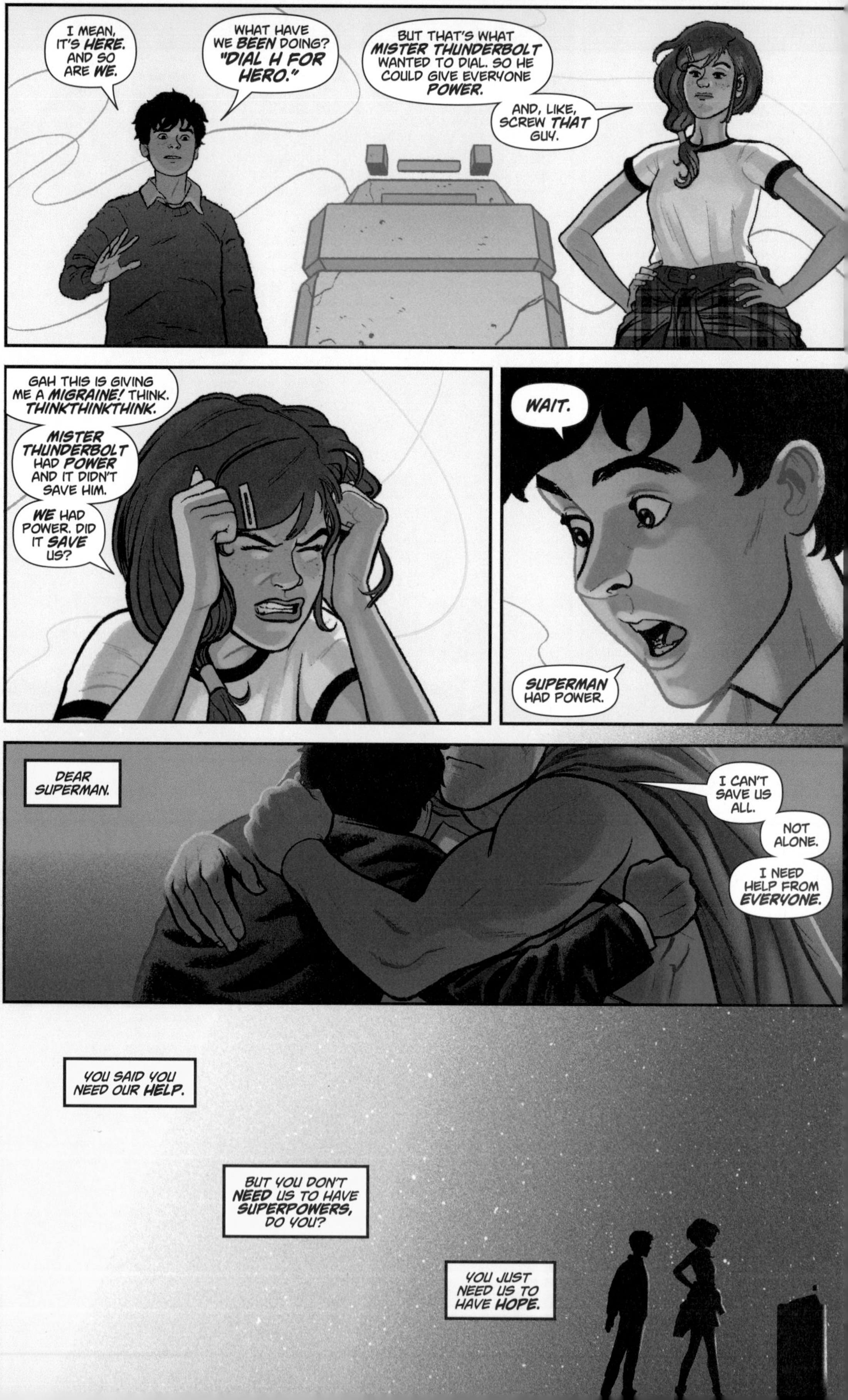
I MEAN, IT'S **HERE.** AND SO ARE **WE.**
WHAT HAVE WE **BEEN** DOING? **"DIAL H FOR HERO."**
BUT THAT'S WHAT **MISTER THUNDERBOLT** WANTED TO DIAL. SO HE COULD GIVE EVERYONE **POWER.**
AND, LIKE, SCREW **THAT** GUY.
GAH THIS IS GIVING ME A **MIGRAINE!** THINK. **THINKTHINKTHINK.**
MISTER THUNDERBOLT HAD **POWER** AND IT DIDN'T SAVE HIM.
WE HAD POWER. DID IT **SAVE** US?
WAIT.
SUPERMAN HAD POWER.
DEAR SUPERMAN.
I CAN'T SAVE US ALL.
NOT ALONE.
I NEED HELP FROM **EVERYONE.**
YOU SAID YOU NEED OUR **HELP.**
BUT YOU DON'T **NEED** US TO HAVE **SUPERPOWERS,** DO YOU?
YOU JUST NEED US TO HAVE **HOPE.**

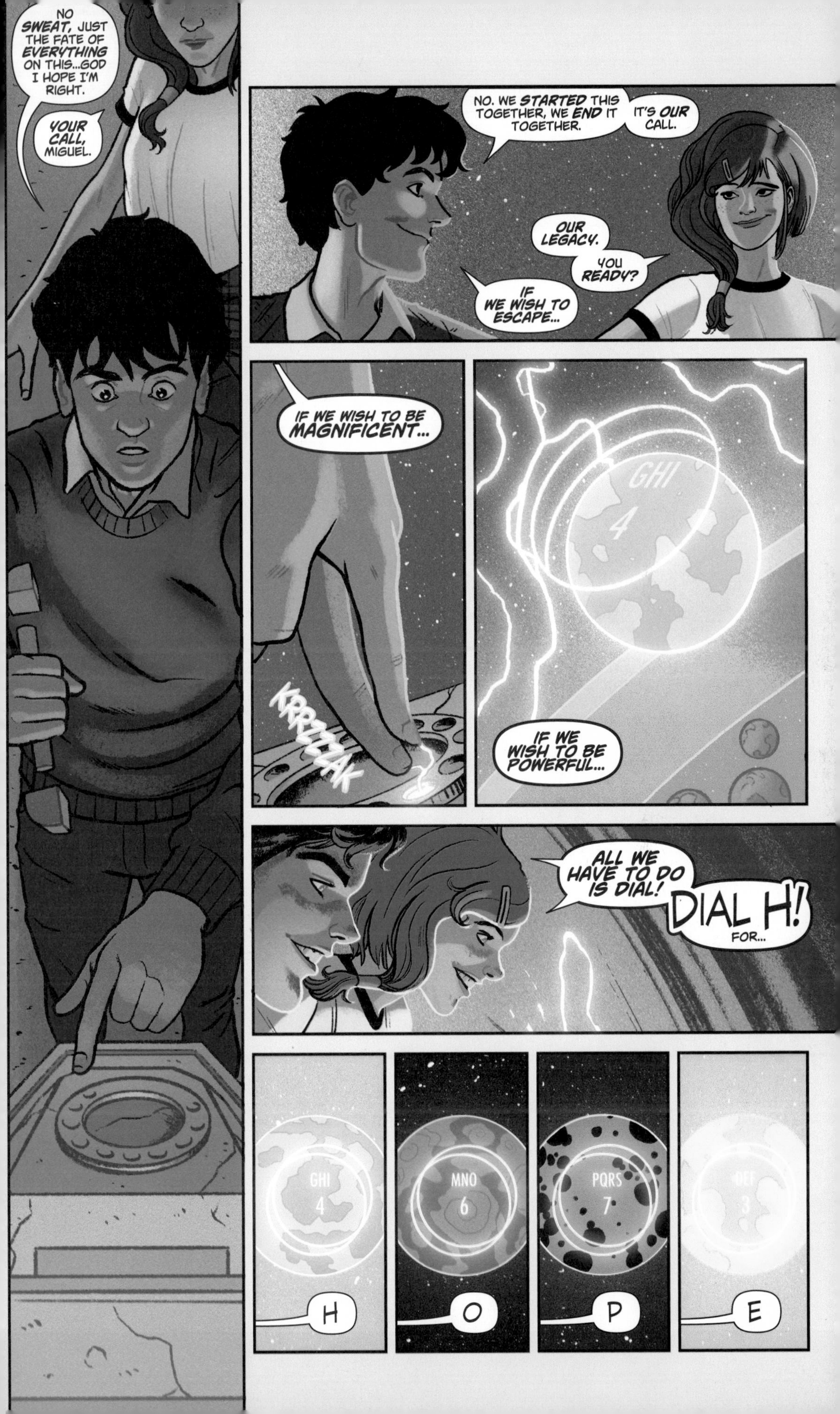

NO SWEAT, JUST THE FATE OF EVERYTHING ON THIS...GOD I HOPE I'M RIGHT.
YOUR CALL, MIGUEL.
NO. WE STARTED THIS TOGETHER, WE END IT TOGETHER.
IT'S OUR CALL.
OUR LEGACY.
YOU READY?
IF WE WISH TO ESCAPE...
IF WE WISH TO BE MAGNIFICENT...
KRRZZZAK
GHI 4
IF WE WISH TO BE POWERFUL...
ALL WE HAVE TO DO IS DIAL!
DIAL H!
FOR...
GHI 4
H
MNO 6
O
PQRS 7
P
DEF 3
E

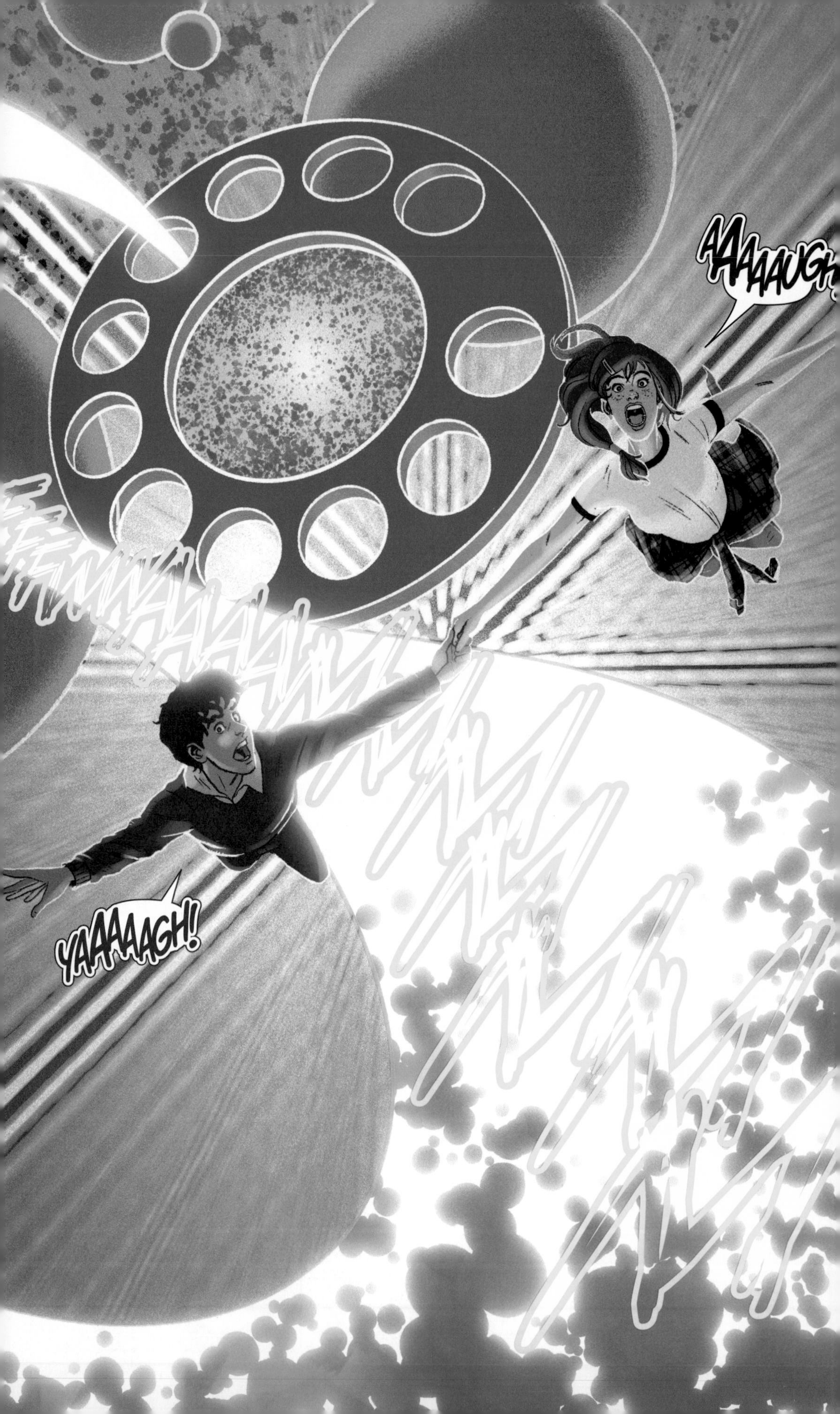
AAAAAUGH
YAAAAGH!

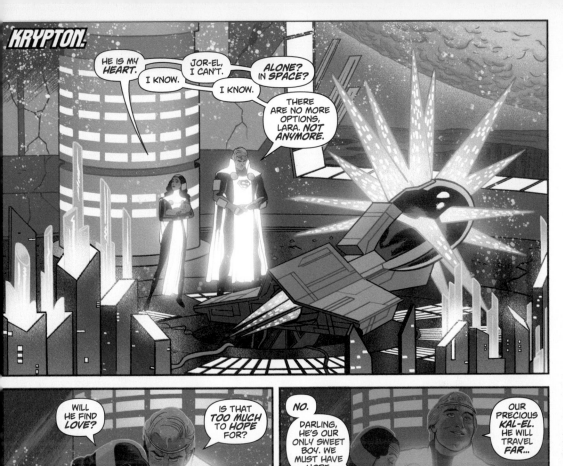

HE IS MY HEART.

I KNOW.

JOR-EL, I CAN'T.

ALONE? IN SPACE?

I KNOW.

THERE ARE NO MORE OPTIONS, LARA. *NOT ANYMORE.*

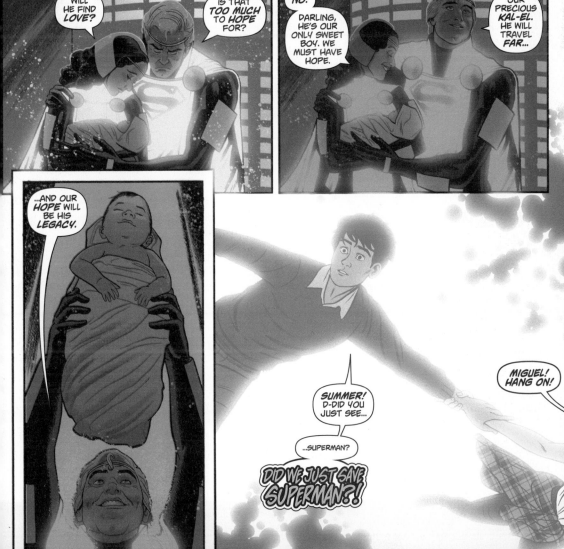

WILL HE FIND *LOVE?*

IS THAT *TOO MUCH* TO *HOPE* FOR?

NO. DARLING, HE'S OUR ONLY SWEET BOY. WE MUST HAVE HOPE.

OUR PRECIOUS *KAL-EL.* HE WILL TRAVEL *FAR...*

...AND OUR *HOPE* WILL BE HIS *LEGACY.*

SUMMER! D-DID YOU JUST SEE...

...SUPERMAN?

MIGUEL! HANG ON!

DID WE JUST SAVE SUPERMAN?!

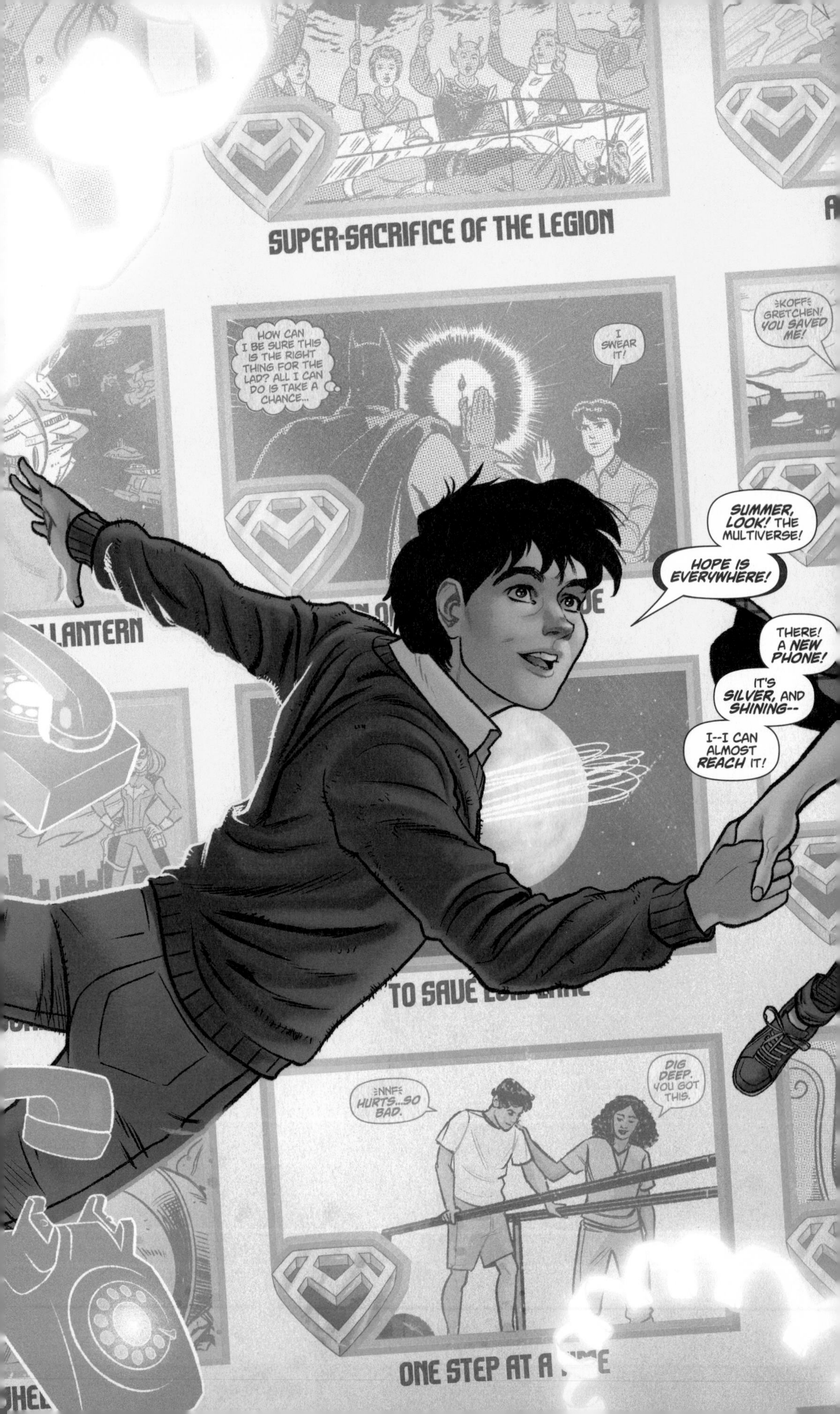
SUPER-SACRIFICE OF THE LEGION
HOW CAN I BE SURE THIS IS THE RIGHT THING FOR THE LAD? ALL I CAN DO IS TAKE A CHANCE...
I SWEAR IT!
KOFF GRETCHEN! YOU SAVED ME!
LANTERN
SUMMER, LOOK! THE MULTIVERSE!
HOPE IS EVERYWHERE!
THERE! A NEW PHONE!
IT'S SILVER, AND SHINING--
I--I CAN ALMOST REACH IT!
TO SAVE
NNF HURTS...SO BAD.
DIG DEEP. YOU GOT THIS.
ONE STEP AT A

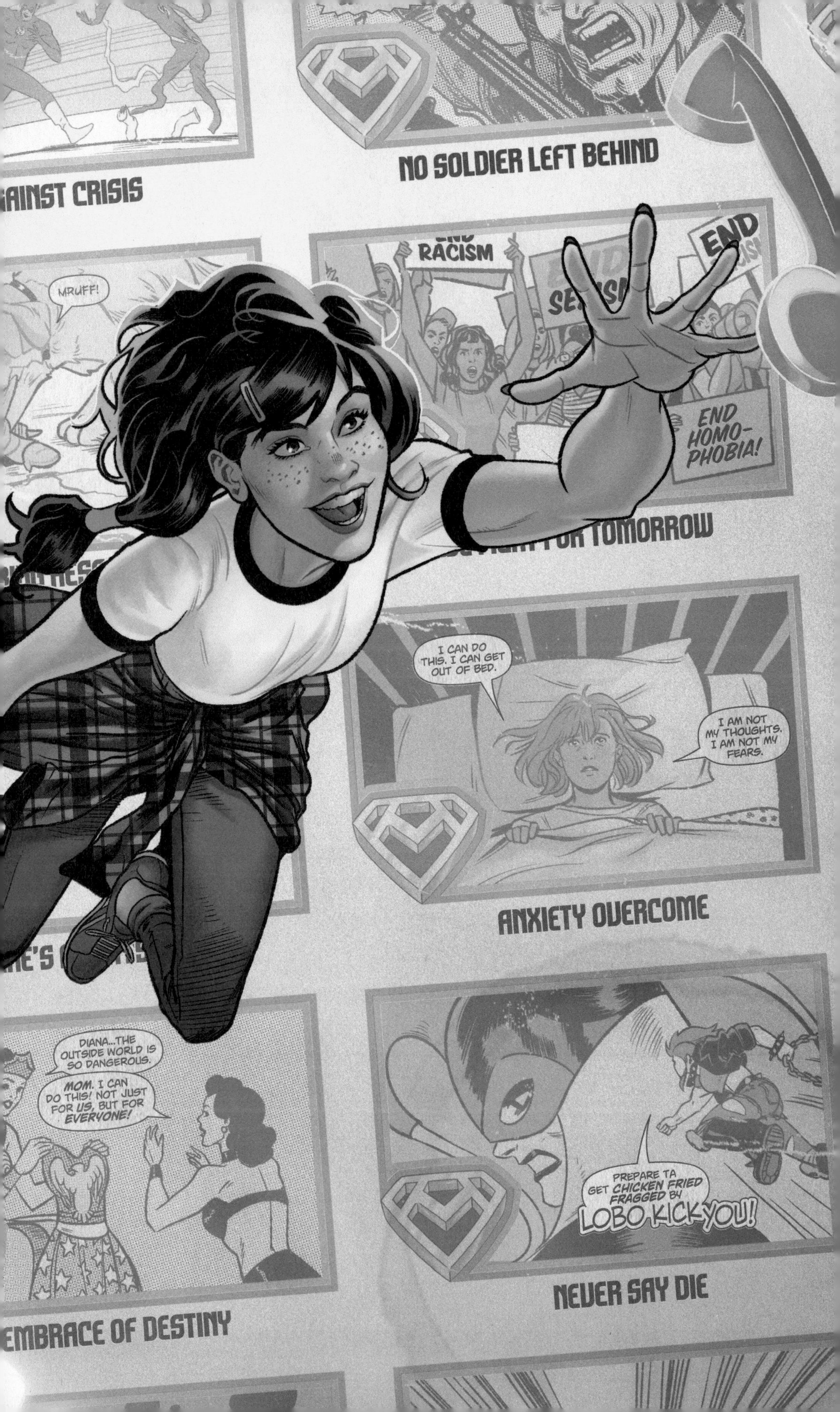
NO SOLDIER LEFT BEHIND
AINST CRISIS
MRUFF!
RACISM
END
SEXISM
END HOMO-PHOBIA!
TOMORROW
I CAN DO THIS. I CAN GET OUT OF BED.
I AM NOT MY THOUGHTS. I AM NOT MY FEARS.
ANXIETY OVERCOME
DIANA...THE OUTSIDE WORLD IS SO DANGEROUS.
MOM. I CAN DO THIS! NOT JUST FOR US, BUT FOR EVERYONE!
PREPARE TA GET CHICKEN FRIED FRAGGED BY LOBO KICK YOU!
NEVER SAY DIE
EMBRACE OF DESTINY

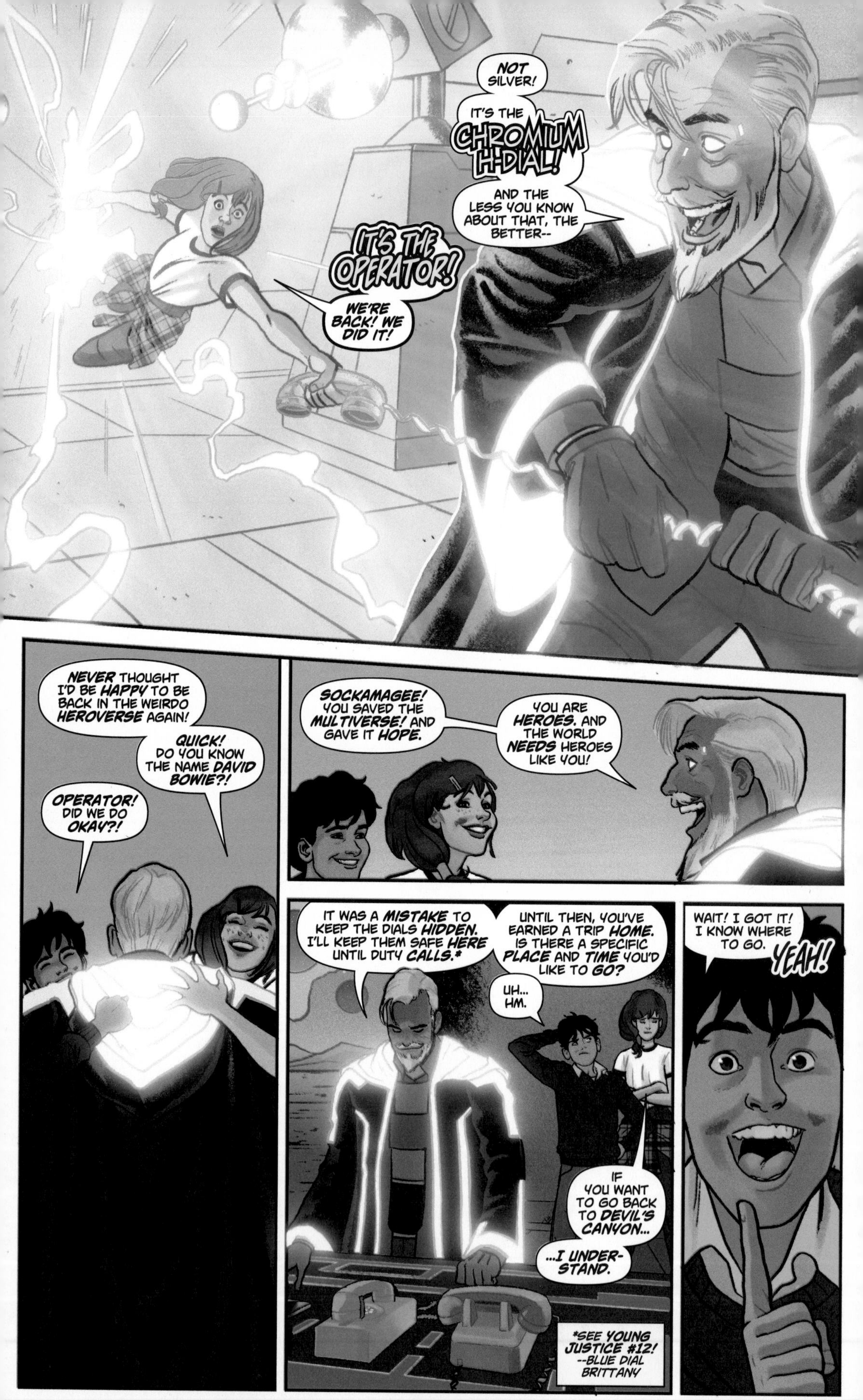
NOT SILVER!
IT'S THE CHROMIUM H-DIAL!
AND THE LESS YOU KNOW ABOUT THAT, THE BETTER--
IT'S THE OPERATOR!
WE'RE BACK! WE DID IT!
NEVER THOUGHT I'D BE HAPPY TO BE BACK IN THE WEIRDO HEROVERSE AGAIN!
QUICK! DO YOU KNOW THE NAME DAVID BOWIE?!
OPERATOR! DID WE DO OKAY?!
SOCKAMAGEE! YOU SAVED THE MULTIVERSE! AND GAVE IT HOPE.
YOU ARE HEROES. AND THE WORLD NEEDS HEROES LIKE YOU!
IT WAS A MISTAKE TO KEEP THE DIALS HIDDEN. I'LL KEEP THEM SAFE HERE UNTIL DUTY CALLS.*
UNTIL THEN, YOU'VE EARNED A TRIP HOME. IS THERE A SPECIFIC PLACE AND TIME YOU'D LIKE TO GO?
UH... HM.
IF YOU WANT TO GO BACK TO DEVIL'S CANYON...
...I UNDERSTAND.
*SEE YOUNG JUSTICE #12! --BLUE DIAL BRITTANY
WAIT! I GOT IT! I KNOW WHERE TO GO.
YEAH!

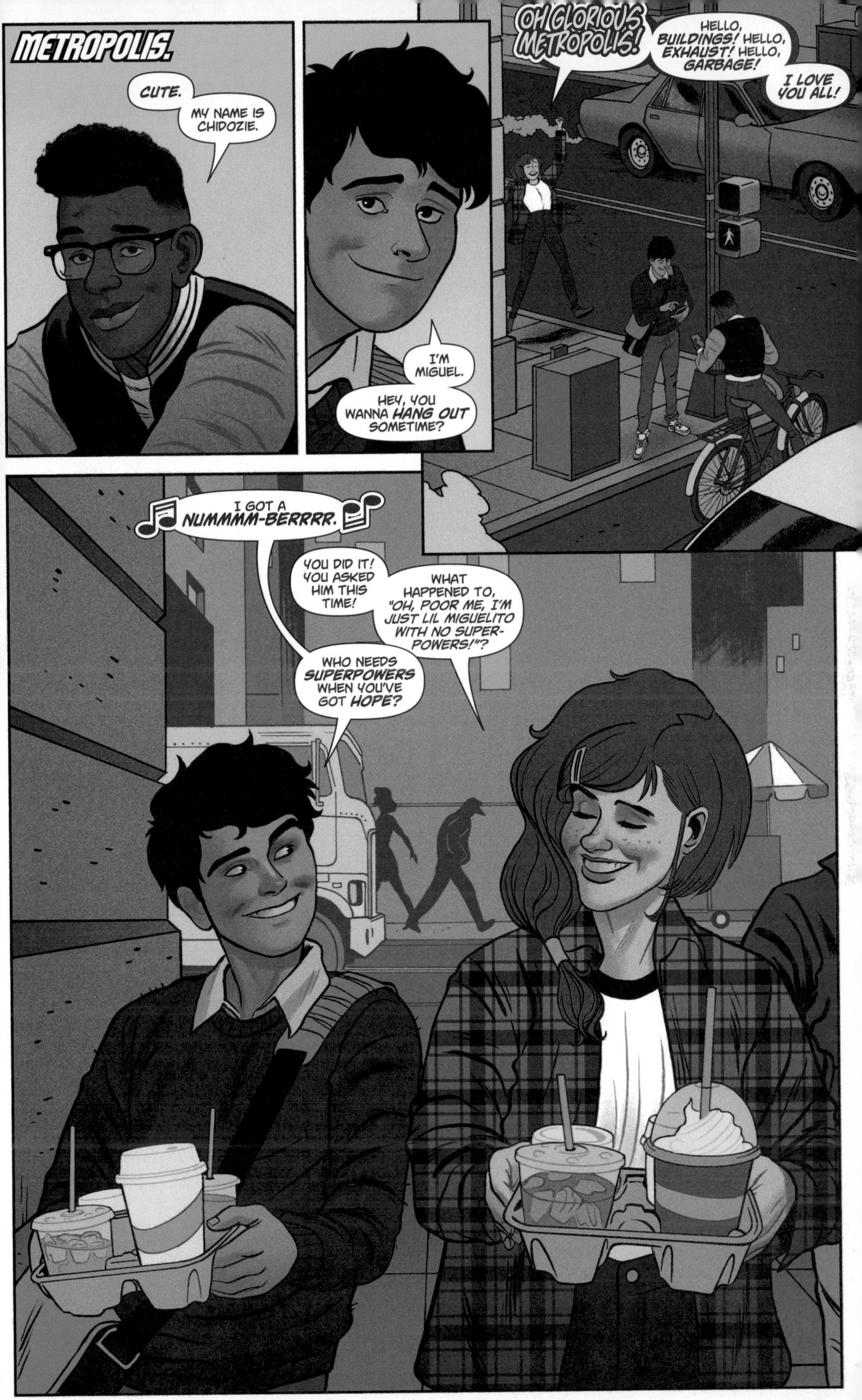

METROPOLIS.
CUTE.
MY NAME IS CHIDOZIE.
I'M MIGUEL.
HEY, YOU WANNA HANG OUT SOMETIME?
OH GLORIOUS METROPOLIS!
HELLO, BUILDINGS! HELLO, EXHAUST! HELLO, GARBAGE!
I LOVE YOU ALL!
I GOT A NUMMMM-BERRRR.
YOU DID IT! YOU ASKED HIM THIS TIME!
WHAT HAPPENED TO, "OH, POOR ME, I'M JUST LIL MIGUELITO WITH NO SUPER-POWERS!"?
WHO NEEDS SUPERPOWERS WHEN YOU'VE GOT HOPE?

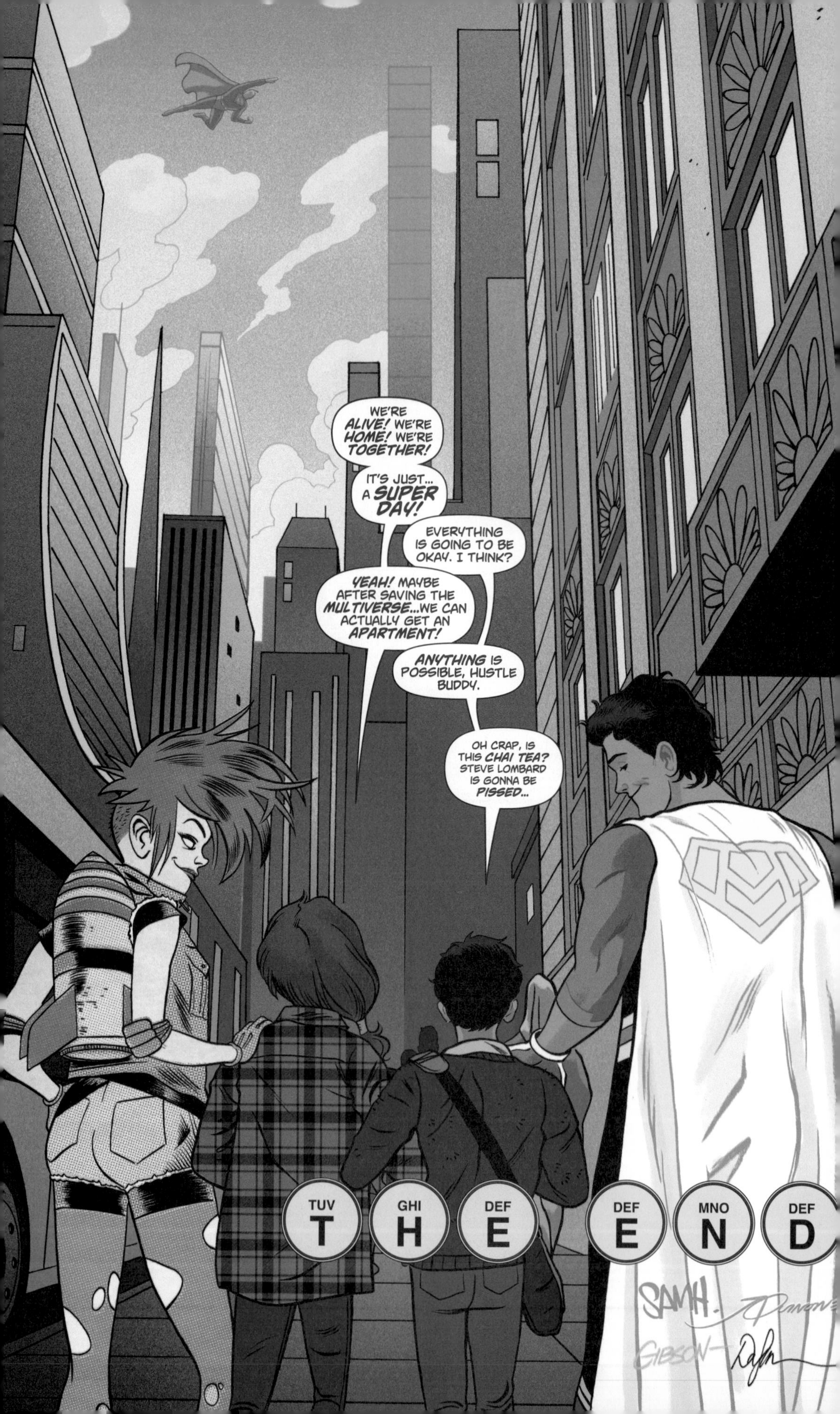
WE'RE ALIVE! WE'RE HOME! WE'RE TOGETHER!
IT'S JUST... A SUPER DAY!
EVERYTHING IS GOING TO BE OKAY. I THINK?
YEAH! MAYBE AFTER SAVING THE MULTIVERSE...WE CAN ACTUALLY GET AN APARTMENT!
ANYTHING IS POSSIBLE, HUSTLE BUDDY.
OH CRAP, IS THIS CHAI TEA? STEVE LOMBARD IS GONNA BE PISSED...
TUV T GHI H DEF E DEF E MNO N DEF D

DIAL TONES

Sketches and character designs by JOE QUINONES

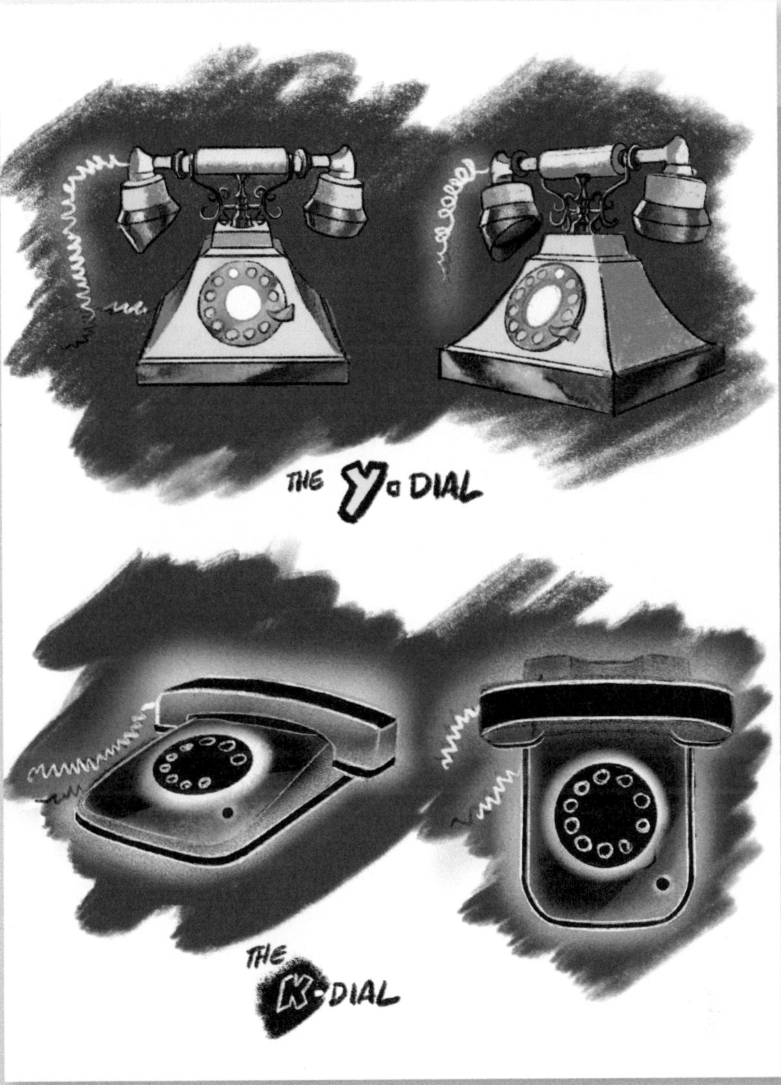

THE Y-DIAL
THE K-DIAL

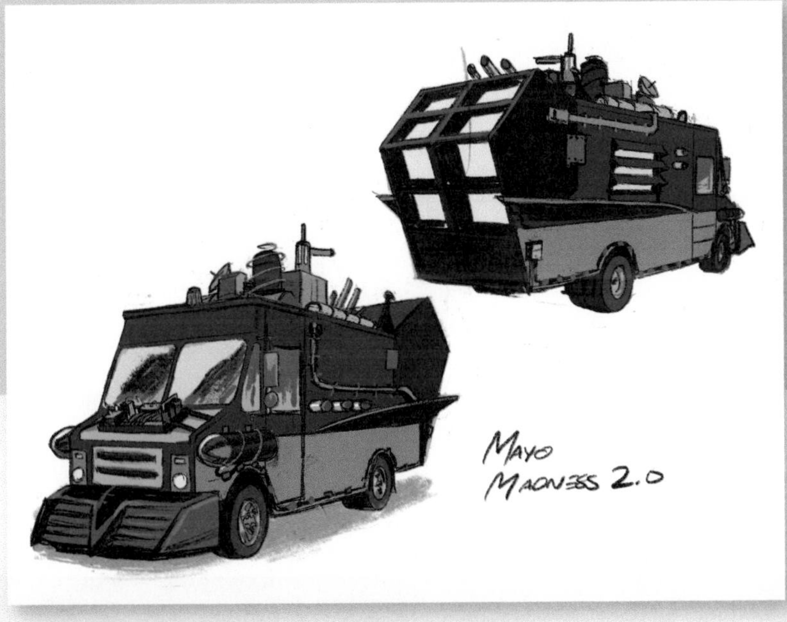

MAYO MADNESS 2.0

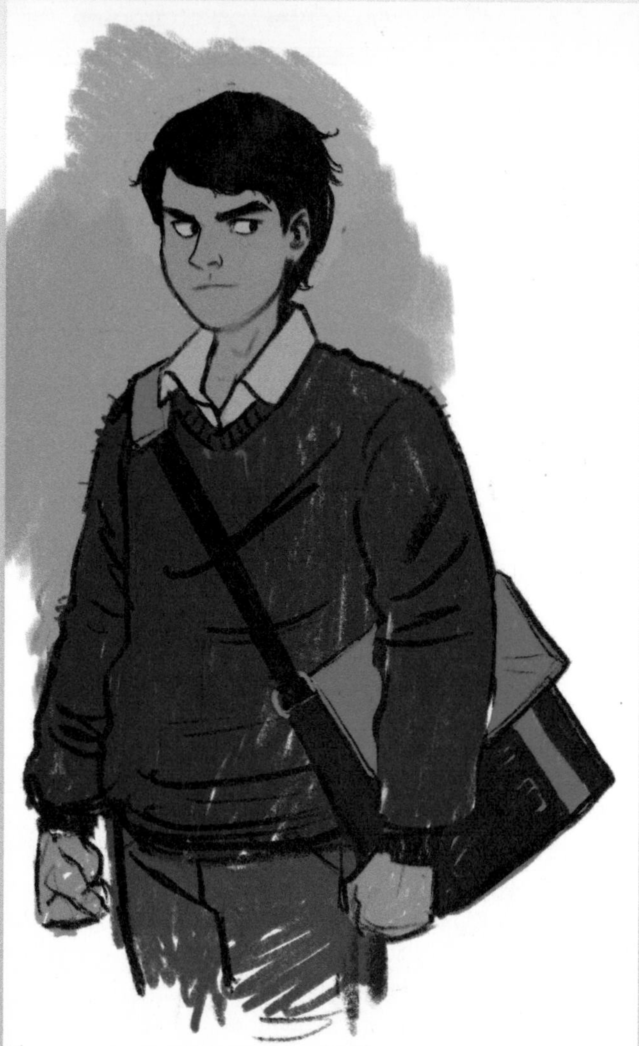
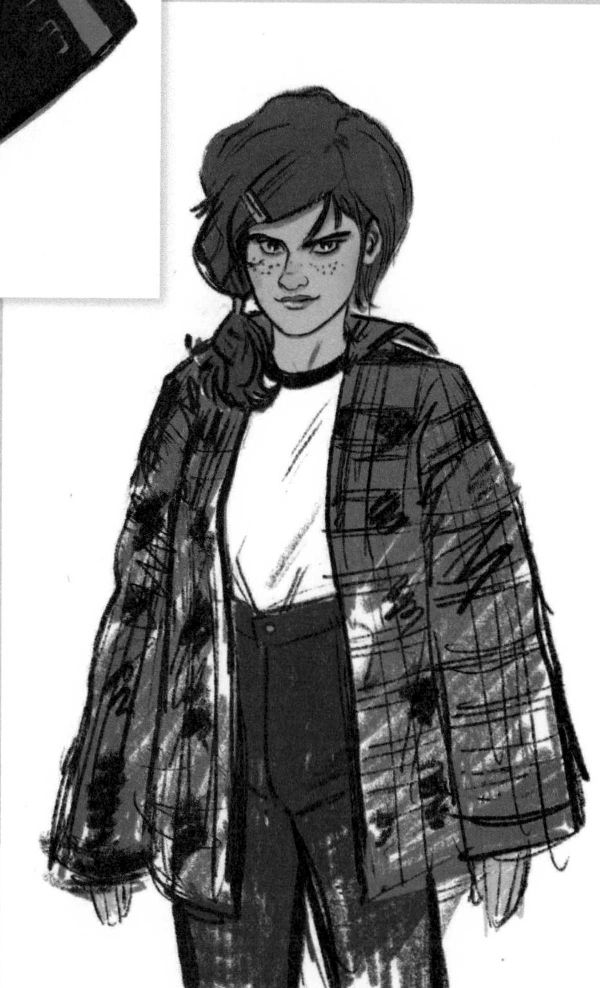

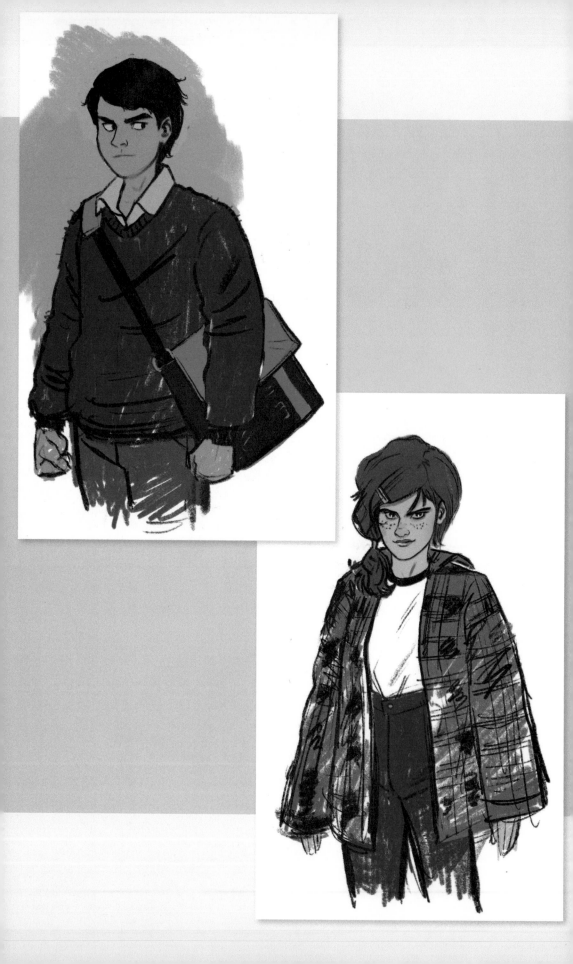

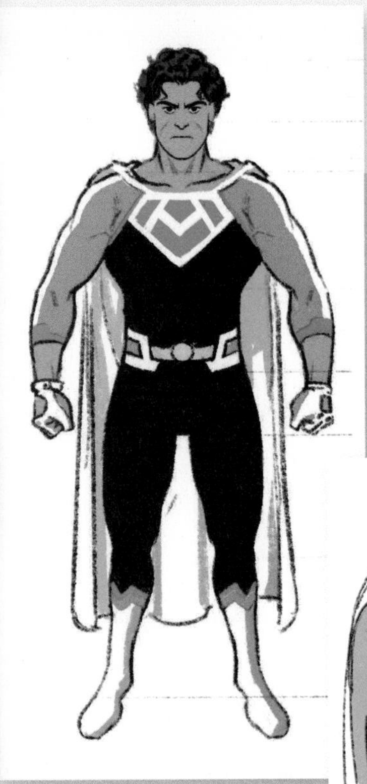

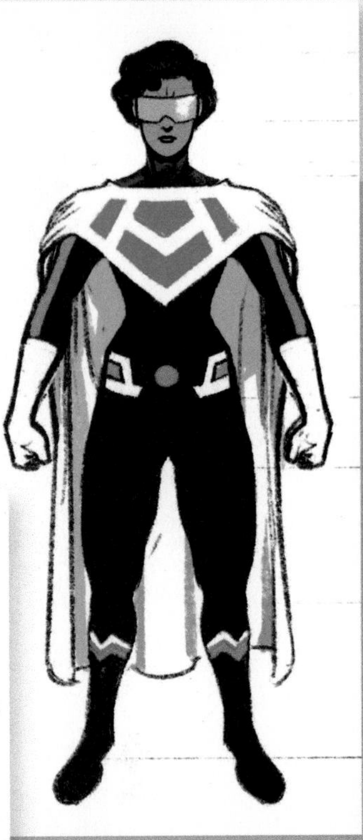

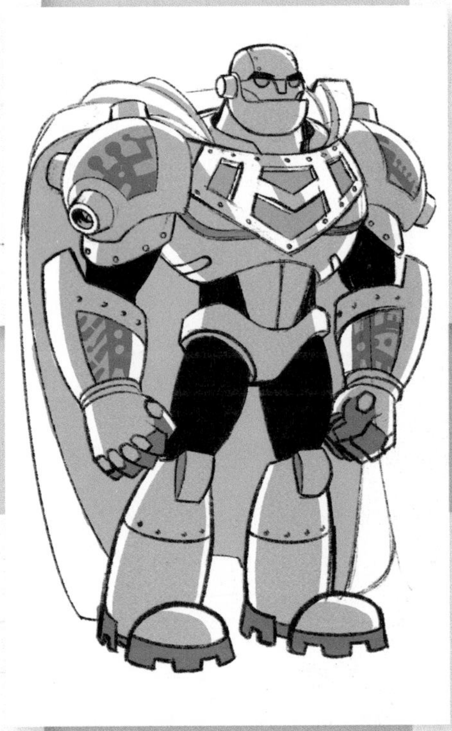

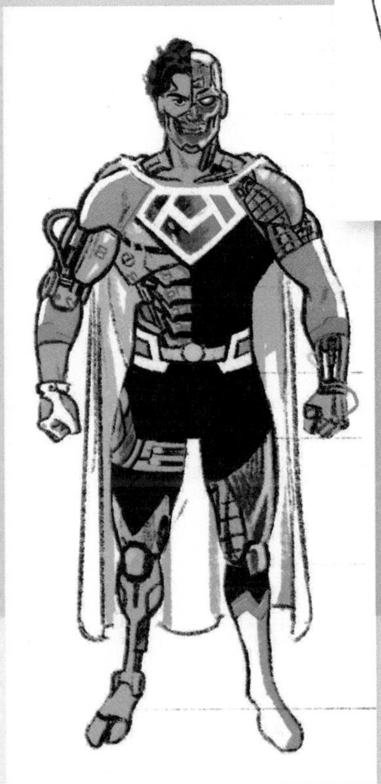

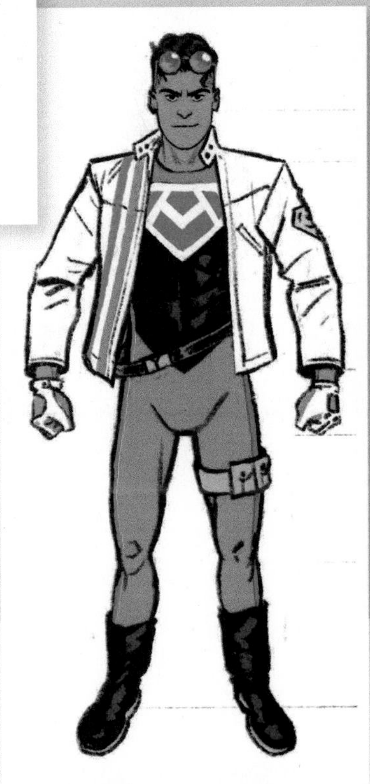

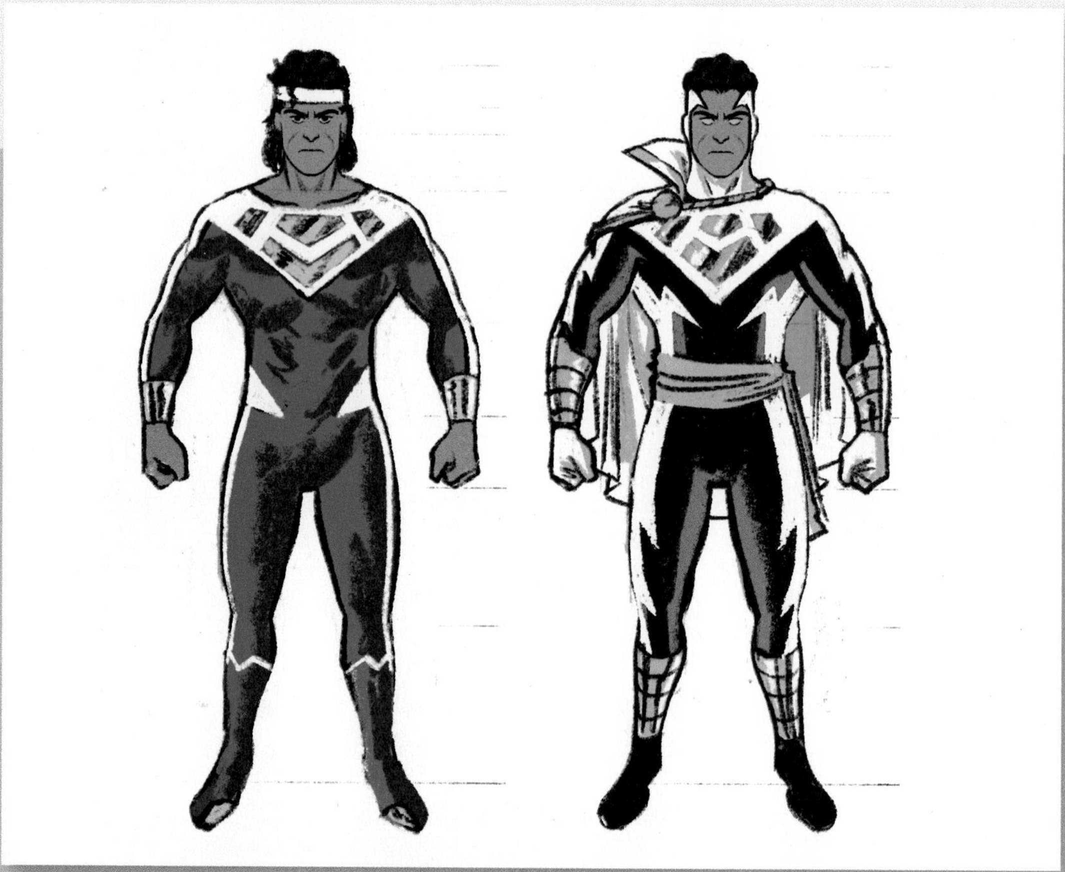

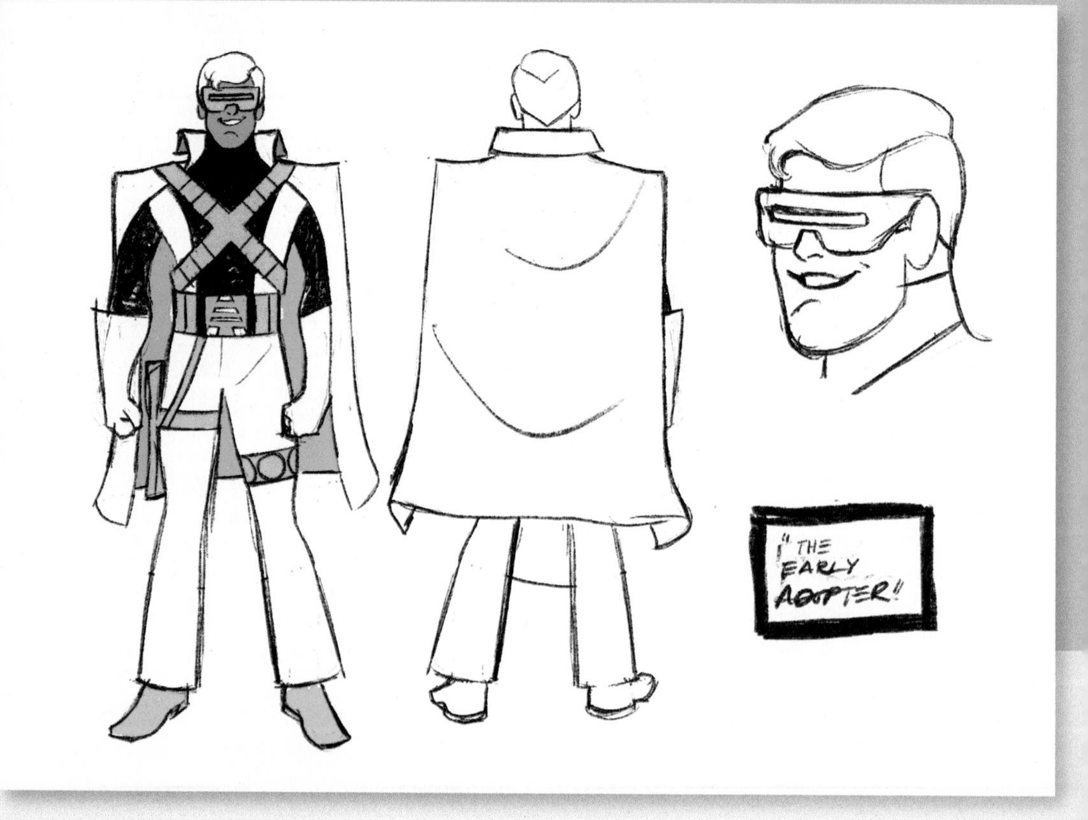
"THE
EARLY
ADOPTER!!

LoLo
Kick
Ya
VER.5

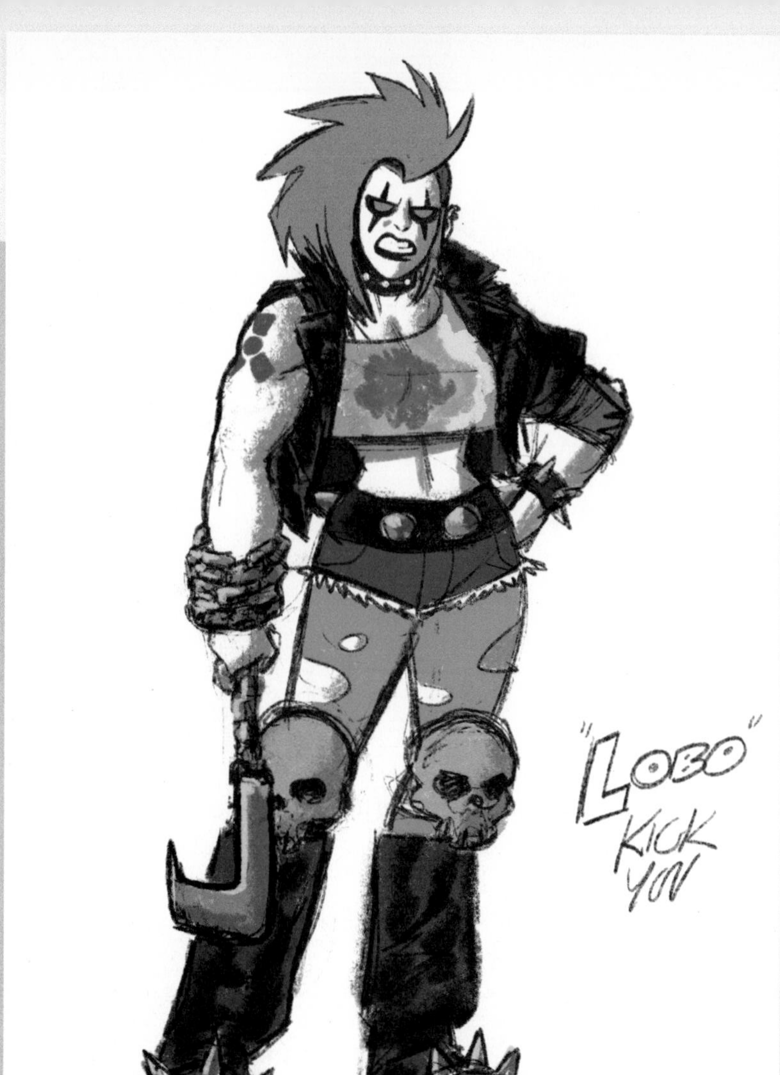
"LOBO"
KICK
YOU

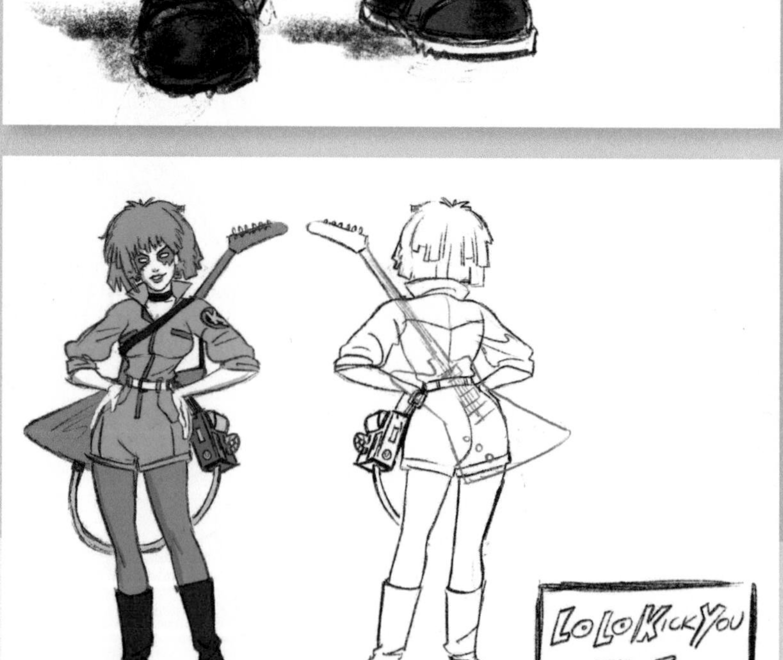
LoLoKickYou
VER 3

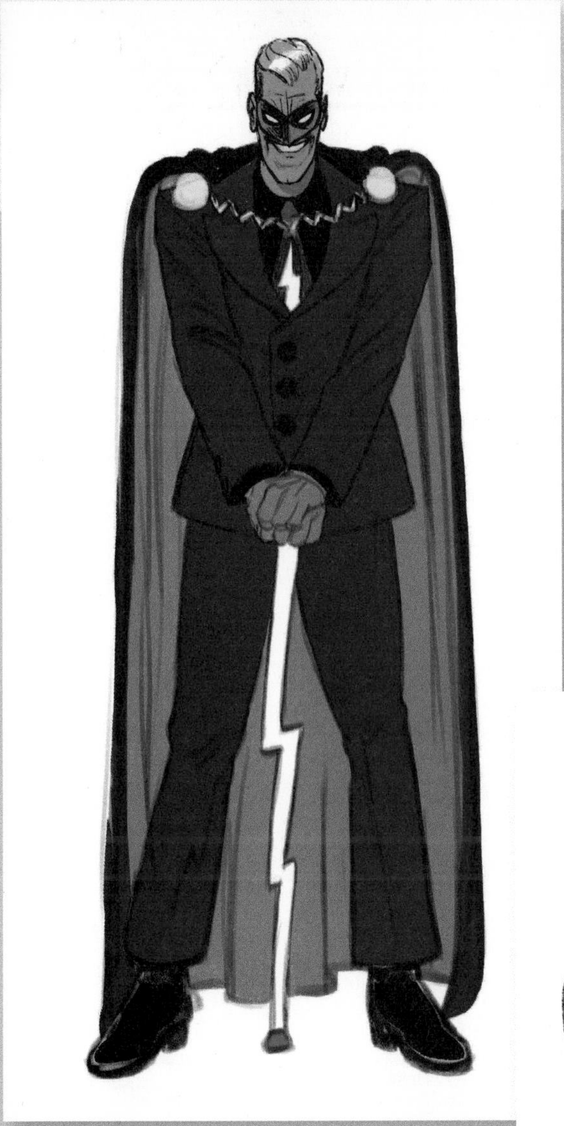

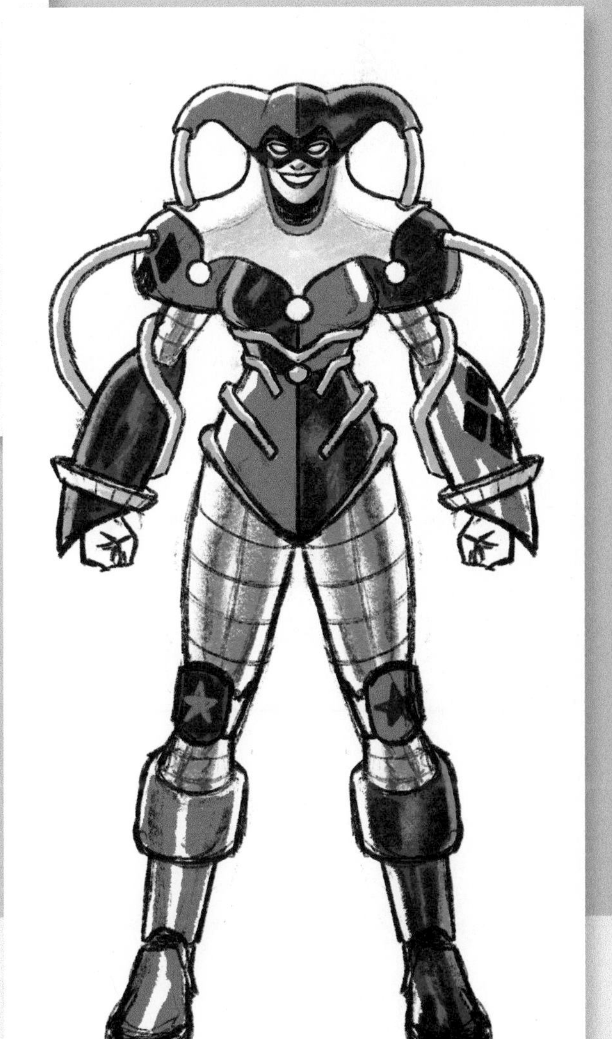

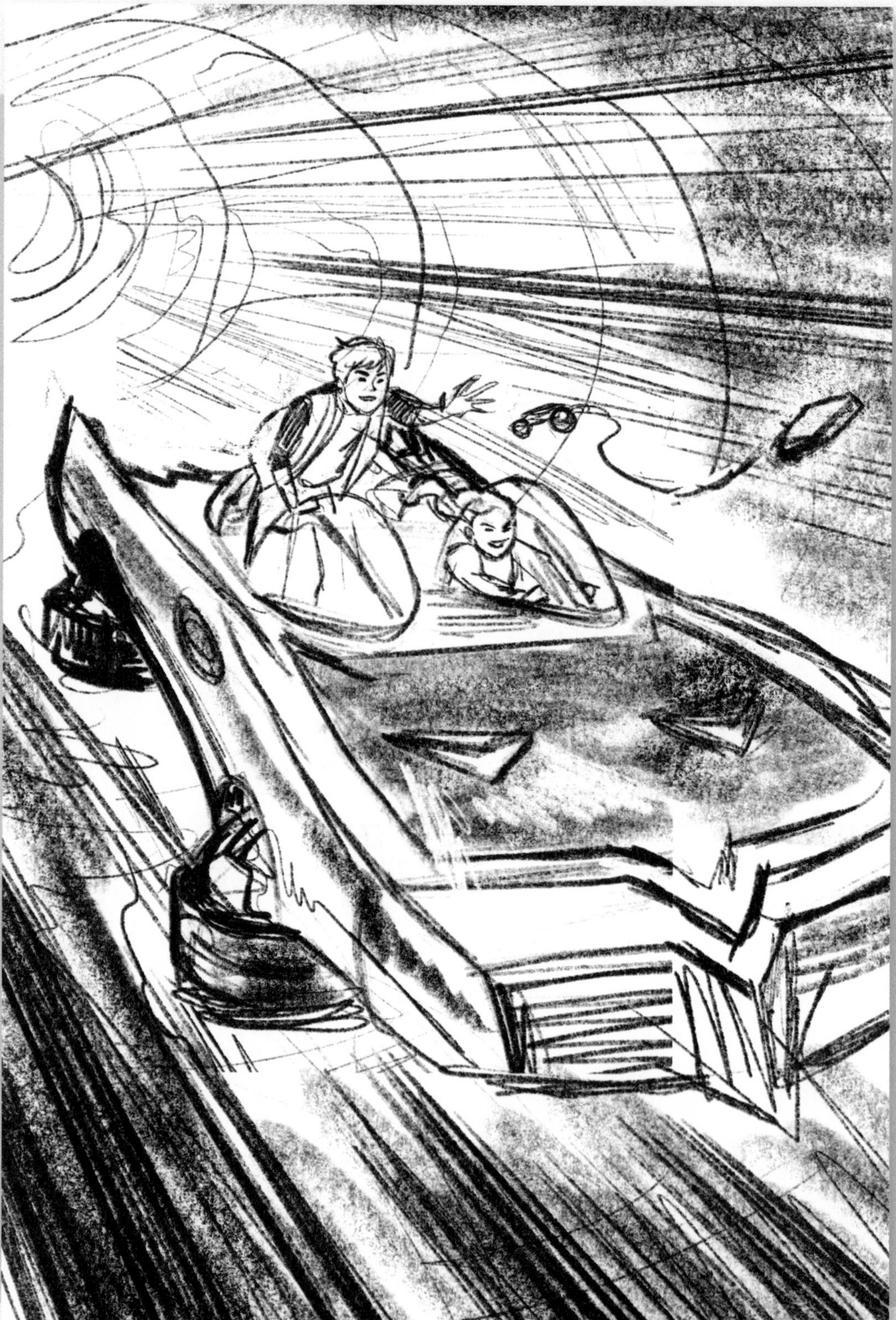

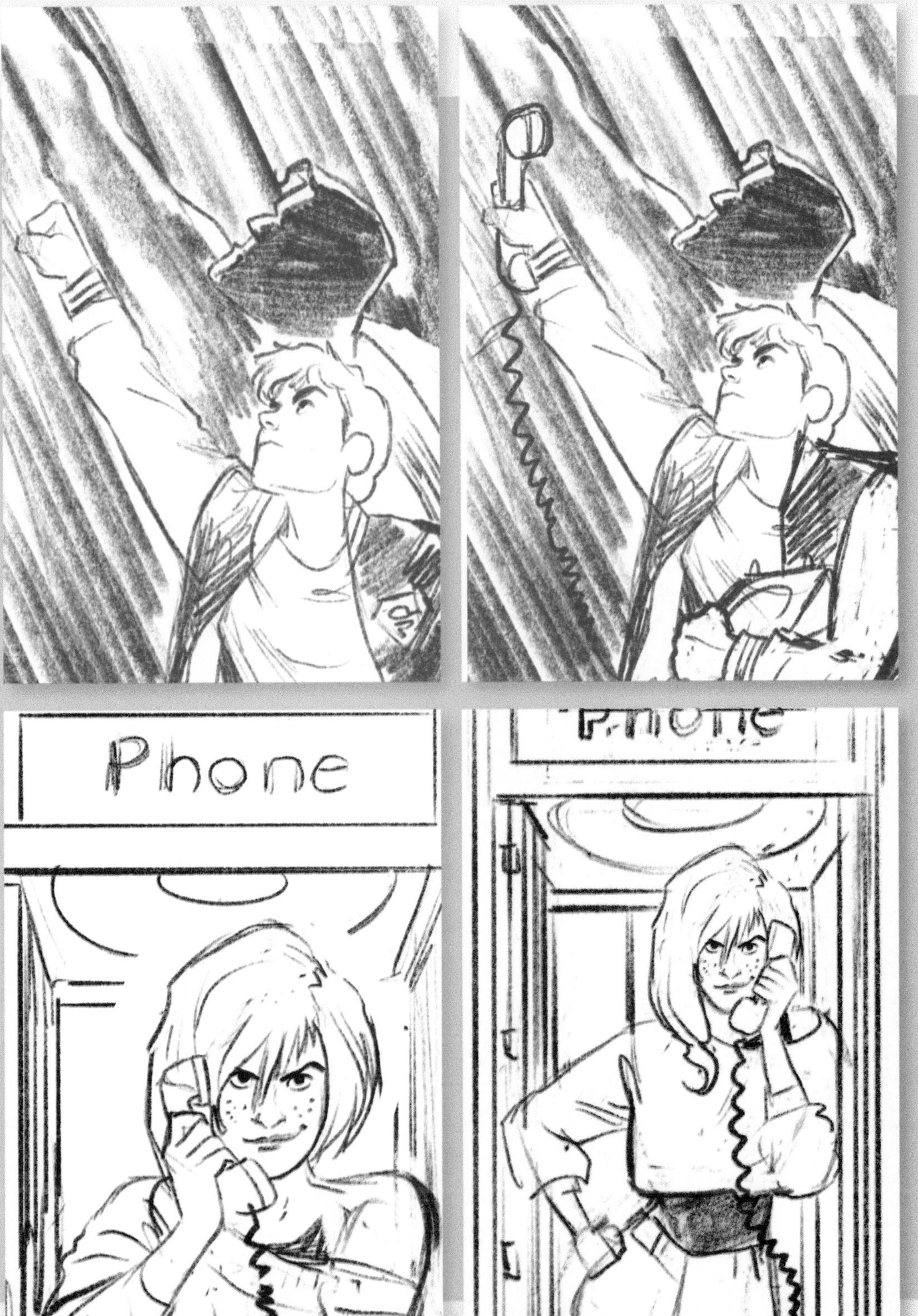
Phone

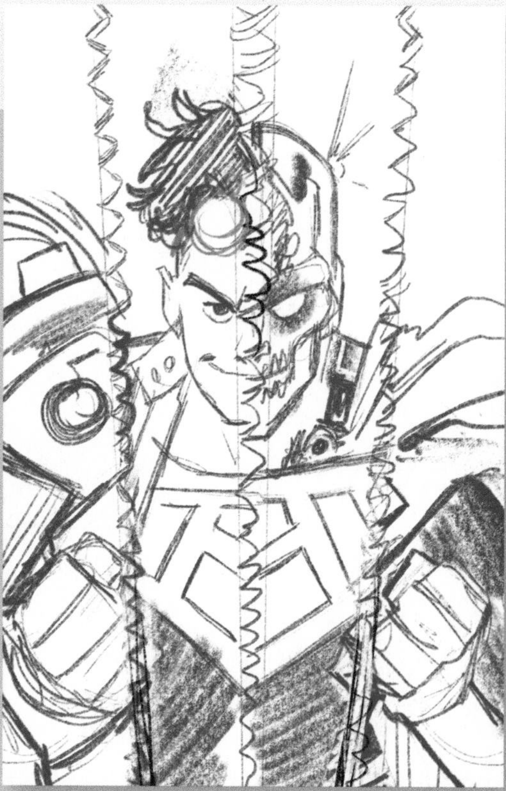
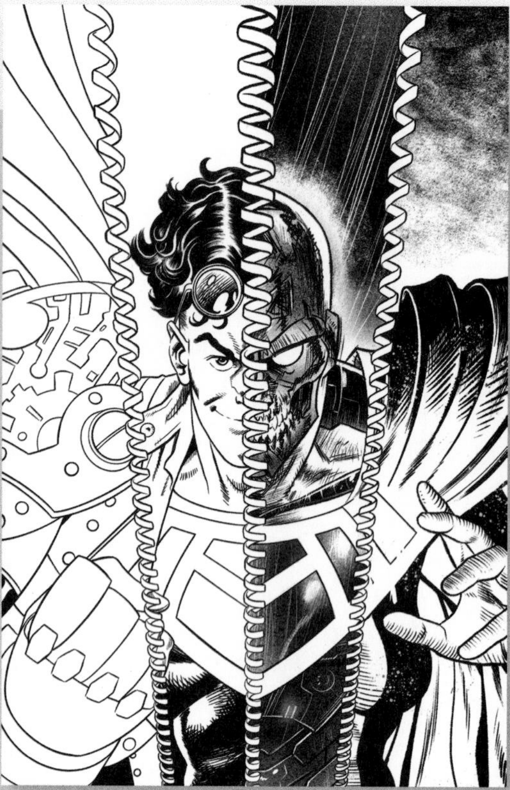
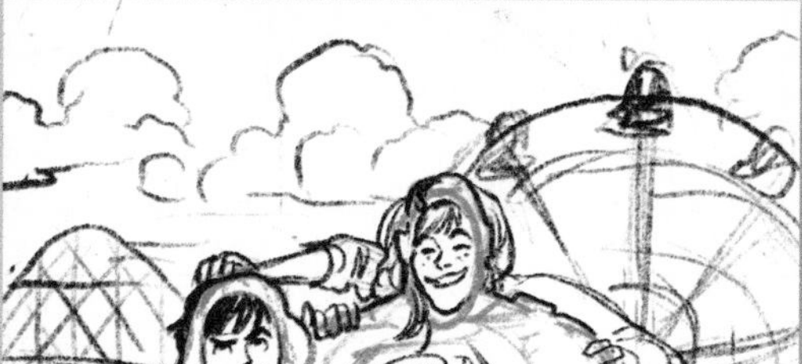
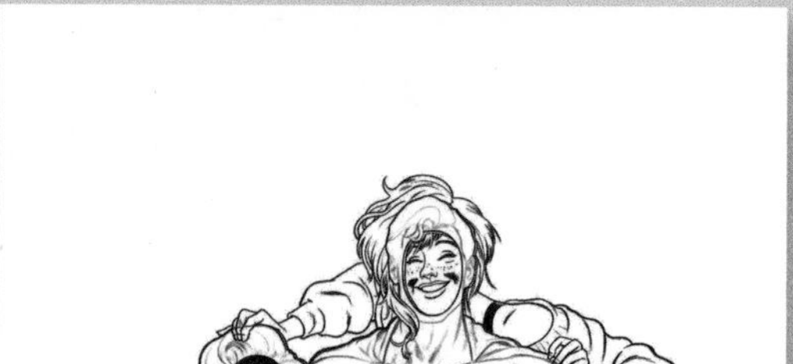

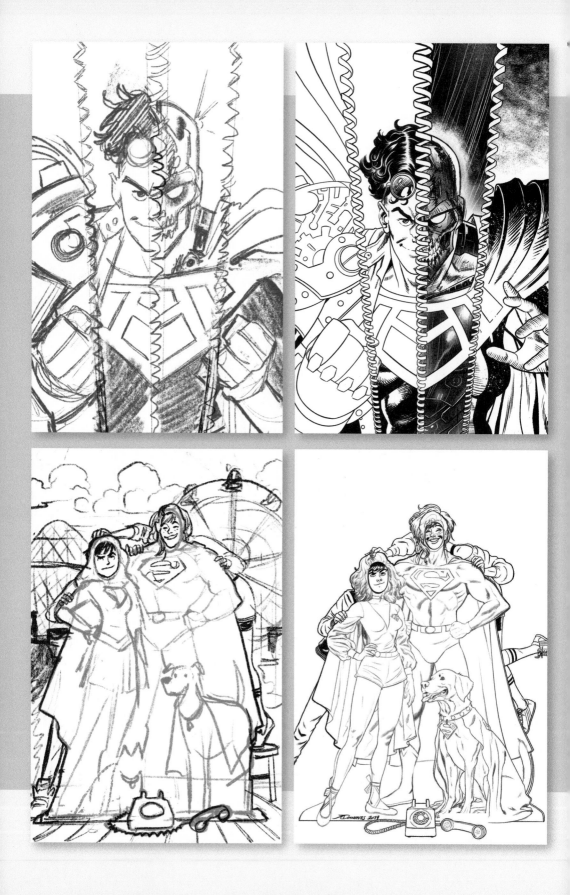

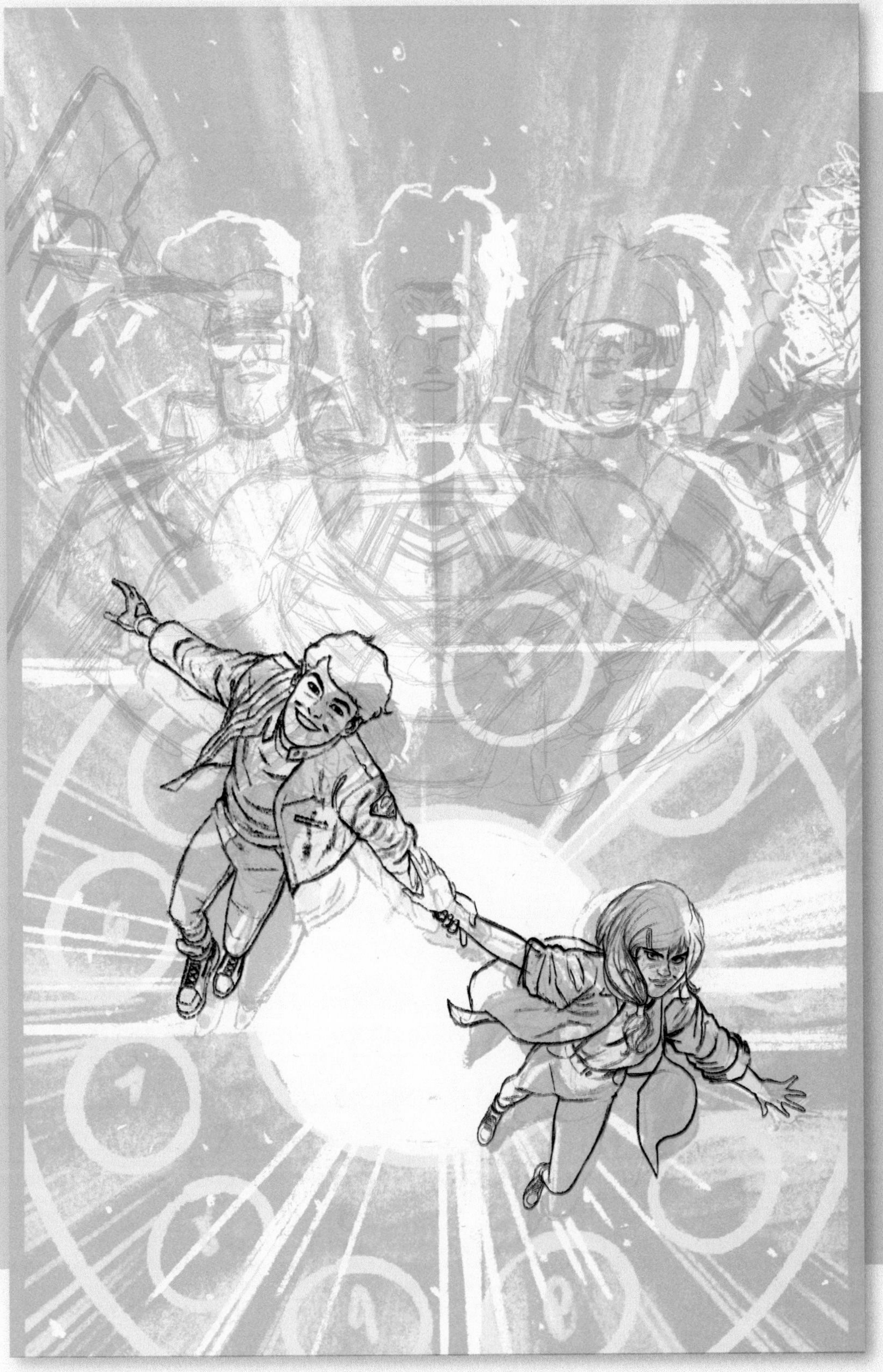

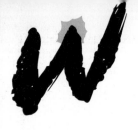

"Bendis reminds us why we loved these characters to begin with."
—NEWSARAMA

YOUNG JUSTICE
VOL. 1: GEMWORLD
BRIAN MICHAEL BENDIS, PATRICK GLEASON and JOHN TIMMS

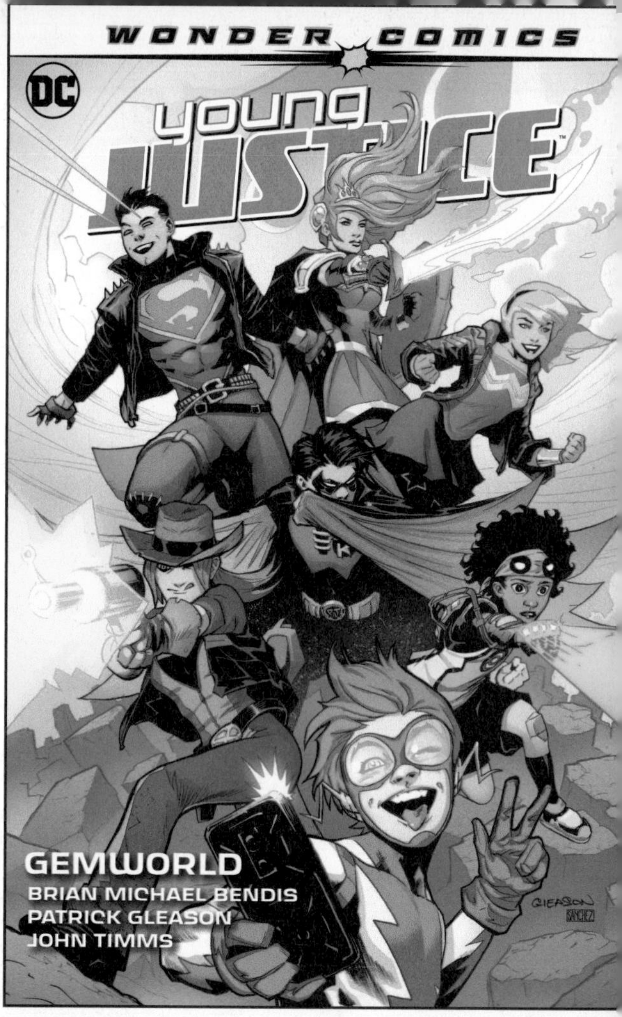
WONDER COMICS
DC
YOUNG JUSTICE
GEMWORLD
BRIAN MICHAEL BENDIS
PATRICK GLEASON
JOHN TIMMS

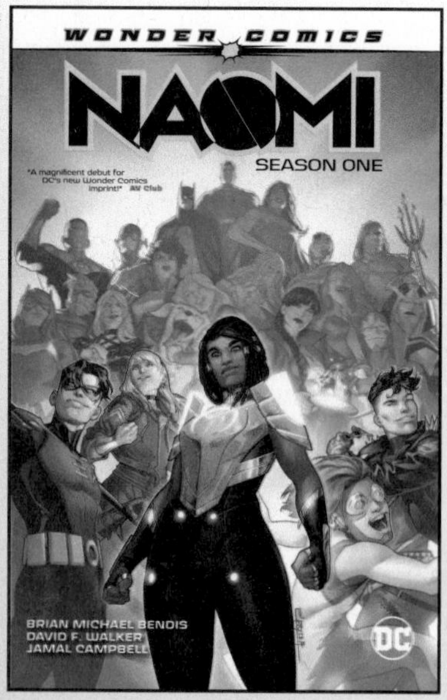
WONDER COMICS
NAOMI
SEASON ONE
BRIAN MICHAEL BENDIS
DAVID F. WALKER
JAMAL CAMPBELL
DC

NAOMI
VOL. 1: SEASON ONE

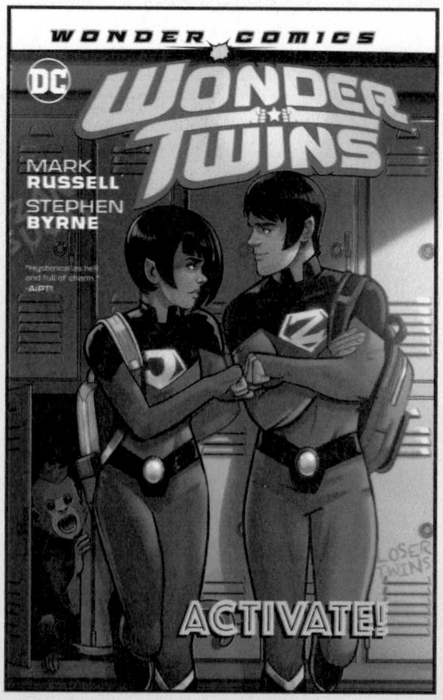
WONDER COMICS
DC
WONDER TWINS
MARK RUSSELL
STEPHEN BYRNE
ACTIVATE!

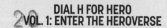

WONDER TWINS
VOL. 1: ACTIVATE!

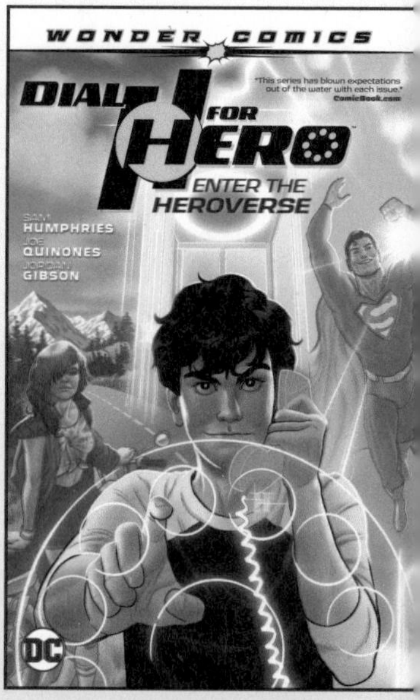
WONDER COMICS
DIAL H FOR HERO
ENTER THE HEROVERSE
HUMPHRIES
QUINONES
GIBSON
DC

DIAL H FOR HERO
VOL. 1: ENTER THE HEROVERSE